Ever Faithful

Ever Faithful

Race, Loyalty, and the Ends of Empire in Spanish Cuba

DAVID SARTORIUS

Duke University Press • Durham and London • 2013

Printed in the United States of America on acid-free paper ∞
Tyeset in Minion Pro by Westchester Publishing Services.

Library of Congress Cataloging-in-Publication Data
Sartorius, David A.
Ever faithful : race, loyalty, and the ends of empire
in Spanish Cuba / David Sartorius.
pages cm
Includes bibliographical references and index.
ISBN 978-0-8223-5579-3 (cloth : alk. paper)
ISBN 978-0-8223-5593-9 (pbk. : alk. paper)
1. Blacks—Race identity—Cuba—History—19th
century. 2. Cuba—Race relations—History—19th
century. 3. Spain—Colonies—America—
Administration—History—19th century. I. Title.
F1789.N3S27 2013
305.80097291—dc23
2013025534

CONTENTS

To visit the Palace of the Captain General on Havana's Plaza de Armas today is to witness the most prominent stone-and mortar monument to the enduring history of Spanish colonial rule in Cuba. Built in the eighteenth century, the palace has served many purposes: as the home of the captain general, the highest-ranking Spanish official on the island; with Cuban independence, the home of the U.S. military governor after 1899; the home of the Cuban president until 1920; as the city hall, municipal archive, and finally a museum.[1] Long since national independence in 1898, Cubans have resisted the influence of foreign powers, but the empire that built the palace as its nerve center has become, with each successive transition, a less commanding symbol of imperial domination. Cubans have confronted problems that had their origins in slavery—economic dependency and racial inequalities among them. The palace itself, though, is now associated with the treasures of a bygone era. Walking through the palace today, it's easy to underestimate the heft of an empire that for almost four centuries variously inspired fear, resentment, and affection from its subjects.[2]

Fernando Ortiz, the foremost scholar of Cuba's African dimension, knew this palace well. It was here that the lawyer and anthropologist learned lasting lessons about the meaning of colonial rule to Cuba's multiracial population. Ortiz spent his formative years in the Canary Islands before returning to Cuba when he was fourteen, just months before the final war for independence erupted in February 1895. Within days of his arrival in Havana, his grandfather took him to the palace to catch a glimpse of Arsenio Martínez Campos, the once and future reform-minded captain general known for negotiating with rebels over the course of a three-decade insurgency. Such conciliation provoked nothing but contempt in the grandfather, a staunchly conservative supporter of Spain. When Martínez Campos entered the room, the grandfather whispered into young Fernando's ear, "Look well at his face; he is a mulatto from Guanabacoa" (see figure P.1).[3]

FIGURE P.1 • Arsenio Martínez Campos, ca. 1870. Courtesy of Prints and Photographs Division, Library of Congress, Washington, DC.

Never say never, but it would be surprising if Martínez Campos—who was born in Segovia, Spain, and whose well-documented rise through the ranks of a mostly segregated military led him to high office—was either of African descent or from a marginal Havana suburb.[4] But this was how the elder Ortiz made sense of the openness toward those who fought for national independence, all of whom he assumed to be black or mulatto—"as if being a rebel was proof that one was colored," his grandson later noted. This episode also illustrates the central topic of this book: the relationships imagined between political allegiance and racial identity.

Fernando Ortiz would eventually dismiss the far-fetched theory as an old man's prejudices, although he still observed that the captain general "looked and he seemed to me somewhat like a light-skinned mulatto." In the same chamber after Cuban independence, Ortiz recounted this anecdote to Tomás Estrada Palma, the first president of the Cuban Republic (see figure P.2). Estrada Palma dismissed with "unforgettable amiability" the story about his colonial predecessor: "Now all that has finished; in Free Cuba we are now all of the same color."[5] And this was the idea that Ortiz reiterated in a speech delivered in that very same space (in what was now the Municipal Palace) in 1943.

FIGURE P.2 • Palace of the Captain General, Havana, ca. 1895. Courtesy of Cuban Heritage Collection, University of Miami Libraries.

He located the writings of independence leader José Martí at the heart of a vision of the Cuban nation that transcended the racial divisions created under colonial rule. He also acknowledged that many Cubans of color in the nineteenth century found it logical to support a national project that placed being Cuban above blackness or whiteness. This was an idea developed in writing by Martí and others and in practice within a diverse liberation army, and it is a national racial ideology that still today stands as one of the most remarked-upon features of the island—one with analogs in many other areas of Latin America.

Although this book began as a social history of those ideas, early discoveries in Cuban archives shifted attention to another intriguing intersection of race and politics: how ordinary Cubans expressed support not for national independence but for the Spanish colonial government, how that government unevenly cultivated and reciprocated that support, and how African-descended Cubans figured prominently among its adherents. Here was a story of political allegiance running parallel to the narrative of raceless nationalism championed by Martí, Ortiz, and many other people who wove it into the fabric of Cuban history. Once I started to tug at the thread of argument about pro-colonial loyalty, that fabric began to unravel. Basic understandings about the nature of Spanish imperialism, African slavery, colonial racial hierarchies, liberalism, and national citizenship all begged for revision.

How, then, are we to reconcile such divergent forms of political allegiance, or to account for a phenomenon that confounds the anti-imperialist orientations of so many struggles against racial inequality? Scholars have acknowledged that the Spanish government had cultivated that support and extended limited rights and privileges, but they have generally understood it either as exclusive to Cubans of full Spanish ancestry or as false consciousness: a "divide and rule" policy, as Ortiz called it, an "immense social lottery" designed to keep most Cubans of color "distracted and diverted from fundamental grievances." Ortiz did not dwell on the question of why Cubans of color might have affirmed colonial rule. In his speech of 1943, he briefly explained it as an elite affair. "Doubtless there existed in Cuba that select group of colored people whose personal interests were selfishly interlocked in the high wheels of the colonial government," he argued, insisting that most of those individuals "were mulattoes with hidden or unconcealed family connections, favored by privileges; mulattoes of blood tinged with blue by amorous relations that placed ebony patches on the noble Castilian heraldry; and mulattoes of blood turned yellow by the embrace of the dark-colored girl with the man who was the color of his gold coins."[6] Like his grandfather, Ortiz associated political allegiance to one cause or another as being linked to blood, ancestry, and color: the key concepts that gave meaning to the idea of race in Cuba.

Certainly, Ortiz was on to something when he linked mixed ancestry to the consolidation of empire. Since the earliest years of the Spanish presence in the Americas, strategic marriages to native elites and the Hispanization of mixed peoples helped make Spanish legal and social norms hegemonic.[7] Yet it is no more persuasive to assume that support for Spanish rule was limited to Spanish ancestry than to assume that Arsenio Martínez Campos's concessions to rebels meant that he was a mulatto passing for white. Nor was loyalty to Spain limited to those who derived economic privileges from colonial rule. Indeed, many wealthy Cubans preferred the stability of Spanish rule to the uncertainties of independence, but so did many other Cubans, and for a wide variety of reasons. Neither economic opportunity nor Spanish descent fully explains popular support for a colonial government that survived mainland Spanish American independence by many decades.

This book argues that alongside persistent associations of pro-colonial sentiment with Cuba's white population lay a conception of race and loyalty that allowed Cubans of African descent—slave and free—to be included in colonial politics as faithful, if unequal, subjects. Reconstructing this history requires looking beyond the dramas that unfolded in the captain general's palace and the imposing mansions of Cubans whose wealth derived from the island's sugar economy, which was built on slave labor. The history of race and loyalty is also to be found in bustling meeting halls and public squares across the island, on plantations transformed into battlefields, and in the barracks of militia soldiers and wartime recruits. These spaces became the staging grounds for mutual and reciprocal interests articulated by the Spanish government and its subjects. Although the focus of the book is primarily on people of African descent, it is more than a social history of those black and mulatto Cubans who explicitly supported the continuation of Spanish rule; it asks broader questions about the centrality of race to the maintenance of the Spanish empire in its final decades in the Americas. In doing so, it questions the neat divide commonly drawn between colonial and national racial ideologies in Cuba and, by extension, political strategies of African-descended Cubans based on identifications as subjects of an empire or as citizens of a liberal nation-state. Chronicling individuals caught between competing racial identities, colonial identity as subjects of the Spanish empire, and race-transcendent national identity, this book explains how Cubans of many different backgrounds shaped the politics of Spain's "ever-faithful isle."

I follow the history of race and loyalty along two principal axes. Military service represented one of the most conspicuous opportunities to demonstrate loyalty in colonial Cuba. Free men of African descent had served the Spanish empire in militias since the sixteenth century, and membership conferred social status and legal privileges recognized by colonials of all backgrounds. Yet militias encountered patchy support by Spanish officials and free people of color alike in the early nineteenth century. After the Haitian Revolution (1791–1804) and independence wars in mainland Latin America, for example, colonial officials doubted more than ever the wisdom of arming potentially rebellious groups. It was not until the outbreak of the first major anticolonial insurrection, the Ten Years' War (1868–1878), that military service regained its earlier importance to defining loyalty, and some free men mobilized to defend Spain against the rebels. The Spanish government also offered slaves an incentive to support the empire as it initiated the gradual process of slave emancipation: those who fought for the Spanish in the insurrection could receive their freedom. Field interrogations of slave-soldiers juxtaposed popular and official understandings of loyalty that determined whether or not a slave would be freed, uncovering, in the process, assumptions about the will and ability of slaves to be loyal subjects.

As a result of the political reforms that followed the Ten Years' War, many more African-descended Cubans asserted their allegiance to Spanish rule, in part because they encountered new opportunities for doing so. The second axis on which I plot race and loyalty tracks the spaces of their public articulation, which expanded significantly in the late nineteenth century. The Spanish state sanctioned the formation of political parties, and it loosened restrictions on press and association. Cubans of color quickly asserted their presence in this burgeoning public sphere by invoking their loyalty to the government that made it possible. Since 1812, when a constitution drafted by the besieged Spanish government radically expanded the citizenship rights of select Spanish American men, colonial and metropolitan liberals had struggled to contain the demands of African-descended and indigenous people within the Spanish system—notably through censorship and control of public spaces. Reforms after the Ten Years' War represented a turning point. Thus, the book moves from the hot, crowded theaters in small towns that hosted political party meetings to the ceremonious patriotic clubs in Havana where Cubans of color delivered florid speeches, attended by colonial officials, that called for slave emancipation and clearer voting rights. In the late 1880s, the slow steps toward an integrated postemancipation society provoked frustration among many African-descended Cubans who had deferred protest in good faith. Spanish political concessions buckled under social pressure for wider inclusion, and by the War of Independence between 1895 and 1898, the separatist movement's explicit commitment to antiracism had done much to displace popular loyalty to Spain, particularly among Cubans of color.

This is a book about the ideological foundations of empire, about reexamining the central themes of Cuban history, and about a prominent but underexplored phenomenon in the political history of the African diaspora. At the heart of the history of race and imperial loyalty is the interplay between an early iteration of Spanish national citizenship and an older form of subjectivity as a loyal vassal of the monarch. This is a story of their conflict, but also of their interdependence.

ACKNOWLEDGMENTS

Conducting research and writing a book can be isolating endeavors. But what immediately comes to mind when I think about the process are the good conversations, good ideas, and good laughs shared with friends and colleagues. Thanking all of them as I wrap up this project has an unfortunate air of finality about it, so I acknowledge their support with the proviso that they aren't off the hook just yet.

Dedicated and inspiring teachers guided me on the journey that led to this book. It emerged from my doctoral dissertation, so first and foremost I heartily thank my advisor, Louis A. Pérez, Jr., for his encouragement, advice, and above all for his patience. Perhaps as no one else can, he taught me a great deal about Cuba and, just as important, he taught me about the act of writing and about the ethical responsibilities of belonging to an intellectual community that spans the U.S.-Cuba divide. I also thank the other members of my dissertation committee—Kathryn Burns, John French, John Chasteen, and Jerma Jackson—whose gifts as writers, teachers, and people continue to serve as examples. Leon Fink and Judith Bennett also provided wisdom and perspective along the way. I became hooked on Latin American history during my first semester in college, and I am grateful to Franklin Knight, Alida Metcalf, Linda Salvucci, Richard Salvucci, and Aline Helg for sparking my curiosity and monitoring my wobbly first steps as a historian.

Over many years, the Instituto de Historia de Cuba in Havana has supported my research in countless ways. Along with the Unión de Escritores y Artistas de Cuba (UNEAC), it has sponsored research visas, facilitated access to archives and libraries, and included me in its conferences and seminars. I thank Belkis Quesada y Guerra and Amparo Hernández for their strenuous efforts to make all of this happen. I also thank the *instituto* for the opportunities to become acquainted with Cuban scholars who have made room for me next to them in the archives; fielded my oddball questions; and shared thoughts, writing, and suggestions. I owe a huge debt of gratitude to Carmen Almodóvar, Manuel Barcia Paz, Barbara Danzie León, Yolanda Díaz Martínez, Mitzi Espinosa Luis,

Leida Fernández Prieto, Reinaldo Funes Monzote, Gloria García Rodriguez, Julio César González Pagés, Silvia Gutiérrez, Oilda Hevia Lanier, Fe Iglesias García, Patricia Cok, Jorge Macle Cruz, María de los Ángeles Meriño Fuentes, Blancamar León Rosabal, Adrian López Denis, Fernando Martínez Heredia, Aisnara Perera Díaz, Carlos Venegas Fornias, and Oscar Zanetti Lecuona. A few colleagues deserve special mention for years of ongoing exchanges and warm friendship: Marial Iglesias Utset, Tomás Fernández Robaina, the late Francisco Pérez Guzmán, Abel Sierra Madero, and Orlando García Martínez, the open-hearted and open-minded former director of the provincial archive in Cienfuegos and president of the UNEAC branch there. I learned some life lessons in Cuba from Marél Suzarte, Gladys Marél García, Berta Linares, Oscar Montoto, Cecilio, Loly, and some guy named Carlos.

Archivists and librarians at the research institutions I visited went out of their way to help me navigate their collections. I want to thank the staffs of the Archivo Nacional de Cuba, the Biblioteca Nacional José Marti, and the library of the Instituto de Literatura y Lingüística in Havana; the Archivo Histórico Provincial de Cienfuegos and Biblioteca Provincial de Cienfuegos; and the Archivo Histórico Provincial de Santiago de Cuba. In Spain, I am grateful to specialists at the Biblioteca Nacional, Archivo Histórico Nacional, Servicio Histórico Militar, and Real Academia de Historia in Madrid; and at the Archivo General de Indias in Seville. In the United States, I benefited from help at the Houghton Library at Harvard University, the U.S. National Archives, the Huntington Library, and the Latin American Collection of the University of Florida's Smathers Library, particularly from its director, Richard Phillips, and Margarita Vargas-Betancourt. Most of all, I thank the good people at the Hispanic Division of the Library of Congress, who for years have provided a calm place to write and more books than I could ever read.

A special bond develops among historians who visit Cuba and overlap in the course of research and conference going. These colleagues have graciously shared leads, advice, and a sense of collective endeavor, I thank Sandra Bronfman, Matt Childs, Camillia Cowling, Alejandro de la Fuente, Ada Ferrer, Jorge Giovannetti, Lillian Guerra, Frank Guridy, Jane Landers, Kathy López, Gillian McGillivray, Jill Lane, Melina Pappademos, Michele Reid-Vazquez, Reinaldo Román, and Michael Zeuske. Early discussions with Rebecca J. Scott helped me formulate some of the central questions guiding this project. Marikay McCabe and I spent a lot of time together in nineteenth-century Cuba; I thank her for making the voyages with me. Her friendship is inseparable from this project but I am grateful that it extends so far beyond it.

At the University of North Carolina and Duke University, colleagues and friends provided critical engagement and distraction. It was a privilege to learn alongside my Latin Americanist *compañeros* Adriana Brodsky, Vince Brown, Mariola Espinosa, Amy Ferlazzo, Mark Healey, Jan Hoffman French, Lupe García, Jane Mangan, Josh Nadel, Rachel O'Toole, Jody Pavilack, Tom Rogers, Devyn Spence Benson, Ivonne Wallace-Fuentes, and Bill Van Norman. Many other fellow graduate students were there for first response and last call: Anastasia Crosswhite, Will Jones, Michael Kramer, Ethan Kytle, Susan Pearson, Erik Riker-Coleman, Blain Roberts, Michele Strong, and Adam Tuchinsky all deserve a nod. Three individuals in particular have helped hold everything together: Sarah Thuesen, my intrepid writing partner; Bianca Premo, whose ideas may have shaped this project more than my own (although any errors are mine alone); and Jolie Olcott, whose support and friendship, and intellectual and political commitments, humble and inspire me. This book feels like the product of many-year-long conversations with these friends, which makes it all the more meaningful.

Through a Latin American history reading group in Los Angeles I became close colleagues and even better friends with Robin Derby, María Elena Martínez, and Micol Seigel. As this project became a book, their humor, encouragement, and whip-smart insights have been invaluable. Other generous colleagues—M. Jacqui Alexander, Andy Apter, Ben Cowan, Lessie Jo Frazier, Jim Green, Ramón Gutiérrez, Pete Sigal, John Tutino, and Ben Vinson—have sharpened my thinking and made enjoyable the hard work that goes into our professional labors. For their comments on parts or all of the manuscript I thank Herman Bennett, Kathryn Burns, Ada Ferrer, John French, Clare Lyons, Jolie Olcott, Bianca Premo, Karin Rosemblatt, Leslie Rowland, Rebecca Scott, and especially Sarah Chambers. Thanks to kind invitations to share my work, my ideas benefited from perceptive audiences at Brown University, the Latin American Labor History Conference at Duke University, Georgetown University, Indiana University, St. Mary's College of Maryland, Tulane University, the University of Chicago, the University of Redlands, the University of Southern California, and the Universidade Federal Rural do Rio de Janeiro in Nova Iguaçu, Brazil. I want to make special mention of the Tepoztlán Institute for the Transnational History of the Americas, founded by Pamela Voekel and Elliott Young. I have never found a more encouraging and exhilarating forum for experimenting with ideas as this annual gathering. I thank its many participants over the years and in particular the other members of the organizing collective. I met my good friends David Kazanjian and Josie

Saldaña in Tepoz. I am buoyed by their support and collaboration and astounded by their generosity.

I thank the staff and faculty of the University of Maryland Department of History for their collective energies on behalf of this book. *Mil gracias e muito obrigado* to my Latin Americanist colleagues—Mary Kay Vaughan, Alejandro Cañeque, Karin Rosemblatt, Barbara Weinstein (ever so briefly), and Daryle Williams—and to a great group of graduate students, for keeping the day-to-day and the big picture in proper perspective. Elsa Barkley Brown, Ira Berlin, Jim Gilbert, Julie Greene, Hilary Jones, Clare Lyons, Mike Ross, and Leslie Rowland have aided this project in ways large and small. Both intellectually and personally, Christina Hanhardt, Jerry Passannante, and Sangeeta Ray helped me keep the world beyond my work in view.

The financial support of many institutions facilitated the research and writing of this book. I carried out most of my research in Cuba and Spain through the generosity of the Conference on Latin American History's Lydia Cabrera Award, The Johns Hopkins University's Cuba Exchange Program, and the Department of History, the Institute of Latin American Studies (now the Institute for the Study of the Americas), and the Graduate School at University of North Carolina. A fellowship at the Massachusetts Historical Society and a Library Travel Research Grant from the University of Florida's Center for Latin American Studies helped identify crucial sources in the United States. Faculty research grants from Whittier College and the University of Maryland provided additional travel opportunities. The Paul Hardin Fellowship of the Royster Society of Fellows at the University of North Carolina allowed me to complete the dissertation, and I am especially grateful to the University of Maryland's Latin American Studies Center for a postdoctoral fellowship that gave me the time and space to widen the frame of this project.

This book simply would not exist without Valerie Millholland. I can never repay her efforts on my behalf. With superhuman patience, she and Gisela Fosado have gone above and beyond the call of any editor's duty. Compassion is not a job requirement for editors, but they have extended theirs to me, and to the pages that follow, in countless ways. I thank them and the whole production team at Duke University Press, as well as the extremely thoughtful and helpful anonymous readers who improved this project greatly.

Some of those people mentioned in this exhausting, and certainly not exhaustive, list are like family—one of the great results of undertaking this project. There are many families that have supported me over the years, and two in particular learned more about Cuba than they had ever planned to and have taught me more about loyalty than the research and writing of this book. Long ago my brother and I decided to take a class together on Caribbean history, and one of us received the higher grade; my late father, a teacher, and my mother, whose passion for learning continues to lead her in new directions, have always given me the space to follow my curiosity. So, too, has a group of childhood friends (and their hangers-on) who still know me best and tolerate me anyway. I thank all of them, in order of having met them beginning at age six: Sarah, Marla, Andy, Phuc, Chris, Kim, Courtney, Brandon, Dan, and Ken. I dedicate this book to all of these loved ones as meager compensation for everything they have dedicated to me.

A Faithful Account of Colonial Racial Politics

At the top of most pieces of official correspondence in nineteenth-century Cuba, from statistics on sugar harvests to investigations of slave unrest, was a seal or letterhead hailing "La siempre fiel isla," the ever-faithful isle. Cuba's loyalty to the Spanish empire became one of its defining attributes during the Age of Revolutions. Travel accounts repeated and reproduced the "ever faithful" motto, as did leading writers throughout the century. By the time that Fernando VII of Spain formally bestowed Cuba with the *siempre fiel* title in 1824, people had described the island with the phrase for decades.

Perhaps the title protested too much. In the wake of successful independence movements in mainland Spanish America from Mexico to Argentina, Cuba, along with Puerto Rico and the Philippines, stood as the remnants of what at the beginning of the nineteenth century had been second only to Russia as the world's largest empire. As Cuban sugar production grew to global dominance during that century—enabled by the vast expansion of African slavery—Spain was as eager for the island to remain in its imperial orbit as Cubans themselves were sharply divided about their political future. Anxiety about maintaining the colonial relationship explained, in part, the spread of the "ever-faithful" motto, adapted to designate cities that were *fidelísimas* (superfaithful) and printed atop the lottery tickets that optimistic Cubans tucked away in their pockets. Its ubiquity guaranteed nothing in terms of people's political allegiance, but neither did it lack symbolic value. In 1899, one year after the conclusion of the thirty-year struggle for Cuba's national independence, court documents still written on the Spanish government's letterhead had the coat of arms punched out of them, leaving a gaping hole at the top of the page.[1]

So much talk of loyalty does not entirely square with common historical associations pertaining to Cuba, namely, the rebellions and revolutions that have given shape to its unique political culture. Today, at the Museo de la Revolución in Havana, the narrative of the Cuban Revolution begins with the resistance of African slaves in the nineteenth century. But at a time in the Atlantic

FIGURE I.1 • Cuban lottery ticket, 1840. Private collection.

world when anticolonial movements in Europe's American colonies gave rise to new national states and the promise (if not the uniform practice) of liberal citizenship, Cuba did not experience revolutionary upheaval and, in fact, prospered greatly as a colony. Cuba's loyalty to Spain was not the outcome of the wishful thinking of the Spanish government, no matter how persistently it affirmed the ever-faithful island. Nor was repressive violence the lone explanation. That allegiance depended on the support of Cubans and on the pervasive ideas about race that shaped Cuban society.

This book attempts to understand that support from the inside out: not as an aberration of Cuban history, nor as a pothole in the road to national independence and citizenship—the benchmarks of political modernity—but as a meaningful political relationship that expressed mutual and reinforcing interests between the Spanish state and Cuban society. Moreover, loyalty to colonial rule did not slowly fizzle throughout the nineteenth century, paving the way for the empire's demise. In fact, at the end of the nineteenth century, popular expressions of allegiance found new means of expression that had been stifled earlier, when colonial authorities more strictly policed spaces for public deliberation and limited citizenship based on race as well as colonial status (and on gender, age, and many other criteria). The fact that these spaces allowed, and sometimes encouraged, the participation of Cubans of African descent helped bind together ideas about political inclusion and social subordination.

Scholars of Spanish and Portuguese American independence have gone to great lengths in recent years to explain the multiple contingencies that converged to effect the end of Iberian rule.[2] With a few exceptions, colonial Latin America at the beginning of the nineteenth century was no powder keg, no combustible mess of tensions and contradictions caused by the worst aspects of colonial rule. Still, the general absence of anticolonial fervor in the Spanish Caribbean perplexed the great liberator of Spanish America, Simón Bolívar: "But aren't the people of those islands Americans? Are they not oppressed? Do they not desire their own happiness?" he wrote from Jamaica in 1815.[3] Popular support for the Spanish empire in Cuba, even if it appeared counterintuitive to Bolívar and still does to many people today, is a topic that pushes us to reconsider much of what recent scholarship has made visible: the agency of African-descended people, the relationship of racial ideology to empire and nationalism, and the ascendancy of the nation-state as the outcome of political struggles in the nineteenth-century Americas.

Loyalty, Race, and Slavery

In many ways, histories of race and loyalty in Cuba are nothing new. Race has long figured prominently as an explanation of Cuba's "ever faithful" political culture during the nineteenth century. By far the most common argument has cited white Cubans' fears of racial reprisal as the African slave population increased to accommodate the explosive growth of the sugarcane industry. John Lynch, for example, writes that "slave revolt was so fearful a prospect that creoles were loathe to leave the shelter of imperial government and break ranks with the dominant whites unless there was a viable alternative."[4] Other scholars, too, have put the decision-making power in the hands of the island's economic elite. This focus makes sense, given the considerable power that the elite held both locally and in their negotiations with the crown for the concessions that enabled the expansion of the slave trade and sugar cultivation. Capital often superseded, controlled, and coincided with the interests of state, and not surprisingly the Spanish empire functioned in ways that distributed power to those who profited from the island's agricultural enterprises. In other words, the choice (to the extent that it could be chosen) between colonial rule and national independence was one made by a small segment of the island's white population, one with deep investments in the stability of the growing slave society.[5] A thin echelon of privileged Cubans benefited both from the coercive and violent powers of the Spanish state and by the state's delegation of coercive and violent powers to slaveowners. The loyalty of the white elite postponed national independence, as common arguments go, and other Cubans endured the mechanisms of social control imposed by the Spanish government, especially those designed to regulate slavery, capture runaway slaves, suppress rebellions, and limit political discourse.

This interpretation is persuasive. But by widening the frame of Cuban history to examine race and loyalty in the context of Spanish America and the African diaspora, more expansive arguments become visible. Instead of locating support for Spain primarily in the Spanish and creole population, and linking them to a particular class experience, historians of the Americas have found the support of ordinary colonials, including those of indigenous and African ancestry, critical in explaining the trajectories of colonial and republican rule. Jorge Domínguez notes "the enormous variety of reasons why a great many people in Spanish America across the economic hierarchies and the color spectrum resisted those who clamored for independence and often fought with their blood and guts" against it.[6] Attention to popular politics has not simply made visible a wider cast of actors; it has also revealed how racial ideology shaped projects of independence, royalism, and many other imagined political communities whose possibilities have been rendered invisible by a near single-minded focus on the formation of national states.

Thus the title phrase "ends of empire." Rather than identifying the generation of wealth for planters and the Spanish state as the sole end, or goal, of the imperial project, this book emphasizes the multiple reasons that empire lasted so long in Cuba, namely because so many individuals looked to colonial rule to attain a wide variety of ends. Among those aims figured formal membership in a political community that was sometimes inclusive of (but never exhausted by) the idea of liberal citizenship. We can also understand the ends of empire to refer to its limits or extremities. Indeed, the history of loyalty in Cuba cannot be told as one of unqualified success. One of the reasons that the concept held so much value throughout the nineteenth century was because at some point just about everyone expressed discontent with Spanish rule on the island. They discovered and tested the limits of empire—where their loyalty began and ended—including the question of whether Cubans of African descent could be considered, and know themselves to be, loyal subjects. Finally, the ends of empire are obviously chronological. No single year marked the end of the Spanish empire, as various areas of Spanish territory declared independence at different times. Moreover, the many new nations that emerged during the nineteenth century felt the effects of colonial rule long after its formal conclusion. And of course, empire in Cuba did not end in 1898 with victory against Spain in the independence war; the intervention of the United States at the end of the conflict signaled a new imperial presence that operated on new terms. Thus, the goals and limits of Spanish imperialism in Cuba intersect with the chronological questions of why empire didn't end earlier and how it eventually did.

Looking to beginnings, in contrast, the importance of popular support for European rule in the colonial Americas had almost always been necessary for the establishment of empire, and for much of the colonial period that support coalesced around the figure of the benevolent and protective monarch.[7] Depending on their legal and social status as slaves, free people, Indians, or women and children, individuals assumed to be inferior could lay claim to royal benefaction by occupying a subject position as humble and loyal subjects with affective ties to empire. For example, Eric Van Young has argued about New Spain that "in the Spanish colony as one descended the social pyramid and found one's self in a countryside still predominantly indigenous in makeup, the sign of the tyrannous monarch reversed itself into that of the defender of his most humble subjects, who became the object of messianic fervor."[8] At the same time, assumptions (and inventions) of indigenous allegiance to the Spanish system allowed independence supporters to cast Indians as backward and unfit for the Mexican nation.[9] The protective ethos could be extended as well to the multiple holders of sovereignty in the colonial world: colonial officials in Spain and in the colonies at the level of vice-royalties, captaincies general, provinces and towns, and even slaveowners. Native elites whose claims to nobility were backed by Spanish authority found strategic reasons to support colonialism: Andean peasants in the Ayacucho region articulated alternatives to the nascent Peruvian state in the language of loyalty to the Spanish crown.[10] Slaves in New Granada identified themselves "his Majesty's slaves" in a petition at the end of the eighteenth century, and racial hierarchies there relaxed as the Bourbon state recognized the political benefits of affirming slaves' claims to honor and respect.[11] With the arrival of the Portuguese court to Rio de Janeiro in 1808, Brazilian slaves used royal courts to advance petitions for freedom, which, though they were rarely successful, affirmed the authority of the monarch over that of slave owners.[12] And Spanish officials actively sought the military support of African-descended subjects, both free and enslaved, during the South American wars for independence. For some free men, this extended their service in free-colored militias and, for some slaves, it represented an opportunity for freedom.[13]

The cumulative impact of these histories encourages a reexamination of the racial politics of Cuban loyalty to Spanish rule. This need not negate the significance of Cuba's Spanish and creole leaders, whose class interests and racial anxieties informed their own allegiance. Rather, it opens up new possibilities for understanding the role of race in nineteenth-century Cuban society, and it broadens a field of politics typically divided into discrete colonial and national units. Indisputably, most Cubans of African descent regularly confronted discrimination, violence, and legal subordination under colonial rule. Many (often those who were legally free) also found opportunities for membership and mobility in Spanish institutions. Separate militia units composed of free black and mulatto men, for example, had existed in some Cuban towns since the sixteenth century. The mass arrivals of African slaves in the late eighteenth and early nineteenth centuries dwarfed but never extinguished the communities of relatively prosperous free people of color, particularly in urban areas. *Cabildos* and *cofradías*, lay brotherhoods and mutual aid organizations, gave sanctioned institutional structure to organizations of free and enslaved Cubans of color that sometimes preserved African ethnic designations.[14] No wonder, then, that the slaves living in the copper-mining community of El Cobre, in eastern Cuba, experienced a highly conditional freedom once the crown confiscated derelict mines. A direct line to royal authority allowed the "royal slaves" to make claims based on their professed loyalty to their king and master. Slaves in the early nineteenth century acted on rumors of emancipation by royal authority, a phenomenon that Matt Childs terms "rebellious royalism."[15] None of these aspects of Cuban society guaranteed loyalty to Spanish rule, but they offered status linked to, and not in defiance of, putatively subordinating racial identifications. The principal contrast between pro-colonial allegiance in nineteenth-century Cuba and the earlier examples in Iberian America is that the figure of the monarch held much less purchase as the embodiment of Spanish justice. Dramatic transformations in Spanish politics throughout the century made forms of republican government—the Cortes (the parliament), various constitutions, and even political parties—a more visible signifier of Spanish sovereignty and the possibility of rights, citizenship, and inclusion.

Running throughout these developments, the political question of whether Cubans of color could express loyalty to Spanish rule was inextricably bound up with the social realm, particularly the quotidian experience of slavery. "Humility, obedience, loyalty," wrote Brazilian historian Katia Mattoso; "these were the cornerstones of the slave's new life." Indexing the terms by which the "good slave" could "acquire the know-how" to improve her or his situation, Mattoso makes clear the paternalistic values common to many slave societies in the Americas, Cuba included.[16] This idealized relationship has played a complicated role in depictions of slavery in the Americas, and it conditioned thinking about obedience and loyalty in its political forms. Countless fictional accounts contain stock characters of docile and loyal slaves who accept their conditions uncritically and sometimes continue to work for their masters after their freedom.[17] In the United States, the figure of Uncle Tom in Harriet Beecher Stowe's novel *Uncle Tom's Cabin* (1852) has been transposed, inaccurately, as a condescending stereotype for African Americans' passive acceptance of discrimination. Narratives about faithful slaves content with slavery and loathe to challenge their legal status, much less political rule, proliferated when slavery was in full swing. They lived on in subsequent histories to be memorialized in ways that reproduced and mollified the inequalities wrought by slavery.[18] Thus, historians in their wake faced an uphill historiographic battle in documenting the resistance of the enslaved and free to the inequalities they faced.[19]

The figure of the loyal slave captured the attention of Cubans as well during the nineteenth century. At their most idealistic, Cuban planters linked the hierarchy between colony and metropole to the hierarchy between masters and slaves, even using the risky rhetorical strategy of decrying unfair conditions under colonial rule as enslavement. Assurances of colonial stability could link royal and private authority through evidence of slaves' supposed loyalty. Writing to the king in 1790, a group of planters recalled the widespread flight of slaves during the occupation of Havana by the British in 1762–63. But "once Your Majesty's august father was restored," they argued, "the slaves themselves sought us out on their own, under no undue influence or persuasion (fugitives, criminals, and the wicked excepted)." Spanish benevolence also explained to them why freed slaves often continued working on the same sugar estates, which they would never have done "if those very same owners had been such tyrants."[20] The fantasy of the submissive slave, as Sibylle Fischer has noted of Cuban literature, gained particular resonance in the aftermath of the Haitian Revolution and, in that fantasy's sublimation of black agency, could have shaped the political imagination of the creole elite. "The possibility of Cuban autonomy and independence," she argues, "depends on the suppression of black insurrection and the substitution of affective, voluntary submission through brute force."[21] A main goal of this book is to revisit questions of race and loyalty without assuming affective and voluntary submission as fact but seeing its figuration as central to Cuban racial politics. That Cubans of all backgrounds could express support for colonial rule does not imply that they did so based exclusively on their whiteness, blackness, wealth, poverty, and so on. They did, however, express that support frequently through language that drew on deeply entrenched ideas about social status, hierarchy, and belonging—including the idea of the loyal slave.

The significance of this story to the history of the African diaspora cannot be understated, even if it can be difficult to document. Enslaved Africans and their descendants constituted one of the populations that felt the inequality, violence, and exclusion of imperialism most severely in the Americas. But they also, against the odds, formed bonds of community, political in nature and sometimes drawing on iconographic vocabularies of monarchical rule and empire. Anthropologist Lorand Matory acknowledges that "the people of the black Atlantic never simply embraced nation-states as sufficient indices of their collective identities." His insights into Afro-Brazilian religious practices confirm that the transnational processes that define the African diaspora perhaps best demonstrate that "territorial jurisdictions have never monopolized the loyalty of the citizens and subjects that they claim, and they are never the sole founts of authority or agents of constraint in such people's lives."[22] Alternative conceptions of community in the diaspora have often been expressed in idioms of culture and religion, and to great effect.[23] But what about politics? To the extent that these frames can be discrete, scholarship about the African diaspora has focused on culture more than politics. To take seriously, as historian Steven Hahn describes them, "the political tendencies of self-determination and self-defense" in the history of African Americans (imagined hemispherically) is to allow the possibility of imperial affiliations in their multifaceted struggles for freedom.[24] It is also an invitation to move past plotting royalist or monarchist ideologies along a spectrum that renders them archaic and retrograde in relation to liberal and national forms, and to consider instead a hidden history of modern politics based on earlier traditions of community and belonging.[25]

Empires, Nations, and Liberal Subjects

What does it mean to be loyal to an empire? From the vantage point of the twenty-first century, questions of patriotism and political allegiance usually target nation-states, while dismissing pro-colonial affinities as the misfires of historical subjects acting against their interests: dupes, victims, collaborators.[26] On closer inspection, answers for the two political forms can be strikingly similar when placed side by side. Asking how loyalty to an empire differs from loyalty to a nation-state implies, at least in part, that the two political forms are mutually exclusive; this was not the case in nineteenth-century Cuba. In the context of the Americas, singling out imperial loyalty as a historical "problem" reinforces an assumed evolutionary progression from colonial rule to national independence, or at least to political affiliations that are non- or postimperial. Those assumptions do not originate with contemporary scholars. Cuban intellectual Father Félix Varela, for example, wrote in 1824 that whatever support existed for King Ferdinand VII of Spain would never survive the march of progress: "Whether Fernando wants it or not, and regardless of the opinion of his vassals on the island of Cuba, the country's revolution is inevitable."[27] The unavoidability of national independence routinely implies that "bad" political traditions originated with colonial rule and that the "good" ones emerged with nation-states, even when their ideals of national rights and citizenship are not fully realized.

The point here is not that colonial rule was good or bad for the Cubans who lived under it, or better or worse than a national government. One purpose of this book is to broadly explore what political practices colonial rule enabled and suppressed, who could practice them, and the criteria for determining that "who." My approach stands in contrast to histories of late Spanish colonialism that adopt the frame of nation-states (and their anachronistic postcolonial names such as Mexico, the Dominican Republic, or Bolivia) and work backward to trace the historical events that led to the successful realization of nations. Instead, I take up Frederick Cooper's challenge to consider "what it meant for a polity *to think like an empire*, to conjugate incorporation and differentiation, to confront problems of long-distance extension and recognize limits of control over large and diverse populations."[28] Thinking like an empire was not limited to its political and economic elites, and it helps explain why the Spanish might have cultivated and received the support of ordinary Cubans.

This approach to empire also restores some contingency to Cuban history by avoiding easy assumptions that the island's trajectory was delayed or out of step, that opposition to Spanish rule was the default position of most Cubans, or that Cuban nationalism was the sole engine of popular politics in the nineteenth century. Ada Ferrer, Jorge Ibarra, and Francisco Pérez Guzmán, among others, have thoroughly demonstrated that the path to Cuban independence was by no means preordained; nor was the race-transcendent vision that developed within it and became central to its purpose.[29] The dramatic transformations that accompanied the independence movement occurred alongside, in reaction to, and sometimes in the shadows of changes happening within a Spanish polity by no means slowly fizzling out over the course of the century. Seeing the dynamism of Spanish rule brings even the struggle for Cuban independence into sharper view as one of multiple and overlapping political projects that attracted popular support.

Extending to Cubans public rights already enjoyed by citizens in Spain, for example, marked a change in the late nineteenth century from earlier policies that excluded Cubans from the promises of Spanish liberalism. Thinking like an empire, it turns out, was complicated when Spaniards thought simultaneously like a nation.[30] Cubans experienced the tensions between nation and empire acutely as their status shifted with the winds of Spanish constitutional politics. The Constitution of 1812 embraced liberal principles earlier than most other European constitutions, and its definition of citizenship in the Spanish nation—which included the indigenous inhabitants of Spanish America but not those of African descent—drew on liberalism as well as early modern Castilian notions of citizenship and belonging.[31] The promise of those rights in Cuba was unevenly fulfilled in the years when the constitution was in effect (1812–14, 1820–23), and even when a new constitution in 1836 explicitly excluded the colonies, aspirations toward Spanish citizenship—by the end of the century, particularly among Cuban men of color—contrasted sharply with the imagined citizenship of an independent Cuba. It also contrasted with the privileges and incentives extended to imperial subjects, which had a long history in Spanish America. It required Cubans to imagine the reciprocities of pro-colonial loyalty in Cuba in terms of both citizenship and rights, on one hand, and privileges and protections, on the other.

If Cuban independence was not the universal aspiration of the island's inhabitants, and if slavery and racial hierarchies (to say nothing of gender distinctions) shut out many inhabitants from claiming Spanish citizenship, there was still another path to political personhood and belonging: the forms of public expression predicated on the inequality, subordination, and vulnerability of being a colonial subject. Throughout the book, I refer to this path, and the kinds of subjects idealized by the Spanish state and Cubans themselves, as loyal subjectivity.[32] Cubans of color, slave and free, could inhabit loyal subjectivity because of, and not despite, the so-called "defects" of their status.

That this mode of political expression infused discussions of citizenship and rights invites a dialogue with scholars of mainland Iberian independence who have recognized the colonial moorings of putatively "national" forms of representation, sovereignty, legitimacy, and inclusion. Excessive attention to the burden of the Spanish past on Latin American nation-states compounded the region's problem of persistence, as Jeremy Adelman has called it, and historians of Latin America have balanced attention between the influences of Spanish structures and ideas and the innovativeness of experiments with liberal citizenship following independence.[33] Cuba can thus be seen as central, rather than peripheral, to the political history of Latin America in the nineteenth century if we understand, following Adelman, that "the ambiguities of sovereignty could not be easily dissimulated in visions of nationhood or political power without the existence of previous deep-seated ideologies to justify them."[34] Loyalty to Spanish rule was always about more than strategic calculations and anxiety about radical change. It was imbued with longstanding principles of political membership expressed affectively and whose traces remained long after independence.

Those principles were by no means unique to Cuba or to the Spanish empire. Given my interest in a diasporic population and a form of politics exceeding a national frame (whether Cuban or Spanish), *Ever Faithful* should not be read as a story of Cuban exceptionalism. The major themes of the book also find parallels in Anglophone, Lusophone, and Francophone colonial histories. And, as Rebecca Scott notes, Cuba was among many slave societies that experienced "pervasive uncertainty over whether persons held as property could, in practice, also be colonial subjects deserving of protection."[35] If colonial loyalty might appear anachronistic within the history of Cuban nationalism, it should appear downright typical in the context of the Caribbean, where the British empire held on until the 1980s, Martinique and Guadeloupe are still departments of France, and the historical presence of the United States challenges easy declarations of the end of empire. Spanish attempts to merge liberal principles with imperial practices exposed the limits of Cuban political inclusion, particularly around questions of race and slavery. Those attempts also resemble other forms of imperial citizenship more closely associated with French and British rule during the period.[36] Loyal subjects were ubiquitous in Europe's African, Asian, and Caribbean colonies, and they were more than understudies in the performance of liberal politics; they shared the stage, and sometimes even roles, with national citizens.

Writing a History of Loyalty

Histories of the people, politics, and culture of Cuba and the African diaspora have for decades circled around the theme of resistance. Given the weighty legacies of slavery, imperialism, capitalism, and their attendant violence, it is of little surprise that attention has focused on challenges to those deep structures. Historians have read sources "against the grain" to emphasize the visibility of people who openly contested their exclusion from power. But what about when those people didn't? Rebellion, revolt, and revolution have been privileged modes of identifying subaltern agency—including African American politics—with the effect that disloyalty is far better understood than loyalty. If the latter may hold less appeal for its associations with conservative or accommodationist politics, attending to it may loosen the tight connection drawn between resistance and agency.[37] Yet attempts to historicize loyalty run afoul of formidable methodological hurdles.

Perhaps the most significant problem lies in the sources themselves. To the extent that pro-Spanish loyalty represented a normative political position against which others were contrasted, it often went unmarked in the historical record—no head counts, no lengthy theorizing, and no generous documentation produced within a fully formed social movement. At the same time, there is the ever-present "Ever Faithful" emblem marked on official correspondence. Its pervasiveness does not prove its sincerity any more than signing "sincerely" at the end of correspondence today. But filtering it out as an irrelevant formality glosses the power relations that shape the material production and reception of documents. Recipients of royal decrees in Spanish America ritually kissed the royal seal on the document and then held it above their heads to acknowledge the monarch's authority.[38] As Kathryn Burns writes of colonial notarial templates, "knowing something about the formulae one encounters in the archive is as useful as having some insight into the relations between the parties involved."[39] The struggles of colonial officials charged with maintaining Cuba's fidelity come into sharp relief when they entertained the possibility of extending privileges to African-descended Cubans persistently characterized as rebellious and unfit for political participation. How well can an official report, then, index political subjectivity when both the language of loyalty and the language of resistance may be so commonplace as to overdetermine even basic description?

Drawing on periodicals, literary sources, and proceedings of associations, political parties, military units, and municipal, island-wide, and Spanish "national" governing bodies, this book draws on a wide range of sources to examine loyalty as something neither merely rhetorical nor a verifiable belief. One case in point bears attention. Scholars who have searched for evidence of resistance and rebellion in Cuba's colonial past have been intrigued by the subversive behavior or African-derived cultural practices that might have been taking place in various urban clubs and associations. They have productively interpreted such documents against the grain of colonial discourse, reading past the language of loyalty and subordination that characterizes the public statements of those institutions.[40] My reading of nineteenth-century documents places this language front and center: as evidence of a mode of engagement with the colonial state that may fit uneasily with the language of liberal citizenship or revolutionary rhetoric but that nevertheless offered African-descended Cubans a public voice for inhabiting loyal subjectivity. For historians conditioned to examine sources for perspectives silenced or forgotten by the archival record, however, there might be good reason to suspect that statements of popular support for empire served as "respectable performances" and little else.[41] But to write them off them entirely as elite fantasies or false consciousness is to miss the chance to glimpse what Ann Stoler calls "the febrile movements of persons off balance—of thoughts and feelings in and out of place." "In tone and temper," she continues, "[archives] convey the rough interior edges of governance and disruptions to the deceptive clarity of its mandates."[42] In other words, summary dismissal prevents us from imagining that the point of contact between subjects and representatives of the colonial state might sometimes identify—uneasily and messily—common ground or a shared ideology of rule, as opposed to exclusively adversarial relationships.

Another problem of grasping loyalty revolves around identifying who supported Spanish rule in the nineteenth century. Attempts to provide a demographic profile of pro-Spanish loyalty in Cuba miss an always shifting target. No matter how hard they tried, Spanish officials could never measure or predict, or document, the demographic dimensions of popular loyalty. Numbers of soldiers, even, were difficult to aggregate, and concealed the desertions and defections common on all sides of the island's military conflicts. Political affiliations never mapped neatly onto geographical regions or census categories, and certainly not racial identifications, in a way that allows for neat conclusions about who might predictably have affirmed colonial rule. Given the nature of the evidence, it is tempting to characterize the Cubans of African descent most likely to support colonial rule as urban, free, island born (as opposed to African born), and overwhelmingly male. Indeed, much of the evidence for this study points to such individuals. But there are plenty of examples of rural, enslaved, African-born men and women who found themselves fighting alongside the Spanish army, traveling to see a politician passing through town, or phrasing a petition in the language of humility and obedience. Despite the exciting evidence of women of color participating in public life and the surprising evidence of slave women engaged in Spanish military campaigns, one definitive demographic conclusion about loyalty is that women faced serious challenges to inhabiting loyal subjectivity, which means that examples of their success might better be understood as exceptions rather than the rule—or, in contrast, that Spanish authorities and other observers had reasons for erasing or understating the presence of women in a public world that operated on paternalistic terms and that posed challenges for subaltern men to make their voices heard.

No matter who claimed it, loyalty was, and is, a slippery concept. It at once occupies an old-fangled and modern place in political imaginaries: on one hand, the feudal pacts between lord and vassal; ancient conflicts between family and community; the thick ties of blood, faith, and status evoke primordial bonds that resist the spaces of modern, secular politics. On the other hand, political allegiance appears in some political theory as a product of the individual will or choice that is constitutive of the modern liberal subject. In fact, thinking about patriotism or affinity is so closely linked to liberal political theory—or to the nation-state—that there seems little room to consider individual choices affecting empires, dictatorships, or other systems reflexively deemed undemocratic or illiberal.[43] In part, this association appears so pervasive because claims about loyalty rest more on theory than on the function of the concept in specific historical circumstances. Historicizing key political concepts has yielded great insights into Latin American society when applied, for example, to the idea of honor.[44] In methodological terms, historicizing loyal subjectivity draws on many of the approaches that historicize resistance; rather than delineating the repertoires of rebellion and revolution so central to Cuban, Latin American, and African American history, this book offers instead a genealogy of consent.

One useful approach to understanding loyalty can be found in Albert Hirschman's classic study of how individuals respond to a qualitative decline in firms. Hirschman postulated three basic possibilities. The first, exit—or leaving—stands in contrast to the second, voice—an attempt to change "an objectionable state of affairs." A third option is loyalty, a "feeling of attachment" and the "reluctance to exit in spite of disagreement." Loyalty benefits institutions (such as states), Hirschman argues, when the costs of exit are low and when alternatives are less than desirable. The "consumer," or, for our purposes, the political subject, finds loyalty beneficial because it opens up possibilities for dialogue and critique.[45] Within the problem-space of colonial and national politics, Hirschman offers a path forward from national histories centered on exits from colonial rule, and he also foregrounds loyalty as an affective posture that allows for the potential to express voice within the world of empire. Jeremy Adelman, for example, has fruitfully brought Hirschman's concept to bear on the South American independence movements, taking care to note the loyalty expressed by most of colonial Spanish America when crisis erupted in Spain.[46]

Bringing Cuba into the picture only amplifies the importance of looking at colonial politics on its own terms, rather than from the outside space of the modern nation. It revives loyalty to colonial rule as an active historical process and a crucial element in cementing Spanish hegemony, rather than an inertial default position obstructing radical change. As useful as Hirschman's framework may be, I try not to remain bound to a single schematic throughout the book. Instead, I try to understand the historical actors I encounter to be theorists of loyalty in their own right: when slave-soldiers explained why they enlisted in the Spanish army; when a colonial official reinstated the militias of color after their abolition; when the editor of a black newspaper explained how racial affiliations could complement, rather than compete with, ties to Spanish rule; or the myriad instances in which Cubans themselves defined loyalty in counterpoint to the disloyalty they believed was always around the corner. Within particular contexts, I also analyze behaviors and actions not named as loyalty front and center but that conform to patterns that people elsewhere commonly acknowledged as loyalty. If we can understand that invocations of loyalty may sometimes have been disingenuous, we should also acknowledge other instances when Cubans grappled with questions of loyalty without actually naming it as such.[47]

Because attention to the issue of Cuba's continued colonial status became acute during the early nineteenth century, or the tail end of the Age of Revolutions, I begin the book with two chapters that survey those decades from two angles. In chapter 1, I consider the implications of the tectonic political shifts in the Spanish empire for Cubans' status as subjects and citizens. The Napoleonic invasion of Spain, the independence movements, and most important, the liberal Spanish Constitution of 1812 redefined the relationship between Spain and its colonies and the categories of political belonging available to colonial subjects. Colonial officials wavered on how these changes would affect political definitions of being Spanish or white, the freedoms of free men of color, and even the status of the inhabitants of Cuba's last two Indian pueblos. With formal citizenship and representation off the table more often than not, chapter 2 explores how Cubans attemped to express loyalty to Spain rule as a historical strategy for gaining privileges, access, and mobility. Colonial policies aimed at stifling seditious activity and slave rebellions restricted opportunities for popular politics in general, but a coherent picture of what a loyal subject was supposed to be still came into focus. Restrictive measures left Cubans at midcentury with an ambivalent sense of belonging to the Spanish empire, especially people of African descent, who saw the militias abolished and reinstituted and who found their desires to be loyal subjects checked by other Cubans.

The initiation of the Ten Years' War (1868–78) reactivated the military dimension of popular allegiance to colonial rule at the same time at which Spain began the gradual process of slave emancipation. Chapter 3 plunges into the wartime drama to reveal a resurgence of active support for Spanish rule, even as the incorporation of slaves and free people of color into counterinsurgent ranks operated on more limited terms than in the multiracial rebel army. The military adjustment to the presence of Cubans of color overlapped with one crucial component of the abolition law, which offered freedom to slaves who fought against insurgents. The interrogations of slave-soldiers provide a rich source for the construction of loyal subjectivity as soldiers and officers often disagreed on its definition.

The last three chapters of the book address the flourishing of public life in Cuba following the war. Cubans of African descent took great advantage of the extension of Spanish constitutional protections in the forms of press and associational freedoms and sanctioned political parties. Chapter 4 examines the amplified meaning of loyalty in the burgeoning public sphere as black newspapers and organizations attempted to prove their readiness for freedom and citizenship. Chapter 5 zooms in on an incident that took place in the southern port city of Cienfuegos just weeks after the formal abolition of slavery in 1886. The racial politics of traveling representatives of the Liberal Autonomist Party blurred the boundaries between robust popular loyalty and violent public disturbance. Finally, chapter 6 looks at the final years of Spanish rule in terms of how the proliferation of political affiliations merged with frustrations about the slow pace of postemancipation improvements to marginalize the role of the loyal subject. The war for independence that began in 1895 only increased the fragmentation on the island, and by 1898 new relationships between race and loyalty emerged as Spain was defeated, the United States intervened, and a race-transcendent vision of Cuban independence faced an uncertain future in a new republic.

Throughout the book, cities and towns frequently provide the setting for the main developments and patterns that I trace. Clearly, Havana, the capital, and Santiago, the second-largest city and main anchor of eastern Cuba, feature prominently. I give particular attention as well to the southern port city of Cienfuegos. This focus emerged at first from encountering the rich documentation in its provincial archive and the effervescent community of scholars who gravitated toward it. Eventually, Cienfuegos developed a purpose inherent to my argument about race, loyalty, and empire. It was founded in 1819 through a Spanish initiative for white immigration to Cuba but quickly developed an economy that, like most other parts of the island, employed

African slave labor. As a large slave population, a smaller free population, and a multiracial society took shape, residents of Cienfuegos—and those governing it—did not miss the transformation from what was supposed to be a white colony. Its role in the independence wars and its extensive public life shed light on some islandwide trends; of more significance, it offers a glimpse into the workings of race and loyalty not conditioned by competing connotations ascribed to Santiago and Havana: a center of potential and actualized anticolonial resistance, for the former, and the center of imperial power and intellectual life, for the latter.[48]

Finally, a note about terminology. Most books about race in Latin America clarify classifications that might seem most confusing to contemporary English-speaking readers.[49] This is necessary and standard practice: readers should understand the synonymy between designations of *pardo* and *mulato* (usually translated as "mulatto" throughout the book)—both referring to mixed African and Spanish ancestry—and between *moreno* and *negro* (translated as "black" or kept as "negro"—references to blackness and sometimes to "pure" African descent. In many cases, ambiguity in the sources prevents distinguishing these groups, so I use the term "Cubans of color" or "Cubans of African descent" when necessary. An increase in references to *gente de color* (people of color) and the *raza de color* took place in the second half of the century, which fused *mulato* and *negro* nomenclature. *Casta,* another ambiguous term, denoted any person of mixed ancestry. There was a dual use of *criollo* (creole) to describe Cuban-born Spaniards (in contrast to *peninsulares,* from Spain) and Cuban-born people of African descent (in contrast to *bozales,* who were born in Africa). We should approach the anachronistic term *afrocubano* with caution, as it speaks more to twentieth-century reckonings of race and nation than to the era of Spanish rule. And above all, readers should realize how slippery each of these concepts could be, as categories overlapped to collapse and differentiate groups and individuals with frequent inconsistency.

For the purposes of this book, equal attention is due to the presumed normative categories against which these racial "differences" became meaningful. A relatively unexplored area of historical research concerns the meaning of whiteness in the colonial world. Being white was by no means inevitably interchangeable with being Spanish. Both categorizations depended on situational and relational criteria that could encompass parentage and place of origin (sometimes verifiable with baptismal records) as much as color.[50] The well-known *casta* paintings of eighteenth-century Spanish America, which visually charted the dizzying number of categories of mixture, placed an *español,*

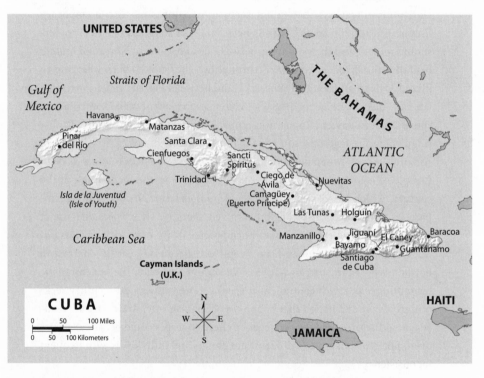

MAP 1 • Map of Cuba with major cities and contemporary political boundaries.

not a *blanco*, at the top of the hierarchy. The conceptual links between race, blood, and place of birth made references to Spanish blood more common than white blood, although in the system's originary trinity of Spanish, Indian, and black, black blood could also be referred to as African blood.[51] Informal estimations of color often identified individuals as white—or sometimes *trigueño*, "wheaty" or olive-skinned—and as the century progressed, more standardized censuses and references to Cubans "of color" elevated the category of whiteness above Spanishness. When the Spanish government established a Comisión Blanca in the 1810s to encourage "white" immigration to Cuba, it initially had peninsular Spaniards in mind, but low interest on the peninsula forced the commission to broaden out to include French and British migrants. Even as Cubans increasingly spoke of "whites"—often in relation to anxieties about "black" (read as slave and free, *negro* and *mulato*) rebellion—they stayed focused on the category of "Spaniard" in light of the Constitution of 1812's provision that anyone residing in Spanish territory could be considered as such. ("Citizen" was a different story.) The shifting uses and definitions of white and Spaniard should encourage readers to avoid easy linkages between the two.

An equally relevant clarification at the outset concerns my references to loyalty. Scholarship that considers pro-colonial sentiment in the Francophone, Anglophone, Lusophone, and Hispanophone imperial worlds regularly deploys the term "royalism" to shorthand various forms of allegiance during the eras of colonialism and independence, and "loyalists" to refer to the people who pledged it. These terms rarely appear in nineteenth-century Cuban and Spanish documents. The meaning of royal authority changed as Spain became a constitutional monarchy, and the monarch, as the source of authority and paternal rule, lost some of the symbolic prominence it had in earlier centuries.[52] The conflicted and interrupted reigns of specific monarchs (such as Fernando VII and Isabel II), moreover, dimmed the luster of things "royal." I tend to avoid the term "loyalists" as well. Reading across the different imperial case studies, supporters of European empires throughout the Atlantic world in the Age of Revolutions often embraced the term. And indeed, one of the richest fields of comparison for this book is that which considers African-descended British loyalists in the Atlantic World after the American Revolution.[53]

On closer inspection, a pattern emerges in these studies: individuals and governments identified loyalists primarily after colonial rule or during the military conflicts that ended it, when the ability to win favors and collect reparations or pensions depended on the guise of permanent allegiance to the metropole. This created "strong identity" (to borrow Frederick Cooper and Rogers Brubaker's term) intended to remain fixed and durable over time.[54] Instead, popular allegiance might better be understood in more flexible terms, as a mode of political belonging strategically invoked by states and subjects alike and, in the case of nineteenth-century Cuba, a concept joined to racial ideology in order to cement Spanish hegemony in Cuba. This is the idea behind my discussion of loyal subjectivity. The decision to avoid cementing allegiance as an "-ism" should not imply that Cubans, particularly those of African descent, were incapable of maintaining durable political ideas. They lived during a period when ideologies and social movements changed radically and rapidly—even, and perhaps especially, liberalism, a practice whose contingency was evident to almost everyone.

ONE

Belonging to an Empire
Race and Rights

The blood of colored men is red, and so is that of warriors, of healthy men: pure and noble blood. The *juntas* established in America have won this class over, granting them the equality for which they yearn. We must win them back with a similar declaration. "Come, *pardo*," I would say: "Do not stray in search of the sweet food you desire. Do not flee your home to seek it, poor wretch (for they are very humble and like to be treated like this). Here at home you can have it."
—José Mejía Lequerica, addressing the Cortes of Cádiz, 1810

Napoleon Bonaparte's invasion of Spain in 1808 prompted a remarkably uniform response from the Spanish American colonies: demonstrations of loyalty to the exiled monarch Fernando VII and the establishment of *juntas* (councils) that would rule in the king's name as Joseph Bonaparte assumed the Spanish throne. Few calls for independence could be heard in the Americas. The Junta Central in Spain called for an assembly to redefine the relationships between the king, his government, and his subjects, and in so doing it began to imagine what it meant for Spain to exist as both an empire and a nation. With French troops advancing south from Madrid, the Junta Central retreated in 1810 to the Isla de León at the southern port of Cádiz, and dissolved to form a Regency Council that called for an assembly to draft Spain's first constitution. It included deputies from across the Atlantic but stopped short of asserting the political equality of the American territories; the deputies instead insisted that they were not from "colonies or outposts (*factorías*) like those of other nations, but an essential and integral part of the Spanish monarchy."[1] So many interested parties from across the empire descended on the city to observe and participate in the proceedings that one onlooker wrote that "Spain had almost entirely been reduced to the walls of Cádiz."[2]

That microcosm bustled with people maintaining an empire entering its fourth century. Among the official delegates to the constitutional Cortes

(Parliament) figured titled nobles, priests, lawyers, and merchants, and they mingled in the city with the sailors, slaves, and artisans who had done their part, too, for the prosperity and defense of Spain. By 1812, sixty-three of the delegates—about a fifth of the total—represented the American colonies.[3] As the port in Spain through which most trade and communication with the Americas took place, Cádiz was no stranger to transatlantic arrivals or to the presence of slaves, who were bought and sold there as they were in other imperial ports. But during the constitutional debates, the presence of Americans and people of African descent—both of them subjected to a subordinate political status—served as a powerful reminder of the limits of the liberal principles being fiercely debated. That some of the American juntas began to favor independence and seek supporters of native and African origins exposed the contradictions in the Cádiz debates even further.

In the midst of the commotion was a free Cuban man of African descent experiencing firsthand how the Spanish state gave political significance to racial difference. José María Rodríguez, identified in documents as a free mulatto and *vecino* (resident) of Havana, spent the early months of 1812 stuck in Cádiz with no apparent role in the constitutional drama. Instead, he was struggling to acquire a passport—in this era, permission to make a single voyage—that would let him travel back to Cuba to take care of urgent financial matters and then return to Cádiz with the money that he needed to conduct business. He was one of several Cubans whose requests to travel stalled as the imperial bureaucracy struggled to stay afloat. Unlike applicants of full Spanish descent, however, Rodríguez had to wait for the Real Audiencia (high court) in Havana to send documentation of his free status back to Spain before he could receive permission to travel.[4] Moving within the empire as well as beyond it irregularly required state documentation for most people, and a passport—a basic document that identified membership in a sovereign political community— presented particular challenges to free people of African descent, whose full legal personhood was not recognized by Spanish law. In contrast, thousands of enslaved Africans continued to travel the Atlantic against their will each year with no such passports; as far as customs houses and officials were concerned they were cargo, property, but rarely individual people with fixed legal identities who required documentation. Rodríguez's hassles occurred as the Cortes of Cádiz was determining the legal status of free people of African descent: whether they could be Spanish citizens or remain Spanish subjects.

The crisis in Spain precipitated an empire-wide crisis of coherence, and people from Cortes delegates to frustrated Cubans routinely used the language of race to formulate their responses. Drawing on old languages of citizenship and inclusion, the Cortes of Cádiz initiated new conversations about the political subjectivity of African-descended people in the Iberian world that became particularly resonant in Cuba as it remained part of the empire. Although the Constitution of 1812 was in effect only briefly (from 1812 to 1814 and 1820 to 1823), it established the terms of debates about who did and could belong to the newly imagined Spanish national empire, despite its long-term inability to reconcile liberalism with an ongoing imperial project.[5] In the context of a French invasion of the mother country, restructuring the Spanish nation had immediate implications for Cubans. In the wake of the Haitian Revolution, French refugees arrived from Hispaniola. Now that the French had seized Spain, did those immigrants obey the same king? Did support for France equate to sedition or solidarity?

Independence movements in mainland Spanish America found their origins less in long-simmering nationalisms than in the chaos produced from competing attempts to reformulate Spanish sovereignty after 1808.[6] In this light, the politics of empire in Cuba merit close attention. The historical developments that postponed violent independence conflicts in Cuba do not necessarily attest to an inherently conservative, backward-looking, or risk-averse political culture. As is well known many well-to-do Cubans preferred Spanish stability to the risks of a violent conflict when both sugar production and slavery were expanding precipitously—in other words, loyalty to Spain represented "the price of prosperity."[7] That explanation leans heavily on the racial anxieties of white Cubans.[8] As the Cortes of Cádiz and other imperial projects reconsidered the privileges and meanings of whiteness in the early nineteenth century, the diverse Cubans who shaped the island's political trajectory did not stop at trying to stifle independence; they sought to reimagine the goals and limitations of loyalty to the Spanish empire and the political languages through which they expressed that support.

Race, Rights, and the Constitution of 1812

Spain's political identity as an empire had long been supported by legal structures and governing institutions that generated interrelated hierarchical distinctions between its diverse subjects. Representative advisory councils called *cortes* dated back to medieval Iberian kingdoms, but throughout the colonial period, the colonies had not figured in what had become a fulsome legislative system. All of the monarch's subjects enjoyed the right of appeal, but the extension of royal justice to social subordinates functioned unevenly and according to paternalistic ideologies that attributed an inherent weakness to women, children, inhabitants of the colonies, and people of indigenous and African ancestry, who required the king's benevolent protection. Measures to ameliorate the conditions of these weaker people made no presumption of their equality or capacity for membership in a polity.[9] The crisis of 1808 effected dramatic reimaginings of these relationships. In the process of drafting a constitution in Cádiz, the question of who could belong to Spain overlapped with the question of how Spain would unite its territories around the world. The answer offered by the Cortes of Cádiz was to envision Spain much more explicitly as a nation, even as it sought to preserve its older imperial configuration and regain territorial control from France. As Henry Kamen explains it, "Spain existed as a nation because absence made it real."[10]

This is not to say that concepts of nationalism and citizenship did not exist before the Constitution of 1812. Among the earliest references to the Spanish nation, even in the absence of a political unit, were contrasts between Spanish *naturales* (natives) and *extranjeros* (foreigners), and indeed, the select few who would claim to be *vecinos* (residents or citizens) enjoyed limited formal rights offered by the crown. Early modern notions of *vecindad* and *naturaleza* were primarily local categories of belonging from which broader concepts of a national community later derived, although the monarch could naturalize foreigners by issuing a *carta de naturaleza* (naturalization letter). Inhabiting those categories involved negotiations and affirmations within towns and cities, and although the boundaries were rigid enough to prevent women from claiming vecindad, early cases of indigenous, mestizo, mulatto, and non-Spanish European vecinos and naturales attest to the fluidity, and perhaps informality, of these designations. What Tamar Herzog notes as a "growing identification between 'Spanishness' and citizenship" in the seventeenth and eighteenth centuries was often checked by individuals who proved their love of community or "a sufficient sense of loyalty," according to one eighteenth-century writer.[11] Thus test cases in the colonies often delineated citizenship's boundaries, as individuals not from Iberia attempted to claim membership and as migrants to the colonies longed for their homeland.

The Constitution of 1812 was a radical document that placed Spain far ahead of other European polities in its embrace of liberalism and its extension of citizenship rights guaranteed by a constitution. It limited the power of the crown and traced its authority to popular sovereignty; it established civil rights and free trade; and it announced the elimination of entail and seigneurial jurisdiction. Beyond the concrete outcomes, the proceedings of the constitutional Cortes in 1810 and 1811 devoted significant time to discussing basic political questions and how they might be applied to Spain and its empire.

What is sovereignty? What is a nation? Who are the people of a nation? What is a citizen? These questions led delegates to test the limits of vague commonplaces; especially vexing were the ideas that the nation was the collectivity of all Spaniards in both hemispheres and that the "voice of the people" resided in the majority. As in earlier negotiations of the meaning of vecindad and naturaleza, delegates routinely sought evidence in the details of colonialism and racial difference.[12]

From the outset, the deliberations in Cádiz had to address the question of the political representation for the Americas. By 1810 the provisional juntas that had been established in many Spanish American cities were no longer reliably supportive of Fernando VII and the Cádiz Cortes, sometimes out of calculated strategy, sometimes out of genuine confusion. Indeed, minor confusion about legitimate political authority punctuated early deliberations in Cuba. When news of the French invasion reached Havana in July 1808, the Marqués de Someruelos, the captain general, authorized the formation of a junta subordinate to the Junta Suprema Central in Spain, but two members of Havana's *ayuntamiento,* or city council, opposed the decision, claiming that there was no precedent or right to do so. Francisco Arango y Parreño, the modernizing political force behind Cuba's expansion of slavery and sugar cultivation, led a short-lived movement to form a Junta Suprema. With equal authority to those in Spain and presumably with the intent of reorganizing the government, the movement nominally claimed a state of exception that justified extraordinary power during crisis.[13] Ultimately, the ayuntamiento requested permission to form a junta on 26 July and in 1810 received a royal order thanking Cubans for "the demonstrations of loyalty and the common feelings in all American provinces of love for the King."[14] The Consejo de Regencia, which replaced the Junta Suprema Central, formed a Cortes in Cádiz and gave Cubans the right to representation in the Cortes in February 1810. When the Cortes first met at the end of September, twenty-seven delegates out of the ninety-nine represented the Americas. Cuba had two delegates: the Marqués de San Felipe y Santiago and Joaquín Santa Cruz.[15] Representation surfaced frequently as the principal problem of including the colonies in the process and nation. Many Spanish deputies understood that guaranteeing representation across the ocean was necessary to maintain the loyalty of the colonies but a threat, in numerical terms, to the dominance of peninsular Spaniards in a representative system.[16] Delegates from the Americas faced the dilemma of advocating for broad categories of citizenship that would include non-European populations in order to increase their proportional numbers, while remaining concerned about the social repercussions of extending rights so broadly at home. In contrast to finding colonies expressing increased frustration with Spanish rule, members of the Cortes worried that Spain had too many loyal subjects—namely the dark ones who threatened to outnumber them.

Despite the low-key presence of the Cuban deputies in the Cortes Constituyentes, the debates that took place had a profound impact on the island and on the way that ideas about race intersected with political rule and political allegiance. Certainly some concerns about who counted as a Spaniard minimized racial distinctions. Pedro Inguanzo, a delegate who consistently argued against the adoption of liberal principles, explained that the majority of the population included women, artisans, menial laborers, *rústicos* (bumpkins), and ignorant people who were too "docile and submissive" even to expect to have a voice, much less know how to represent "the people."[17] And the question of who could become a Spaniard was sometimes less about who lived within Spanish territory than who came from beyond it. The French intervention weighed heavily on the minds of delegates, and Francisco Javier Borrul, a delegate from Valencia, thought it appropriate to require a foreigner to live in Spanish territory for at least ten years before seeking naturaleza, "in order to ascertain his love of the nation and firm desires to follow our laws."[18] Belonging to the empire, in other words, depended on affective ties and avowed subordination—fundamental components of pro-colonial loyalty as its adherents frequently articulated it.

Several delegates recognized the incongruity between the embrace of liberal ideas and the continued existence of slavery, and proposals in July 1811 to abolish slavery and the slave trade were one of the first debates into which Cuban delegates actively entered. José Miguel Guridi y Alcocer and Agustín de Argüelles, who did the most to introduce the principles of liberalism into the constitutional debates, submitted proposals to abolish slavery in July 1811. Concerned, too, with property rights, Guridi y Alcocer proposed to require current slaves to "remain in servile condition" so as not to "defraud their owners of the money they cost them."[19] Argüelles, however paired his proposal to abolish the transatlantic slave trade with a call to abolish torture "tan bárbara y cruel [so barbaric and cruel]" and to live up to "the liberality and religiosity of the principles of Spain's criminal code."[20] Andrés de Jáuregui, a Cuban deputy, spoke against the proposal, promising that Cuba "today enjoys profound tranquility," and he worried about the political effects of altering "domestic peace" by abolishing slavery in "one of the most precious parts of overseas Spain." Domestic peace was a constant concern of Jáuregui to the extent that he requested that all discussions of slavery be conducted in secret sessions so that news of the proceedings did not reach Cuba and generate rumors of emancipation.[21]

Francisco Arango y Parreño, Cuba's great enlightened reformer and voice of the planter elite, regularly expressed concern that Cuba's place in the Spanish empire would be in jeopardy if slavery were abolished. No enemy of liberalism, Arango y Parreño was perhaps the greatest ideological exponent of free trade in Cuba, which he had been advocating for since he joined Havana's ayuntamiento in the 1780s, when he was still a legal minor. He epitomized the reconciliation of free market economics and slave labor that, as Dale Tomich has noted, was "at once a defining feature and a central paradox of the nineteenth-century Cuban slave regime."[22] The proposals by Guridi y Alcocer and Argüelles led Arango to author one of the great defenses of Cuban slavery and persuade the captain general and Havana ayuntamiento that the question of slavery would be the one issue that might determine Cuba's loyalty to Spain.[23] In this case, Arango's fear was less that a slave insurrection would cause the demise of colonial rule than that the Cuban elite would revolt if slavery fell victim to the Cortes's commitment to liberal principles.

It should come as little surprise that the Cuban deputies felt so strongly about maintaining slavery. In the preceding two decades, the island had experienced a degree of economic growth unprecedented in its three-hundred-year history under Spanish rule. Coffee and sugar production had reached a level of profitability previously unheard of within the Spanish empire.[24] The boom coincided with the decision by Spain in 1789 to allow free trade in slaves for Cuba; that is, in contrast to a closed system in which the Spanish government gave *asientos* (contracts) to specific slave traders to sell a limited number of slaves in specific locales, foreigners and Spaniards alike could now sell any number of slaves to multiple ports. The Cortes of Cádiz took place in the midst of massive importations of Africans: between 1774 and 1827, the slave population of Cuba grew from around 39,000 to 287,000, from composing 23 percent of the island's residents to composing 41 percent.[25] In 1811, Cuba's wealth resided in slaves and the agricultural endeavors that employed them. Abolishing slavery, in the minds of Cuba's political and economic elite, would transform the island's economy and society beyond recognition.

The Cuban deputies appeared less interested in questions of race and citizenship than in the slavery debates, despite the consequences that the former would have for the island. When the Cortes debates turned to the political status of indigenous- and African-descended subjects, slavery rarely emerged as a topic. On its most basic level, citizenship was a status premised on freedom. Thus discussions of the legal equality of indigenous people merited little discussion. Their juridical freedom had been acknowledged since 1542 with the qualification that they remain legally separated from Spaniards: a republic of Indians complemented the republic of Spaniards for the purposes of guaranteeing Indians' acceptance of Catholicism and paying tribute in exchange for designating them Christian vassals. On 7 January 1812, both indigenous tribute and forced labor were abolished, and the end of the system of separate republics signified the formal end of Spain's tutelary evangelical project. Cuban delegates had little at stake due to Cuba's scarce indigenous population. Despite anxieties about their social consequences, most proposals affirmed the citizenship of Indians more out of principle than by practice.

Debates over the summer of 1811 yielded a definition of Spaniards as "free men born and domiciled in the Spanish domains," naturalized foreigners, and "freedmen from the time they acquire liberty in the Spains," and a definition of vecinos as "Spaniards who on both sides trace their ancestry to the Spanish dominions of both hemispheres," including indigenous Americans, who were considered native to what was now Spanish territory. As fall approached, discussion of Article 22, about the status of free men of African descent, began with the following draft:

> For those Spaniards who on either side derive their origin from Africa, the door of virtue and merit is open. In consequence the Cortes may grant letters of citizenship to those who have rendered eminent services to the fatherland, or to those who distinguish themselves by their talent, application, and conduct, provided ... that they be the offspring of legitimate marriages, the children of free parents, themselves married to free women, and resident in Spanish dominions, and that they exercise some useful profession, office, or industry and have capital of their own sufficient to maintain their homes and educate their children honorably.[26]

The debate set off by this proposed article far exceeded the simple question of adding to the numbers of Americans who qualified for representation and augmenting the American presence in the Cortes. Spanish delegates were predictably wary of American delegates who inflated the number of citizens they would represent. They decried the hypocrisy of creole, or American-born, representatives from the colonies who had not spoken up for the rights of people of African descent when they were carefully claiming their equality with *peninsular* (Spanish-born) Spaniards as well as indigenous people and *mestizos* (people of mixed Spanish and indigenous ancestry).[27] But for most deputies involved, at issue was the nature of the colonial project and the loyalty of the African-descended men whose legal status was on the line.

Opposition to the proposed article came as swiftly from those who felt that it went too far as from those who felt that it didn't go far enough. Some delegates criticized the inconsistency of Article 21, which granted citizenship to the sons of foreigners in Spanish territory for a single generation, while denying the same rights to men whose "foreign" ancestors from Africa "had established themselves in the Spanish monarchy for the long period of two hundred years." If indeed the love for and service to Spain was learned over generations, there was no reason to give primary emphasis to "the quality or accident" of dark skin, one of "the variety of colors in the human species" over "the influence of parents on their children."[28] A Peruvian deputy, Francisco Salazar, explained in detail the demonstrated loyalty of African descendants: the free-colored militias had been the first military units to pacify Peru in 1780 as the Túpac Amaru Indian revolt ignited; at that very moment, black troops were defending Buenos Aires, Guayaquil, and Callao, near Lima, from anticolonial attacks. Was it wise, he asked, to question their moral capacity and deny them rights when their loyalty to Spain was most crucial?[29] As with the earlier debates about American representation, citizenship and inclusion, then, also fell within an affective register that acknowledged the affinity for Spanish rule that had moved so many African-descended men to defend the empire from attack.

Agustín de Argüelles, who had fought to preserve slavery, gave the preliminary speech establishing the terms of Article 22, but admitted during its formal debate that he lacked firsthand experience of the situation in the Americas. Those who did—except for the Cubans—painted a picture of the colonies that brought into relief the instability of racial categories. Antonio Larrazábal, from Guatemala, drew parallels between castas and indigenous people, emphasizing the smooth integration of Indians and even mulattoes into political affairs, with long-functioning Indian *cabildos* (municipal councils) capable of producing administrators and officials in their communities.[30] José Ignacio Beye de Cisneros, a Mexican delegate, insisted that some measure was needed to ratify the existing prominence of some African-descended men in Mexican society. He explained that he had "known mulattoes who had been counts, marquis, *oidores* [magistrates], canons, coronels, and knights, surrounded by intrigue, bribery, extortion, false information, perjuries, doctored books or public registers, and I have seen those who have acquired their positions and distinctions by reproachable means, despite knowledge of their mixture . . . they were taxed shamelessly for their respective honors . . . [and] Spaniards, of European and American birth alike, marry their daughters, principally for the money." To ignore the concerns of Article 22 and ignore the gap between law and practice, for Cisneros, betrayed Enlightenment ideals: "We deceive ourselves; in the darkness and without light, all are black."[31] Perhaps the most conspicuous American participant was the indigenous deputy Inca Yupanqui, a member of Cuzco's indigenous nobility who had moved to Spain with his family during the Túpac Amaru revolt. Speaking of free men of African descent in Peru, he explained that "there being nothing but love in domestic matters, it follows that they cannot but look with horror when society acquires certain distinctions." He added that in the militias of *pardos* and *negros* "their officials are of the same *castas,* including those of the staff of the regiments . . . many *bachilleros* [university graduates] of color, those writers knowing that souls are neither white nor black."[32]

The arguments that won out over the eloquent statements in support of citizenship for free men of African descent doubled back on the language of vecindad and naturaleza. In arguing that African origin should be treated no differently from any other foreign origin, delegates who sought to include castas opened themselves to explain the distinction between forced and voluntary migration. African-descended Spaniards might be immigrants, but their ancestors made no deliberate choice to relinquish membership in one community for another. With the passage of Article 22 by a vote of 108–36, the Cortes weakly affirmed the possibility of African-descended men being granted Spanish citizenship under extraordinary circumstances. It resolved that "virtue and merit" was the channel for free men with African descent in either parental lineage. Measuring virtue and merit by reasonable services performed for the nation echoed the power of monarchs to naturalize loyal vassals of foreign origin, and made clear what an exceptional privilege citizenship would be. The conditions and exclusions in Article 22 might invalidate any claim to liberalism's universalistic pretensions, but the "exclusionary impulse," as Uday Mehta calls it, was endemic to the liberal tradition.[33] In the case of Spain, that impulse followed a racial logic imbued with the sedimented discursive residue of will, foreignness, and loyalty.

What should we make of the virtually silent Cuban deputies? They made no mention in deliberations of the critical role of free-colored militias in defending Spanish authority during two turbulent decades in the Caribbean, or even a rhetorical flourish about the unwavering loyalty of free people of color to make a common illustrative contrast with the slave population. Because of their near single-minded attention to preserving slavery and free trade (including the slave trade), Cuban delegates skipped the debates about race that tested the limits of liberalism's universal claims. They were also nervous about vague promises of citizenship spreading to Cuba. For as much ink as Jáuregui spilled on the issue of slavery, his reports to the Havana ayuntamiento hardly mentioned Article 22 aside from a brief summary on 3 October. "What I always feared has happened," he explained. "Exalted principles and dangerous doctrines forced by publicity that in my judgment will bring many ills to America."[34] Clearly opposed to the measure, he nonetheless remained silent in the Cortes, concerned that additional discussion would only lead to more claims to citizenship by castas, and resolved that "it is politic and prudent to surrender to the circumstances." His parenthetical reaction to Article 22 on 14 November offered little in terms of political strategy: "We should place our destinies and our existence in the hands of Divine Providence."[35]

The Constitution Comes to Cuba

In the midst of the Cortes debates about slavery, Jáuregui shared his concerns about secrecy to the Havana ayuntamiento in April 1811. Invoking *patria* (fatherland) to refer to Cuba rather than the Cortes's definition as part of the two Spains, he recounted his efforts to "*conjurar* [ward off] the storm" threatening his homeland. The closed sessions he persuaded the Cortes to hold about the abolition of slavery attempted to prevent "murmurs among our servants that might finally degenerate into frightful conclusions." Jáuregui regretted that his votes against further discussion of slavery could not be published in the record, explaining that "too many explosive issues have already been mounted to allow me to amplify their volume." The other Cuban delegates—Joaquín Santa Cruz and the Marqués de San Felipe—had not been present at the sessions, and so it was up to him, he claimed, to protect his country from "this destructive bolt" that would likely produce "the havoc that I understandably fear and that has not been avoided by those who wish to exploit the slaves at the wrong time, leaving no help for free people."[36] Protecting Cuba took priority over constitutional principles for Jáuregui, and the free-speaking Cortes delegates, not just rebellious slaves, posed a threat to order and stability on the island. The promulgation of the 1812 Constitution gave decisive shape to the continuity of empire in Cuba, but not the effects that Jáuregui imagined on the basis of his worst assumptions about slavery and racial difference.

The fretting of Jáuregui and other Cortes deputies about the circulation of news about the constitutional deliberations may not have been unfounded. A significant minority of African-descended inhabitants of Spanish America figured among a literate colonial public attentive to the political deliberations affecting them, and anxieties about their knowledge of the Cádiz Cortes acknowledged, if indirectly, that elite white Cubans did not monopolize Cuban political discourse. As part of the reforms made by the Cortes, freedom of the press had been proclaimed in 1811, despite the maintenance of the Junta de Censura (censorship board) in Havana.[37] Censors, customs inspectors, and police sought to control news of slave uprisings in other parts of the Americas, and they were particularly nervous about information regarding the Haitian Revolution. While still alleging a predisposition toward rebellion on the part of most Cuban slaves, officials noted that many free people were not opposed to Spanish rule or social peace. In 1804, the captain general worried that an issue of the *Gazeta de Madrid* detailing negotiations between Haitian revolutionary general Jean-Jacques Dessalines and French general Jean-Baptiste Donatien de Vimeur, the count of Rochambeau, would corrupt the loyalty of "the people of color of this Island, some of whom are educated, come from good origins, and deserve to be thought of well among the rest of their *especie* [kind]."[38] In 1811, the governor of Puerto Príncipe informed the captain general that a priest residing in Jamaica had sent him news that the *Gaceta de Jamaica* was publishing paragraphs "offensive to the *tan acrisolada* [proven] loyalty that the inhabitants of this Island are known for."[39] Attempts to reassert the integrity of Spanish territory met their limits as ideas and people circulated across borders throughout the Caribbean.

Indeed, the proceedings in Cádiz sparked conversations in Cuba about the possible effects of a liberal constitution that might threaten the slave trade, slavery, and racial hierarchies. Even critiques of the Constitution and its unsettling potential drew on the language of freedom and rights. An anonymous cleric in Havana, for example, drafted a sharp critique of the Cortes deliberations about ending slavery for failing to clarify "an undefined freedom" that might await slaves. He saw no contradiction between slavery and a political community guided by the principles of liberalism. In this he might have found agreement with Francisco Arango y Parreño, but advanced through a different logic. Whereas Arango y Parreño drew on Adam Smith (and looked past Smith's critique of slavery) to argue that slaves could not have the same self-interest in private property that wage earners did, the cleric writing from Cuba looked to Spain's legal tradition not to argue for slaves' exclusion or subordination but to show how they already enjoyed rights. They had "the freedom for the use of their natural rights to enter into matrimony, to change their owner, and consequently to improve their fate in service occupations." As for their capacity to be political subjects, he distinguished between slavery during the classical era, when slaves were "civilized men who formed the body of the nation" who were deprived of law by the privations of slavery. In contrast, Cuban slaves were men of "different castas; or African tribes among which, it can be said, have not encountered social relations: stupid; without regular legislation, without fixed populations." Humanity, he claimed, was already favoring Africans by removing them from the wars among "those nations," but they were not suited for membership in "the great world Republic" as slaves in classical times were.[40] Invoking natural rights, law, and nation allowed the cleric to fashion a similar argument on the same terms that some delegates in Cádiz used to define the limits of citizenship.

Once the constitution arrived in Cuba—now clear in its exclusion of rights to almost all African-descended subjects—colonial officials did an about-face. No longer did they work to keep news of it under wraps. Strict instructions came from Cádiz about the formal means of circulating the constitution. And circulated it was. On receiving a copy of the constitution, the "chief or judge" of each town would read the document in its entirety in a prominent location, to be followed that night by bells, fireworks, and gun salutes. On the first religious holiday, an official would read the constitution again during mass, following up with a catechistic exchange: "Do you swear by God and by the evangelical saints to guard the political constitution of the Spanish monarchy, sanctioned by the general and extraordinary Cortes of the nation, and be loyal to the king?" Once the congregants replied affirmatively, they would sing the Te Deum. The same exchange was required of every corporation, university, religious community, government office, and all military troops—even members of the free-colored militia, who might have been alternately encouraged or frustrated about Article 22 once they heard about it.[41] Spreading the news across the island did not have the sole purpose of informing a handful of Cubans that they now enjoyed constitutional rights. It also sent a message loud and clear to most of Cuba's inhabitants that no matter how much value their loyalty had to Spain, their exclusion from a new form of political membership rested on a new set of arguments.

It was lost on few officials in Cuba that after years of attempting to regulate information about the Cortes of Cádiz, the orders to disseminate the constitution so widely came at a delicate time. A series of slave revolts proliferated on the island in 1812, and suspicions of a coordinated movement pointed to José Antonio Aponte, a captain in Havana's free black militia. This intensified scrutiny of the militia members. Urban militia companies—including those composed separately of blacks and mulattoes—had been spruced up and given new uniforms and weapons, as much to prepare them to combat rebellions as "to stimulate their zeal and energize their patriotism," according to Puerto Príncipe's governor.[42] The outbreak of slave revolts in the early months of 1812 confirmed the fears of those Cubans who had worried about the intersection of slavery and the liberalizing measures discussed in Cádiz. Andres de Jáuregui, at least, preferred measures of vigilance "outside of common order" to attempt to suppress the slave revolts. Clearly committed on one level to the rule of law—and, as his actions in the Cortes attest, to a large slave population—he expressed little faith in the structures of Spanish rule in the face of widespread unrest: "I do not believe there is a law, rule, or anything to prevail over the urgent need to save the patria."[43] Nevertheless, the new laws and rules that accompanied the 1812 Constitution became widespread knowledge no matter what their effects were on containing popular unrest.

Evidence of free African-descended men taking advantage of the "open door" of Article 22 is frustratingly slim. A search through countless archival bundles in Spain and Cuba reveals just one attempt. Manuel Marciel, a mulatto from Santiago, submitted a petition on 30 March 1813 for the "grace" or favor that would grant him and his descendants "the character of citizen and the class of white." But why ask for whiteness, rather than citizenship? African-descended Cuban men could claim to be Spanish without recourse to petition, but whiteness, nowhere mentioned in the constitution, would ostensibly have been purchased through the royal privilege of the *gracias al sacar*.[44] Instead, Marciel cited Article 22 of the constitution in his petition for citizenship and then apparently added on whiteness as a bonus requiring no payment for a certificate. Nimbly couching his image in the likeness of the idealized exceptions provided for by Article 22, Marciel noted that he had served for thirty years as a member of the pardo militias in Santiago and Bayamo and was regarded by various individuals as "a good man, peaceful and obedient to his superiors, who provides a good education for his children." He was married to a free parda, María Antonia del Pozo, and his parents had been free from birth and married in a church. He possessed two houses, two parcels of land, some slaves, and a copy of his father's will identifying Nicolás Antonio Marcial as a native of Galicia. A little over one year later, Manuel Marcial became a white citizen of Spain.[45]

But by 1816, after Fernando VII had nullified the 1812 Constitution, it appears that even the exceptional achievement of Marcial's citizenship had limited public affirmation. A list of contributors to a provincial fund for expeditions to capture runaway slaves includes Marcial donating six pesos, but his name lacks the honorific "Don" that appears next to most other men's names.[46] Even without the status of citizen, which excluded all Cubans after 1814, the social status that Marcial might have claimed or have acknowledged by other *santiagueros,* whether through his putative whiteness or having proved "virtue and merit," appears illusory.

Ultimately, affirming loyalty to the imperial project may have been what offered more secure footing than Article 22 to some free men of color; this new circumstance arose not despite the widespread unrest on the island and in the Americas but precisely because of it. What some Cubans came to realize in the years of imperial crisis, as they watched other regions of Spanish America dissolve into violent conflict, was that loyalty—as opposed to exit—offered a relatively stable position from which to negotiate within the empire, particularly in the midst of crisis.[47] Even before the constitution came to Cuba, Pedro Galdíz, a lower officer of the pardo battalion in Havana, successfully lobbied for a portion of normal monthly pay during the months of rest. In 1811, he appealed "with no pretension but obedience and hope for the return of our legitimate sovereign to his throne" for a type of recognition that would not have been granted by invoking the constitution.[48] Whether or not Galdíz knew of the Cortes deliberations, the constitution seems not to have mattered when he looked to imperial politics to advance his request.

Throughout the period of Spanish rule in America, the crown played a mediating role between Spanish colonists and the colonized populations of indigenous and African descent. It was not a static role. In the wake of the Haitian Revolution, the beginning of insurrections on the mainland, and the unfolding of the Aponte Rebellion of 1812, Spanish officials appeared more intent on policing slaves and safeguarding the loyalty of the creole elite than offering opportunities for free people of color to become citizens. Slaveowners, when giving attention to the coherence of Cuban society, might have been influenced as much by recent slave revolts as by the offers of political rewards by Spain. In his study of the Aponte Rebellion, Matt Childs documents how judicial officials and colonial authorities in Havana bought the freedom of slaves who denounced the Aponte Rebellion, in part because their owners refused uncompensated manumission: in other words, "Loyalty carried no discount for a slave's price of freedom."[49] Other Cubans within reach of citizenship also reacted with hesitance. In the case of two unique towns in Cuba, the offer of citizenship to a surprising group of racialized subordinates produced stunning responses.

Becoming Spanish in the Indian Pueblos

The constitution's declaration that indigenous men were now citizens affected vast numbers of people and countless communities in Spanish America, far more than the population of African descent affected by the constitution. Residents of Mesoamerican and Andean regions with indigenous majorities faced imposing decisions about how political change would affect social stability.[50] In contrast, Cuba's indigenous population fell victim to Spanish disease and by the middle of the sixteenth century had experienced catastrophic population loss. It was not a complete extinction. Understandably, indigenous citizenship in Cuba has merited little attention by scholars. Yet in 1812 there were two remaining indigenous pueblos, Jiguaní and El Caney, in eastern part of the island. The ambivalent promises of liberal citizenship set in motion decades-long debates between residents and officials about the meaning of citizenship and the significance of "pure" races.

News of the constitution's promulgation took a while to reach the people of El Caney and Jiguaní. Their *protector de indios* (an official legal advocate for Indian pueblos), reported that after the document was read and discussed in Havana, *alcaldes* (mayors) and cabildos of smaller towns relied on rumors until official copies arrived midyear. Once word spread, the ayuntamiento of El Caney quickly erected a monument in honor of the constitution in its main plaza on August 14.[51] On hearing the provisions of the constitution's extension of citizenship to Indians, the leaders of Jiguaní and El Caney asserted to the protector, Luis Maríon de Arce, that they had independent jurisdiction from the Spanish government and would decide for themselves between Spanish citizenship and the older protections enjoyed by Indian *pueblos,* such as limited self-government and corporate land rights. The questions that emerged from the conflict this ignited were as material as they were conceptual: now that Indians could claim Spanish citizenship—in other words, were Indians still entitled to special protections? And did they even want them? Officials in eastern Cuba struggled to take seriously the idea that Indians could become Spanish citizens on equal standing with white Spaniards. Free from the tutelage and surveillance of a protector, would their loyalty to Spanish rule wane?

"They want to be Spaniards!" Arce wrote to the Audiencia in Santiago, but he was reluctant to abolish the protections they received as legal subordinates. Residents of the towns could not agree: in September, the leaders of El Caney told the Audiencia that "in light of the Constitution they do not need a Protector"; five residents of Jiguaní wrote in November that over three centuries they "never abused, nor will ever abuse the graces, donations, and privileges that His Majesty with his liberal and caring hands has conceded." They took a swipe at what they perceived as the ignorance of El Caney and petitioned in February 1813 for the Audiencia to clarify the constitution's meaning so that they could keep their protector and their historic privileges. The mediating role of Arce complicates the story. On one hand, he wrote eloquently about the fragile condition of the pueblos: despite the implications of the "wise Constitution," and that "in other times it had been proven that Indians would be better managed without protectors," he went on to warn that "this is a time motivated by the human heart, although among us are evildoers capable of abusing, to sinister ends, the ignorance and simplicity of the Indians." He specifically referred to the influx into the region of French émigrés from Haiti and their "slaves of the rebellious race" who were capable of corrupting and exploiting the Indians. Arce pleaded that even if the Indians gave up all of their other privileges, the loss of their protector was not a disgrace they should suffer. On the other hand, Arce's most impassioned defenses were of his own indispensability—this, after all, was a man in danger of losing his job.

The struggle with Jiguaní over its protector continued well past the revocation of the constitution in 1814 (legal squabbles continued until 1846), but officials remained determined to abolish pueblo privileges, with or without the promise of citizenship. In 1818, Jiguaní lost its protector under conditions that the Audiencia tried hard to cast as good news. It bestowed the title of *villa* on the community, "with the same prerogatives that Spanish pueblos enjoy," and it declared Jiguaní's residents "among the most faithful vassals, giving to said pueblo the title of *Leal* [Loyal]."[52] In other words, the Indians were declared Spaniards free of protections in reward for their loyalty. The decision drew on a report made in 1814 by Pedro Alcántara—an Audiencia member and former Cortes deputy—which claimed that "the spirit of those vecinos has been influenced by the new order of things in their municipal government" and that "the *casta* [mixed population] there is entirely extinguished by the general mix of whites, Spaniards and Isleños [Canary Islanders], and of *cuarterones* [quadroons] and pardos, such that the natural physiognomy of Indians has disappeared entirely."[53] Again, the shady role of the protector confounds an easy interpretation. Alcántara argued that Arce's contempt for the constitution betrayed the good faith support and patriotism he enjoyed within the pueblos—Juan Miguel Randón, the Indian alcalde of Jiguaní, called him "one of the most refined constitutionalists."[54] Ultimately, Alcántara accused Arce of having long abandoned his responsibilities to protect and manage these unique communities, but the profit to be gained from preserving their designation trumped the principles of racial difference, constitutionalism, and citizenship to which he paid lip service.

In consultation with the Audiencia in Caracas, a royal order in 1821 eliminated the office of the protector de indios in Santiago de Cuba because the Indians needed their equality restored, noting that after 1814 they had been left in "a state of minority when before they were subjects" and "should be made equal" like Spaniards in both hemispheres.[55] The archives do not give a clear indication of what happened in Jiguaní and El Caney between 1823 and 1837, but we can infer that the abandoned constitutional guarantees of Spanish citizenship explain the appearance of yet another paper trail in the 1840s, revealing that the towns still had a protector. By now, officials in Madrid worked assiduously to eliminate what they viewed as an exotic and arcane institution. The ultimate demise of the office of protector in 1846 came when Spanish officials acted on the authority to govern by "special laws" and on the grounds that there was no longer a *raza pura* [pure race]" of Indians that necessitated protection. Although the Audiencia blamed the office for leaving the community "backward on the March of Civilization and general progress," the census suggested that living in the backward community remained an appealing option for many Cubans. In 1837 there were 1,708 individuals living in El Caney, and 1,206 were identified as indios; there were 111 Spaniards, 134 free people of color, and 257 slaves. More telling is the prevalence of identifying as Indians the children of mixed descent—in other words, white Spaniards and African-descended residents had children with the Indians of El Caney and strategically "increased" the Indian population by designating their children as such. To colonial officials this was a farce; to the residents of El Caney, Indian privileges—whether the residents "were" Indians or not— may have represented a means of commanding resources in the absence of claims to Spanish citizenship.

As with other indigenous communities in Spanish America, under colonial rule or in new republics, transformations occasioned by liberal ideals often occasioned loss more than opportunity. Despite periodic enthusiasm for the constitution, particularly in El Caney, the inhabitants of the Cuban pueblos— "pure" Indians or not—recognized the vulnerability of Spanish citizenship. Over thirty years later, when at long last the Spanish government successfully abolished pueblo status and the office of the protector de indios, the impoverished residents of those communities found themselves denied both special protection and Spanish citizenship.

Commissioning Whiteness

In his insistence on maintaining slavery and the slave trade in the Spanish empire, Andrés de Jáuregui counted as one of his great victories in Cádiz the silencing of debates about abolition. Yet privately, he expressed concerns to officials in Havana about how the "inferior condition" of slaves and free people of color exacerbated the critical situation of the monarchy. Invoking the example of the Haitian Revolution, he encouraged officials in Havana to find in Spain's crisis opportunities to attract laborers to the island who were not of African descent. Spanish provinces such as Galicia, Asturias, and the Canary Islands "abounded in population and their naturales" were "quite valuable for their good habits." Although the constitution itself could not mandate an increase in the Spanish population of Cuba, Jáuregui noticed an opportunity for the new government and "the liberality of its principles" to encourage migration from the peninsula to the Caribbean colonies.[56] Jáuregui was not the first person to advocate increased "white" migration to Cuba as a means of naturalizing allegiance to Spanish rule, but his timing was auspicious, coming as it did when the Haitian Revolution, threats to Spanish hegemony in the colonies, and new political categories of belonging redrew the boundaries of race and loyalty.

Heightened attention to who came and went from Cuba preceded the crisis in Spain and the Constitution of 1812, when instability in St. Domingue sent many of its inhabitants to nearby Cuba. Not all migrants enjoyed the same status. An edict by Captain General Luis de las Casas in 1796 prohibited the entry into Cuba of foreign blacks who were not *bozales* (slaves brought directly from Africa), targeting slaves from islands that had experienced revolts.[57] French and creole refugees fleeing the upheaval of the Haitian Revolution arrived in numbers too great (approximately 18,000) to solicit individual cartas de naturaleza, the naturalization certificates historically linked to trading and travel privileges. An 1803 report from Santiago noted that families from Port-au-Prince were "seeking hospitality" and that their former slaves were allowed to disembark (sometimes taking loyalty oaths) only because of their "indispensability" to the families, whose French nationality did not mitigate the advantage of "acquiring the largest number possible of good white inhabitants" in Cuba.[58] By 1804 the king had suspended issuing cartas de naturaleza altogether to French immigrants from Saint-Domingue, ending local concessions of cartas in Santiago "with the idea of developing the agricultural arts and population." But newly arrived immigrants still received opportunities to buy land in the interior once they had taken an oath of loyalty and vassalage.[59] If the crown, then, became reluctant to extend Spanish political personhood to émigrés, it nevertheless offered them material support in the name of cultivating more "good white inhabitants."

Other foreigners seeking to enter Cuba encountered fewer problems than those from Saint Domingue. The island experienced a sharp increase in the number of individuals migrating from mainland Spanish America in the midst and wake of violent independence conflicts. Patriot forces deemed slaves and the many property owners who supported Spain "royalists" during and after the wars. Thus insurgents sent captured slave soldiers to Cuba and often confiscated the property of other Spanish sympathizers. Those free individuals often came to Cuba voluntarily, following kin and commercial networks as well as opportunities for state support. Simón Bolívar's own sister fled to Cuba from Venezuela and received a pension from the Spanish government after identifying herself as one of "the defenders of the cause of the King."[60]

Lingering concerns about the destabilizing presence of French émigrés extended debates about natives and foreigners in the empire. Most Saint-Domingue refugees had been expelled from Cuba in 1808 and 1809 because of their unclear loyalties after the French invasion of Spain—and out of fears that they and their former slaves would spread news of the Haitian Revolution. The gradual return of some of the expelled only intensified doubts about racial identification trumping political affiliation. The abrogation of the constitution in 1814 ceased to offer Cuban-born men citizenship, but those men still joined peninsulares in publicly distinguishing themselves from the French, doubting the intentions and political affiliations of the new foreign residents. Suspicions foiled attempts to subsume national differences in the interests of a unified "white" population. By 1815, with the monarchy restored, Havana's cabildo reiterated concerns to Madrid about the presence of French. Nevertheless, attempts by St. Domingue refugees to return to Cuba after the restoration of the monarchy encountered a slightly improved political climate. They had to take oaths of loyalty to Spain once they arrived, but otherwise met with fewer restrictions.[61] Even financial complications in their resettlement received resolution: widows of military men demanded pensions based on their husbands' service alongside Spanish troops in Hispaniola and generally found sympathetic treatment.[62]

These tensions about race and loyalty, in combination with concerns about economic growth, had deepened interest in increasing the "white" population—specifically named as such with greater frequency. In 1812, members of the Sociedad Económica de Amigos del País, Havana's premier intellectual and economic society, established a Comisión de Población Blanca. In June 1816, members Francisco Chacón and Andrés de Zayas assumed responsibility for the commission, charged with avoiding the "imminent risk" posed by "vecinos of all democracies" of the "states of the American federation."[63] The efforts of the commission resulted in a royal order issued by Captain General José Cienfuegos in October 1817 that affirmed the need for white immigration and free trade, both of which were advanced by leveling the privileges of foreigners and natives. Even with the suspension of the Cádiz Constitution in 1814, naturaleza rights, if not full citizenship, could still be granted and claimed in the interests of fomenting a loyal population in Cuba dedicated to productive endeavors.[64] And cartas de naturaleza became the principal legal conduit through which migration to Cuba took place. In part because of insufficient initial interest on the part of Spaniards to migrate, whiteness, as defined in the development of the immigration project, broadened to include any European Catholic (and even some Protestants)—and was likely also judged by appearance and on the spot by local officials in Cuba or by consulates in other areas.

Public discussions of the commission's deliberations linked questions of white immigration to political loyalty but disagreed as to whether whiteness or legal freedom was the better indicator of allegiance. In 1817, Pedro Alcántara de Acosta argued for measures to increase the white population "for the enrichment of those loyal vassals whose love for their sovereign has never diminished." Yet he declared it no less important to recognize "the necessity of conceding to the free blacks of the city of Santiago de Cuba the military gracias they requested for their conduct. It is only with those that their loyalty can be assured, and with the social education we have *prestado* [lent] them ... nobody in this eastern part [of the island] fears those free blacks; the slaves, yes." Alcántara carefully defended the "*dulce y humano* [mild and humane] commerce" that brought Africans out of "ignorance or malice" and developed the "*bien real y moral* [real and moral good] that they possess in the good treatment of the owners of this island."[65] If loyalty to Spain represented the goal of white immigration, Alcántara argued that other means besides whitening the population could achieve the same end. Slaves, however, received none of the benefit of the doubt that Alcántara and other officials extended to free people of color.

The final guidelines of the Comisión Blanca in 1818—now assuming more durable form as the Junta de Población Blanca—laid out rules for any foreigners who wanted to migrate to Cuba: they had to be Catholic, they had to take an oath of loyalty and vassalage, and, as an incentive to migrate, they did not have to pay tribute or taxes on anything but their slaves for the first five years. This initial exemption recalls the paradoxical double meaning of *derecho*—tax or tribute to the crown, as well as rights—insofar as the "freedoms" of citizenship did not immediately accompany the instant freedom from taxes guaranteed to immigrants. After five years in Cuba, immigrants and their legitimate descendants would acquire the rights and privileges of Spaniards. As property, any slaves held by those immigrants traveled according to their masters' designs but with no state regulation or documentation besides a tax paid on them. Slaves, then, traveled as property, not as people, and thus existed for official purposes as heads to be counted for tax purposes and not always subjects with privileges or rights.

A project to attract white immigrants and their slaves presumably required little discussion of free people of African descent, but after several years of deliberation, the Comisión Blanca made an unexpected proposal to the captain general. If the point of white immigration was to increase a loyal Cuban population that could balance the effects of an increasing and potentially restive slave population, it argued, then free people of color could tip the balance toward order and stability. Echoing Alcántara's logic, the commission recommended issuing cartas de naturaleza to free men of color residing in Cuba who met requirements virtually identical to those in Article 22 of the now defunct Cádiz Constitution. The commission explicitly invoked the language of citizenship and legal identity: it sought to give the captain general the authority to "confer the document" to those who sought it, stating that free people would "earn the rights accorded to the same class of naturales on the island." The proposal pivoted on the distinction between nativeness and foreignness. The commission sought to extend the right to those free people born in Cuba or other Spanish dominions and exclude from consideration anyone of African descent who had come directly from Africa or who worked for a recently arrived white immigrant.[66] At once a significant revision and as well an enhancement of the terms of political belonging laid out in the 1812 Constitution, the proposal placed a tenuous right of citizenship within reach of free African-descended Cuban men. Yet the right itself, in the absence of any constitutional guarantees, may have lost some of its luster.

The final guidelines for white immigration projects did not adopt this novel amendment, but its mere proposal helps qualify the significance ascribed to whiteness in explanations of Cuba's loyalty to Spain. As Pedro Alcántara de Acosta pleaded from his official post in Santiago de Cuba, white immigration alone could not reduce the threat of Mexican insurgency, Haitian aggression, and a growing slave population.[67] By contrasting the loyalty of free people with the natural ignorance and malice of the slave population, he imagined a supportive and mediating role for free people of color. But they could not guarantee Cuba's allegiance on their own either. Correlating race with loyalty never yielded a universal rule that extended to Cubans of different backgrounds. When colonial elites and authorities attempted to formulate such a rule for whiteness alone, they quickly ran afoul of complications from both within and beyond the island.

The Wagers of Whiteness in Cienfuegos

After Spain regained control of Havana after the British occupation in 1762 and 1763, settlement projects gained momentum from the twin impulses of military defense and economic development through commercial agriculture. A number of towns and cities founded in the late eighteenth century later developed into sizable communities: Mariel, Manzanillo, Santiago de las Vegas, Güines, Cárdenas, Caibarién, San José de las Lajas, Pedro Betancourt, and others. With the institutional support of the Comisión Blanca, the goal of increasing the island's white population became a third goal alongside defense and profit. Although some emphasis fell on increasing the white populations of well-established cities such as Puerto Príncipe, bureaucrats and private entrepreneurs focused their energies on new sites that became Guantánamo, Jaruco, Santo Domingo, and Reina Amalia (on the Isle of Pines).[68] The policies of the Comisión Blanca initially favored the equivalence of whiteness and Spanishness. As high as expectations rose that white colonists would be ideal members of the Spanish empire, the projects themselves faced formidable obstacles in agreeing on the terms of the whiteness of white immigration, affirming Spanish rule, and checking the growth of the slave population.

Of the towns created with the encouragement of the *comisión,* the establishment of Cienfuegos perhaps best illustrates the challenges of creating a white population. Although no long-standing Spanish settlement existed around the Bahía de Jagua, the region was not new to Spaniards: Christopher Columbus was said to have landed there in 1494, and in 1511 the "Protector of the Indians," Bartolomé de Las Casas, was granted an *encomienda* (a grant of Indians under his care) on one of the peninsulas in the bay.[69] By the late eighteenth century a smattering of people inhabited the area, but its economic potential as a major port for southern Cuba was not lost on the individuals who periodically floated settlement plans to the Spanish government. Several navigable rivers fed into an enormous and well-protected bay, and dense forests had already been exploited by residents of nearby Trinidad. A proposal in 1798 to develop areas around the Bay of Jagua led to the establishment of Nuevitas slightly inland, but the incentives offered by the white colonization project of the 1810s led to a successful bid by a naturalized Spaniard.

Louis de Clouet was a Bourdeaux-born lieutenant, a *coronel* (colonel) in the Spanish army, and a resident of New Orleans, and he made an immigration pitch in January 1819 to Captain General José Cienfuegos and Intendant Alejandro Ramírez, drawing explicitly on the *real cédula* (royal decree) promoting the growth of Cuba's white population.[70] In his proposal, De Clouet gave himself the power to apportion land to individual colonists—any white man or woman over eighteen years old—that would be granted for distribution within two years. He also put himself in charge of arranging the transportation of families, distributing the six months of daily stipends provided to settlers, and serving as "moderator and judge" of disputes and disagreements among colonists. What made his proposal especially notable was the background of the families he proposed to attract. The core of them were not from Spain or Cuba, but Louisiana, "old naturales or vecinos" who had been "vassals" of the king of Spain and "always wanted to be so and establish themselves in Spanish territory."[71] All settlers would need to document that they were Catholic, and those who had not been born "Spanish vassals" were required to obtain letters of *domicilio* and *naturalización*. By April of the same year, he had arrived on the parcel of land provided by Captain General José Cienfuegos for de Clouet to distribute among the forty-six families he brought with him from Bordeaux.[72] By the end of the year, the 232 residents of the colonia Fernandina de Jagua (named for Ferdinand VII) were a surprisingly diverse group: 123 from France, 31 from the United States, and 28 who had left Saint-Domingue during the Haitian Revolution, as well as Irish, Spanish, German, Italian, Portuguese, and Belgian settlers.[73]

As ships arrived from New Orleans, Bordeaux, Baltimore, and Philadelphia, new arrivals did not easily congeal into a population united by a shared identification with being "white." Inhabitants faced steep challenges in fighting off yellow fever and sharing the responsibilities of building roads, houses, docks, and functioning farms, and the pressure of work coupled with scarce resources seems to have produced routine disagreements. The conflicts that arose often laid bare deep distrust among people originating from different locations and backgrounds. A robbery, for example, might provoke competing accusations leveled against the Spanish and French colonists en masse.[74] De Clouet acknowledged that the work of unifying the population might better be left to future settlers, suggesting in an 1823 report that it would benefit the colony to attract families from the Canary Islands, who over time "through their marital bonds with foreigners will result in all becoming Spaniards."[75] That same year, a colonist from mainland Spanish America organized Los Yuquinos, a group that plotted to liberate the settlement from Spanish rule. It targeted the French inhabitants as those deemed most loyal to Spanish rule and circulated rumors of a French plot to rid the region of Spanish control. A tense standoff narrowly avoided violent confrontation, but uncertainty lingered about the political allegiances of newly arrived migrants under the auspices of white colonization.[76] Frustrations with de Clouet's iron-fisted control over the city led to an assassination attempt in 1832 organized by Spanish and Cuban inhabitants, who called themselves "The Rivals" in opposition to the residents from non-Spanish territory, who referred to themselves as Los Fieles (The Faithful).[77]

If the diversity of immigrants to the region muddies the definition of whiteness, the presence of an African-descended population confuses the meaning of white colonization. African slaves figured among the early arrivals to Cienfuegos, and in the early records of the settlement an eagerness to record "firsts" among the white population—the first white child born, the first marriage between whites, the first white person to die—met its limits when the first two baptisms that occurred were of Roque and Victoria, two slaves belonging to de Clouet.[78] His original proposal made clear that settlers would pay no duties on bozales, as they were considered "instruments of agriculture" which—like food provisions and tools—were considered necessary enough to require a concession from the government.[79] De Clouet appointed a notary in 1820 to document the increasing number of transactions of land and slaves.[80] The African slave trade to Cuba officially ended in 1820 as arranged in an 1817 treaty between Britain and Spain, which meant that ships carrying captives from Africa could not legally disembark on the newly built docks on the bay. In practice, slaves continued to arrive illegally through the 1860s, often making use of bays and inlets close to major port cities to accommodate slave ships. In the case of the colonia Fernandina de Jagua, the nearby Bahía de Cochinos (Bay of Pigs) became an important site for the arrival of ships from Africa.

New settlements did not always embrace plantation export agriculture immediately, and slaves in the early economy of Cienfuegos likely labored in many other endeavors: felling trees for wood and to clear farming land, cattle ranching, and small-scale tobacco and coffee cultivation. Such an economy in uneven formation may have proved favorable to slaves who sought their freedom, and indeed a free population of African descent developed almost as early as the slave population. But as sugar cultivation expanded around Cienfuegos during the 1830s, demand for slave labor intensified, the number of slaves increased considerably. So, too, did slave resistance.[81] In 1832 the ayuntamiento had to ask a judge to create a separate space to hold captured runaway slaves, who were crowding the municipal jail.[82] Periodic slave revolts during the 1830s likely reminded inhabitants of the principal motivation of the white colonization project and helped bridge the gap between shared European descent and whiteness, as over time their benign identification with the city's French origins posed less of a threat to Spanish order than a potentially restive population of African descent.

By the time that Fernando VII bestowed town status and the name Cienfuegos (after the captain general) on the settlement in 1827, it had accumulated 1,129 white inhabitants, 125 free people of color, and 301 slaves. In other words, eight years after the city was established to increase Cuba's white population, 27 percent of the city's residents were of African descent. The rapid development of sugar production accelerated the trend. By 1846, with seventy-one sugar mills operating in the city's jurisdiction, that proportion had increased to 44 percent.[83] By then, the majority of white residents had come from Spain, the Canary Islands, or other parts of Cuba. When the Sociedad Patriótica de la Habana organized a statistical report on Cienfuegos in 1838, it complained that the colonization project did "not progress as it was intended," noting that African slaves outnumbered white individuals engaged in agricultural labor three to one.[84] Despite the gap between expectations and outcomes, the development of Cienfuegos generally counted as a success for Spain: having fashioned a white population out of individuals of multiple national backgrounds, residents had overseen the creation of a profitable economy even before sugarcane cultivation developed in full force during the 1830s and 1840s. They had also built a church, formed an ayuntamiento, and developed other institutions that identified them as members of a stable community oriented toward the reproduction of loyal subjects of the Spanish empire.

Rights and Wrongs: The End of the Cádiz Experiment

The revival of the Cádiz Constitution in 1820 following a military coup breathed new life into Cubans' struggles for political representation and citizenship, with more enthusiasm among the population than among the principal authorities. Demonstrations in support of the news occurred again in major cities in March, with militia companies leading cheers and with processions, singing, and dancing filling Havana's streets.[85] But orders emanated from the captain general's palace to temper that enthusiasm. Concerns about social order intensified as struggles for independence were now succeeding in most parts of Spanish America. In a bold move, Fernando VII extended the right of free association to Cuba when he returned to the throne, but the captain general declined and asked that the offer be kept secret. He expressed to Madrid his reservations about allowing free Cubans of color to organize when talk of independence was in the air: "The class of free pardos and morenos, although generally loyal to the nation, would not cease to be seduced by it, stimulating their pride and leading them to hatch the idea of an exact equality with the same principles as those naturales who have gone astray on the mainland."[86] Cuba's representatives in the Cortes—restored after elections had been nullified three times—were similarly reluctant to extend the liberal policies that the agents of Spain's "liberal revolution" encouraged. As one of the Cuban deputies to the Cortes, Father Félix Varela argued liberal positions so radical that they eventually led to his death sentence for sedition: the abolition of slavery, self-government for Cuba, and celebrating the independence of the mainland colonies. In an 1822 essay, however, he expressed wariness about the prospects of African-descended Cubans embracing constitutionalism and liberalism:

> I must warn the Cortes that among people of African origin there is a well-known discontent with the Constitution, for they have never given the slightest sign of happiness, when it is well known that in any fiesta or public celebration they are always the first to create a scandal. Sensible people observed that when the news of the reestablishment of the system arrived in Havana, it seemed as if the earth had swallowed the blacks and mulattoes, for one could count on one hand those that were in the streets, despite the general rejoicing, and for some time they maintained a somber and imposing air. Do not believe that they did this out of ignorance, or out of adherence to the old system, for we already know that they have tried twice to overturn it, declaring themselves free, and I am sure that the first person to mount the call for independence will have almost all of the people of African origin on his side. Let us not fool ourselves: Constitution, liberty, equality, are synonyms; these terms are polar opposites to the words slavery and inequality of rights. It is in vain to try to reconcile these opposites.[87]

Attempts to reconcile those opposites indeed came to define much of Cuban politics during the nineteenth century. Varela's warning carefully avoided assessing the dispositions of the rest of the Cuban population, pointing a finger instead at what was already the most suspect group. In the short term, slavery and inequality of rights won the battle. The end of the "Liberal Triennium" in 1823 signaled another abrupt end to the Cádiz Constitution. Beginning in 1823, Fernando VII ruled Cuba and Spain without a constitution, and not until the end of the bitter Carlist War in Spain was the possibility of constitutional rights and citizenship again raised for Cuba.

Thirteen years later, an insurrection in La Granja, Spain, prompted liberal-minded ministers to reinstate once more the Constitution of 1812. A royal decree of 13 August 1836 specified that the new constitution only applied in Spain, not its colonies. Thus the remaining Spanish colonies lost whatever claims to citizenship they had hoped for—ironically, during the same months that the Cortes finally gave formal recognition to the independent Spanish American nations. A parliamentary report argued for "national pride" in observing how members of "that large family . . . have reached that stage of education and maturity which enables them to take leave of their mother."[88] On 29 September Manuel Lorenzo, the provincial governor of Santiago de Cuba, reprinted the Constitution of 1812 and circulated it throughout the city with a broadsheet addressed to "CUBANOS": "Twice the celebrated law of Cádiz has been proclaimed in our ancient monarchy: twice the evil genius expelled it from the *suelo patrio* [patriotic soil]. The third time it arrives brought by the Mother of Iberia . . . Long live the constitution of 1812! Long live the immortal Governor Queen! Long live the constitutional Isabel II! Long Live Spain!"[89] This was not the kind of patriotism that colonial officials wanted to hear. Captain General Miguel Tacón blockaded the Bay of Santiago and demanded that Lorenzo roll back his constitutional pronouncements. Lorenzo refused, Tacón relieved him of his duties, and the Santiago cabildo drafted a defensive statement on 4 November affirming their support for Spanish rule.[90]

Forced out of office, Lorenzo explained in a pamphlet from 1837 his frustration with Spanish rule in Cuba as a story of broken promises and unrequited loyalty. What Tacón and his supporters in Madrid had understood as rebellion was, as he put it, an affirmation of Spanish government as embodied in the liberal principles established by the Cortes of Cádiz and revitalized on the peninsula. He (mis)read back onto the Constitution of 1812 that "it specifies the enjoyment of citizenship rights with relation to the castas," and he defended himself against attacks that he "armed the blacks and mulattoes to support the pronouncement." If he understood himself to be following the inclusive provisions of the constitution, "How could I," he reasoned, "tyrannize with the same tool forged to destroy tyranny?"[91]

Other Cubans who had not gone to such extremes were no less frustrated by their exclusion, yet again, from the rights and citizenship guaranteed by a Spanish constitution. Although José Antonio Saco did not support Lorenzo's radical move, he also leveled a damning critique of Spanish republicanism. In 1835 he had been nominated as the Cuban representative to the Cortes, and his reflections on his short-lived debut in Spanish politics advanced some surprising arguments. Saco wrote extensively of his reservations about a system of slavery that populated Cuba with dangerous and uncivilized people. Ending the slave trade, then, was not a moral position but a practical necessity to guarantee the island a prosperous future with as few influences of African descent as possible: "We are left with only one remedy: whiten,

whiten, and then we will be respected."[92] By 1837 he complained that treating the colonies differently by basing their proportional representation only on their white population violated the spirit of equality set forth in the Constitution of 1812, "still the fundamental law of the State."[93] The entire adult male population of Cuba, he contended, deserved to be represented.

Saco still asserted that white Cubans fostered a special love of freedom and equality through their direct exposure to those who did have it, compared to Spaniards on the peninsula, for whom "freedom is nothing more than a right"; but "when society is composed of slaves and masters," he wrote, "freedom is not merely a right but a rank, a privilege, and, if one wants it to be, a matter of vanity."[94] Here Saco got to the heart of the contradictions of Spain's liberal experiment. It was not simply that the persistence of slavery and colonial rule made discussions of free individuals as the bearers of universal rights ring hollow. Protesting the denial of rights with the language of rank and privilege, as Saco did, disrupted a progressive narrative of the victory of liberal ideas over putatively archaic forms of authority grounded in hierarchy and particularity. Moreover, it laid bare the limits of the freedom promised by liberal citizenship in contrast to the freedom defined against slavery. It situated Cuban elites somewhere in between what Saidiya Hartman describes as the "unencumbered individuality of liberalism," derived from the knowledge and enjoyment of freedom, and "the excluded, marginalized, and devalued subjects that it engenders . . . the fleshy substance that enable[s] the universal to achieve its ethereal splendor."[95]

But can individuality only be unencumbered through national independence? Certainly the events of 1837 shattered the hopes of liberal inclusion. One historian during the early years of the Cuban Republic noted that the suspension of constitutional guarantees "can be considered as the origin of the armed revolutions that ended with the independence of the island."[96] Setting aside the search for the origins of Cuban nationalism and independence, Spain's imposition in 1837 of "special laws," rather than constitutional government, marked the beginning of a search among Cubans for new ways to advance their goals under the colonial rule of Spain. That some of those approaches continued to draw on the language of loyalty and privilege rather than citizenship and rights suggests that Cubans never abandoned older forms of engagement with the Spanish state in the absence of a viable project for anticolonial rebellion and the liberal practices and principles that might—or might not—have inspired it.

Evidence of a widespread public crackdown in Cuba is abundant in the years after 1836, although it is difficult to claim definitively that this represented a real increase in resistance or repression—as opposed to an increase in state surveillance by the Comisión Militar, a repressive institution sanctioned in 1825. Both possibilities speak to the bleak political outlook in Cuba. Among the well-documented cases of disloyalty, one case in particular sticks out. In 1838, Fernando Estrada, described as a moreno, was caught on the streets of Bayamo in eastern Cuba talking to anyone who would listen. He was reading from a pamphlet entitled *Ejemplo de la libertad civil* (Example of Civil Liberty), which had been published in 1813 in Puerto Príncipe to explain how the rights guaranteed by the Spanish Constitution of 1812 affected Cubans.[97] By conjuring the ghosts of the Cortes of Cádiz, Estrada favored an incarnation of Spanish citizenship and representative government that, setting aside his own likely exclusion from the system, was no longer a possibility. Yet he was decidedly not advocating independence from Spain. That the Comisión Militar snuffed out his activities as swiftly as they would direct challenges to Spanish sovereignty reveals how far Spain and its agents in Cuba retreated from attempting to reconcile liberal practices, including national citizenship, within an empire that was radically smaller than it had been in 1812.

NO LESS THAN KARL MARX attributed the unfulfilled promise of the Constitution of 1812 to popular discontent rather than monarchist foibles: when "the sudden disappearance of their social sufferings" did not occur, he wrote in 1854, "the very overstrained expectations which had welcomed it turned into disappointment, and with these passionate Southern peoples there is but one step from disappointment to hatred."[98] Certainly, popular discontent with the limitations of imperial citizenship reached Cuba, but restive African-descended subjects, not fiery Spaniards, figured as the "Southern peoples" whose disappointment most worried politicians and colonial officials who sought to keep Spain's empire intact.

As much as Spain's experiments with liberalism in the colonies tells a story of dashed hopes, they also shed light on Cubans who sought the rights of citizenship within the empire or, when denied them, pursued other channels toward inclusion, political personhood, and a greater voice in Cuban society. Colonial rule denied people rights, reinforced social hierarchies, and all the while attracted some degree of popular support as a system that might allow for mobility, privileges, and protections. When Louis de Clouet, the founder of Cienfuegos, found himself appealing a legal decision in 1845, he invoked the Constitution of 1812 and the Constitution of 1837 in his defense. As a Spanish citizen, he claimed that he should not be treated differently in Cuba than in

Spain. But he emphasized the particularity of his citizenship, too, not as a French immigrant with a carta de naturaleza but through the title of nobility he earned in 1821 as a reward for his leadership in developing the island's white population. Even among the Cuban "creole" elite, the rights of citizenship both intersected and clashed with the privileges awarded to favored subjects of the crown.[99]

Beyond blanket condemnations of political ineptitude or naively optimistic assessments of liberal nationalism lies a more useful understanding of the Spanish imperial state in the nineteenth century. Policies about racial inclusion and exclusion, about conceding privileges and guaranteeing rights, were nothing if not inconsistent; and perhaps that was precisely the point. As is the case with other empires, such a sprawling political system was not well equipped to accommodate universal principles that could be uniformly applied. Scattered policies administered by multiple and shifting institutions allowed the Spanish government the flexibility to adapt its administration to alternating moments of relative stability, crisis, and emergency.[100] It also furnished colonial subjects with multiple political vocabularies through which to express their aspirations. Conflicts over liberal citizenship and older interpellations of the colonial subject established the terms on which rights, privileges, political inclusion, and categories of belonging could all be discussed. Both depended on affective ties to Spain—loyalty and love of country above all.[101] How those bonds conditioned the participation and exclusion of African-descended Cubans in colonial politics is the subject of the next chapter.

TWO

Suspicious Affinities
Loyal Subjectivity and the Paternalist Public

The following morning when all the people were at church, a free servant called me aside, and in a whisper, said to me, "my friend, if you suffer it is your own fault; you are treated worse than the meanest slave; make your escape, and present yourself before the Captain-General at Havana, state your ill treatment to him, and he will do you justice"; at the same time showing me the road to Havana.
—Juan Francisco Manzano, 1840

When the Prussian scientist-explorer Alexander von Humboldt visited Havana in 1800–1801 and 1804, his observations affirmed the deep opposition to slavery he had held before he left for Spanish America. Horrifying conditions in Cuba contradicted the benevolent and protective slave laws and regulations enacted by the local authorities—or better put, as Humboldt clarified, the rich landowners who populated Havana's *ayuntamiento* (town council), the Consulado, and the Sociedad Patriótica. He hoped that a more responsible government, supported by "rich and enlightened citizens," would improve Cuba's prospects for order and prosperity. If the nominal safeguards of government, which Humboldt saw as a vehicle for wealthy interests, cloaked the violence and degradations of slavery, what Humboldt saw as the empty language of loyalty veiled similar injustices. He was annoyed by "perspicacious writers" given to idealizing the supposed loyalty of free and enslaved Cubans of African descent to the government and to their masters. "With the ingenious fictions of language," he claimed, they "have invented the terms 'black cultivators of the Antilles,' 'black vassalage,' and 'patriarchal protection'" to distort the image of social relations in a slave society.[1]

Humboldt was neither the first nor the only skeptic of the language of loyalty. The "wily sophisms" at which he took aim became a common target among critics of the Ever-Faithful Isle, who often took aim at the protections and vassalage associated with colonial rule, slavery, and racial hierarchy. Here was a fine example of a public transcript: an expression of relations between dominant and subordinate groups as defined by the privileged and powerful—a flattering "self-portrait," as James Scott called it, of how they wish to be seen. Subordinates might endorse those terms in the presence of superiors, as the documentary record of slaves, colonial subjects, those racialized as black or mulatto in nineteenth-century Cuba frequently makes evident. But according to Scott, subordinates also express a hidden transcript, a dissonant message expressed offstage, behind the scenes, or beneath the surface, which might draw on elements of the dominant discourse if only to undermine it. Thus even when colonial subjects wrote of their love of country, or when slaves' petitions went on and on about how humble and loyal they were, their language served to "clothe their resistance and defiance"—opposition for which, in the Age of Revolutions and in a slave society, there were plenty of extant models.[2]

This innovative framework for understanding popular struggle and politics has shed bright light on questions of resistance and rebellion, especially for the history of slavery in the Americas. It has also had the effect of compressing a wide range of affiliations and actions within the categories of resistance and agency. As observers of the past, should we expect subaltern historical subjects to have confronted their subordination in the terms of our contemporary political vocabularies and expectations? What are we looking for—and what do we obscure—when we do?[3] Actions and beliefs not easily characterized as resistance invite us to step back from an instinctual association of agency with resistance, from assuming resistance as the default position of subordinate groups, and perhaps from the framework of resistance, agency, and accommodation as a whole.[4] For much of the nineteenth century, expressing loyalty to Spanish rule figured as the principal mode of political self-assertion on the island, and Cubans of African descent joined most other Cubans in locating themselves in a position of political or social subordination. (Perhaps loyalty maintained its purchase given popular disappointment from piecemeal Spanish experiments with liberal and republican practices of freedom, rights, and citizenship.) If this appears to hew too closely to a "public transcript," one that did little to challenge ubiquitous inequalities, it might encourage us to pay a little more attention to the historical logic of ingenious fictions of language, as Humboldt called them, and to rethink what a public is in the first place.

Contrasting a public to a hidden world takes for granted widespread access to established spaces and forums of exchange, and in early nineteenth-century Cuba, hardly anyone took those for granted. After each suspension of constitutional rule, colonial officials, sometimes more so in Cuba than in Spain, tightened their grip on most mechanisms of public life, and fears of slave rebellion and race war became their routine justifications for restricting press and associational freedoms for the entire island. The point is not to declare that Cubans of color really were truly rebellious or truly loyal, but to argue that this very dichotomy conditioned the terms of public discourse. If, in the first decades of the century, Cubans met with limited success when they entered the field of politics by claiming the rights of citizens (or, in a few cases, by declaring independence), expressing themselves as loyal subjects represented more than a poor substitute. Loyalty grounded claims to membership in the Spanish empire that could allow the pursuit of various ends in the context of inequality by design.

Could anyone, then, become a loyal subject? This was the question that perplexed and energized those who sought to accumulate the symbolic capital sufficient to enter public life—and those who sought to manipulate it. It is also the question that this chapter pursues, and it was a question that loomed large during turbulent moments in the first two-thirds of the nineteenth century: the Napoleonic invasion and implementation of the 1812 Constitution; the 1823 Soles y Rayos de Bolívar conspiracy, led by Colombians determined to rid the hemisphere of Spanish rule; the decision in 1837 that Cuba would be ruled by "special laws" rather than constitutional guarantees; and the brutal repression of an alleged conspiracy between slaves, free people, and British abolitionists in 1844 known as La Escalera.

The Loyal Subject

For the authors of the so-called antislavery novels of the 1830s and 1840s, the ideal Cuban slaves were submissive, loyal to their owners, and possessed of innate nobility. Sab, the slave and title character in Gertrudis Gómez de Avellaneda's 1841 novel, claims to be the son of an African princess and explains that slaves "drag their chains patiently."[5] Francisco, the intelligent and attractive protagonist of Anselmo Suárez y Romero's novel, communicates with tears more than words, and he serves his mistress faithfully while enduring relentless beatings. Other slaves in the novels—secondary characters, nameless masses—hint in the background at more defiant responses to the brutalities of plantation life. Far from dismantling tropes of African barbarity and racial inferiority, the authors of these novels sought to show the pervasive decay that slavery caused to an island like Cuba, decay visible even in the paternalistic depictions of the authors themselves. One writer later praised Suárez y

Romero for departing from "the ridiculous habit or error of depicting a selective society: the society, white only, isolated . . . it is necessary, indispensable, to see the *negritos.*"[6] Writers thus carefully featured loyal slaves so that even the problems their presence exposed—dangerous intimacies and an ineluctable sense of humanity—would appear preferable to more violent alternatives.

Yet it was difficult for Cuba's literate population to read any of these novels, since government censors had prohibited their publication on the island for decades. Juan Francisco Manzano's *Autobiography* appeared in London in 1840 and Gertrudis Gómez de Avellaneda's *Sab* was published in Madrid in 1841, but Suárez's *Francisco,* written in 1839, was not published until 1880, and *Cecilia Valdés* did not appear until 1882. In 1859, censors rejected a request to publish Félix Tanco y Bosmeniel's *Petrona y Rosalía,* written in 1838, and it remained unpublished until 1925. That even these novels, deemed too risky for Cuban readers, depicted slaves as submissive and docile reveals just how deeply rooted that idealized type was in Cuban society, not surprising during a period when a growing slave population fueled growing fears of rebellion. This tendency also underscores a tension running throughout early nineteenth-century Cuba, experienced by everyone from writers to planters to administrators to common people of all backgrounds. How could expressions of loyalty speak to a sense of social and political cohesion when public restrictions were so tight that even expressions of support or stability might be routinely prohibited or denied? That paradox lay at the heart of loyalty to Spain, given that constitutional guarantees of citizenship and rights, whether within the Spanish empire or as an independent nation, could not reliably ground claims to political personhood.

Certainly, neither censors nor writers expected antislavery literature to serve as how-to manuals for slaves themselves, or that fictional representations of loyal slaves could seamlessly model colonial political relationships, either in affirmation or critique. As Sibylle Fischer has persuasively argued, the figure of the loyal slave in these works can be understood through the prism of fantasy, a negotiation with the values and anxieties of a slave society, in particular the fears of repeating the events of the Haitian Revolution. Thus a fictional loyal slave could perform useful labor in support of proslavery arguments as well as antislavery ones. To relate the character to a "debate about the 'truth of slaves,'" either through "the paradigm of realism or a reflection theory of ideology," she cautions, "would be to seriously misdiagnose the ideological operations of the narratives."[7]

We might deepen our understanding of these dynamics by seeing the fictional loyal slave as but one manifestation of a widespread valorization of loyalty as a virtue and practice. It was an ideology that accomplished considerable work in holding together a slave society and a colonial regime. Loyalty almost always implied hierarchy, and it was through multiple and overlapping hierarchies—polar extremes such as master and slave, colony and metropole, white and black (followed by intermediate categorizations), male and female, parent and child, rich and poor—that most Cubans understood themselves in relation to each other and the institutions that governed them. Individuals and groups commonly inhabited subordinate positions and understood that location as a regular point of departure for making claims. Cast in religious terms, it might ennoble the loyal as suffering martyrs. In the case of the antislavery novelists, invoking loyalty allowed them to foreground the humiliations of slavery. For others, it often seemed like the only viable, or most successful, mode of expression; individuals and groups might successfully petition their superiors as humble and loyal servants, whereas they would have less luck making demands as equals who could threaten rebellion or independence. Such positioning recalls the dual meaning of "subjection" explained by Judith Butler as a "fundamental dependence on a discourse we never chose but that, paradoxically, initiates and sustains our agency."[8] Discussions of loyalty, then, may not reveal a "truth about slaves" or anyone else, but they relate to lived experience and the material world through their ability to shape common understandings of how society and politics functioned on the island.

Cubans were never dependent on banned novels for models of loyalty. They heard other examples in sermons, read them in newspapers, and learned them through the daily experiences of various hierarchical relationships that depended on the language of loyalty to appear natural or normative. The Covarrubias dictionary, for example, defined loyalty with the example of a wife's obedience to her husband.[9] An 1824 school primer issued by the Sociedad Patriótica of Havana attempted to imbue in children the value of loyalty and obedience beyond personal relationships, instructing them that "love of country is an obligation of social man."[10] Furthermore, newspaper advertisements identifying slaves for sale often boasted slaves' loyalty as one of their most important qualities. One slaveowner described a *mulata* cook he was selling as "very efficient and untiring at work, *fiel* [loyal] and humble"; a washerwoman "of the *lucumí* nation" selling for 640 pesos was described as "very loyal, healthy, and without defects."[11] Advertisements in newspapers for slaves—whether for sale, for rent, or wanted for purchase or rent—routinely valued loyalty and obedience. Predictably, advertisements attempting to locate runaway slaves, which ran alongside these other notices, tended to emphasize negative characteristics in the absence of any behavior that could be described as loyalty.

Within the political culture of Spanish American colonialism, locating sovereignty with the monarch allowed the king's subjects to envision a subordinate and personal identification with empire that was routinely expressed in terms of loyalty. It was not a discourse that was necessarily emasculating or lacking in honor. In the highest social strata, an economy of favors rewarded elites with titles and professional advancement for what was understood to be their loyalty to the crown.[12] Indeed, an aristocratic upper crust centered in Havana had maneuvered deftly in the early decades of the nineteenth century to support the kind of government that would guarantee stability and profit. The rhetoric used by this elite was saturated with effusive protestations of loyalty to Fernando VII, who rewarded some of them with titles of nobility as he simultaneously nullified the 1812 Constitution.[13] These privileged subjects frequently joined less favored plebeians in large public ceremonies in towns and cities that celebrated Spanish authority: carefully arranged processions for a monarch's new child, oaths sworn to a new monarch, or the arrival of a new captain general. Plebeian Cubans gathered in squares and other public spaces to hear royal edicts read or to watch bullfights, fireworks, and parades that commemorated royal power and offered symbolic proximity to the king.[14]

Social and political hierarchies, however, never overlapped perfectly, and transposing loyalty from a private virtue to a public one posed multiple problems. Familial ties and tropes of sobbing plantation slaves and trusted domestic servants all point to a feminization of loyalty in the private sphere that made an ill fit for a public milieu dominated by patriarchs. Assumptions that adult men would speak for, and not with, women, children, slaves, and servants regarding political matters raised questions about how social subordinates might make public their allegiance to Spanish rule, whether imagined as the king, the constitution, the Cortes, more localized institutions of state, or broader cultural affinities.[15] The absence of a male head of household might require a supplicant to amplify the language of loyalty (read especially as patriarchal subjection) even more: the benefactors of Havana's Casa de Maternidad prefaced an 1833 request for more funding by noting that the women and children "do not have nor are able to have any other father than the Sovereign."[16]

The changing physiology of the body politic in the nineteenth century meant that colonial subjects had to revise what they understood the object of their loyalty to be. The long popular refrain of colonial critique, "Long live the king! Death to bad government!" had ceased to carry the weight that it used to with the instability and of the monarchy itself. Fernando VII, the Spanish king, lost power to Joseph Bonaparte with the Napoleonic invasion, supported the 1812 Constitution that implemented a constitutional monarchy, nullified that constitution when he returned to power in 1814, and remained a vexed and complicated figure of Spanish authority until his death in 1833. Subsequent regencies, child monarchs, and military coups further diminished the all-powerful image of the monarch. Also, the monarchy had not given way completely to ideas of secular government or popular sovereignty, and Cuba and the other Spanish colonies remained on the margins of formal political representation for much of the century.

Although the weakened monarchy may have rattled the vertical links holding together the political logic of community in Cuba, the Spanish empire in the nineteenth century was by no means on a clear path to substituting this older order with horizontal ties of popular sovereignty among a unified *pueblo* (people or community). Celebrating the popular sovereignty articulated in the 1812 Constitution may, in one moment, have been understood as a supreme act of loyalty that in another moment—after 1837 in particular—could have been treated as a seditious denunciation of Spanish rule. Critics of colonial policies still relied on the language of loyalty more than that of rights and citizenship, even though they were less likely to contrast bad government with a benevolent king. The Condesa de Merlin drew on the figure of a well-placed slave to demonstrate the extent of popular discontent with Miguel Tacón, the particularly harsh captain general in the late 1830s. Her reflections in 1841 on Cuba included an anecdote about a dinner hosted by the Marquesa de Arcos, daughter of the Marqués de Casa Calvo, a Havana noble targeted by Tacón. The captain general himself was in attendance and filled up on the food of "the negro Antonio," the marquesa's slave and supposedly the best cook in Havana. In appreciation for the meal, the captain general made the paternalistic gesture of offering the slave his freedom (and a healthy gratuity), but Antonio—apparently aware of Tacón's offense against his mistress's family and against Cubans in general—responded, "Tell the governor that I prefer slavery and poverty with my owners to riches and freedom with him."[17]

Who better to voice discontent than someone who had far fewer privileges to lose and much more to gain relative to his wealthy owners or an elite Spanish visitor? And how better to illustrate disdain for Tacón than identifying someone who would prefer enslavement to freedom and money from a tyrant? Writers, nevertheless, recognized the limits of locating the plight of all Cubans in the character of a loyal slave. In Cirilo Villaverde's *Cecilia Val-*

dés, Dionisio—the literate, cultured, African-born slave with a "fondness for dances deemed appropriate only for whites," reveals some limits. Coincidentally, he was a well-regarded cook for the Gamboa family, had met several captains general, the Condesa Merlín, and even Louis Philippe of Orléans. Yet he knew with one word when his masters thought he had crossed the line and presumed too close an affinity with his esteemed company: "Dionisio knew very well that he shouldn't say a word from the moment that his masters began to use the formal *Usted* to address him. That was a sure sign that the tide of their wrath was rising."[18] Merlin and Villaverde knew that popular political grievances ventriloquized through a slave had to be carefully contextualized to avoid collapsing altogether the differences between slaves and the elite circles they sometimes inhabited, or opening up the space for popular demands for rights and reform.[19]

For colonial officials, acknowledging the political allegiance of Cubans also required nimble rhetoric, especially when creole elites justified their criticism of Spanish policies with their continued presence within the empire. Some Spanish observers defended policies in Cuba by invoking the peculiarities of the "Latin race" that made other, usually more lenient, colonial policies in the British and French Caribbean unsuitable for the island.[20] Others extolled the loyalty exhibited by Cubans and argued that the Latin race cohered politically "because it has the same origin, because there the same language is spoken, the same holy religion is venerated and the customs and habits are the same."[21] Official organs such as the *Diario de la Marina* regularly reminded readers that the government's "active and intelligent authority" and *vigilancia tutelar* (tutelary vigilance) were the sources of its economic well-being, its security, and its education in refining its habits and customs.[22] Specifically, the newspaper drew a sharp contrast to the lawlessness and disloyalty that characterized the struggling mainland Latin American republics, warning Cubans what was possible "if the societies of our race, by habits and ideas, do not conceive of power as strong and unitary."[23] The language of custom and habit here vaguely resembles references to *usos y costumbres* common in colonial Spanish America that described local, often indigenous, forms of rulership and governance. As Cuban officials used it, allusions to custom and habit expressed similarity and identification between Spain and its colonies rather than denoting cultural differences that justified local autonomy. Cubans' loyalty could thus be considered a naturalized cultural affinity rather than a calculated political strategy.

In response, Cuban politicians, reformers, and writers took the colonial government and its promoters at their word, and often invoked a racially charged concept of loyalty to their "Hispanic" brethren on the Iberian Peninsula when pressing for political rights. During the tumultuous 1840s and with new possibilities for reform in the 1850s and 1860s, white Cuban writers regularly positioned themselves as loyal subjects. In an essay in 1851, José Antonio Saco identified related internal and external dangers to Cuba that "posed a new test of its unchanging loyalty."[24] Namely, as the covetous gaze from the North intensified, a growing movement among Cubans favored annexation by the United States. A longtime advocate of white immigration to Cuba as an alternative to slave labor, Saco sought to exclude the population of color as a factor in offering rights to white Cubans in order to maintain support for Spain. He explained that "the Indian and African races remained completely excluded" from earlier colonial reforms that Spaniards wrongly assumed to have led to mainland independence. Cuba's new threats, he insisted, did not "originate in a clash between blacks and whites."[25] With only white Cubans in the picture, then, Saco deployed metaphors of bondage without fear of inviting enslaved Cubans to press their demands as well. He asked rhetorically what the benefit of support for Spain might be in the face of increasingly visible alternatives: "Why are political chains the compensation for such loyalty?"[26]

Collectively, the deliberate exclusion of Cubans of color by these Spanish writers and by Saco would suggest that people of African descent could only be loyal subjects in the realm of fiction. And even there, it is not coincidental how few characters of African descent express opinions about colonial politics. Slave allegiances beyond the plantation were rare in antislavery novels, and authors placed at a safe distance the idea that the noble slaves they endowed with humanity would ever make claims on political personhood. Gómez de Avellaneda might have acknowledged the alienation of the Middle Passage, but she was not ready to offer her characters a new *patria*. Sab explains that he is "alone in the world," without his parents, and further laments, "Nor do I have a country to defend, because slaves have no country."[27] Of course, Cuban slaves might have imagined themselves capable of having multiple countries: African ethnic and political identifications (often called *naciones*) persisted throughout the nineteenth century, and some rebellions and legal challenges by slaves had as their goal new rights, privileges, and local political practices.[28] The pattern in Cuban fiction of excluding slaves from the realm of formal politics certainly mirrored the laws and policies in place to guarantee that prohibition in practice. Beneath both patterns lay suspicions that if Cuban slaves comprehended the presence of Spanish government at all, they would instinctively oppose it.

The historical record reveals a far broader range of political subjectivities. The royal slaves of El Cobre stand out as Cuba's most celebrated historical example of slaves whose rhetoric of loyalty and subordination helped win them concrete rights and ultimately their freedom. As mentioned briefly in the introduction, 271 slaves working in derelict copper mines near Santiago de Cuba became property of the king when the crown confiscated the operation in 1670. Royal slavery was a common, if not widespread, practice in which slaves owned by the crown and laboring in public works projects or short-term military defense might encounter opportunities for manumission, but the slaves of El Cobre experienced multigenerational proximity to state power of a different kind.[29] For over a century the slaves and their descendants used their special subordination to royal authority to petition for rights to land, tax relief, pueblo status, and limited self-government. They cited their military service to the crown in defense, mining, hunting down runaway slaves, and the construction of a church at what was becoming Cuba's principal Marian shrine. Just as important, their petitions were replete with mentions of loyalty, obedience, servitude, and allegiance to a king who was also their master—not the cruel, heartless master of antislavery novels but a benevolent protector. Thus actions that officials and masters could view as contentious when other slaves undertook them—protests, legal complaints, and the like—could be tolerated from the *cobreros* as loyal subjects pursuing the appropriate channels of Spanish justice.[30] Seeking royal privileges as a corporate group, rather than demanding individual rights or openly rebelling, served the cobreros well throughout the eighteenth century. The language of loyalty that the cobreros used continued to hold purchase throughout the nineteenth century as a mode of self-fashioning among all slaves, not just the king's, and especially for the free population of color in Cuba and beyond.

Dynamics among free people more clearly exposed the gendered conditions of loyal subjectivity. In contrast to the feminized valence of loyalty in the private realm, what constituted the free man of color as a loyal subject of the state was military valor, skilled occupational status, and social relationships that included, among other things, "authority over subordinates."[31] Public service that might require the use of force or physical labor frequently appeared in the documents attesting to the loyalty of free men of color: participation in territorial defense, the suppression of runaways, and labor on public works projects as militiamen. Exercising authority over subordinates might be demonstrated through marriage, childrearing, or officer status in a militia. Depending on their circumstances, and certainly in comparison to slaves, free men enjoyed greater opportunities to attain normative markers of honor: better chances of accumulating wealth and property, maintaining families and other social solidarities, and acquiring an education. The 1841 census identified just over half of all 152,848 free people of color (about 15 percent of the total population) to be *pardo,* or *mulato,* indicating that a sizable number of free people could assert partial Spanish descent—although questions of parentage and legitimate birth might complicate reputational consensus.[32] If loyal subjectivity for free people seemed to rely on mimetic proximity to Spanishness, that may have had less to do with perceived descent or physical appearance—after all, racial purity and adherence to patriarchal ideals also figured into estimations of honor—than it did with the ability to inhabit social roles whose primary characteristic was not African descent. In *Cecilia Valdés,* a master tailor explains to his assistant that "His Majesty the King has declared our art to be a noble one, as is the occupation of cigar makers, and we have the right to use Don before our name. Tondá, even though he's a mulatto, has his 'Don,' thanks to the King."[33]

In a similar vein, the "stain" of African blood precluded the possibility of equal status to loyal white subjects not simply because of racial purity but, not surprisingly, because free people's social, occupational, and, above all, political allegiances were never guaranteed. Although colonial authorities learned time and time again that nobody's loyalty could be assumed, nor determined by race, free people of color posed to them a particular threat. In the minds of many Cubans, they were as likely to marshal their resources in support of anticolonial projects or to incite slaves to demand their freedom as to support the current order. The very "in-betweenness" of free people of color made their suitability as loyal subjects a heated political issue in the first half of the nineteenth century. The result was that even when free people and slaves behaved in ways that would suggest support for Spanish rule and public order, they confronted two responses: either an acknowledgment of their loyalty framed as an exception to a general rule of black rebelliousness, or outright denial in line with Sab's observation that "slaves have no country."

Here was the flip side of claiming loyalty from a subordinate position: it reinforced the power of superiors in ways that did not always inspire a benevolent, protective, or reciprocal response. This point would not have been lost on most of the enslaved, who lived under the constant threat of violence no matter how they positioned themselves. Even the authors of the "antislavery" novels acknowledged this. Cuba's creole elite and free men of color learned this lesson, too, when Spain would shut them out of political life. Nevertheless, faithfulness to one's superiors routinely stood as the necessary precondition for political voice, and under the right conditions those who could inhabit the role of the loyal subject could bend the ear of those in power. If loyalty was the magnetic north of colonial rule, the position from which all other political orientations would be measured, there were mutual and reciprocating benefits to viewing Cuba as an island of humble servants.

Whispers of Revolution: The Soles y Rayos de Bolívar

The tight grip of colonial officials on public spaces, publications, and associational life intended to limit opportunities for subversion. It had the same effect on loyalty. Restrictions on mobility, information, and public expression already concentrated on Cuba's population of African descent, slave and free. With scrutiny by colonial officials on the activities of all of its subjects, popular expressions of loyalty were frequently suppressed, denied, or doubted. This reality came to the fore during the first large-scale challenge to Spanish rule in Cuba emerged in 1823, the movement of the Soles y Rayos de Bolívar (The Suns and Rays of Bolívar). The involvement of slaves and free people in alerting authorities to the threat did little to curb suspicions that they might understand themselves, or be understood, as loyal subjects.

Beyond the island, Cuba acquired a reputation during the 1820s throughout Spanish America as a loyalist refuge. Spanish authority from Mexico to Argentina crumbled with the success of various independence movements, and exiles from new republics and refugees from the wars arrived in Havana. Recall that one of them was María Antonia Bolívar, sister of the Great Liberator.[34] The Spanish government shifted military and administrative resources to Cuba and used Havana as a launching point for defensive engagements in the remaining areas of mainland control. But such a visible symbol of Spanish power attracted attention. Throughout the Americas, agents and supporters of independence—espousing varied combinations of republican fervor and anticolonial grudges—made Cuba the setting for their next, and possibly last, attempt to rid the hemisphere of Spanish authority.[35] They no doubt had sympathetic potential collaborators on the island, but without a blueprint for identifying and organizing them, foreign agents of Cuban independence faced similar challenges to those of the Spanish state: through what institutions and mechanisms could Cubans be compelled to support one political project over another?

One of the most elaborate of the foreign plots to "liberate" Cuba used secret societies to organize clandestinely on the island. The restoration of the 1812 Constitution in 1820 and ensuing Trienio Liberal (1820–1822) allowed a brief reprieve of associational restrictions, which independence supporters exploited. Despite the role of Masonic lodges in many mainland independence movements, Cuban lodges traced origins and ongoing relationships to counterparts in Spain and generally survived intense government scrutiny, as did non-Masonic secret societies founded by foreigners, such as the Soles y Rayos de Bolívar.[36] By the early 1820s, this organization provided some of the organizational structure sought by José Francisco Lemus, a resident of Havana who left Cuba in 1817 for Philadelphia, Florida, and Madrid, where he maintained contacts with supporters of Bolívar. He returned to the island as a colonel in the Gran Colombian army and an agent of Colombian conspirators for Cuban independence, quietly plotting until 1822, when he received orders from his Madrid allies to implement plans to incite popular revolt.

Those plans unfolded slowly as agents in various part of the island struggled to spread information to gather popular support without inciting uncontrollable slave unrest. As in other independence movements, leaders strained to avoid complete social upheaval, and some forms of unrest trumped others: a co-conspirator from Guanajay called for postponing action "until seeing to a matter involving the *negros,*" and Lemus accordingly waited several months before proceeding.[37] Even with the openings offered during the Trienio, the absence of a well-developed print culture, associational life, and widespread clandestine support that could enable rapid communication and mass mobilization forced Lemus and his co-conspirators to remain constantly on the move, shuttling between cities and the countryside to gather support. Responsibility for organizing various parts of the island (with an emphasis on the western provinces) fell to a small group of individuals, mostly Cubans, that included tradesmen, professionals, a *capitán del partido* (an administrative and judicial official), and a parish priest.[38] José Tolón, who covered Matanzas and its environs, reportedly gathered "all of the blacks and mulattoes" at the beginning of December with the goal of arming them for a march to Havana.[39] Still unresolved was the role that those blacks and mulattoes should play in an islandwide revolt against Spain.

In August 1823, proclamations circulated as broadsides that could be easily transported and, literacy allowing, read privately or publicly. They appealed to Cubans as "Españoles," as "free men, enlightened, lovers of independence," and called for an end to three centuries of "false and monstrous politics" by a faraway government. Some of them identified Lemus as "General of the Republic of Cubanacán." Others raised the specter of a British invasion and argued that only independence would prevent Cubans from remaining pawns of European politics—"humble serfs and vile slaves." In general, they took aim at what the leaders of Soles y Rayos imagined as the source of many Cubans' continued support for Spain: the increasingly distant promise of constitutional rights. Reminding readers how quickly those rights had been revoked in 1814, the broadsides noted that those who "answer to the glorious call of the Constitution" should never be called rebels. As long as Cubans willingly consented to an unequal political system, the distinction maintained between vassals of an empire and citizens of a republic, the leaflets cautioned, would devour the Spanish nation from within. For Cuban *españoles* whose ancestral links to Spain might inform their political allegiances, creole leaders in the new American republics offered an alternative, imploring Cubans to join with mainland patriots, "united with us through the tightest bonds of flesh, the social spirit and life."[40]

A racially (and gender-) exclusive appeal to white Cuban men is not terribly surprising. Even as they modified and selectively dismantled colonial social hierarchies, including the *sistema de castas*, many independence leaders wavered on the question of incorporating black and mulatto patriots into the upper ranks of armies and governments. Bolívar, for example, worried about the rise of a "pardocracy" of free mulattoes whose goals would shift from seeking legal equality to seizing control of the government.[41] On the other hand, as Marixa Lasso notes, Colombian nationalist ideology, as it developed in the 1820s, asserted the "equality and harmony" of its multiracial population."[42] These two visions presented competing rhetorical strategies for extending independence beyond Colombia, and the organizers of the Soles y Rayos, by singling out white Cubans, would more closely identify with the former.

But strengthening the "tightest bonds of flesh" was not their sole strategy. Organizers of the Soles y Rayos circulated a different broadside to selected Cubans of color that used a quite different political vocabulary than the one circulated among españoles. On 22 August Luis de Vargas, a soldier in Havana's pardo battalion, noticed a sheet of paper lying at the door of the militia barracks and immediately delivered it to his superior. In the nearby battalion, José de Soto, a soldier on night patrol, descended his barracks' staircase around midnight to find a large number of soldiers gathered to read a letter, which he quickly confiscated. The documents discovered in the colored militia barracks did not demonstrate a common recognition of citizenship associated with being Spanish. Instead, the so-called español was portrayed for the *milicianos* (militiamen) as a tyrant who had sustained "the chains that barbarism and ambition were able to invent and that still have not sated the Spanish cannibal after three hundred years." Independence was a goal to be pursued, it said, for "your protection," rather than for the promise of citizenship. The subordinate terms of the milicianos' possible participation—they must fight so that they would be better protected—may have rung familiar given the colonial rhetoric that recognized their respectable status as subordinate loyal subjects. Moreover, shifting the loyalty of well-placed Cubans of color required recognizing Lemus as a champion of freedom, but that freedom was ambiguous in its invocation of slavery, more as a political metaphor for colonialism than as a lived experience.

The proclamations did not completely ignore the social disadvantages that blacks and mulattoes with militia status might have faced, including access to literacy. Identifying as one of the "true sons of Bolívar" and identifying oneself to others did not have to hinge on reading, writing, or even speaking: milicianos were encouraged to communicate their allegiance to the *junta americana* by donning a hat with a colored feather and a coat with a small ribbon of the same color. The broadsides gave little suggestion of seeking extensive support from free or enslaved people of African descent in a rebellion, despite the presumably wider channels of communication that this might occasion. Instead, the Soles y Rayos cultivated the support of militia members, an elite group assumed to have felt the insult of Spanish subordination more acutely than others and whose capacity for patriotism and love of country could be placed in the service of a "united call" to end Spanish rule—albeit a unity that may have left intact many of the legal and racial hierarchies maintained under colonial rule.[43]

Despite these attempts to ignite a rebellion for independence, slaves and free people appear to have been instrumental in alerting authorities to the Soles y Rayos de Bolívar conspiracy just days before the planned actions were to begin. Indeed, Captain General Francisco Dionisio Vives himself learned of the conspiracy through a network of slaves and servants. On 23 July, he received a visit from Bonifacio Duarte, a "well-known person in Havana," according to the main government investigator of the conspiracy. Duarte's household included "an old man of color" who was "in his sphere, a highly respected man." That old man was also the *padrino* (godfather) of a slave woman whose companion was an African-born slave, Tomás, who worked at the Havana printing press of Miguel de Oro. Duarte brought his servant and the two slaves to meet with Captain General Francisco Dionisio Vives and deliver a copy of the broadside that Tomás had been printing on Oro's request. Although he could not read, Tomás had begun to notice his owner working furtively, with the doors shut, so that no one could see him.[44] Tomás shared a copy of one document with his girlfriend, who took it to her padrino, who realized that the broadside was a call for Cuban independence and immediately consulted Duarte. Their collective visit to the captain general and the subsequent apprehension of Miguel de Oro revealed the extensive network the Soles y Rayos movement in Havana comprised—and the central role of a clandestine print culture in its organization.

The success of these underground circuits of communication until this point must have irked Vives. Less than two weeks earlier, he had made explicit his attempt to shut out Cubans of color from political discussion when he rejected a royal order sanctioning free deliberation among and within associations. He wrote to Madrid that free pardos and morenos, "although generally loyal to the nation, will not cease to be seduced, encouraging their *amor propio* [self-esteem] and leading them to hatch the idea of an exact equality with the same principles of natural law as those who have strayed on the mainland." There was "infinitely more to fear," he argued, from allowing slaves access to political discussion.[45] Justifying strict control of the population based on anxieties about black rebellion was a familiar policy. What did it mean for this strategy to fail so blatantly? Not only did anticolonial conspiracy circumvent limitations on public political discussion; contrary to racialized assumptions about loyalty and rebellion, it was mostly white conspirators who comprised the Soles y Rayos, and Cubans of color, including some well-connected slaves, who had halted it.

Despite the clear barriers they imposed, illiteracy, slavery, and African origins did not exclude a slave like Tomás from the world of print and political intrigue; in fact, because of his presumed powerlessness, such "defects" may have made him an appealing choice to place in close proximity to sensitive material. By mobilizing formal and informal networks of kin and patronage that existed among slaves, free people, and even Havana's elite, an *esclavo prensista* (press slave), as he was called in government reports, made common cause with the highest colonial official on the island.

Traces of the restricted print culture in Havana proper were scarcely visible just outside of the city. Still, even there illiterate Cubans of color found themselves target audiences of printed propaganda. Bruno Aristegui, a free moreno and a shoemaker living in the nearby community of Guanabacoa, had encountered a piece of paper on the back patio of the Santaya dance hall late at night on Saturday, 23 August. Since he could not read, he visited Doña María Ignacia Loysa the following morning and asked her to read it to him. She told him that the paper was a "bad thing" and would keep it herself. The following day, Aristegui retrieved the paper in order to try his luck with Father José Alayeto, a priest who likewise refused to divulge the message on the paper and instead delivered it the following day to authorities in Havana. They were shocked by what they read: a salutation from "the Junta Americana designated by the honorific seal 'The Republic of Cubanacán'" to "all of the Americans of Guanabacoa." This was yet another rhetorical strategy of the Soles y Rayos: not one exclusive to white or African-descended Cubans but a general appeal to all. Hours later, Aristegui found himself in Havana and under interrogation, still, presumably, with no knowledge of the seditious message written on the paper he found.[46] But his knowledge was less important to the police than his potential to spread news of rebellion to other Cubans of color. Although white officials in the highest levels of Guanabacoa's municipal government ended up linked to the Soles y Rayos (Lemus had lived in the town at some point), it was Aristegui who endured the strictest scrutiny from investigators.[47] Whatever privileges could befall loyal subjects seemed well out of reach.

Aristegui, Tomás, his companion and her godfather, and the milicianos Luis de Vargas and José de Soto: each of them had either resisted the call of the Soles y Rayos or had been instrumental in unearthing its subversive intentions. Yet they received no official recognition, and their support never merited a description of "loyalty" in the documentary record. This was not what officials wanted to see. In the aftermath of the conspiracy, investigations—if not punishments—disproportionately focused on slaves, free people, and sympathetic white Cubans, such as local priests, who might influence them. Only one free pardo appears to have been among the detained or exiled, but authorities seemed as intent to determine the loyalty or disloyalty of Cubans of color as they were to trace the flow of information and public dissemination of the Soles y Rayos message.[48] Rooting out conspirators might resolve the immediate conflict, but leaving their circuits of communication intact— especially if they allowed exchange between cities and the countryside—left the island vulnerable to future conspiracies.[49] Investigators generally exonerated illiterate milicianos and slaves because of their presumed ignorance, but the role of slaves and free people in uncovering the conspiracy did not alter the worst suspicions of high-ranking officials. In one statement Captain General Vives wrote to Madrid that the free-colored militias, "who express the loyalty they have for the King," had helped prevent the conspiracy, although he was cautious "to avoid that they unite among their party."[50] In another statement, he attributed Cubans' pacification to the "intimate relations they have with the peninsula, where they maintain relatives and friends." He explained that the current laws might let him preserve order if the island was inhabited only by these presumably Spanish-descended residents, but those laws were "for countries that did not have the inconvenience of slaves and free people of color like this one."[51] By attempting to attribute allegiance only to Spaniards and creoles, Vives betrayed the facts of the conspiracy—a testament to how deeply ingrained anxieties could trump the wide applicability of loyal subjectivity

To contemporaries, the narrative of the conspiracy did not break down along expected lines: a Spanish and creole population resistant to an anticolonial plot and a population of African descent itching for rebellion. Nevertheless, that story circulated to the benefit of those who continued to believe that the propensity for rebellion was racially specific. The subsequent tightening of public space and information did not exclusively suppress Cubans of color—Vives declared the creole-predominant Masonic lodges illegal in 1824— but they remained the best threat that officials could cite in order to place strict controls on political discussion.

The Soles y Rayos conspiracy does not clearly emerge as a proto-national movement of Cubans or as a foreign import wasted on a population content with Spanish rule. It does seem difficult to ignore the significant role of a handful of slaves and free people in defusing a potential independence plot. That it was easy for officials in the moment to do just that underscores the limits of loyal subjectivity as a political position that Cubans of color could inhabit without scrutiny or suspicion. The conspiracy also tells us about two other aspects of the political culture of Spain's remaining empire in the 1820s: the strict limits placed on public forms of political expression and the privileged status of the men in the militias of color, representing both their potential for political leadership among other Cubans of color as well as the contingency of their political leanings, which made them alternately trusted and feared.

Paranoia and the Public

The portrait of public life painted in the Soles y Rayos conspiracy is a bleak one. Clandestine meetings, secret societies, broadsides left outside doors, passed hand to hand, and discussed in stairwells: these were briefly effective but ultimately poor substitutes for visible and sanctioned networks of associations, publications, and physical spaces where political discussion could occur. The conspiracy occurred less than a year after the end of the second constitutional period in Cuba (1820–1823), which ostensibly broadened opportunities for more Cubans, citizens or not, to engage in political discussion. But even those liberties had their limits: government censors issued 147 denunciations to various licensed newspapers in the course of the Trienio.[52] After major turning points away from expanded rights—in 1822, in 1837, with the announcement of "special laws," and after the slave revolts and La Escalera conspiracy in the 1840s—moderate reforms coming from Madrid often faced skepticism from officials on the island, such as Vives's refusal to permit associational freedoms to continue just weeks before the Soles y Rayos conspiracy came to a head. Such refusals, common in the first half of the century, transformed the political landscape, leaving figures such as Father Félix Varela, once a Cuban delegate to the Cortes, to relocate political discussion off of the island—in Varela's case to the United States, where he published *El Habanero* in Philadelphia and advocated Cuban independence. The restrictions placed on public space and association, political discussion, and publications may have been intended to squelch seditious and revolutionary activities, but they also confined public expressions of support for Spanish rule.

Not surprisingly, a great deal of knowledge about the public sphere in the early nineteenth century comes from the government officials who were concocting plans to eliminate or restrict it even further. Thus public life was at least visible enough for censors and governors to target it. The continuity of colonial rule in Cuba set it apart from the independent mainland republics where, between the 1820s and the 1850s, "Spanish America experienced a veritable explosion of the public sphere of civil society," according to Victor Uribe-Urán.[53] Nevertheless, in the moneyed and literate circles of the island's major cities, profits from agricultural expansion underwrote limited developments in cultural life. Manuel Moreno Fraginals notes that between 1824 and 1834, what was known as the "ominous decade" in Spain, Cubans experienced "an age of cultural splendor and growing refinement in the dominant sector."[54] At the center of it was the Sociedad Económica de Amigos del País, founded in 1793 as the Real Sociedad Patriótica. Composed of Havana's creole elite, its members established a public library and championed education and scientific research, as well as laying the groundwork for an academy of literature. They also tended to fill the posts of the government's civil censor boards and actively removed children and teachers of color from schools, thus occupying a dual role as patrons and police.[55] The Sociedad provided a crucial and visible linkage between a public "patriotic" institution and the white elite, a link that its publications tended to affirm. In 1830, the society's history section published a narrative of the island's past that decried the poor treatment of indigenous Cubans in the sixteenth century, who "as our historians suppose," were "less barbaric" than Africans and "did not put up so much resistance."[56] Although the Society did not always enjoy cozy relations with the colonial government, it usually adhered to the norms of acceptable public discourse set forth by the Spanish administration.

Those norms frequently hamstrung the periodical press and people's access to it. Newspapers, as Benedict Anderson famously noted, were pivotal among the "creole pioneers" of Spanish America in developing a sense of nationalism; for authorities on the island, news of anticolonial or revolutionary movements had to be stifled at all costs—and not just from white creoles.[57] In 1804, the captain general acknowledged that enough literate Cubans of color existed to warrant measures attempting to keep news about the Haitian Revolution out of their hands. Although "some portion of the people of color are educated, are of decent backgrounds, and merit esteem," he worried that news about Haiti published in the *Gaceta de Madrid* might confuse even that group into assuming that that the Spanish government endorsed the revolution.[58] Sporadic press restrictions during constitutional periods led to short runs of newspapers throughout the island. Yet even before the 1837 decision to rule the island through special laws, Cuban officials doubted the idea that Cuba and Spain could enjoy equal freedoms. Miguel Tacón, perhaps the most severe of the captains general in the early nineteenth century, wrote to Madrid in 1835 that freedom of the press was the principal manifestation of the "principles of absolute equality" being expounded in Spain, principles he found "incompatible with the old colonial regime."[59] Government control of print culture extended beyond newspapers. As in nineteenth-century Brazil, when the Portuguese court moved to Rio de Janeiro, the imperial government made use of the press to attempt to shape public opinion.[60] In addition to regulations and statistical reports, government presses also published fiction, poetry, and dramatic works, presumably to guarantee the absence of subversive messages in popular entertainment. Loyalty was a prevalent theme, from syrupy poetry celebrating the regency of María Cristina to an allegorical play, *Lealtad cubana*, starring Commerce, Religion, Justice, Agriculture, the Diplomatic State, and the Arts—and with *El Pueblo* as a silent supporting character that was rarely on stage.[61]

Colonial authorities extended restrictions on public life beyond publications to specify practices that, at first glance, did not seem particularly threatening to public order or colonial rule. Form became as dangerous a threat as content. One of Tacón's first acts on becoming captain general in 1835 was to prohibit patriotic songs and marches in public, for even those could awaken "the spirit of indiscipline and disorder."[62] Several years later, for the same reason, he prohibited applause during and after performances in theaters, including the colossal new one he had built in Havana that bore his name. J. M. Andueza, who visited Havana in 1841, noted that the applause ban "converted the theater into a church, so religious was the silence and restraint."[63]

Richard Henry Dana, traveling to Cuba from the United States in 1859, mentioned an opera singer being fined and imprisoned for refusing to substitute *lealtá* (loyalty) for *libertá* (freedom) in a performance of Puccini's *I Puritani*. Dana went on to describe the entirety of public life as vulnerable to the state of exception: "The power of banishing, without a charge made, or a trial, or even a record, but on the mere will of the Captain-General . . . hangs at all hours over the head of every Cuban. Besides, that terrible power which is restrained only by the analogy of a state of siege, may be at any time called into action."[64] For all of the limitations on what could be said and done in public, the very act of setting the limits was a public one with a clear message: that the power of the Spanish government, especially as embodied by the captain general, was absolute and arbitrary—all the more reason for Cubans to attempt to become loyal subjects deserving of benevolent paternal concern.

More often than not, justifications for these restrictions cited the potential for unrest among Cubans of color, even with qualified acknowledgment of their loyalty. For those prominent Cubans who sought a greater role for the island in Spanish politics, assessing the political nature of Cubans of color presented difficulties. Emphasizing loyal slaves and free people could persuade opponents that extending rights and reforms would not unleash violence or demands for racial equality. But attributing that docility to successfully repressive state measures did not help their case if less repression was their goal. Allowing for the possibility of willful political choices on the part of slaves and free people only underscored the contingency of their loyalty and the possibility of equally willful rebellion. Authors, then, tended to displace the less appealing aspects of political agency onto savage Africa. Juan Bernardo O'Gavan, writing in 1821, itemized the backward politics and "horrible ceremonies" of the African polities from which *bozales* originated, explaining that "there had never existed a government more tyrannical" than those of the *reyzuelos* ("despotic petty kings").[65] The Cuban "Africanization scare" of the 1850s, when British pressure for emancipation clashed with the possibility of annexation to the United States, only amplified damning descriptions such as O'Gavan's.[66]

Stigmatizing many aspects of African culture and politics became a common gesture in reformist political discourse, but there often remained the possibility for Cubans of color to learn from white Cubans to respect property and "paternal authority," in O'Gavan's words, in a way that could simultaneously preserve social order and eradicate barbaric influences. Domingo Dulce, a reformist captain general during the 1860s, went so far as to cite the "progressive amalgamation of races" in the Spanish empire as the main reason to begin eliminating laws that distinguished free people of color from white Cubans.[67] This was but one iteration of "whitening" rhetoric that aspired to purging traces of the African past from Cuba's colonial future. More reserved captains general, censorship boards, and local authorities often restricted even statements like these.

Echoes of Africa

In practice, however, "African" culture, as it was revised and re-created in Cuba, provoked mixed responses. Even when they characterized them as barbaric and inferior to Spanish customs, observers of African-derived cultural practices noted advantageous overlaps with Spanish colonial political culture. *Cofradías* (Catholic lay brotherhoods) and *cabildos* (mutual-aid societies), the sanctioned institutions in which Africans and African-descended Cubans could gather publicly, were of Spanish origin, even as they preserved African ethnic identifications (*naciones*). The cabildos became especially visible on 6 January during the Fiesta del Día de Reyes, or the Feast of the Epiphany, when members would take to the streets, celebrate the presentation of gifts to Jesus by the Three Kings, and crown their own kings and queens of each cabildo. Here was a moment of reprieve when slaves and free people could take to the streets without excessive surveillance, proceed through the city or town in *comparsas* (carnival bands or processions), and end up at the residence of the captain general or other high representative to ask for *aguinaldos,* or gifts of money doled out on special occasions.[68]

African-descended Cubans' identifications with Spanish culture never guaranteed uncritical acceptance of the colonial order or slavery, and paranoia about Cubans of color turning any opportunity to gather into subversion occasionally rang true. In 1838, the slaves on an estate in Manacas used the Día de Reyes celebration as an opportunity to plan a rebellion, and other plots launched elsewhere around Easter or Christmas led to regulations calling for heightened vigilance of stores, taverns, cabildos, and plantations during these religious observations.[69] By the 1840s, as slave revolts proliferated and government officials looked high and low for causes and conspiracies, the embrace of Catholicism and Spanish cultural practices by some Cubans of color had become as suspicious as the presumed barbarity of African culture that persisted among others. In 1843, a typical report warning of conspiracy reached officials in Havana from an "honorable Spaniard and rich landowner" in Puerto Príncipe concerned by the formation of a cabildo of over 1,200 slaves and free people, both African born and creole. Although the "consummate stupidity" of the bozales, he asserted, prevented them from organized action, their support from literate, skilled creoles—who themselves could have ties to blacks in Haiti or Jamaica—could prove fatal on the island. Moreover, the election and coronation of Miguel Linares as king of the cabildo, with accompanying appointments that "imitated" Spanish institutions, appeared less as a celebration of empire than an attempt to "parody state dignitaries."[70] After investigators traced suspected La Escalera conspirators to cabildos, Captain General Leopoldo O'Donnell called for the extinction of the societies.[71]

On the other hand, observers of these supposed imitations often reduced to the symbolic complexity to fit their high hopes or dark suspicions.[72] Travel accounts from the 1850s describe the persistence of cabildos and the Día de Reyes celebrations as carefully balancing African, Spanish, and Cuban cultural idioms. When Antonio de las Barras y Prado visited Havana from Spain in 1853, he noted generally that Cubans of color at that point were prohibited from sharing public space with whites—separate spaces in theaters, separate dances, and so forth, with churches being the only integrated spaces—but he was impressed that the Kings' Day festivities brought the cabildos to the heart of Spanish authority:

> Once the cabildos are organized they take to the street, presided by their respective kings or queens, carrying Spanish flags or those of other colors, which they wave in the air, and continue this way, playing and dancing and asking the *aguinaldo* of so many whites they encounter, until from eleven to one they swarm the palace of the Captain General, on whose patio each *tango* is allowed a brief dance. . . . The Captain General sticks his head out from time to time from the balconies and throws them cigars and some *reales,* to which they respond with shouts of "Long live Spain! Long live Isabel II!"[73]

In its performative dimension, this demonstration of loyalty seems pro forma: in expressing gratitude to the captain general, the cabildos acknowledged that taking to the streets on this special day was a privilege he granted. The use of Spanish flags is slightly more complicated. Barras y Prado speculated about the resentment the flag might have provoked among those who came from Africa (or, more likely, their ancestors) on ships that bore the same standard—or, in the case of recent arrivals, people who might have seen Spanish ships in the Gulf of Guinea to load up on palm oil.[74] In his study of Afro-Cuban religions, David Brown considers the possible meanings of the flags in the "miniature neo-African monarchies" of the cabildos.[75] Kings or queens led most of them, or sometimes presidents or *capataces* (bosses), and sometimes surrounded by a court with other members carrying military or royal titles. Flags, then, reinforced the status of the cabildos as political, even "national," units. Given, however, that the cabildo flags might also index an affiliation with both a Catholic saint and an African deity, the flags may have served to send multiple political messages or rework the obvious ones. This practice itself had African antecedents. Kongo Angola and West African groups had "built much of their royal and martial iconography upon European imports" so that "iconographically hybridized royal displays" tell a far richer story about diasporic cultural practices than one of black mimicry of Hispanic norms—as if mimicry could ever be "mere" or simple.[76]

At critical moments, the simpler mimetic reading captured the attention of contemporaries in ways that connected the survival of the cabildos to their intimate relationship to the state. On 3 January 1852, just days before the Día de los Reyes festivities, Mariano Mora asked the Matanzas police to intervene in a dispute within the Congo cabildo. According to Mora, the cabildo was composed of five "nations or tribes": Musundi, Bongoma, Cabo Verde, Luango, and Reales. Each nation had a *capataz* (overseer), but a *primer capataz* enjoyed the privilege of bearing "the royal flag with the Spanish national banner" behind all of the other flags. Mora claimed that he was the rightful heir to the title. He alleged that a rival named Valentín Castillo contested the claim on behalf of the Luangos and Reales, so he sought the assistance of a *celador,* an official charged with neighborhood peacekeeping, to resolve the dispute.[77] Why invite the authorities who policed public life to intervene in the internal struggles of the cabildos? Although a Spanish flag could denote any number of political affiliations, its symbolic capital, in this case, provided Mora the outcome he sought with Castillo and the Luangos and Reales backed by Spanish authority and endorsed locally by the celador. As long as each of the nations sought this particular flag, its political specificity could be activated, however momentarily, to find resolution through a mutually respected authority. And the request provided benefits to the celador as well: new access to monitor the cabildos, a chance to shape the reception of one of the most visible emblems of colonial rule, and evidence that—despite multiple and overlapping allegiances—cabildo members expressed some degree of respect for Spanish rules and institutions.

Many of the quotidian activities of urban Cubans of color might have been stigmatized and criminalized under the rubric of "public order," yet cabildo leaders, free-colored artisans, and militiamen (sometimes the same people) remained visible alternative "types" with greater social acceptability and fuller integration into populations and practices associated with pro-colonial loyalty than slaves, for example. Similarly, Cubans of African descent, slave and free, living on the island generally garnered more trust than those from other countries, which explained the ban placed on free blacks on foreign ships from disembarking in Cuban ports. Fewer distinctions, however, applied in areas of rural Cuba with large slave populations, where any collectivity of Cubans of color could set off fears of unrest that might not differentiate between slavery and colonial rule as its target. Militiamen sometimes remained a notable exception, especially when they reinforced their distinction as free men by hunting down runaway slaves and *palenques,* the communities runaways formed. In doing so, according to a military commander in 1816, they fulfilled "obligations owed in service to the King and of the Patria and of the commander they respect and obey."[78] But although slave resistance and communication occupied the lion's share of concern and scrutiny, their potential to communicate with those free blacks who had resources and subversive ideas, frequently fueled accusations of conspiracy, most notably with La Escalera in 1844. Prosecutions by the Comisión Militar in the wake of that conspiracy would interrogate slaves and free people "for having had a dangerous conversation."[79] Controlling these plantation publics was primarily a matter of private authority, with slaveowners adhering to the standards of treatment set forth in slaves' codes and allowing dancing, drumming, and late-night gatherings in the *barracones* (barracks) only to the extent that those enjoyments might prevent tensions from coming to a boil. Educating slaves did not appeal to many owners, but an 1846 report on slave suicides by a state attorney recounted the long history of missionary education of Indians as key to a successful colonial project. Despite its potential to give slaves access to a reading public, education—the official noted—would "teach the savages to be men first, teach them to be religious later, and finish by encouraging them to submit to the Sovereignty of the Country."[80]

Provincial Publics: The Case of Cienfuegos

If anxieties about race war and skepticism about constituting African-descended Cubans as loyal subjects conditioned the limited terms of public life in most of the island, white colonization projects such as Cienfuegos might presumably offer better prospects for open and heterogeneous political discussion and public expression. In fact, the development of Cienfuegos reveals a process of gradual adaptation to the public norms of a slave society rather than offering an alternative or antidote to them.

As of 1833, the town ceased to enjoy the protections and exemptions granted to it as a white colonization project. This was partially the outcome of an investigation in the wake of some calamitous disputes among the founders and leaders, culminating in the shooting of Louis de Clouet, the settlement's founder and governor. Mismanaged funds set aside for the purposes of increasing the white population weakened an already complicated project, with some early heterogeneous settlers still not assimilated as a fully Hispanized population: some of the interrogations conducted to investigate the corruption and shooting still required French interpreters.[81] A second reason that Cienfuegos lost its status is that, as a white settlement, it was not so white anymore. Hopes for projects such as Cienfuegos to maintain a white majority in Cuba could offset neither the continuing demand for African slaves nor the increasing volume of the clandestine slave trade. If slaves constituted a common form of property, it should not be surprising that white residents brought slaves with them and, over the years, bought even more slaves, sometimes transferred and sold from Santiago but frequently from a less conspicuous port than Cienfuegos itself—in the nearby, swampy Bay of Pigs.

By the 1830s, those slaves did not just labor in small numbers for residents of the town, Spanish merchants, or owners of small rural estates. Although ten small sugar estates could be found in the hinterlands of Cienfuegos in 1830, the following two decades witnessed a rapid expansion of cane cultivation, and, consequently, the slave population. A measurable free population of color in Cienfuegos was apparent in an 1830 census, showing men working as tailors, carpenters, and masons, some of whom owned slaves themselves. By 1838 there were 26 sugar estates employing 1,502 slaves and only 71 white workers, as well as 469 smaller farms that, on average, had one or two slaves working on them.[82] By 1846, nearly one-third of Cienfuegos's 29,000 residents were slaves, in addition to almost 4,000 free people of color. And by 1862, with a total population at 28,648, Cienfuegos's slaves and free people of color outnumbered whites by almost 4,400.[83] So much for a white colony: competition between racial purity and economic prosperity had a clear winner in Cienfuegos and a lesson in how a white settlement colony could evolve into a slave society.

Although slaves in any situation might create opportunities to change or end the terms of their bondage, a fledgling settlement with unstable economic and social foundations may have provided more favorable conditions for resistance and manumission than, say, a region where intensive plantation enterprises encouraged stricter control of slave populations. The Cienfuegos ayuntamiento received enough requests for intervention with questions of slavery and freedom to add a *síndico,* an official charged, among other things, with ensuring the applications of Spain's laws regarding slavery and negotiating the legal transfers of slaves.[84] By 1824, two palenques had developed in the Bay of Pigs, prompting one adjacent resident to request the removal of two unfazed officials who allowed the communities to flourish. (Not incidentally, the resident embraced the language of humility with gusto, offering the sacrifice of, as he put it, "my few goods and even my life . . . in honor of the government and religion we profess" in exchange for the governor's "help and protection.")[85]

Rebellions and conspiracies increased, as did public vigilance, as more plantations and larger workforces came to typify the regional geography. Policemen in 1840 overheard a conversation one night at a store in town between a group of slaves plotting an attack on the army barracks. Not all of their words were intelligible, but whispered mentions of Santo Domingo, ostensibly referencing revolutionary action in the mold of Haiti, caused immediate alarm. Fifty soldiers dispatched to the docks, since the slaves mentioned something about using a ship's arrival to signal the start of the rebellion. Of ten slaves interrogated, all were African born; had backgrounds variously identified as Congo, Gangá, and Carabalí; and were engaged in trades ranging from carpentry to tobacco rolling to cooking. Anxieties about bozales were often more acute than fears of creoles, but the rest of the alleged conspirators' profiles—urban, skilled workers sufficiently trusted to circulate in the city on their own—heightened alarm among cienfuegueros precisely because they did not resemble the predictable cast of characters for a slave revolt, namely, rural plantation workforces.[86]

As with fears of anticolonial rebellion, anxieties about slave revolts could not be separated from questions of their organization and the circuits of public or private communication that could facilitate them. Police investigating the 1840 conspiracy were sure, "or at least one should suppose," they qualified, "that this plan is communicated to everyone of color in this town and possibly beyond it." That slaves might "speak bozal," a nineteenth-century shorthand to refer to African languages and African-inflected dialects, further complicated the ability to surveil and control communication.[87] During a moment of island-wide panic about slave conspiracy, the governor of Cienfuegos wrote to the Captain General in July 1843 to request a prohibition on slaves beating on drums. The drums could get loud, he noted, and thus allowed slaves to communicate from long distances to plan gatherings. Three months later, when a hurricane barreled through the district, rumors abounded that slaves were conspiring to capitalize on the unrest and kill all of the white men and take their women.[88] The informal circulation of information both about and among slaves—through rumor, drumming, or whispered conversation in taverns and stores—remained as much of a concern to authorities as the strict control of public spaces, organizations, and publications.

Controlling the slave population remained a top priority as the presumed loyal white population decreased proportionally to the growing numbers of slaves and free people of color. A circular issued in September 1864 to the ayuntamientos of Cuba's largest cities expressed concern about an increase in criminal behavior among slaves, free people of African descent, and Chinese indentured laborers. It requested the formation of councils to investigate matters locally and to suggest means of inculcating "Christian morality" in these populations and remedying the social ill. The Cienfuegos report concluded that the slave population posed few problems to social order and in fact exhibited "better behavior than the free class of color." Slaves were obedient and docile, and—thanks to concessions from their owners—industrious, "such that they do not have time to acquire the vices so common by misfortune in the heterogeneous free class."[89] In other words, there were not enough institutional constraints on the free population to ensure their loyalty—either to employers or to government. It thus may have been the absence of such reciprocities, not repression, that explained the problem that the ayuntamiento had raised. Although colonial authorities were seeking out the loyalty of Cubans, their own policies could leave them with few places to look.

For all of its limitations, social life in Cienfuegos also accommodated cabildos, although they were subject to more scrutiny than other forms of association. According to municipal ordinances approved in 1856, cabildos had to meet in spaces designated by the teniente gobernador (deputy governor) or face a fine between three and five pesos. They could only meet on Sundays, special occasions, and feast days. They could neither march "with flags or other insignias," nor "congregate publicly." The regulations made exceptions for the feast days of the Santos Reyes (Epiphany), San Juan, San Pedro, and Santiago, important feast days for African-derived religious practices.[90] Less formal gatherings faced fewer restrictions. On one summer Saturday night in 1865 three different dances were featured: one at the Sociedad Filarmónica, one in a private residence, and one "of color," as the newspaper *El Telégrafo* reported it.[91] The fault lines of public life could not be clearer: a sanctioned philanthropic association and racially segregated private gatherings. The heavy hand of government officials in determining the conditions of cabildos' public expressions—legal freedom, no flags, designated spaces, synchronized to Catholic feast days—resembled patterns across the island.

Not that public life among respectable residents escaped surveillance. Newspapers and literary publications also fell under the scrutiny of government censors and ensured that the community of *letrados* (lettered men) in Cienfuegos would remain small and exclusive.[92] Luis Martínez Casado, the conservative second editor of *El Fomento,* installed a lithographic press in 1861 and published two issues of *El Apuntador,* a theater publication. Enrique Edo y Llop, the city's illustrious historian, used the press a year later to publish *El Chismoso,* a journal of literary criticism with drawings, lithographs, and caricatures, but censors closed the operation after he published the second issue in 1865. *El Negro Bueno* (The Good Black), a weekly journal published by Jacobo Domínguez y Santí, lasted from 1869 until the government closed it the following year. None of these publications challenged the Spanish empire per se, but rigid guidelines about what it meant to exercise public voice meant that extinguishing sedition marked only one of the ends of censorship.

When the slave and poet Ambrosio Echemendía arrived in Cienfuegos from nearby Trinidad with his master in 1865, the local elite organized banquets, evening parties, and other charity drives throughout the year to raise the necessary money to purchase Echemendía's freedom. Once organizers had obtained a book of Echemendía's poetry, published in Trinidad as *Murmurios del Táyaba* under the pseudonym Máximo Hero de Neiba, they enlisted him to recite his poems at their functions and persuaded Jacobo Domínguez Sanctí, then the editor of *El Telégrafo,* to offer glowing critical praise: "Our hand has extended with pleasure to the humble servant in whose gaze shines the golden ray of genius, slowly obscuring the mark of color. The prospective *liberto* [free man] relies fervently on the protection of the patriotic inhabitants of Cienfuegos, remembering with gratitude the promises they have made to him."[93] Not only had the residents of Cienfuegos accumulated the five hundred pesos necessary to free Echemendía by the end of 1865; they had also provided him with five hundred pesos to begin a new life as a free person.[94] They had also reinforced the paternalistic terms of public life in no uncertain terms.

Echemendía's manumission figured as one of several examples of slave poets, always described publicly as loyal and humble, patronized by the elite of cities and towns. The most famous of them was Juan Francisco Manzano, the slave and poet who ultimately became the cause célèbre of Domingo Del Monte's Havana literary circle, which became implicated in the supposed La Escalera conspiracy of 1844. Impressed by a sonnet Manzano recited at the group's meeting, the *tertulia* (salon) raised enough money in 1836 to free the thirty-nine-year-old slave, whom Del Monte admired for being "docile and humble."[95] (Of course in Manzano's narrative he identified the precise moment at which he "ceased to be a faithful slave" and "a humble submissive being.")[96] With the elite's embrace of Echemendía, Cienfuegos could claim its own Manzano.[97] While Echemendía remained in popular memory as a poet from Trinidad, it was cienfuegueros who claimed to recognize his valor and attain his freedom. His celebrity and Manzano's speak to the most optimistic and exceptional promises paternalism. In cases like these, public merit and honor was recognized not through engagement with the state but through private philanthropy and mutual aid. In the process, private values such as gratitude, protection, and patronage—which grounded relationships like the one between Echemendía and the urban elite of Cienfuegos and Trinidad—became markers of public virtue and patriotism. So long as they could be interpellated as loyal subjects—not of Spain, necessarily, but of a civic-minded urban elite—select Cubans of color might be offered subordinate roles in the paternalist public.

Beyond Cienfuegos, other poets of color, many of them already free, gained similar notoriety in Cuba's literary circles, and often on the same hierarchical terms as Echemendía and Manzano. Cuban writer Francisco Calcagno published a survey of these poets in the 1880s and identified José del Carmen Díaz, a slave in Güines, who published his work in local newspapers; Agustín Baldomero Rodríguez from Villaclara, who had excelled despite the "abject ignorance" of his family; and Vicente Silveira, a pardo from Guanajay.[98] Antonio Medina was a free pardo born in Havana who wrote and published plays, poems, and *zarzuelas* (Spanish light opera) in the 1840s and 1850s. In 1878, Calcagno visited the fifty-year-old Medina at his house, which also served as a school for Cubans of color, and noted how happy Medina was "to encounter a white not dominated by unjust prejudices." Then Calcagno went on to marvel at how obedient Medina's wife and daughter seemed, and how a "noble smile of gratitude" appeared when Calcagno rewarded Medina with a gold coin after receiving a free copy of Medina's work.[99]

This kind of paternalism met its limits in the case of the most famous and prolific poet of all, Plácido (Gabriel Concepción Valdés). His execution in 1844 for his alleged participation in the La Escalera conspiracy made him a cause célèbre. Subsequent critics throughout the nineteenth century debated the political contents of Plácido's work, often depending on whether they wanted to view him as a loyal subject or a proto-nationalist martyr.[100] Race and allegiance were clearly never far from the surface. Critics dwelled on Plácido's European and African blood when discussing his "half savage" writing, and Calcagno found evidence of the "essentially Cuban" Plácido's "liberal spirit" in his ode to Isabel II.[101] In contrast, those same critics assumed the writings of Echemendía and Medina to be politically inoffensive; to be fair, Echemendía thanked his owner for such kind treatment in one of his poems. Echemendía and other poets of color made their way into literary society and literary canons as loyal and ennobled exceptions in a slave society where resistance and retaliation were presumed to be at a constant simmer. As Cienfuegos developed into a society structured by slavery, the culture wars between the various wagers of whiteness gave way to efforts to subjugate slave and free people of color, both through policing their activities as well as defining them within the discursive scope of the loyal subject.

The Free-Colored Militias and the Limits of Loyalty

If the restricted opportunities to publicly claim loyalty or have it affirmed left many Cubans in a precarious political state, members of the free-colored militias enjoyed a long history of a recognizable loyal subjectivity. If agents of the Soles y Rayos conspiracy and the government it challenged agreed on anything, it was the prominence of the men serving in the free-colored militias. It was no accident that conspirators targeted the militia barracks with their broadsides. The milicianos were the only legally armed Cubans of color on the island, and the cultural capital derived from military service afforded them a status recognized across racial lines. It may also have been no accident that the milicianos reported the conspiracy right away to colonial officials. Kings, captains general, and local officials had long recognized the allegiance of the soldiers, and the militias survived until the end of colonial rule despite a weakened status after their banishment in 1844. That suspension, and their reinstatement in 1854, support the point made by Matt Childs that the sugar revolution catalyzed the erosion of esteem for the militias in the nineteenth century.[102] Surprisingly, free Cubans of color became active participants in that erosion by the 1850s and 1860s.

Milicianos' claims on loyalty dated back to the earliest moments of Spanish rule. The militias first appeared in Cuba in 1600, when the governor of Havana organized one hundred mulattoes into the *Compañía de Pardos Libres* (Free Mulatto Company). Throughout the seventeenth century, separate companies of both mulattoes and blacks developed in tandem with white companies. Milicianos guarded forts, fought pirates, captured runaway slaves, and sometimes even engaged in military expeditions and battles outside of Cuba. In rare circumstances, slaves themselves took part in the military defense of the island, which enhanced their leverage with the state. The leader of the royal slaves in El Cobre in 1677, for example, used an occasion of military defense to petition for more rights for his community. Sidelining the issue of potential rebellion, Captain Juan Moreno invoked the loyalty of the slaves as a reminder that "when the occasion comes up we never fail with ardent zeal what our superiors have ordered us," and he pledged a "desire for greater opportunities in the royal service."[103]

Milicianos and their superiors in Cuba and Spain routinely expressed mutual and reciprocal interests in a common colonial project, albeit interests contained within strict military and racial hierarchies. In 1714, Philip V praised the mulatos and negros in the Cuban militias, "considering them as *vasallos míos* [my vassals]," and he declared that they "should be given the good treatment they deserve."[104] At the time of the British occupation of Havana in 1762, two-thirds of free-colored heads of household in Havana served as militia members.[105] By the nineteenth century, militias bolstered the military presence Spain maintained in response to the Haitian Revolution, turbulence in Florida, and eventually the independence conflicts igniting throughout Spanish America. Maintaining racially segregated militia units continued to benefit Spain, as assertions of equality, rights, and citizenship based on military service—claims heard throughout the Americas during the Age of Revolutions—could be addressed differently based on their claimants. White members of the national militia formed during the Trienio suspended their citizenship when they joined militias—they were to "return to the common class of citizen" on completing their service—and officers were only supposed to "conduct themselves as citizens and direct other citizens."[106] This practice differed strikingly from republican notions of the armed citizen in a militia, although some regular soldiers in Spanish America were also prohibited from active citizenship while they served. That military service might be held as a competing or separate corporate identity from citizenship had origins in the *fuero* rights that relocated an individual from civil to military jurisdiction. Occupying an intermediate subject position between vassals and citizens, militiamen found no clear path to obtaining concrete political rewards for their professed and demonstrated loyalty.

Some men of color simply bought their status once Spain opened officer positions to them. Despite the clear exclusion from these rights, free-colored *militianos* no longer had exclusively white officers. When Leandro Varona of Havana's pardo battalion offered 1,000 pesos in 1818 to be promoted to captain, Spain's war minister instructed the captain general to take the money and forthwith accept payment from men of color who were willing to pay for officer status, upping the amount for captain to 1,700 pesos.[107] The *milicias de color* in 1830 made up three battalions and twenty-six companies, as well as three full companies of artillery.[108] Carefully ordered processions during religious festivals and major events of state regularly included the milicias de color, and the documentary record of these events is replete with colonial officials taking special note of their good behavior. They lined up in full uniform with other units of white militiamen and the Spanish army and paraded through their towns for celebrations. In Trinidad in 1825, for example, they brought up the rear of the Corpus Christi procession.[109] During the six days of festivities in 1833 observing Fernando VII's death and Isabel II's regency, an ayuntamiento member in Holguín singled out the pardo and moreno militias with admiration, commending them one day for conducting themselves in a dignified and praiseworthy manner and another day for their discipline and fine disposition.[110] But such effusive compliments often papered over anxiety about what officials noted as frequent episodes of militia insubordination.

Certainly, the execution in 1812 of José Antonio Aponte, a militiaman suspected of organizing an island-wide slave revolt—and whose confiscated sketchbook drew on the iconography of both the militias and the Haitian Revolution—signaled the exhaustion of any easy linkages between militia service and support for colonial order. Of course, many rebels interrogated during the Aponte Rebellion claimed to be acting against the French as loyal vassals of the Spanish crown.[111] For many of the nineteenth-century conspiracies, however, government suspicions of milicianos usually superseded clear evidence. With the exception of the Soles y Rayos, organized resistance did not always rely on writing anyway and left few paper trails. What these moments reveal, more than a verifiable sense of the suspects' motives, is how quickly colonial officials and other observers could shift their language to characterize suspects differently. The discourse of loyalty and obedience easily yielded to accusations of seditiousness, rebelliousness, and contempt for Spanish institutions. An article from 1823 in this vein in the newspaper *La Fraternidad* provoked a collective written rebuttal from Havana's pardo and moreno militias, in which they questioned such fickle opinions: "How is it possible that a subject could have dictated such inflammatory ideas, in spite of the fact that we have repeatedly and unequivocally proven our loyalty and submission to the governing laws and the authorities that dispense them? Why insult us so, when there is not the smallest glimmer of suspicion, nor the most trivial motive of distrust to fear?"[112] Many skeptics of milicianos' loyalty routinely expressed a common goal: preventing a race war in the image of Haiti that would end colonial rule and the prosperity it brought to well-placed Cubans.

Additional suspected conspiracies in 1835, led by Juan Nepomuceno Prieto—a cabildo capataz and retired sergeant—and in 1839, led by León Monzón—a former captain of the moreno militia—only compounded authorities' skepticism about unconditionally believing milicianos' allegiance.[113] A report in 1839 acknowledged the public distrust of the pardo and moreno militias but suggested political reasons for sustaining them, namely that members came from "the most visible and notable families in the country" and were otherwise excluded from pursuing the "noble career" of military service.[114] On the other hand, a royal order from the end of that year called for heightened vigilance of the militias in order to identify "symptoms of seduction or desires for innovation."[115]

In such a precarious climate, militia members struggled to maintain the privileges and esteem that they had long enjoyed, such as guarantees of fuero rights and *preeminencias,* the latter of which occasionally exempted individuals from paying *servicios* (monetary contributions), to the crown.[116] The ordeals of José Joaquín Pompa, a Santiago barber and twenty-year veteran soldier, derived from the decay of informal networks connecting militiamen to other prominent inhabitants. When Pompa appealed in 1843 to the captain general to reaffirm his fuero privileges, he found himself insolvent and imprisoned after a mishandled case in the civil court system. The indignities he endured resembled the experiences of most individuals who sought legal action: long delays, inattentive clerks, and lawyers who disregarded his requests. But if fuero rights could circumvent the process, all the better, and Pompa's own letter made no use of formulaic gestures of humility. He resented his lawyer's "spirit of condescension," and he cited documents dating back to 1769 supporting his argument; a postscript concluded, "I ask for justice, like I did above."[117] Neither deference nor paternal benevolence characterized these encounters. Pompa was demanding the recognition of honorable status.

When a wave of slave resistance developed across the island in the early 1840s, the militias faced their most intense scrutiny. José Erice, a moreno sergeant from a Matanzas militia company, alerted the new captain general, Leopoldo O'Donnell, of potential unrest that preceded the La Escalera conspiracy. Free people of color fell under such disproportionate suspicion in 1844 that even avowedly loyal militia leaders found themselves suspect. If public anxiety shrouded members' activities in distrust, the milicianos themselves could not have been clearer in their public displays of subjection. They took advantage of the public commemorations of Isabel II's ascent to the throne to display their support for Spanish rule. This particular performance of patriotism and social order carried special weight, since Havana's cash-strapped ayuntamiento openly fussed about its ability to pay for the celebrations and they barely happened. On 9 and 10 February 1844, in addition to the usual processions, verses appeared on the door of the pardo barracks that included the following stanza:

El batallón por siempre de leales,	The battalion of the ever faithful
Tremolo sus banderas cual crisoles	Waved its flags during tribulations
[H]Ace más de dos siglos y graboles	For over two centuries, and etched upon them
En su servicio lauros inmortales.[118]	Everlasting honors in your service.

The milicianos gave the same kind of public performance as their predecessors had done for centuries, but the government to which they showed their support no longer reciprocated. By the end of March, the captain general had instructed the governor of Matanzas to confiscate the weapons of the milicias de color and the *bomberos* (firemen) as a "precautionary measure."[119] In June, the government eliminated the milicias de color altogether on the grounds that they were complicit in La Escalera.[120] The wide extent of the brutal crackdown has been chronicled elsewhere, but of particular note is the targeting of free people of color in positions of authority and artisanal occupations. O'Donnell prohibited blacks and mulattoes from working as dock foremen or as teachers or master craftsmen, or to send their children to trade schools.[121] Whatever symbolic capital the free population of color had accumulated through centuries of service and loyal subjectivity had been exhausted.

To be sure, the backlash from La Escalera inaugurated an era of intensified state violence, with the African-descended population—slave and free—as its disproportionate target. The dissolution of the free-colored militias, the silencing of the island's most prominent intellectuals, and the setback to abolitionism took a heavy toll. But historians have frequently portrayed La Escalera as a point of no return, signaling the end of public freedoms, the consolidation of Spain's repressive regime, and rule by arbitrary and illegitimate force as the norm. To borrow Walter Benjamin's terms, one can find in La Escalera and its aftermath both lawmaking violence and law-destroying violence: "If the former is bloody, the latter is lethal without spilling blood."[122] Just under the surface of these arguments lay the idea that milicianos and other Cubans of color harbored anticolonial, and possibly proto-nationalist, sentiments that would continue to grow. In contrasting the participation of slaves and free people of color, some historians have searched for the locations of revolutionary consciousness that foreshadowed anticolonial insurgency.[123] Other historians recognize La Escalera as a moment caused by the culmination of social tensions and contradictions that would resurface again only in 1868, with Cuba's first war for independence.[124]

Rather than ending the story of the militias—or of early nineteenth-century politics altogether—on a bleak note in 1844, extending the chronology allows for a different interpretation. The free-colored militias reappeared in 1854 as part of a broad attempt, in the words of one commentator, to "invigorate in the spirit of the population of color an unlimited adhesion to the political interest of Spain in the island of Cuba."[125] In the formal announcement that appeared in the *Gaceta de la Habana,* Captain General Juan de la Pezuela attributed the policy shift to the "rigors of the climate" in Cuba that raised special military needs and "the loyalty, suffering, and spirit with which the pardo and moreno *voluntarios* have upheld the Spanish flag on diverse occasions."[126]

Why reestablish an institution deemed just a decade earlier as too dangerous? One of Pezuela's political contemporaries commented that "not everyone agreed" with his "annoying" decision; slaveholders, remarked Richard Henry Dana, "are more impatient under this favoring of the free blacks, than under almost any other act of government."[127] Spaniards who sought to keep Cuba in the imperial orbit, in contrast, applauded the decision. Mariano Torrente argued in a pamphlet that Cuba would never become independent from Spain, since the crown "could always resort to recruiting colored volunteers, who have been constant in their loyalty to the Spanish throne."[128] Pezuela's decision was one of a series of reforms enacted shortly after his arrival in Havana in December 1853 that aimed to make good on Spain's treaty with the British in 1817 to halt the transatlantic slave trade. He imposed stricter penalties for individuals attempting to import slaves and clearer laws about the free status of intercepted *emancipados,* African captives intended to be sold into slavery. Drawing on the military threat of filibustering expeditions, Pezuela enhanced the military presence to protect Cuba from the United States, which sought to annex Cuba as a slave state. Reviving the free-colored militias would strengthen the military and lay a groundwork for a social order with a constantly increasing creole population. With a focus on urban and military strength, Pezuela hoped to minimize the threat of social unrest by relocating people to what they perceived to be an ordered, modernizing, everfaithful city in opposition to the restive countryside.

The new militias got off to a slow start. The Sección de Guerra y Marina of the Consejo Real approved the new *reglamento* (regulations) in 1858, and in 1859 the Ministerio de Ultramar laid out plans for sixteen militia companies of 125 members each. By another accounting, the additional 7,680 pardos and morenos in service would increase the military presence on the island by over 50 percent, given the (segregated) peninsular force of 14,400 soldiers.[129] Thus, authorities recruited thousands of free people of color from urban and rural areas alike to receive training, clothing, and pay similar to that of their white counterparts—and, among other duties, the responsibility for capturing *cimarrones* (runaway slaves).[130] The captain general specified by locality whether the militia companies would be composed of pardos or morenos: Bayamo and Trinidad/Sancti Spíritus organized companies of pardos; Villaclara/Cienfuegos and Manzanillo/Baracoa raised companies of morenos; Havana, Matanzas, Puerto Príncipe, and Santiago de Cuba maintained both types.

The blueprint for militia service outlined in the reglamento emphasized willful participation and patriotic duty on the part of the soldiers and the social status they received in recognition of their fidelity to Spanish goals. It defined militia service as an obligation of free men of color but placed priority on its voluntary nature. Chapter Two, Article Four stated that the monarch was "eager to avoid if possible the personal losses that this obligation can create" and that the captain general would promote voluntary enlistment, "making clear to the people of color the advantages inherent in service to these Militias, the same as those granted to the white *disciplinados* [militias] of the Island." That said, the reglamento recommended enlistment for at least eight years with the possibility of continuing indefinitely. Although the officer corps was to consist of militia veterans (white, mulatto, and black), and the government gave explicit preference to a free person of color over a white veteran. Perhaps anticipating that the militias would get off to a slow start, the captain general received a census of the militias each March, and if the companies did not fill voluntarily, he had the authority to draft individuals. Lotteries at the beginning of May would identify drafted individuals, who needed to be between twenty and thirty years old, strong, and over five feet tall. Most important, the reglamento stipulated that the milicias de color "enjoy the same fueros, preeminencias, and other exemptions as those of the white militias of the Island." Following a decree in 1769, free-colored widows and children of militiamen who died in wartime action would receive the same benefits as their white counterparts. The new regulations clarified ambiguities about the status of the free-colored militias before La Escalera and proposed measures that placed them in closer proximity to white militias and the standing army.

Whether it was from a lack of willful participation or patriotic duty, enlistment often proceeded as slowly as the reinstatement. When slots did not fill in 1859, the captain general exercised his authority to hold a draft. In Cienfuegos, for example, the district government became responsible for filling one-fourth of the tenth company of morenos in the Western Department of the island, which amounted to only thirty-three individuals. The town fared better than most with only two slots remaining empty in June. But the wide net that officials cast—eighty-four potential draftees from various locales and professions—hints at the determination, even desperation, to fill every slot, and probably carry out some surveillance at the same time.[131] When nine of the morenos named in the draft did not even present themselves to authorities in May, they were declared fugitives and captured in September.[132] Beyond their youth (the oldest was twenty-three) and predominantly rural backgrounds, the "runaways" did not fit a type. Some were married, and some were single. Only one of the nine—a carpenter named Manuel Maya—was from the city itself; the other eight hailed from the city's hinterland. One was African born. A demography of (dis)loyalty was elusive.

By 5 August 1859, Cienfuegos had filled its thirty-three slots in the company of morenos, but not before an exhaustive review of the draftees. Most of them tried to avoid militia service.[133] Investigators deemed some cases valid: one draftee named Eulogio Navarro had a broken leg that exempted him from service. The board exempted José Curbelo after three (white) witnesses testified that he cared for his mother, who was in her eighties, as well as a brother who had been paralyzed since birth. It did the same for Juan Tardio, who cared for his mother, who was in her sixties, and his five brothers of minor age. Florencio Quesada offered evidence that he was an only child who provided for his mother and that he "suffers flights of dementia from time to time that make him useless except for the job of selling cigarettes on the street." Others referred to baptismal records to prove that they exceeded the age limit for militia service; Juan Crisóstomo Taltabull, born in Africa, could refer to no such record and instead presented his letter of freedom to prove that he was forty-seven years old. His letter also identified his nationality as "Lucumí Ayllo" and his provenance as a slave brought from Africa on a Spanish ship intercepted by the British in 1832.[134]

Competing social identifications exempted two of the draftees. In one case, José Mariano Varona presented a letter from a parish priest in Puerto Príncipe citing the book and page number of the church's baptismal register. The priest affirmed that he had baptized José Mariano himself as the legitimate child of two pardos libres and the godson of a white man and woman. Had

Varona still been living in Puerto Príncipe, he might have had to serve in that city's company of pardos, but since Cienfuegos only had a company of morenos, he was in luck. Juan Vilche, from the partido of Cumanayagua, also argued for an exemption because he was a pardo, not a moreno, but he had no written records to support his claim. The commission noted that because "it was not obvious by looking, this impeded physical recognition" of his racial categorization, and it did not grant Vilche an exemption until he produced evidence that he was an only child caring for his seventy-year-old mother. Was it impossible, then, for a *padre de familia* (patriarch or head of household) to be a militia member? Were distinctions between pardos and morenos so stark as to disqualify men whose status was confused? In their deft management of the privileges and obligations ascribed to various social groups, the maneuvers by the free men, and the commission too, echo the arguments put forth in freedom suits initiated by slaves.[135]

The rural backgrounds of many of the draftees revise a long-standing image of militia service as an exclusive opportunity for urban free people of African descent. Without documentation of the final composition of the militia, it is impossible to make generalizations about who actually filled the ranks. But in the geographically diverse composition of the draftees, fewer than 20 percent of them from the city, several features of the state's intentions for the militias emerge. A force of thirty-three soldiers severely limited the possibility of militia service as a widespread opportunity for social status or mobility and thus the maintenance, in Pedro Deschamps Chapeaux's words, of a "petite bourgeoisie of African descent."[136] Perhaps the La Escalera crackdown disillusioned urban free men of color about militia service. It remains unclear, however, if government officials were also deliberately trying to incorporate more rural freedmen as loyal subjects, further sidelining the urban population in the process. Clear answers are hard to come by. But between the efforts of Cienfuegos draftees to avoid service and the routine recourse to drafting milicianos throughout the late 1850s and 1860s, militia service no longer cemented close relationships between free-colored communities and Spanish colonial rule.

Just as administrators in Cuba were realizing that the new militia system was not working as it used to, events across the Atlantic cast the Spanish empire and its military prowess in a new light. In 1859, Spain's cresting frustrations with Morocco led it to claim the ports of Ceuta and Melilla and occupy Tetuán until Morocco agreed to sign a peace treaty the following year. The push to war came from Leopoldo O'Donnell, the Spanish prime minister (and Cuba's captain general during the 1840s) who sought—in Raymond

Carr's estimation—"to stimulate patriotic enthusiasm and keep the army occupied."[137] The relative success of the mission did not come easy, but it produced the intended public response. Formulaic outpourings of patriotism and loyalty occurred throughout Spain, and in Cuba and Puerto Rico as well.[138]

Despite doubts about the aims of the war with Morocco, Spaniards and Cubans alike recognized a new, concrete interest in Spanish expansion into Africa.[139] The war gave rise to the idea of (re)connecting African-descended Cubans to Africa that would reappear periodically throughout the rest of the century. This sits oddly with the regular concern of colonial authorities that Cubans of African descent could harbor loyalties to polities and places beyond the Spanish empire. But the idea gained slight traction anyway. A Havana resident named Martín de Arredondo proposed to the captain general in February 1860 the formation of a battalion of pardos and morenos to take part in combat in Morocco. "Guided by patriotic instinct," Arredondo imagined a battalion adapted to the African climate, a familiar and dubious racial logic that frequently justified putting African-descended people to work in awful conditions. He reminded the captain general that "the loyal pardos and morenos of Havana took an active part" in past military expeditions. He predicted that Cuba's role in Spain's expansionist designs would earn it the respect of the metropole and, presumably, a more advantageous bargaining position in colonial politics. An assistant to the captain general quickly expressed his doubts about the proposal, citing the existing difficulty of filling the regiments in Cuba, the cost of transporting milicianos from Cuba to Africa, and the deleterious effects on Cuba's artisanal workforce, "as almost all free people of color are artisans [because of] the disgust that the whites have for those trades." The plan never came to fruition, and Cuba's most significant contribution to the war effort came in the monetary donations that individual towns and military units collected.[140]

Arredondo's proposal may not appear so far-fetched in the context of other imperial policies in the Caribbean. British West Indian troops helped settle the Sierra Leone colony beginning in the 1800s, and regiments had assumed garrison duties in British forts in the Gold Coast in the 1840s.[141] As Spain clashed with Britain over control of the island of Fernando Po in the Bight of Biafra, Caribbean troops of African descent were already present. Rather than worrying, as British colonial governors did, about native Africans adopting the poor habits of the black men of the West Indian Regiments, Arredondo expressed optimism about the advantages that Cuba's milicianos de color could bring to Spain's colonial project and to Africa.

For those equally worried about the effects of native Africans on the Cuban milicianos, redirecting the soldiers to Spain instead became a popular idea to ensure their continued identification with Spanish rule. In a public discussion about the future of slavery in 1867, the Conde de Vegamar circled around ideas about the inevitable end of the illegal slave trade, freedom for children born to slave mothers, and compensation for owners. He also explicitly looked to British and French examples of imperial consolidation, adding his own twist to ensure that free adult men remained productive and loyal. He advocated their passage to Spain to serve in "black battalions," a practice he attributed to the British, or their incorporation into the navy, as both the British and French had done.[142] As proposals like these came and went, the question of the militias remained an open one. Their loyalty and enthusiasm for militia service no longer guaranteed, Spanish and Cuban officials mused about the significance of soldiers of color in the colonial project.

IN THIS CHAPTER there have been countless examples of Cubans of color, slave and free, expressing their support for Spanish rule, and a mix of recognition and suspicion by watchful officials and a lettered Cuban elite that often aligned with the interests of slaveowners. Loyalty assumed different guises during decades when prominent examples of ruptured allegiances— independence movements and social unrest in other parts of the Americas— captured the attention of many Cubans. Fidelity to empire served many ends: it could ground appeals for justice and privileges, justify a critique of Spanish rule, or reinforce the multiple and overlapping vertical relationships that proliferated in Cuba, not least of which was the bond between slave and master. A wide array of social subordinates could figure as loyal subjects, yet in times of crisis, obliging acknowledgment of their loyalty could be slow in coming if colonial officials considered a confrontational response to be more effective. Slaves might have been instrumental in disabling the Soles y Rayos conspiracy, but the captain general who met some of them himself doubted their contributions. In the history of the free-colored milicianos, their faithful service to Spain emerges more prominently than their isolated episodes of rebellion, but the presumed perils of acknowledging them as loyal subjects left their actions unrewarded. Whether valorized, ignored, encouraged, or suppressed, loyalty—more than freedom, emancipation, or equality—represented the key term of vernacular politics in Cuba.

The early decades of the nineteenth century were a period when constitutionally backed equality before the law eluded Cubans because nominally universal liberal principles proved a poor fit for a slave society whose coherence depended on structured inequality. Inclusion based on declared loyalty to Spanish rule—a practice whose origins stretched far back in Spanish America—had the appearance of being universal itself, which presented a problem to those who held authority in Cuba. The creole elite, and free people more broadly, frequently realized the dilemma in attributing loyal subjectivity to slaves and free people of color: it was the same subject position that most of those superiors themselves had to inhabit in the colonial world. The prospects of being lumped together with subordinates threatened a social and political order that was imperfect but preferable to collapse. This is why the mimicry of cabildos' identifications with Spain met with mixed responses. The "ironic compromise" struck between the wide array of loyal Cuban subjects speaks to what Homi Bhabha has called the ambivalence of colonial discourse.[143]

Lest we reify loyalty as a force unto itself that could regulate its own meaning—as a principle somehow independent of historical circumstances—we should recognize that conflicts throughout the early nineteenth century over the loyal subject depended upon the willful action of Cubans (and Spanish officials, too). The recognition of willfulness on the part of slaves and free people of color gave pause to those in power. If the faith of the island's ever-faithful demanded active support, then their activities guaranteed that the discourse of loyalty could not enjoy limitless and unchanging influence in Cuba. If ideology is as pervasive as the air that people breathe, we might learn from José de la Luz y Caballero, the formidable and influential author who explored the essence of *cubanidad* early in the century: "It is necessary to change the atmosphere in order to recognize the impurity of the air."[144] As they invested meaning in their faithfulness, loyal subjects challenged ubiquitous inequalities and abuses of power, and the recipients of that fidelity cautiously shaped a public atmosphere intended to root out disloyalty. The political limits of that public could not accommodate sharper critiques that circulated on the island, and the beginning of Cuba's first war for independence in 1868 set more dramatic atmospheric changes in motion. In doing so it made loyal subjectivity all the more urgent.

THREE

The Will to Freedom
Spanish Allegiances in the Ten Years' War

A lusty, sonorous name echoed in your ears and engraved itself upon your minds: *National Integrity!* And the vaulted roof of the national assembly hall echoed with the unanimous cry: *Integrity! Integrity!*

Oh! It is not really so beautiful or so heroic, this dream of yours, for there can be no doubt that you were dreaming. Look, look at the image I shall paint for you, and if you do not shudder with fear at the wrong you have done, if, aghast, you do not curse the face of national integrity that I present you with, then I will turn my eyes in shame from this Spain that has no heart. . . .
—José Martí, "Political Prison in Cuba," 1871

Contrary to what nervous colonial officials had long anticipated, the instigators of the first large-scale threat to colonial order were not rebellious slaves but disgruntled planters. European liberalism, not African retribution, inflected the Grito de Yara, the call for independence proclaimed in October 1868 by Carlos Manuel de Céspedes, a sugar planter from Manzanillo. Spain's own liberal "Glorious Revolution" the same year, and the fluency of rebel leaders in the language of liberalism, inspired conspirators in eastern Cuba to give voice to their grievances. Even members of *cabildos* (town councils), lower government officials, and priests joined in what José Abreu Cardet describes as the "infidelity of the faithful."[1]

For decades, Cuban and Spanish officials had been fixated on preserving order, maintaining a productive economy, and keeping Cuba in Spain's imperial orbit. These objectives touched virtually every aspect of Cuban life on the island, and the concept and practice of loyalty linked them. In the most optimistic appraisals of those who benefited most from this system, slaves would not challenge colonial order if they did not challenge their masters. Loyalty to Spain and loyalty to one's superiors blurred into an imagined unitary allegiance to empire. The rebellion of 1868 tore apart these bonds.

Opposing slavery did not overlap neatly with opposing empire. Some slave-owners declared themselves independent from Spanish rule and freed their slaves. Other rebels hesitated to support abolition. Still others remained committed to Spanish rule while their slaves ran away to fight as *ciudadanos cubanos* (Cuban citizens) in the insurgent forces or simply fled to escape servitude. And as some masters rebelled against Spain, their slaves remained loyal by continuing to work on farms and plantations, or by fighting in the Spanish army.

Throughout the Ten Years' War (1868–1878), neither Spaniards nor Cubans could unhinge the bonds of race and empire. In that wrenching decade, the discourse of loyalty acquired added resonance precisely because incidents and accusations of perceived disloyalty proliferated throughout the island. Now, more than ever, those hailed as loyal subjects could not be guaranteed to respond. Struggles over who could play that political role continued to spotlight racial issues during the war, as did debates within the insurgency about how widely to define a fraternity of Cuban citizens. Many on the island defied legal and social conventions in seeking personal and national autonomy. This was the formative decade for the separatist movement and the development of a nascent Cuban nationalism, and it also occasioned major realignments in Spanish strategies to maintain popular support.

On both sides of the conflict, people of African descent fought alongside creoles and *peninsulares* (peninsular Spaniards). At the same time that authorities warned of the black and mulatto presence among the rebels and invoked the threat of race war, they worked actively to counter that presence by cultivating comparable allegiance to Spain. That loyalty, valued unevenly in the early nineteenth century in the face of routine repression, appreciated during the urgency of an anticolonial war that necessarily reconfigured the means and ends of long-standing colonial reciprocities. Did the war enable ordinary Cubans to advance more and different claims within the Spanish empire—or expand the ranks of its loyal subjects? If the military support of Cuban men (and some women) of color shaped Spain's prosecution of the war, what effects did it have on the military itself? Transformative possibilities emerged, too, with the legal initiation of gradual slave emancipation: the Moret Law of 1870 included a clause offering freedom to slaves who supported the Spanish during the war, and records of hundreds of officers' on-the-spot interrogations of slave-soldiers provide an unparalleled opportunity to witness participants reconciling competing definitions of loyalty.

In various locales, distinctions between loyalty and disloyalty sometimes remained secondary to more pressing realities. The insurrection did not touch all regions of Cuba equally, as the intense fighting in eastern Cuba never spread as much as rebels hoped to the plantation-intensive areas of central and western Cuba. Yet the Ten Years' War affected almost all Cubans—even those uninvolved in military engagements. It certainly syncopated the rhythms of rural society. Food shortages threatened lives and disrupted productive activities; tens of thousands of people died from illness and in battle. In cities, public life often continued as before, with stepped-up vigilance against unrest or disorder and with heightened military fortification from militias and army soldiers. Leaders policed the boundaries between enslaved and free African-descended Cubans much as they patrolled the borders of loyalty and disloyalty, especially as increasing numbers of slaves gained their freedom. Thus authorities monitored the political dispositions of free people of color with one eye on the immediate conflict and the other eye on the future. "National integrity," the oft-used phrase that so irked the young José Martí, more often than not referred to the unity of Spain and its colonies—a unity under assault during the Ten Years' War—but it was also a term that signaled within the Spanish orbit an unresolved relationship between empire, race, and nation that the insurgency's competing national vision brought into relief. In the course of the Ten Years' War, national integrity also acquired social meaning, as racial divisions among supporters of Spain raised new questions and opportunities about the kind of integrated polity that might emerge from the conflict.

Loyalty Challenged and Affirmed

The political and economic grievances of white island-born elites in the east erupted in 1868 and sparked rebellion, with many people of African descent leaving their towns, farms, and plantations to join the insurgent ranks. Many rebel leaders freed their slaves and called for immediate abolition. The leadership's sometimes egalitarian tone encouraged black and mulatto support, in part by valorizing the term *ciudadano cubano* (Cuban citizen) as a model of political inclusivity within an imagined Cuban nation.[2] The promises of emancipation that Carlos Manuel de Céspedes and other leaders made were lukewarm and conditional, at least at the outset, but they were strong enough to attract slaves to join the rebel forces. Free men of color also joined, not as militiamen in segregated units, but as fully incorporated soldiers and officers who ascended the ranks of the rebel army to high levels of leadership. One Spanish official in Cuba foresaw unrest on plantations when he noticed slaves looking to the rebel flag "as a symbol or promise of freedom." Worse yet, he worried, Spain would earn the scorn of Britain and the United States by not freeing enlisted slaves as some insurgent slaveowners had already done.[3] For many supporters of Spain, the insurgency came into view as threat to the island's social and economic stability and as a vexing issue in the international politics of antislavery. At stake, then, were nothing less than the prosperity and moral standing of the Spanish empire.

Civil and military authorities, increasingly aware of the social threat of the insurgency, moved quickly to put down the rebellion. They did so against considerable disadvantages. Spain itself was in the midst of its own turmoil in which a rebellion (whose liberal leaders held close ties to Cuban planters) had temporarily driven Isabel II into exile.[4] With financial and military resources concentrated on the Iberian Peninsula, leaders in Cuba looked to loyal militias and volunteers, including units of free-colored soldiers, to control cities and rural areas until regular troops from Spain could arrive. The militias constituted a force well adapted to local conditions despite a disorganized officer corps and deficiencies in supplies and training, likely a result of denied resources.[5] Spain worked quickly to mobilize the *milicias de color*—a little more than a decade after their reestablishment—to work on the local level with other militias, army volunteers, and the Civil Guard to locate and disable pockets of insurgency.[6] Enlistment in new free-colored companies had begun late in 1868, when the captain general authorized the formation of "a battalion with the *negros* that want to go to combat the enemies of Spain who they call, in their picturesque language, *cimarrones blancos* [white fugitives]." This was a clever inversion of the word usually reserved for runaway slaves and a strategy of making even white rebels legible through racialized language. An article from a military newspaper reported that three hundred people of African descent were already prepared to enlist at the time of the authorization.[7]

Fighting initially centered around Bayamo, where leaders constituted the first revolutionary government, and Puerto Príncipe. Armed confrontations spread west by February 1869, touching Cienfuegos, Santa Clara, Trinidad, Remedios, and Sancti Spíritus. Captain General Domingo Dulce requested six thousand soldiers in addition to the five thousand already on their way to fight in the east.[8] Local populations responded far more quickly to the outbreak. By February, twelve telegraph lines between Havana and central Cuba were operating again, and military officials in the provinces had a clear sense of their enemy. Insurgents in central Cuba were led by Adolfo Fernández Cavada, who had fought in a Philadelphia regiment during the U.S. Civil War and was serving as U.S. vice-consul in Cienfuegos. His ties to the United States prompted Captain General Francisco Lersundi to suspend the U.S. vice-consul in Cienfuegos and the consul in Trinidad.[9] The creation of volunteer regiments stirred patriotic sentiment on the island, more often tied to Spanishness (and its racial connotations) or "Spanish Cuba" than anything resembling the rebels' extension of citizenship . The *ayuntamiento* in Cienfuegos, for example, hailed the members of Batallón Voluntarios de Cienfuegos, a cavalry militia protecting rural areas, for recognizing "with pride its origins and the Spanish blood that circulates through its veins."[10]

Racial distinctions thus conditioned the symbolic and material contributions to the war effort on behalf of Cuban men of color, both slave and free. Those who entered the conflict were not immediately armed and sent into combat. Among the Spanish and rebel forces, slaves and free people also performed auxiliary services somewhat distinct from the kind of military service that accorded status in colonial society. They served as stretcher bearers, trench diggers, cooks, couriers, and countless other jobs that placed them in close quarters with their white Spanish and Cuban counterparts.

Proximity between white and non-white military men did not guarantee acceptance, respect, or any presumption of egalitarianism, as the actions of one civil official demonstrated. Hipólito Reina Capetillo worked with military officers in Holguín, and just as rebels entered the city 30 October 1868, he needed to sneak across town to the civil hospital—a Spanish stronghold—without rebels taking notice. So, hoping to conceal himself in the dark of night, he went in blackface: with burned cork he colored his face, neck, arms, hands, and feet. He wore a colored kerchief, mockingly called himself a *carabalí* (the ethnic "nation" associated with the slave port of Calabar), began to *charlar a lo negro* (talk black), and danced around for other officials, to great amusement, before leaving. Following Capetillo's success, a second mission required the delivery of a letter to one of the insurgent leaders who had invaded Holguín. This time the commanding Spanish officer chose instead a streetwise *bombero* (fireman) named Belis, described as agile, "*de la raza de color,* and with the heart of a brave man." Belis pushed himself through the crowds to deliver a message that apparently upset the rebels, who were organizing the bells, luminarias, and dances to celebrate the city's liberation. Belis emerged the hero of the day.[11] Alongside the offensive spectacle of Capetillo and the other Spanish supporters was a specific acknowledgment of his respectable position as a free man of color.

What might Belis have thought had he watched Capetillo's blackface caper? No matter how laudable his service to Spain may have been, he still had to endure the bigotry of white soldiers and officers who did not seem predisposed to tearing down racial barriers, even as they worked together closely. The incident in Holguín offers another insight into wartime life: setting aside

Capetillo's excuse of traveling in the dark, his choice of blackface to traverse the city streets and the Spanish officer's selection of Belis for the second task hint at distinctive abilities for Cubans of color to circulate in public during moments of acute conflict, in these cases with no apparent assumptions about their affiliations (or possibly the assumption by the rebels that Cubans of color allied with their cause). If, as Jill Lane argues, blackface performance in Cuba "offered a useful, perhaps necessary, alternative technology for mobilizing, organizing, and otherwise constituting anticolonial public subjectivity," Capetillo's actions complicate that insight and suggest that it extended to *colonial* public subjectivity as well.[12]

By the end of 1869, thirty-three thousand Spanish soldiers had arrived from the peninsula, although the early and sustained participation of slaves in counterinsurgent forces aided Spanish forces significantly.[13] The Spanish army struggled to find its place in Cuba and to find a place for Cuba, especially its soldiers of color. An 1870 patriotic album published in Spain, for example, catalogued portraits of most of the major Spanish officers leading the forces in Cuba, but one staged image of ordinary soldiers sticks out: "Defenders of National Integrity," as the photograph was titled, depicted a lone Cuban soldier of color in the group (figure 3.1). Next to him stared a white soldier, his head whipped around to regard his comrade. Was he gazing with admiration? With anxiety? With disdain? Disbelief? Given the uneven reception of Cubans of color in the counterinsurgency, all of these reactions were within the range of possibility.

Two Conscripts of Empire

Because civil and military authority overlapped in policies made from Madrid, decisions about colonial appointments considered the image of Spain that military officials might project, both to officers and troops and to the general public. Officers, troops, and bureaucrats often circulated throughout various parts of Spain's empire, and positions and relationships built elsewhere could be mobilized or transformed in Cuba. Moreover, as the government called on the support of its subjects to put down the rebellion, popular responses to the insurgency could, in turn, potentially shape colonial policy. Domingo Dulce, an abolitionist and reform-minded captain general appointed in 1869, initially eased press censorship and offered amnesty to rebels who surrendered but quickly reversed course when *voluntarios* (volunteers) reacted violently against any concessions to the insurgency. Rumors circulated that he secretly sought autonomy, if not independence, for Cuba, and he left after only six

FIGURE 3.1 • *Defensores de la integridad nacional* (Defenders of national integrity), in Gil Gelpi y Ferro, *Álbum histórico fotográfico de la Guerra de Cuba* (Havana: Imprenta Militar de la Viuda de Soler y Compañía, 1870). Courtesy of Latin American Collection, George A. Smathers Library, University of Florida.

EL GENERAL PUELLO.

FIGURE 3.2 • General Eusebio Puello, from the newspaper *La Ilustración de Madrid*, 12 February 1870. Private collection.

months. His replacement, Antonio Caballero de Rodas, offered the firmer hand that the voluntarios and many creole elites seemed to prefer. His arrival provoked acclamations of loyalty from troops who had served with him in the Philippines. After he delivered a speech at a banquet in his honor promising public calm with the support of "such fine Spaniards," voluntarios took to the decorated streets with large candles and music.[14]

With voluntarios and officers alike ambivalent about men of color serving the Spanish cause, the lower ranks of Spanish defense opened up to accommodate more Cubans of color. Restrictions on access to the upper echelons of the military remained predictably tight. The great and notable exception was General Eusebio Puello (figure 3.2), one of a handful of Dominicans of African descent who had, against the odds, attained officer status in the Spanish army during the military conflicts that began and ended the Haitian occupation of eastern Hispaniola (1822–1844). Born in 1811, Puello enlisted at age thirteen and, after each of his successive victories, earned promotions and responsibility for larger campaigns. Having fought against Haitian forces in many engagements and against insurgents after Spain's reannexation of the Dominican Republic, Puello was no stranger to rebellion and Spanish counterinsurgency. He was as emphatic about the importance of the "free, natural, and spontaneous sentiment" of the Dominican people as he was about military success to the strength of Spanish rule in the Caribbean. "Burning with enthusiasm for the defense of national integrity," as he described it, Puello arrived in Cuba and initially commanded all troops in Sancti Spíritus, Morón, Remedios, and Ciego de Ávila.[15]

As rebel leader Ignacio Agramonte closed in on Puerto Príncipe in June 1869, Puello relocated to the city and assumed the position of comandante general of central Cuba.[16] His arrival immediately provoked resistance from officers, soldiers, civilian officials, and even the Audiencia. Overlooking the wide-ranging experience Puello had developed during a career of nearly fifty years, complaints within the military centered on one particular skill Puello boasted about that proved vital in the most recent Dominican insurgency: his valiant performance with a bayonet in trench battles. Officials in Puerto Príncipe conceded that it had served him well, but argued that Cuban rebels with rifles could fire constantly and required different tactics. They mocked what they thought was his sole meritorious recognition by the government, calling it an *aureola de lealtad* a (halo of loyalty) to Spain, although he had previously received at least three such commendations.[17] Puello suffered a resounding defeat in January 1870 by the forces of rebel leader (and ex–Confederate general) Thomas Jordan, leaving three hundred Spanish soldiers dead and forcing Puello, surrounded by insurgents, to hole up for seventeen days in the abandoned house of the Arroyo Hondo estate.[18]

A black Dominican Spanish general and an ex–Confederate general in the Cuban rebel army? These men are not among the cast of characters typically associated with the struggle for Cuban independence. In Puello's case, contemporaries in the nineteenth century were no less confounded. Antonio Pirala, a Spanish historian reflecting on the Ten Years' War during the 1895–1898 War of Independence, claimed that Puello lacked "the proper education of European generals"; he blamed Cuban society, though, rather than Puello, for its inability to support the leader. Admittedly, Puello had rattled some Cubans with his presence, but "perhaps those who claim that the customs of each country should be respected are correct," he added, arguing that Puello's presence stirred up the slaves in and around Puerto Príncipe. They were already "almost in systematic disobedience to their owners," and some of them were rumored to have "said with arrogance to their owners 'that if a *tiznado* [bastard] like him was going to order around the whites, it was proof that he was equal to them, and there was no reason that they shouldn't all be free.'"[19] This was precisely the conclusion that had worried Spanish officials when they first opposed the migration of the black Dominican officers to Cuba. Were Puello a supporting cast member in the drama of war, his successes and failures might not have caused such a stir. As a lead actor, the audiences he attracted became a justification for ushering him offstage.

Despite his long record of achievement and the respect afforded him in Spain, Puello's reputation suffered in the wake of his lost battle. When the captain general relieved Puello of his duties later in the year, he publicly cited the general's bad health but privately accused Puello of "lacking the energy and disposition for leadership of such importance." Puello himself noted this in an commemorative volume (1872). Newspapers, too, had attacked him for his lack of military knowledge, which he dismissed in the face of the "loyalty and honor" he had displayed a thousand times. This merited as much consideration as a set of self-evident truths about war craft "which are written into the ruggedness of the hills."[20] In a more confessional tone, Puello recalled stating publicly in Puerto Príncipe that he was a strong soldier yet knew little about the work of government, "but what I lack in intelligence I make up for with *voluntad* [determination]."[21]

Will and determination were vital in battle but were not, at the outset, requirements for the freedom ultimately offered to slaves who lent their labor to the Spanish army. In large part, the will of slaves rarely mattered to owners or the state. In the process of freeing slave-soldiers, however, their volition became as important to the officials interrogating them as it was to Eusebio Puello's confidence in his contributions to the Spanish cause. Loyalty to colonial rule, as we have seen repeatedly, was not a passive position to be contrasted to an active decision to join the insurgency.

Although leaders on both sides of the conflict could not easily assess the motives and rewards for those acts of will, an instructive contrast between Puello and mulatto rebel officer Antonio Maceo highlights the different terms on which Spaniards and rebels comprehended racially diverse leadership. Maceo distinguished himself as a guerrilla fighter early in the war and quickly achieved the rank of sergeant, then captain, and then by 1872 a colonel; by the end of the war he had become major general. His superiors, and even some Spaniards who saw him in action, routinely praised his skills. With resurgent campaigns in 1874, authors of Spanish propaganda began to accuse Maceo of inciting a race war, while rebel troops in Las Villas refused to accept him as their commander. There are echoes of Puello's trajectory here: rapid distinction for military successes, fast promotion, public admiration, and racist reaction. But their responses to that prejudice differed in meaningful ways. After waiting a full two years, Maceo responded, characterizing the slander as an attack on the ideals of Cuban independence. His letter of 16 May 1876 accused his "brother" rebel critics of forgetting republican principles and the idea of a nation "that does not recognize hierarchies."[22] For Puello, hierarchies were off the table. In contrast to the political vocabulary of the insurgency, the logic of Spanish rule made hierarchy one of its fundamental tenets. Appeals to liberty, equality, and fraternity—not just the motto of the French Revolution but also a phrase invoked, too, during the Haitian Revolution—resonated far less in Spanish Cuba than his combination of deference and determination. Even so, Puello's leadership left many Cubans skeptical of his ability to command authority.

His image in Spain, however, suffered few of these doubts. Less than a month after his defeat near Arroyo Hondo, an article in *La Ilustración de Madrid* praised his heroism and dedication. Never mind that he blurred the sharp distinction Spaniards regularly made between the "sons of Spain" defending the empire and insurgents, characterized as blacks who embodied the barbarity associated with African origins. Puello, in fact, provided the best evidence of Spain's inclusive ethos. The article's author praised how Puello had taken trenches controlled by over twice as many rebel soldiers as he commanded, and hailed "the sincerity of the affection he inspires in his adopted country." But the writer didn't stop there: he used the example of Puello to show that myths about Spain's brutality and prejudice would be revised substantially if observers were to search "the catacombs of our archives" instead of propagating the "Black Legend." Compared to the "relative mildness" of Iberian slavery, "Yankees" and Europeans had little room to argue about the treatment of blacks. As exemplified by Puello, he stated, "no color difference alters anyone's consideration for his patriotism."[23] The author here replaced the Black Legend with a legendary black who redeemed Spanish empire in its ideals and in its practice.

José de la Gándara had been one of the most important generals in the reannexation campaign in the Dominican Republic, and he recalled the valor of Eusebio Puello well in his memoir of 1884, frequently referring to him as "the loyal Puello." During the conflict, Gándara had begun to take notice of a younger officer whose bravery resembled that of the black general, and he made multiple attempts for Puello to meet the subordinate. At one point the two men were in the same place, but they were so involved in their various exploits that the encounter never occurred. So it was that Eusebio Puello narrowly missed meeting a young officer named Valeriano Weyler (figure 3.3).[24]

By 1898, if anyone remotely familiar with Cuba wanted to embody the whole of the Black Legend in one individual, that individual would have been

FIGURE 3.3 • General Valeriano Weyler. Courtesy of New York Public Library.

Valeriano Weyler. Cubans, and especially the U.S. press, called him "The Butcher." His policy of reconcentration from 1896—a euphemism for the forced relocation of over 300,000 Cubans to isolated areas to clear the path for counterinsurgency operations—killed somewhere between 150,000 and 170,000 civilians, an estimated 10 percent of the island's population.[25]

As recently promoted thirty-year-old officer, Weyler was an early advocate of employing Cubans of color in the Spanish military. When various Havana businessmen in 1870 financed the creation of Cazadores de Valmaseda—a special volunteer force—the responsibility of recruitment fell to Weyler, and he saw in this new force a possible solution to the military challenges posed by the Cuban rebels. Early conflicts in eastern Cuba alerted him to how "the principal action of the enemy" did not conform to the tactics of standard armies but rather to "dispersed forces, experts on the places where columns pass, using natural features to harass the enemy." He described the battle at the Salado River in January 1869, for example, in which six hundred rebel "negros" on the banks of the river waved a white flag of surrender but opened fire when Spanish troops approached them "with unpremeditated trust." When it came to recruiting volunteers, then, Weyler looked not to men with distinguished militia or police experience but to those who more often found themselves on the other side of the law. He quickly assembled "a good number of white and colored Cubans, as well as some foreigners from various countries in Europe," but he left no paper trail of his efforts because he had enlisted "many fugitives or released prisoners and not a few who had unfinished business with the law."[26]

The new soldiers each received thirty pesos monthly, a Peabody rifle, and—because of Weyler's worries about their dubious backgrounds—unyielding discipline. Weyler threw a punch at one soldier who complained "disrespect-fully," and he had another soldier sentenced to death on learning that he had wandered the streets of Cienfuegos shouting subversive statements. However, Weyler also expressed respect for his multiracial troops. After a bumpy start they achieved victories in Las Tunas and Holguín, and Weyler ultimately commended their "unbreakable loyalty." Two months after a successful surprise attack on rebel general Vicente García, the Cazadores de Val-maseda joined with a Spanish brigade to attack a rebel contingent near the Río Chiquito. In a footnote in his memoirs Weyler mourned a black soldier named Joseito—"one of the bravest of my guerrilla[s]"—a death made all the more poignant on finding in his horse's saddle a number of bottles and foods, "without doubt intended *festejar su santo* [to celebrate his saint] the next day."[27] This oblique reference to one of the principal African-derived religious practices (constitutive only much later of *santería*) sticks out as perhaps the most surprising example of Weyler's degree of sympathetic engagement with the black soldiers.

Such a sentimental aside sits awkwardly with the image of Valeriano Wey-ler. What can we make of his younger self and his affection for Joseito? Within the context of military camaraderie, even between social and military unequals, affection between men could safely express itself as a show of patrio-tism.[28] But assumptions about racial difference never vanished from cooper-ative efforts during wartime. Just as continued prejudice qualified the effusive praise for Eusebio Puello's high-profile loyalty, Weyler's appreciation of his troops accompanied an estimation of those men less as loyal subjects than the hardscrabble denizens of the *mala vida,* the illicit world of thieving, gam-bling, and vagrancy, whose lives on the margins taught them useful lessons to exploit in combat. In other words, these men were conscripts of empire: historical agents acting within the ideological and institutional structures of colonial rule.[29] Puello, Weyler, and many others demonstrated their support for Spain in a context of presumed racial (and racist) antagonism that was hardwired into the circuitry of imperial power.

Legislating Loyalty: The Moret Law

Segismundo Moret, the *ministro de ultramar* (overseas minister) in 1870, knew well from civil and military officials in Cuba how to extend and institutionalize the practice of freeing slave-soldiers that was already taking place. His law that set the terms of gradual slave emancipation included an article stipulating that "All slaves who have served under the Spanish flag, or in any manner have aided the troops during the current Cuban insurrection, are declared free. The State will compensate owners their value if they have remained loyal to the Spanish cause; if they belonged to the insurgents, there will be no occasion for compensation." Well before the Cortes considered the Moret Law, the captain general had been consistently relaying to Madrid two conflicting reports about Cuban slaves: their attraction to the anticolonial insurgency's promise of citizenship and their continued support of Spanish rule. He boasted that in April 1870 thirty-two negros presented themselves in the town of Puerto Príncipe to claim unanimously that "they very much prefer to be Spanish slaves than free Mambís."[30] Less than a month later, he wrote that "many individuals of color have given excellent services, taking up arms for our cause. Backed by provincial laws, I have granted freedom to those who have distinguished themselves making public the resolution to stimulate it further."[31] When he freed slave insurgents in a jail, they volunteered to fight in the *contraguerrillas* (counterinsurgent forces) or to serve as spies against their former comrades. In arguing before the Cortes about his proposed law for gradual emancipation, Moret spoke eloquently about the presence of slaves in the Spanish ranks "who have fought on our side, who have taught the Spanish soldier the hidden road, the rugged path, the narrow passage where one could look for the enemy or get out of the tangled jungle: these slaves cannot return to [slavery]; the Spanish flag, waving before them, has converted them into free men."[32] Moret's colleagues in the Cortes generally agreed that slaves who fought with Spain deserved their freedom. Free people of African descent had been crucial in defending the island in the beginning of the rebellion, and deputies in Madrid had few reservations about striking a bargain with slaves: exchanging military service for freedom. As one deputy noted, "Our laws, since ancient times, have conceded freedom to slaves who have lent great services to the Patria or to their owners themselves."[33]

With the practical benefits of cultivating and rewarding the loyalty of slaves established in debates over the abolition law, the Cortes shifted its concerns to the economic and political effects of Article 3. Less consensus about the article existed about reconciling the freedom of slaves with the property rights of their masters. In this aspect Moret and his colleagues fiercely disagreed on the question of compensation for slaveowners. Like many of his colleagues, he was resolutely opposed to compensating rebel slaveowners, and he even expressed doubts about compensating loyal owners. Some owners who had fought for Spain since 1868 had voluntarily freed their slaves, having "recognized the principle of freedom without compensation." Moret argued, "It would be an incredibly strange thing if the Government were to recognize a right that they had begun to renounce."[34] Deputies such as Luis Padial and others disagreed. Owners loyal to Spain would be compensated the price of the slave if freed by the state.

Insurgent slaveowners, however, would be stripped of those "assets" and in effect have their slaves "embargoed," or confiscated by the government. In a North Atlantic political climate favorable to abolition, this proved an embarrassing matter for Spain. Rebel leaders in Cuba and the United States publicized that although they were willing to free their slaves, the Spanish government subsequently might try to capture and reenslave them.[35] Article 3, then, in its final form, embodied conflicting aims. It cultivated the loyalty of Cuban slaves to the colonial government at the same time that it tried to assuage observers throughout the North Atlantic world concerned that the war would prolong slavery. Once the Cortes passed the Moret Law, the binding power of the state backed Spain's promises of freedom in a way that insurgent leaders' abolitionist policies could not yet achieve.

Spanish press coverage recognized how the Moret Law could help the movement to defeat the insurrection but questioned whether or not slaves or former slaves could be loyal subjects. The editors of *La Iberia,* for example, hoped that Article 3 would extinguish slave allegiances to separatism, "one of the most cherished hopes of the insurgents." Instead, the new law could seize on the dispositions of "the negros, held close to their masters, treated with solicitude and affection on the part of their owners." It went on to say, "The Government has comprehended the loyalty of those *negros* to Spain, their affection for Spaniards, and so the project declares them free, compensates their owners."[36] Articles in the liberal daily *El Sufragio Universal* were more skeptical. As a measure to stimulate slaves freed by the Céspedes proclamation to abandon their encampments, Article 3 could not possibly compel slaves from Baracoa to Cinco Villas "to change their real and true freedom that they win in the battlefields, freedom conferred by their owners, to go in search of a fictitious manumission like that offered by the Spanish government, whose domination is considered extinguished in that vast expanse of territory." For slaves in western Cuba, whose loyal owners had not freed them, the government faced a moral trade-off between encouraging slaves "to change the hard labor of barbarous and cruel slavery, to seize the weapons of a soldier, with the incentive of freedom," and "to use slander and accusation against their owners."[37] *El Puente de Alcolea* warned of a potential labor shortage catalyzed by slave enlistment. It looked to the case of Brazil, which "opened its ranks to the servile class" during the war with Paraguay, such that "the mining blacks responded in huge masses to look for their freedom fighting against López."[38] Another newspaper, *La Voz del Derecho,* accused Moret and certain deputies in the Cortes of underestimating the selfless ties that slaves might have toward Spain. Arguing that slaves might fight without recompense, one journalist surmised that Moret "has believed that the colored race could not have affections for the *patria*," thereby reducing loyalty to Spain to a desperate bargain for freedom. By separating "within the same race" freed loyal slaves from vanquished rebel slaves, Moret fostered the type of resentment among slaves that had taken violent, disastrous turns in the past. Once again, the specter of Haiti loomed large: "Unfortunately," the article lamented, "Señor Moret has forgotten the lessons of history."[39]

The initial Spanish press reaction to the insurrection itself did not immediately express fear of racial reprisal and sometimes downplayed the participation of Cubans of color. One editorial in the *Diario de Barcelona* dismissed parallels to earlier Latin American independence movements, as well as the notion that a "new race" born of the "crossing of races, united by the influence of the tropical climate" was to blame for the rebellion. The author claimed to know many rebel leaders personally and assured readers that "the Cubans, then, in their immense majority are white, of pure Caucasian race and all of European origin," adding that "the people of color are, in their near totality devoted and loyal." He understated the presence of mulattoes among the rebels, who were "insignificant as much by their number as by their position and influence." The driving force of the insurrection, instead, lay in the hands of white men "driven by ambition and greed and infected by the predominant ideas in the United States."[40]

Spanish writer Gil Gelpi y Ferro looked to the past and the future when he celebrated the military achievements of African-descended Cubans for their contribution to a reinvigorated empire. He reported in 1871 that rebels constituted a minority of Cubans, in contrast to the "many peaceful workers in the countryside of all conditions and races." He praised how African-descended Cubans, "little knowing what to expect from the so-called *regeneradores* [reformers] and how much they owed to Spanish laws and Catholicism, have contributed on their part to combat those who have neither *patria* nor beliefs." He singled out the "valiant negros" of Havana's milicias disciplinadas and bomberos "that with such enthusiasm and patriotism have gone when the Government commanded it." He specifically credited a battalion in Punta Pilón, Camagüey, with defeating a massive attack by black rebels who had united "in order to surprise the negros who guarded that point: the valiant voluntarios of color, to the shout of '¡Viva España!,' a shout that might cause horror among certain people, obligated them to flee hastily, leaving the countryside covered with cadavers."

But Gelpi reminded his readers that Spain's soldiers of color demonstrated loyalty to more than their patria; they had achieved success through the cooperation, if not supervision, of white superiors. He bestowed equal praise upon white Spaniards in Havana, Cienfuegos, Matanzas, and Cárdenas who "negotiated with the notable Spanish negros just as the French negotiated with their neighbors in Senegal, the British in Sierra Leone, and the Portuguese in Angola."[41] It was a bold suggestion: imbued with the spirit of indirect rule that was solidifying Europe's imperial claims in Africa, Spaniards and creoles could, for Gelpi, usher in a new colonial era in Cuba that built on the alliances forged by blacks and whites during the war. Before Spain could assume a respectable place alongside Europe's other national empires, it would need to demonstrate that the alliances produced the intended outcome of negotiating with "Spanish negros." Incorporating Cubans of color into the war effort had largely been an improvised and instrumental measure, not one with the legally backed bargain codified by Article 3. Would modifying the means of preserving empire also change its ends?

Measuring Loyalty: Field Interrogations of Slaves

Despite issuing a decree establishing obligatory military service in the insurgency, Carlos Manuel de Céspedes criticized the Spanish army for forcing Cubans "against their will" to join their ranks.[42] At the same time, he required that any slaves seeking to join the ranks of the rebellion required the permission of their masters.[43] There were few clear answers to questions of voluntarism and decision making on the part of individuals in choosing sides. Whether allegiance to a cause required proof of willful intent remained a vexed question for both sides in the conflict.

Arming slaves, whatever its successful historical antecedents, required a degree of trust between military leaders and slaves that did not always prevail over officers' perceived threat of reprisal. Indeed, some slaves quickly deserted the Spanish ranks with weapons that they subsequently used in the insurgent army. The conditions of freedom under Article 3, however, depended on the conditions of enslavement and emerged from interrogations in Spanish army camps that expressed little concern about the anticipated behavior of freed slaves. As superiors questioned slaves and their fellow fighters, proceedings often focused on rewarding services rendered rather than welcoming slaves into a brotherhood of free subjects of the Spanish crown. In an examination of over three hundred of these interrogations, it becomes clear that labor and service were necessary, but not sufficient, conditions for freedom. Determining the merits of slaves' affiliations with Spain became a process of reconciling competing definitions of loyalty. Officers encountered slaves with different ideas about what behaviors and arguments made them deserving of freedom.

The first order of business in applying Article 3 was to determine the specific contributions that slaves had made to the war effort. As they often did in the insurgent ranks, slaves performed menial labor for voluntarios and standing regiments as often as they engaged in armed combat. Nicolás Gonzalo, a thirty-year-old member of the Batallón de Antequera, is one example. Guillermo Bell, who fought in the Batallón Cazadores de Bailén, worked as a stretcher-bearer and a muleteer, and sometimes took up arms.[44] José Caimares, who had joined the army on 7 June 1869, was described as "lending his services of *camillero* [stretcher bearer], *acemilero* [muleteer] and others analogous to his class."[45] The majority of slaves interrogated responded similarly. Yet freedom did not depend solely on armed combat: Alejandro Néstor, a slave from the Perseverancia estate and a member of the Third Company of the Batallón de Matanzas, claimed in his interrogation that "he was always *fiel* [loyal] to the cause of the Spanish Government, performing the services of muleteer and stretcher-bearer."[46] Although these auxiliary activities may not have carried the symbolic power of combat, they nevertheless justified freedom. In the case of carrying bodies, slaves performed a service as important for sanitary reasons as for symbolic ones, given the frequency of illness and death during the war. Slave recruits in the rebel army frequently performed the same labor. A North American war correspondent described stretcher bearing in the rebel forces during the 1895–1898 war: "Stout negroes were detailed to carry the helpless. Hammocks were borrowed from those who had them to lend, and the wounded were borne in them, slung on poles on the shoulders of their comrades. Two men carried a pole for a hundred yards or so, and rested it on crotched sticks that they drove upright in the ground at each halt, while they caught their wind and mopped their sweaty brows."[47] Much of the labor performed by slave-soldiers, then, seems to have been labor that voluntarios and Spanish soldiers avoided.

Attentive to the unity and diversity among African-descended Cubans, officials took great interest in the ethnic self-designations of the slaves under interrogation. When asked about his "primitive nationality," Guillermo Bell responded with the ethnic designation "Gangá." When asked if there were other slaves with his surname—presumably from his same plantation—who fought with him, he replied that one was "Congo" and two were creoles. During the interrogation of Félix Bell, another slave from the Perseverancia sugar estate near Santiago, officials cross-checked Bell's ethnic self-identification with an eye toward spotting falsification. Félix himself took great care to explain how his name differed from the one on his baptismal records. Creole slaves apparently did not garner suspicion for identifying as Cubans. When asked of his place of origin, Ignacio Calixto, a slave from Bayamo, responded with "his *patria* Cuba."[48]

In the course of their interrogations, slaves sometimes provided military officials with intelligence about insurgent slaves and masters. Their knowledge of local conditions provided critical information about the composition of the rebel forces and the contours of disloyalty. Slaves who identified rebel owners alerted officials to estates that could be embargoed. Still other slaves traded information about insurgents not for their freedom, but for special privileges and mobility. Eustaquio Adelín, who one official estimated to be nineteen or twenty years old, offered a detailed analysis of the recruiting efforts of the rebel general Donato Mármol. In exchange, he asked only to be able to see his mother, Leocadia, "slave of his owner Don Amá, who is still on the *cafetal* (coffee plantation)."[49] In other cases, slaves fled from insurgent owners. Instead of holding the slaves as embargoed property or punishing the slaves for escaping, Spanish officials freed them for having actively sought out Spanish troops and offering their services. Such was the story of Luciano Sosa from Cienfuegos who had fled an owner and somehow made his way to the eastern part of the island in the Spanish army.[50] Having a rebel owner often aided the cases of slaves obligated to show that they had presented themselves voluntarily to Spanish forces for enlistment. Manuel Olivares identified his owner, Ramón Rubio, as the head of an insurgent battalion, thus demonstrating that his service was not performed only at the command of his master.[51] Andrés Aguilera, a creole slave from the Santa Gertrudis estate in Manzanillo, identified his owner as rebel general Francisco Aguilera. When his insurgent owner and the estate's overseers abandoned the plantation, the workforce dispersed to the Santa Isabel hills until Andrés, with "his woman the *negra* Ursula" and three other male slaves, presented himself to the Fifth Battalion Cazadores de San Quintín to work as a stretcher bearer.[52] Many slaves admitted that they did not know what allegiances their owners had, which also bolstered their claims to voluntary participation.[53] These slaves all affirmed that they had voluntarily presented themselves to the Spanish army for employment.

Other slaves ended up with the Spanish after a stint in the rebel ranks, a shift that elevated the issue of *voluntad,* or will. Even when slaves did not explicitly affirm loyalty to the Spanish government, they improved their cases when they demonstrated a choice to support the Spanish army. Interrogators might even ask a slave "if he had presented himself voluntarily or induced by a second person or if he was forced into it."[54] While some slaves strategically switched sides during the Ten Years' War—depending on resources, patronage, or perceptions of which side was winning—others expressed less of a choice in their military participation. Vicente del Castillo, a slave who worked as a pan maker in Santiago de Cuba, declared that he presented himself to the Conde de Valmaseda of the Spanish army during a battle in Saladillo, "being that the insurgents, against his will, had taken him from the ingenio La Unión, his owner's property."[55] The relative weight ascribed to the accomplishments and intentions of slaves seeking their freedom through Article 3 shifted to will in later years, but even during these early moments interrogators attempted to discern the nature of slaves' allegiance.

Many of the early interrogations of slaves in eastern Cuba referred to the rebel general Donato Mármol as the driving force behind slave recruitment for the rebel army. On a trip to the Esperanza coffee estate, Mármol organized about forty of the slaves and swore to the Virgen de la Caridad that all slaves would be freed if the insurrection succeeded. He then led the slaves to a point near Sabanilla, where nine thousand other soldiers were already stationed. The slaves performed manual labor—digging trenches to keep the Spanish from advancing and building fortifications—and during an engagement with the Batallón de Matanzas, led by the Conde de Valmaseda, at least one slave switched sides, fought for the Spanish, and earned his freedom.[56]

In the testimony of Felipe San José, who worked on a cafetal in Guantánamo, the easternmost region of Cuba, he explicitly related his status as a slave to his decision to fight: "Asked how he found himself in the actions in Saladillo between rebel parties and the Spanish government and not at the cafetal where he was a slave, and who induced such a defection, or if it was voluntarily, he said that accustomed by his condition to blind obedience, he put up no resistance, without conscience of disloyalty, to heed the order that the *mayoral* [overseer] Eduardo Pochet gave to follow the party commanded by the leader Donato Mármol to join the campaign." Pochet, the French overseer, had been approached by Mármol to recruit from the plantation's workforce, and it was only after the slaves joined the insurgent ranks that Felipe and Santiago—a slave from the same plantation—were taken prisoner by a general in the Spanish army, "recommending to [them] fidelity hereafter to the Spanish government." Felipe and Santiago assented to this recommendation, "remained loyal ever since," and thus only months after the passage of the Moret Law, their circuitous route to the Spanish army—and to a situation they could describe as "loyalty"—led them to freedom.[57]

The contradictions in Spanish policy become starkly visible here. Loyalty could be a morally neutral category or a virtue disconnected from a particular value or cause. And in the encounter on the coffee estate, loyalty worked to the disadvantage of Spain. Felipe San José's "blind obedience" was to his insurgent master, not the Spanish government. The loyalty that won Felipe and Santiago their freedom was voluntary, a willful allegiance to Spain if not a decisive rejection of the insurgency.

But a slave's alleged loyalty to Spain did not always necessarily trump loyalty to an owner. Interrogations routinely attempted to ascertain from slaves if they had continued to work on the plantation in the event that their owners had abandoned them to fight in the insurrection. In November 1870, officials promptly denied Antonio Abad's petition for freedom because he had neither offered meaningful services to the Spanish army—he had simply camped out among troops for several days—nor had he fled his master for any good reason acceptable to the authorities. His offense: "resistance to obedience."[58] Loyalty to Spain was a necessary but insufficient condition in the practical application of Article 3. Slaves had to demonstrate moral freedom—that is, evidence of an unforced choice—as a condition of juridical freedom.

Slaveowners, too, had to navigate the variable currents of loyalty and disloyalty when their slaves became free. The Moret Law stipulated that only loyal slaveowners would be compensated when the government freed slaves who had served in the army. Some insurgent slaveowners had freed their slaves at the outset of the rebellion. Others had already had their property, including their slaves, embargoed by the government. But those owners whose loyalty was still in doubt when their slaves petitioned for freedom had to make the case for her loyalty to be compensated. When an urban slave named Felipe sought liberty through Article 3, Juana del Castillo—the widow of an army captain—had to argue on behalf of herself and her daughter Luisa for compensation. In the midst of the rebellion's turmoil, the two women had slipped out of the city of Puerto Príncipe to the seclusion of a friend's rural residence. They left Felipe, a chocolatier and meat vendor, in the city to continue working to pay off the debts they had accrued during the war. The women returned to the city as Felipe was gaining his freedom "for the fine qualities that distinguish him" but with none of his earnings to be found. They aroused suspicion because they had abandoned their slave and left town; cities typically remained Spanish strongholds during Cuba's independence wars, whereas the untamed countryside promised less stability. Ultimately, the Consejo de Administración in Madrid ruled that they were "of good moral and political opinion" and had not acted with negligence with Felipe.[59] But the case revealed that Article 3 allowed the Spanish state to examine and monitor the relationship between masters and slaves that undergirded colonial stability. Thus, officials often seemed as intent on ascertaining the allegiance of slaveowners as they were the loyalty of the slaves they considered freeing.

After the initial years of the war, regular arrivals of numerous Spanish troops reduced the urgency of slaves' military contributions. Assuming that slaves learned about the nature and stakes of the war as it progressed, officials gave greater attention to the intentions and motivations of slaves to join the Spanish cause. Other Cubans worried that the insurrection threatened the obedience of slaves to their owners. Even travelers frequently affirmed the idea that the institution of slavery guaranteed the loyalty of naturally rebellious people of African descent. Antonio Gallenga, on visiting a sugar estate in Güines, noted with no lack of hyperbole that "the Negro in a state of slavery is as efficient and willing a labourer as the master can desire. I have seen crowds of them clustering round Señor Zulueta, on their knees, joyously crying, '¡El Amo! ¡El Amo!' as if the master were a demigod to them and his presence among them an angel's visit." But the planters he spoke to—conscious of slavery's long-term unfeasibility—worried that immediate abolition would be tantamount to "leaving to their own devices an enormous mass of slaves, indolent by temperament, placed above all want": "The immediate emancipation of the Negroes would soon bring back the whole black race to the instincts of its native African savagery." Because "Negro sympathies" buoyed the insurrection, Gallenga implored planters to develop strategies to phase out slave labor while maintaining the obedience of black and mulatto workers that would stave off rebellion and ruin.[60] In this sense, granting freedom only to those slaves who had "proven" their loyalty to Spain through military service provided nervous planters and colonial officials with a gradual and regulated approach to the ties that held Cuban society together. It also gave institutional weight to their definitions of loyalty over those of the many slaves who sought their freedom by contributing to the war effort.

The Will to Freedom • 115

Other Loyalties

In poring over the hundreds of Article 3 cases, it becomes clear that slaves' understandings of the master-slave relationship consistently collided with military officials' assessments of the political loyalty of slave-soldiers relative to their fidelity to their owners. In the process, labor relationships made visible and disrupted by anticolonial rebellion came to condition social relations—and the possibilities for mobility—within Spain's counterinsurgency. Yet to imagine slavery as the only labor arrangement on the island, or to take the master-slave relationship as the root metaphor for all social order and hierarchy, submerges other unequal relations in Cuba that operated by different but related rules. Abundant "others"—in particular, Chinese contract workers and enslaved and free women—experienced wartime instability that pulled them into the increasingly urgent issue of popular loyalty to Spanish rule.

By the beginning of the Ten Years' War, African slaves and free people of color had been working for years alongside Chinese and Yucatec Maya contract laborers who arrived through migration schemes borne out of anxieties about the suppression of the transatlantic slave trade. Working long and illegally extended periods of indenture, these workers often experienced the brutality that characterized African slavery, as employers rarely honored the stipulated freedoms laid out in labor contracts. The dislocations of war affected these workers as well as slaves and raised concerns about their fidelity to their contracts, their employers, and to Spanish rule.

When the Chinese government formed a commission in 1873 to visit Cuba and report on the conditions of Chinese laborers, general concerns about the violation of labor contracts on plantations led investigating authorities to inquire whether "Coolies serve their employers faithfully." They concluded in their report from 1876 that the Chinese "cannot be otherwise than obedient, through the terror inspired by the administrator and overseers, by the chains at their side, and by the rods and whips which goad them into labor." A petition from ninety workers and oral testimony from seven others painted a picture of forced obedience; for example, Chung Shêng, one of many workers forced to continue laboring after the contract term had ended, explained that "I was against my will constrained to continue labor, and had open to me no course but obedience." Since insubordination and flight were among the offenses that employers and government authorities could cite to discipline contract laborers, including extending their period of indenture, the commission scrutinized the actions and statements of the Chinese workers to understand their ideas about loyalty and disloyalty and the pervasive threat of violence against them.[61]

What happened when wartime disruptions led plantation discipline to break down? Like slaves whose masters and overseers had left their estates to join the rebellion, Chinese workers also faced choices about how to proceed. The commission could not reach rebel camps to investigate the presence of Chinese insurgents, but individuals who offered oral testimony or written petitions argued for their adherence to established hierarchies.[62] The petition of Chang Luan and thirty others claimed that despite the many planters rebelling and "endeavouring to induce the Chinese labourers to do likewise," the number of Chinese rebels "is not considerable." As they saw it, a Chinese worker, "born in a country where the principles of right are respected," was "able to refuse to attach himself to disturbers of law and order," although skeptical Cubans denied the "display of such feelings" and thus "use this denial as an excuse for fresh prohibitions and restrictions." Other Chinese emphasized that they continued to work despite the transformations around them; one "remained, and worked for the new owner"; another "attached [himself] to a gang of labourers and worked under its head." Displaced Chinese who could not document their free status were imprisoned or otherwise confined, and sometimes destined for public works projects, which could include military defense. The report estimated that 1,827 of the 1,932 people dispatched to the *trocha*—a massive fortified line intended to prevent the rebels' invasion of the prosperous west—were Chinese. And several men explained that once their masters joined the insurgency, they sought out Spanish forces for service. Wang T'in-kuei, for example, disobeyed his master—"I refused to go with him"—but "ran away to the Government officials, one of whom I served as a cook."[63] Without the promise of freedom, loyalty did not carry the legal weight that it did for African slave-soldiers, but the Chinese involved in the conflict still seemed to recognize the value of loyal subjectivity as they testified to their exploitation.

Slave and free participation on all sides of the war shook up established assumptions about race and about master-slave relations, even though many such arrangements continued unchanged in regions less affected by battle and within cities. If civil and military officials fretted about the long-term consequences of the changing legal and social climate of slavery, they were far less speculative about the toll taken on the institution of the family, another social institution metaphorically frequently linked to the political order. The war was no less disruptive to masters and slaves than it was to Cuban families, but normative gender and domestic arrangements or structures were to be protected at all costs. The Spanish held long-established associations between the cohesion of the family and the cohesion of colonial rule. Rural evacuations sent white women, children, and the elderly to cities for protection, and rebels and Spaniards alike recognized the moral authority to be claimed by guarding their safety.[64] Slaves who built family and kin networks against much greater odds struggled to maintain bonds, often in the face of greater labor burdens placed on them in the wartime economy and multiple relocations. Despite these conditions, most women could not anticipate significant changes in their status as a result of the war. When insurgents gathered in April 1869 to approve the Constitution of Guáimaro—a new vision of national government and citizenship that did not achieve sovereign authority—there was no proposed change in the political status of women. In the context of nineteenth-century constitution making in the American republics, this comes as little surprise; but as a vision of citizenship conceived in reaction against Spanish rule and proposing broad social changes, the constitution's denial of women's citizenship made for a notable continuity.

In contrast to the opportunities it held for men, military service rarely offered an avenue for freedom for slave women. But several dozen of them gained their freedom through Article 3 for the kinds of domestic work that were extensions of the gendered labor they might have done within households and for masters. Cooking, nursing, cleaning, washing clothes, and even ironing all qualified these slave women to receive letters of freedom.[65] After three years of performing all of those tasks, Juana Sariol, for example, was able to leave the camp at Las Parras, near Las Tunas, where she had come in 1870 after fleeing her insurgent owner. Despite receiving only a single ration of clothing in her years of service, Sariol had often "helped out all by herself with the most zealous efficiency."[66] Manuela Betancourt, an African-born slave from the community of Las Minas, near Puerto Príncipe, had spent almost three years with troops—cooking and cleaning—and in a hospital—caring for soldiers stricken with cholera—before being returned to her owner at the Serecá estate at the end of 1873. Officers actively intervened on her behalf. Four of them went to the provincial governor to testify to her contributions, and Manuela brought along her husband, Anselmo, in order to seek his freedom as well in recognition for his own service to the Spanish troops. Such a demonstration of support by so many superiors led the governor to free them both as an expression of "protection for his loyal subordinates."[67] And with that one phrase, the governor constituted and rewarded Manuela and Anselmo as loyal subjects using a catch-all shorthand that reinforced multiple paternalistic relationships. Never mind that Manuela was the one who took the initiative on behalf of her husband; even if that constituted a violation of patriarchal norms that paired men's protection with women's obedience, she and Anselmo experienced plenty of other structured inequalities that provided ample ground for their subjection as loyal subordinates.

Although the services that these slave women performed normally justified freedom to the authorities charged with hearing the petitions, concerns about their voluntad were never far from the surface. How much agency could a slave woman exert without threatening the normative social relations that routinely negated and subordinated those like her? Interrogators carefully noted that Juana Sariol had arrived "spontaneously" to the encampment of Spanish troops when she left her rebel master. In contrast, once an African-born slave named Manuela Betancourt and other workers had been left on their own in Puerto Príncipe, they marched "without knowing where," and with unclear intentions, according to the overseer at the Serecá estate.[68] Other slave women confronted doubts and challenges when they articulated their motives for supporting the Spanish army, sometimes witnessing their claims to freedom recast as affairs of the heart. A *mulata* slave named Candelaria Almaguel infiltrated several insurgent camps around Holguín, ascertained the whereabouts of Donato Marmol's encampment in the Lomas de Miranda, and enabled a major victory for Spanish forces. Despite a commander's endorsement of her freedom request and testimonies that she had acted voluntarily, the governor of Oriente province denied the claim because Candelaria acted "with no other motive than being in love," following a man to whom she had taken a fancy. He also claimed that she was pursuing her freedom by "acquiring the protection of a *gran señor* [prominent man] by seducing him." And so Candelaria returned to her owner, who claimed that he had raised her "in his house, more as a daughter than as a slave."

Caridad Zaldívar had petitioned the captain general directly for her freedom in 1872, and her case—reassigned to military officials in Puerto Príncipe—was complicated by her status as a *coartada* (a slave in the process of gradual self-purchase) with seven hundred pesos more to pay for her freedom. There were few doubts about her contributions, which differed from those made by most slave women. Zaldívar had made her way to a Spanish column near Puerto Príncipe "voluntarily without being advised by anyone," but left several times "to the hills" to round up insurgents and present them to Spanish officers.[69] At least fifteen rebels—officers and soldiers, morenos and blancos, men and women—ended up facing Spanish officials because Zaldívar had either persuaded or ordered them to return to the city.

After Spanish officers testified "applaudingly" to Zaldívar's efforts in her Article 3 petition, the summary report declared that her efforts "did not amount to much"; it seemed unlikely that a woman "on foot with a child in her arms" could wield the necessary influence to affect the voluntad of the insurgents, especially the four officers who presented themselves. Rather than grant Zaldívar her freedom in recognition for her work, officials reframed her petition as the "weak essence of a poor sick woman who has lived shackled by the chains of slavery since birth." Her owner received the balance that Zaldívar owed on her freedom thanks to the government's "innate and magnanimous feeling of goodness."[70] The paternal state's concerns for its weaker subjects, not the willful allegiance of a loyal subject, informed the gendered logic of Zaldívar's claim. Characterizing enslaved women's volition in ways that reaffirmed paternal authority could just as easily raise suspicions about their motives for aiding the Spanish.

Defining as auxiliary the labor of women—whether performed by slave, free, Spanish, or creole—enabled its equation to the work done by noncombatant men of color. The early victory by rebels in Holguín in the initial months of the war left the Spanish volunteer lieutenant Luciano Martínez with a bullet wound in the ass. A city leader, Antonio José Nápoles Fajardo, reported that the *señoras* who tended to him included the wives of other officers who "acted as nurses" despite having no practical training, relying instead on their abilities "to alleviate and console those who suffered." By their side at all times was Antonio Orozco, a black phlebotomist from the *cuerpo de bomberos,* whose skilled contributions were folded into the *buenos servicios* performed by all of them, including a woman whose outsized "humanitarian sentiments" were attributed by Nápoles to having had "no family." Nápoles recounted a dialogue between Atilano Mustelier, a bombero, and his wife, Dolores Castillo, who had nursed him back to health just in time for him to resume fighting the insurgents:

—"I'm going to the Castillo."
—"They'll kill you on the way," the woman responded.
—"They'll kill me here, too," said the bombero. "Why not just join those troublemakers? Therefore, I'm going."
—"Then I'm going with you," Dolores said. "But our children?"
—"Leave them in the care of one of your sisters. Duty calls and I'm going. I'm not telling you to accompany me, but it will make me happy if you come. God will save us."

The choice here was for Dolores to make. Framed as a decision Dolores made of her own volition—putting support for the Spanish and her husband even above the care of her children—the description of her actions strays from common assumptions about women of color.[71]

Together, these cases further muddy the misleading distinction whereby "female slaves preferred to emancipate themselves through legal routes while men, according to mainstream historiography, preferred to fight."[72] Indeed, they broaden the horizons of loyal subjectivity to include Chinese laborers, women, and others whose will was rarely even expected, much less measured.

Loyalty Resurgent: The Final Campaign

Rebels had regained their footing in the war by 1873 and 1874 and mounted new offensives against plantations and Spanish military fortifications—albeit with fewer resources and in smaller groups. Spain, too, revitalized its efforts. After a second rebellion late in 1874, the liberal Republic collapsed and Spain restored its monarchy under Alfonso XII. With this transition came more energy and resources to end the stalemate with insurgents. In 1875, the reformist general Arsenio Martínez Campos arrived with a force of 25,000 Spaniards to share command with Joaquín Jovellar y Soler and put an end to the rebellion in Cuba. In many parts of Cuba, they confronted incinerated crops, demolished ingenios, and exhausted soldiers and civilians. The military campaign led by Martínez Campos, combined with his conciliatory policies that promised amnesties and pardons to the rebels and moderate land redistribution, contributed to the ending of most fighting by late 1877.

Yet this wave of fighting was not limited to eastern Cuba. By December 1873, officials in Cienfuegos noted a growing number of bandits circulating in outlying areas, and by February 1874, the ayuntamiento had mobilized the militias and approved the formation of a new forty-two-member guerrilla force for six months to extirpate a band of rebels active in the Cumanayagua district.[73] This required, for the free-colored militias, the appointment of four captains of color. The new guerrillas were to rid the countryside of any threat to the region's agricultural wealth. Thus charged, they searched out and attacked armed groups, captured runaway slaves, and guarded the sugar mills of dozens of estates.[74] Milicianos from across the island were to be organized into eight batallones de color. Prestación (the loaning or lending of slaves) followed the padrón (estate census) of 1871 and owners were permitted to substitute white men or free men of color for slaves. Distinct from the prestación was a draft of 1 percent of the entire male population. Slaveowners were required to send 1 percent of their slaves to work in fortifications and on the trocha, and those slaves would be declared free at the end of the war, with 1,000 *duros* for each slave in compensation to the owners.[75]

Like the beginning of the Ten Years' War, in which Spanish victories came on the heels of initial fighting by the voluntarios and milicias of color and by slave soldiers, Spain's renewed campaign in the mid-1870s followed a second wave of black and mulatto recruitment. A circular in February 1874 for Santa Clara province, for example, called for mobilizing the milicias de color and augmenting the bomberos with offers of a tax exemption in return for their service. Suspiciously, the circular did not call for the formal enlistment or even the willful loyalty of slaves. Instead, it called for the prestación throughout the region, including sugar plantations.[76]

Municipal leaders in Cienfuegos did not wait for approval from Madrid to step up plans to suffocate the insurgency. Late in 1873, the Junta de Armamento y Defensa of the new Casino Español pushed through the ayuntamiento a new tax that would finance a new and larger army to defend the city.[77] In February 1874, the council called for a new guerrilla force of forty-two soldiers and two officials to fight new rebel bands that had descended on the city's hinterlands. In May and June, it called for a draft for new militias comprising single white men between 20 and 45 and single men of African descent between 20 and 30 who were not already voluntarios. The different age guidelines may have served to sustain rural and urban economies, already disrupted by war. The draft raised a milicia de color of 140 soldiers and a *milicia de blancos* of 150.[78] On hearing the news of the restoration, *cienfuegueros* held a parade in which the bomberos and voluntarios marched. The ayuntamiento sent "an expression of loyal and monarchical ideals" to the crown; the Casino Español hailed the "salvation of the loyal" and honored "such generous and loyal blood" that bound Spaniards. Despite the continued recruitment of Cubans of color, public rhetoric about wartime efforts still adhered to the racially charged association with Spanish blood.

Reports of slave recruits trickled in to military leaders in Havana from Santa Clara, the administrative seat of Las Villas. In early March, officials in Sagua sent news of fifty-four slaves yielded from the draft; Remedios had organized seventy-one. By mid-March, no other regions had responded, and the numbers from Sagua and Remedios did not correspond to their respective slave populations. A worried defense of the low numbers came from one official in Santa Clara on 20 March. On 28 March, a telegram announced 256 more slaves for the prestación from Sagua and Remedios. On 3 April, word finally arrived from Cienfuegos: José de Merás notified the military command from Cienfuegos that the region's owners had eight days to comply with the draft.

Combined with the four slaves taken from the *depósito* (jail), the city had contributed 136 slaves in total, followed by 30 more on 8 April. Trinidad reported the formation of "a section of slaves," but did not provide numbers. In most cases, local authorities defended the lag time and low numbers by citing the difficulty of rapid communication and of finding able-bodied soldiers among the drafted slaves.[79]

The delay may also have had something to do with the reluctance of slaveowners to yield to the government's decree. The new method of slave recruitment caught planters and slaves alike off guard, albeit for different reasons. At the beginning of the war, hostilities had so disrupted the lives of many on plantations or farms that slaves looked to the conflict as an alternative path. In this later phase of the war, on the other hand, the Spanish government actively targeted plantations and farms that had maintained a fragile order amidst the chaos. Cooperative planters had provisioned Spanish troops and continued to produce sugar, even as both sides of the conflict routinely demanded, or simply stole, a portion of the food crop yield. Depending on the perceived loyalties of estate owners, Spanish troops burned cane fields and mills. To compound those losses, planters now had to send part of their workforce into battle, even as they paid taxes on each slave to cover the costs of administering the Moret Law. The cost of loyalty—in this case, a concrete sacrifice of labor and provisions—had begun to impinge on planters' profits and property rights.[80]

Perturbed overseers on the Santa Rosalía estate in Cienfuegos, for example, routinely reported receiving orders from Spanish authorities demanding the loan of particular slaves. As late as 1877, Manuel Blanco (who had assumed ownership of the estate one year earlier) received requests for the *prestación* of one particular worker. Juan de Dios received orders to join a battalion in January 1877 from officials in the nearby town of Arimao. When he still had not appeared by March, a stern letter from the province's military command summoned him once more. Traced through plantation ledgers and work rosters, the long-term trajectory of Juan de Dios's life offers a telling contrast to the Article 3 manumissions of the earlier phase of the war. Although Article 3 and specific statutes in the 1874 *reglamento* (regulations) promised freedom to conscripted slaves, Juan de Dios's subsequent military service did not lead to his freedom. He continued to work alongside Santa Rosalía's unfree workers through emancipation in 1886. Even a decade later, when he was in his fifties, plantation ledgers recorded him working nearly every day.[81] The Spanish military "borrowed" hundreds of slaves from the Cienfuegos region alone, and probably thousands from Santa Clara province, and "returned" most of them to their owners without freeing them. Prestación provided a means of dodging the loyalty bargain of Article 3, and even avoiding its own provisions to free slaves.

The need for military reinforcement from slaves and free men of color became less urgent in the new wave of fighting than during the first four years of the war, when a desperate need for soldiers facilitated the freedom of many slave-soldiers based on their service. Now, the Spanish government backed away from that earlier pact. Their loyalty unrewarded by Spain, slaves fought nonetheless to preserve colonial rule even as officials in Madrid and Havana continued to mount a racialized smear campaign against the insurgents. Sizable numbers of Article 3 freedom claims persisted nonetheless through the remainder of the war, but with an added emphasis on voluntad. In his own hand, an African-born slave named Ramón Gangá petitioned for his freedom in 1874 based on aiding in the defense of Puerto Príncipe. He put love of country—"so he could fight against the enemies of his beloved Spain"—above the limitations of his advanced age. He made no mention of his specific services, only robust statements of willful participation and support for Spain: he gave his services for "Integridad Nacional," he fought for the "glorious Spanish flag and always-Spanish Cuba," and he offered his plea "with the greatest voluntad and submission" from the national prison in Havana, where he claimed to have been unfairly placed.[82] His successful suit mirrored many others that emphasized will and the language of loyalty above specific accomplishments as soldiers or auxiliaries.

For many free men of color, the second wave of the war appealed less than earlier in the war, likely an outgrowth of concern about their ill-defined social roles. Although military participation offered status and compensation on par with those for Spaniards, potential recruits still resisted leaving their productive and profitable routines. Furthermore, the labor expected of them in military campaigns often remained relegated to manual labor and auxiliary services. On Captain General José Gutiérrez de la Concha's inspection of Júcaro in October 1874, he described the miserable conditions of sick and hungry soldiers who had the freed blacks in the Duero battalion carry their baggage and supplies above their heads. He complained, too, that exemptions for bomberos and regular volunteers impeded his ability to form more battalions of milicias de color. He found more success, however, in central Cuba with the slaves "who in great number voluntarily joined the companies de *libertos*, in which they served full of the greatest enthusiasm."[83] In Cienfuegos, the draft for the milicias de color provoked two attempts to excuse a free person of color from service. Juan María Arrillaga, a white resident, presented one thousand pesos to the ayuntamiento in February 1875 to exempt *"el mili-ciano pardo libre* Rafael Díaz" from service. In a parallel case, Rufino Gersa offered one thousand pesos for the exemption of José de la Rosa Román Artillera. Neither man was excused from service, but rather "returned to the bosom of his family." The ayuntamiento flatly refused the offers and returned the money to prevent the men from deserting. Although the rebuff by the government may have revealed how seriously it needed to fill the ranks of anti-insurgent units, the requests alone shed light on the trajectories of Díaz and Román. That white residents offered the money for the exemption sug-gests deep personal or material ties to the free milicianos. The economic bond seems the more likely scenario: one or both of the men in each situation saw fit to pay the government over two years of militia wages (members earned forty pesos per month) in order to devote themselves to other, presumably more lucrative, productive activities. Yet the statement's allusion to family reveals consequences, if not motivations, that went beyond materialism.[84] Like all men recruited in 1874, free people of color could substitute another person in their place, but Jovellar's pronouncement prohibited buying one's way out of service.[85] The property rights of slave owners ultimately trumped the rights of many slaves to their freedom through military service—and even trumped Spain's claim on the obedience and allegiance of those slaves.

THE SURVIVAL OF Spanish rule by the end of the Ten Years' War produced ambiguous outcomes for Cubans of color. One concession granted to the reb-els in the Pact of Zanjón in 1878 was the freedom of slaves who had fought for Cuban independence, finally backing the rebels' longtime promise with a le-gal guarantee. Yet the overall numbers of slaves freed by military service for Spain remain unclear. By 1875, five years after the passage of the Moret Law, over fifty thousand slaves had probably been freed through its various mea-sures. One newspaper account in 1870 surmised that Article 3 could possibly have freed no more than three thousand slaves.[86] Other estimates were sig-nificantly more moderate, numbering in the hundreds. Beyond tallying actual manumissions, Spanish officials were more careful to note the symbolic con-tributions of people of African descent to the Spanish military during the war, even when white voluntarios received the lion's share of attention. And although debates in the Cortes strategically characterized the rebellion as a race war, its deputies also consistently lauded the loyalty and heroism of Spain's African-descended troops.

Although a postwar overhaul of Spanish policy regulating the press and associational life gave new life to expressions of that support, the war itself set in motion a fundamental reframing of loyalty for Cubans of color. After ten years of war and division, an individual's conscious choice became a more consistent defining condition of the loyal subject, and much of the evidence favoring this shift came from attributing will and intent to the words and actions of slave-soldiers and free men in the Spanish forces. But choice had its limits. The war also made visible the limits of willful loyalty as the Spanish reinforced gendered understandings of work and choice, namely by valuing women's auxiliary labor over their value in military engagements. Hopes of universalizing the possibility for freedom through Article 3 were dashed with the turn to slave prestaciones near the end of the war. Especially as they interacted with Spanish officials, though, slave-soldiers gave meaning and shape to the loyalty sought by Article 3 of the Moret Law, and in negotiating a particular kind of unfreedom as slaves, they began to etch the initial outlines of a particular kind of freedom under Spanish rule.

Do the strong voices and assertions of will in the Article 3 interrogations evince what Frank Tannenbaum celebrated as the "moral personality" of Spanish American slaves? That quality—sporadically, if ever, transposed to a legal personality—supposedly derived from Catholic doctrine and "ancient" Spanish laws regarding slavery that made "new Negro slaves automatically endowed with the immunities contained in ancient prescription."[87] That it took until 1870 to codify the freedom available to slaves for military service makes that endowment anything but automatic, but it had precedents nonetheless. The interrogation of each slave-soldier—by no means a broad swath of the island's slave population—revealed so many different paths to freedom that Article 3 might still be better understood as a strategy for individual mobility rather than an affirmation of universal assumptions about slaves' morality or personhood. The futility of searching for the origins of the Cuban liberal subject should caution against overrreading the significance of will and choice into the slave-soldier interrogations and other testaments to the participation of military support by Cubans of color.

The significance of national integrity, on the other hand, only grew during the war as pressure mounted on the war's antagonists to clarify the roles to be played by diverse actors in ill-defined polities. Peter Beattie notes in his study of Brazilian military reform that Cuba, the United States, and Brazil all experienced military mobilizations in the second half of the nineteenth century that weakened slavery and its institutional supports. Comparing the struggles of Cuban rebels to those of Brazilians in the Paraguayan War and North Americans during the U.S. Civil War, he notes that "in all cases, belief in racial hierarchies hampered efforts to imagine a leveled and homogenized 'race' as the basis of an organic nation-state."[88] This was only slightly less true for Spain's national empire than it was for the Cuban insurgency. Neither the Spanish government nor the independence movement unanimously and wholeheartedly espoused the goal of a homogenized "race." The idea of an organic nation-state held appeal on both sides of the conflict, but those sides expressed similar positions in radically different terms. Thinking like an empire, to borrow Frederick Cooper's term, limited the ability to imagine a Spanish nation-state that incorporated the colonies in any organic way that extended the same rights and representation to those enjoyed on the peninsula. Despite the efforts to preserve Cuba as a part of Spain's whole, political inequality stood in marked contrast to the rebels' aspirations of ending slavery with their own liberal constitution. And Spain's maintenance of slavery hampered a transformation of racial ideology that would homogenize racial differences—not that race only performed the work of sustaining slavery. Even the role of the loyal subject could not fully be homogenized. The political vocabulary with which insurgents spoke of racelessness and nationhood embraced citizenship, freedom, and rights. Hierarchies may have remained, but Spain's experience of the war preserved a system of inequality by design within the folds of national integrity—a system that nevertheless continued to enjoy the support of many Cubans of color.

To examine the war by thinking like an empire we can revisit the explanatory power of race—that is, the idea that racial subordination automatically drove African-descended Cubans to the cause of separatist nationalism. Moreover, the ambivalence about claiming Cubans of color as adherents to a cause, wavering between rewarding their service and denouncing their supposedly rebellious nature, reflected an inability to predict loyalty and disloyalty in terms of race. The transition to peace relocated this ambivalence to a dramatically remapped political terrain. It also amplified questions about how the wartime valorization of loyalty would affect planters, soldiers, slaves, and free people alike and, just as important, the spaces and terms through which Cubans of color could make their loyalty publicly meaningful.

FOUR

Publicizing Loyalty

Race and the Post-Zanjón Public Sphere

On the contrary, the constitution of the Metropolis has done nothing to benefit any particular group, but all Spaniards, be they white or black. It is not the birthright of those who have more or less clear complexion. It does not inspire the absurd privilege of color. It represents what is called politics, in what is called government, to all organisms.
—Rodolfo de Lagardère, 1887

As rebel leaders and Spanish officials met on 10 February 1878 to sign the treaty officially ending the Ten Years' War, more radical members of the anticolonial insurgency continued fighting. Among separatists, conflicts over ideology and between civil and military authority led some of them to denounce the Pact of Zanjón after seven months of negotiations. In March 1878, Antonio Maceo, now a major general, issued the Protest of Baraguá, in which he and 1,500 troops continued fighting for ten additional weeks in defiance of the compromise reached by more moderate rebel leaders. Early in 1879, Calixto García led a new military campaign that he had planned in New York, but poor strategy and war-weary soldiers weakened its impact. The participants in the Guerra Chiquita, or Little War (1879–1880), frustrated even the fragile alliance that had taken shape during the war: they continued to oppose Spanish rule, but now they also opposed those rebel leaders who were pursuing peace. Ultimately they failed to achieve the scale of military engagement comparable to that of the Ten Years' War; the leaders struck a far more radical tone than the original insurrection, with black rebel leaders acquiring increased prominence and some white insurgents, aware of a propaganda blitz by Spanish officials warning of a race war, distancing themselves from the changing composition of the rebellion.[1] With the end of war operations in 1880 came small but enduring pockets of military and social resistance that would acquire the peacetime label of "banditry."

The wars redrew the boundaries of loyalty. They posed for the loyal subject concrete, if flexible, political choices to make willfully, in contrast to fewer alternatives prior to the war. Colonial officials could no longer rely on previous methods of suppressing public discussion, since those efforts, as they learned with the outbreak of the Ten Years' War, had been unsuccessful in squelching the networks of communication and organization that allowed the insurgency to take shape. After a lengthy and unforgettable reminder that the allegiance of its subjects could not be assumed or coerced, Spanish authorities gambled that widening the spaces for public expression would raise the volume of loyalty talk and possibly drown out the *gritos* (shouts) of revolution.

Those same officials also had on their mind the end of slavery. In 1880, it ended in name with the establishment of an apprenticeship period called the *patronato*. It offered "former" slaves, or *patrocinados,* meager wages and left intact their work routines and limited mobility. Working through local and provincial Juntas de Patronato (apprenticeship boards), so many slaves had obtained their freedom that it made sense to some deputies in the Cortes to end the period two years prior to the 1888 target date.[2] These developments gave dramatic shape to the social instability that preoccupied so many Cubans and officials after the war.

As for former insurgents, reintegrating themselves into peacetime society required a public disavowal of their anticolonial affiliations. In material terms, expropriation decrees robbed self-identified and suspected rebels of their property. No matter how insistently they comported themselves as loyal subjects, even remote suspicions of prior separatist affiliation excluded Cubans from administrative positions. Confronted with new limits on exercising voice, many frustrated insurgents (and ex-insurgents) chose exit: they left Cuba altogether and joined expatriate communities in other parts of the circum-Caribbean, in Europe, and especially in the United States.

Plotting another rebellion from afar presented communication and transportation problems, especially for African-descended rebels whose return to the island confronted legal bans on disembarking in Cuba on arrival from foreign ports. A group of "Blacks and Mulattoes residing in Jamaica" submitted a letter to Spanish authorities in the "year 1879, and 378 of our enslavement," protesting the maritime policy.[3] Their tone did not particularly evoke the voice of loyal subjects. They attacked the "arbitrary power" and "pedantic bureaucracy" of the colonial government that left them "excluded from the regular life of civilized societies," and their exclusion, they contended, "negated the justice that helps us aspire to enter the banquet of the public."[4]

To what banquet were they referring? The meager offerings of the paternalist public before the war favored famine over feast. The reforms in the wake of the Pact of Zanjón began to satisfy a healthy appetite for public exchange. That Spain had made these policies is a decision that might perplex scholars who consider the relationship between the public sphere and national (and proto-national) states. Jürgen Habermas, whose generative study of the public sphere examined bourgeois society in Western Europe, might have recognized in Cuba the prominent political idiom of loyalty and tight state control of press and public spaces, that had existed in Western Europe, but as a much earlier phenomenon that nationalism and the public sphere had displaced.[5] Benedict Anderson, who identified mainland Spanish American creole leaders as pioneers of nationalism, even ahead of Europe, linked the phenomenon in part to new print cultures that circulated ideas crucial for imagining independent states.[6] Without understanding the post-Zanjón reforms as a response to Cuban rebels, Spain's decision to allow an expansion of press and associational life immediately following a separatist war appears poorly timed and contrary to the goal of maintaining rule in Cuba. What the public sphere enabled was what Geoff Eley has called "an ideal of critical liberalism" *within,* and not against, Spanish colonialism; insurgent demands and the calls for change in the 1880s and 1890s constituted a public that was "as much an effect of its emergence as a cause."[7]

When the Cubans of color in Kingston wrote that they "have nothing to look for in the shade of the Castilian flag," they differed from Cubans who benefited from rebel pressure on Spain that encouraged public political deliberation on the island. If anticolonial criticism of Spain "caused" the extension of press and associational rights to Cuba, were opportunities for intracolonial criticism—especially that which aspired to the rights of citizenship—opened up for loyal subjects? At the limits of those opportunities was the persistent question of who could be a loyal subject, a question now reoriented to consider citizenship by Cuban men of color. Spain had opened up deliberate spaces hoping for a more vocal affirmation of colonial government; doing so enabled Cubans to link its norms and very existence to citizenship. This chapter traces the contours of the flourishing of public life in the 1880s with an eye toward critical liberalism's limits and possibilities.

Repressing Revolution in Santiago de Cuba

One of the first proclamations by Carlos Manuel de Céspedes and other rebel leaders vowed that if Spain recognized freedom of reunion, press, and conscience, it "would find in Cuba a loving daughter."[8] After the Ten Years' War,

Cubans experienced unprecedented opportunities to exercise political voice, and many of those Cubans expressed themselves in the language of loyalty.

The peace treaty made some significant compromises with those who turned against colonial rule in the preceding decade. Spain offered a general amnesty to rebels, who nevertheless continued to face persecution, and it appeased demands for immediate and total slave emancipation by freeing those slaves and Asian indentured workers who had fought in the rebel army, thus neutralizing one of Spain's most radical incentives for attracting slaves' loyalty.[9] On the economic front, Spain made no real concessions, working quickly later in the year to impose taxes that would place the burden of wartime expenses on Cubans. But by loosening press and association restrictions and sanctioning political parties, and allowing Spanish liberal Arsenio Martínez Campos to police them as captain general of the island, the Spanish had given Cubans a starting point from which they could contribute to an emerging national/imperial agenda.

The pact bestowed upon Cuba some of the limited measures of tolerance and inclusion that Spaniards had recently won in the Constitution of 1876, which the Restoration monarchy hoped would stymie revolutionary currents within Spain. For the first time since 1837, Cubans had representation in the Cortes: twenty-four deputies to be chosen from the six newly delineated provinces on the island.[10] On 28 December 1878, the Cortes promulgated an electoral law for Cuba, albeit one that imposed far stricter qualifications for voting than those that existed in Spain. All voters in the Spanish system paid a tax based on either their commercial and industrial assets or on their rural and urban properties. The 125-*peseta* flat tax for Cubans was a remarkable burden in comparison to the 25 pesetas that Spaniards paid on property and 50 pesetas on assets. The explicit rationale for the increase was to exclude Cuba's growing middle class, its small landholders and petty merchants all believed to be susceptible to separatist ideas. Although no slaves could vote, the Cortes did not restrict suffrage or office holding to whites. Those African-descended Cuban men who had been free for at least three years and who paid the tax could vote, and those who had been free for at least ten years could, in theory, hold office.[11] The law also allowed for more inclusive municipal elections and political parties, and by the end of 1878 Cuba had inaugurated versions of Spain's Partido Liberal (often called the Liberal, Autonomist, or Liberal Autonomist Party in Cuba) and conservative Partido Unión Constitucional (often called the Conservative Party).[12] (The Partido Revolucionario Cubano, organized by José Martí, formed in exile in New York and Tampa because separatist politics were not accommodated by the post-Zanjón reforms.)

Yet efforts to draw Cubans back into the Spanish orbit did not end with limited electoral participation. Spain extended to Cuba the civil rights guaranteed to Spaniards by Article 13 of their constitution: "Every Spaniard has the right: to freely utter their ideas and opinions, in word and in speech, having access to press and to other similar methods, without subjection to the prior censorship; to meet peacefully; to associate for the purposes of human life; to direct individual and collective petitions to the King, the Cortes, and the authorities."[13] Note the absence of references to citizenship: the language defining this public right reproduced the distinction between Spaniards and citizens made in the 1812 Constitution. In other words, the constitution extended new rights to public expression and reaffirmed old privileges of petition to those born in Spanish territory without necessarily extending citizenship to them. To administer the new demands that the reform would generate, the government created a Registro de Asociaciones, by which old and new associations would formally register with the state, and it created a press tribunal in Madrid to evaluate alleged infractions. For the many Cubans prevented by poverty, low status, or sex from voting, these additional reforms allowed them to engage each other and the colonial government in public discussion.

Exercise of these public rights began immediately. In October 1879, a little over a month after the Guerra Chiquita began, the leadership of the Casino de Artesanos de la Clase de Color (Club of Artesans of the Class of Color)—a social organization of free tradespeople of color—sent Santiago's provincial governor a *protesta de fidelidad y adhesión* (demonstration of loyalty and support) to "our dear Country and to His Majesty the King." Signed by the eleven members of the *casino*'s executive committee, the letter condemned the "criminal acts" of the insurgents who "hurl the country again into the stormy sea of revolts." The casino asserted that Santiago's artisans of color were "lovers of liberty" who would support Spain unconditionally: "In Spanish territory they have been born; Spaniards they are, and they have defended Spain for ten years, as individuals in the corps of Voluntarios, as enlists in the corps of Bomberos [firemen]."

As we have seen, the Ministerio de Ultramar in Madrid wavered on conceding that black and mulatto Cubans could justifiably call themselves Spaniards—"*compañeros* and sons," as the artisans claimed in their letter. But the governor's office was sufficiently moved to reward such "spontaneous declarations of patriotism and loyalty" as the artisans' statement with a three-day run in the *Boletín Oficial,* its official newspaper.[14] The military service cited by the casino's leaders represented loyalty to the Spanish nation that validated their claims to inclusion, and the publication of the letter signaled in some small measure that the colonial government took those claims seriously.

In the middle of a rebellion articulating a language of multiracial citizenship, the provincial governor and the Ministerio de Ultramar had good reason to publicize the loyalty that Santiago's artisans of color pledged to the crown. But the artisans' declaration went beyond the formulaic proclamations of loyalty that appeared in times of crisis or transition, and also beyond bet hedging or political clientelism.[15] Casino officials demonstrated that they were policing disloyalty in its most basic expression. The supervisory committee advertised that the casino had "entered a new era . . . to exclude once and for all the number of members of the Casino who directly or indirectly are supposed to have taken part in the criminal rebellion . . . against the Government and the existing legality."[16] Earlier in the month, the casino had purged members who sympathized with the separatist cause.

Also, when they recounted their history of military service for the crown, they claimed in their letter that "it would be a great error to suppose [the artisans] capable of abjuring all of those antecedents after the new institutions with which they have acquired rights and conditions that before they did not have." The artisans drew a direct connection here between their loyalty, evidenced through their military service and their expulsion of rebel sympathizers, and its reward: rights and access to the traditional institutions of the public sphere in order to engender new forms of political voice. As late as 1883, squabbles within the casino over membership drew on ambiguous and sometimes arbitrary distinctions between insurgents and their sympathizers, on one hand, and those supportive of Spain and grateful for the newly bestowed rights, on the other. Juan Díaz, one of the vice-presidents, writing about dozens of members who had joined in the previous month, complained of subjective decisions to exclude those who, on this evidence, were declared to be former insurgents. And like the *cabildos* of earlier decades, he asked that Spanish authority be put to use in resolving disputes among members.[17]

In addition to Cubans who left the island, those in municipalities and in the countryside distanced themselves from the separatist cause as they sought to reestablish order in their uprooted communities. Residents of eastern Cuba, in which much of the combat had taken place, tried their best to put the upheavals of war behind them and to convince wary officials that the flames of insurgency had been extinguished. In the immediate aftermath of the Ten Years' War, prominent white pro-Spanish residents of Santiago expressed their confidence in the post-Zanjón reforms' potential to quell resistance by openly including African-descended Cubans in two significant public events. In January 1879, Néstor Rengifo y Sánchez had invited a large group of blacks and mulattoes to his residence to convene the first meeting of the Casino Popular, Santiago's first *sociedad de color* or *asociación de color* (society or association of color) registered under the new associational guidelines. After poetry readings and an orchestra performance, members proceeded to the chambers of the Gobierno Civil for formal approval of their organization, which enjoyed the patronage of two white residents.[18] Seven months later, Santiago's *ayuntamiento* (city council) staged an elaborate ceremony to honor two particularly loyal defenders of Spain: the *voluntarios* (Spanish volunteer forces) and the Batallón de Bomberos. According to the newspaper *La Bandera Español*, Comandante General González Muñoz addressed the large crowds gathered and thanked the bomberos, "gathered today under the flag to which they dedicate themselves," for having "come to demonstrate with their presence the loyalty of their patriotic sentiments and their love of order."[19] In contrast, officials had acted quickly just two months after the Pact of Zanjón, anticipating the formal provisional associational laws established in June 1878, to shut down the cabildo Cocoyé Francés after a dispute about the unbecoming nature of the club's dances, although the official justification was that the members had neither organized themselves nor registered according to new practices.[20]

But by January 1880, patriotism and love of order had not sufficiently cemented the members of the new Casino Popular. The morenos and pardos who had joined the organization had resisted being grouped together under the umbrella designation "de color," and they preferred remaining separate to glossing racial differences.[21] Moreover, military officials still reeling from the Guerra Chiquita's radicalization feared the consequences of African-descended people entering into public life. Adolfo Jiménez Castellanos, an infantry colonel in the Spanish army, offered advice in 1883 to other officers on how to curb subversive activity in Cuba. He warned of the rising expectations among African-descended Cubans as slavery waned: "The *negro*, once free, wants to have the same rights as the white: he wants to harangue in *casinos* and *ataneos*—black professors!;—he wants to rub elbows with the white in all social activities, to learn his ways, to sit in comfortable orchestra seats in the theaters, to enter brand new cafes, to show up at *tertulias* in a frock coat and a crown, to celebrate his meetings and discuss everything imaginable." In other words, Jiménez worried about the integrationist public stance that many civil authorities hoped would improve social conditions—an abandonment of uncivilized African practices for more refined Iberian culture. But for Jiménez, the trappings of the public sphere would induce the "prideful negro" to "want to subjugate everything, sweeping away everything he finds in his path; to plant destruction and death, burning the house where he was born and lived, and ruining the *patria* that converted him to a free man. This has been the thanks that they have given us for abolishing slavery."[22] In the wake of major reductions in the number of troops and the amount of military expenditures for Cuba, many military officials grumbled about the threats still looming after more than a decade of conflict.[23] Unlike the fighting, which had remained focused in the eastern parts of Cuba, the expectations of African-descended Cubans indeed rose across the island, and participation in the public sphere became more difficult to suppress.

The records produced by government officials attending sociedad meetings reveal just how precariously they ascertained the political allegiance of members. In the steady handwriting of an official scribe in 1879, the names of Guantánamo's Casino de Artesanos leadership committee named nine men; in a much shakier hand, likely that of one of the members themselves, are notes about several of them: "good behavior, honorable, and has no other knowledge than his work"; "is not familiar with seditious ideas"; "it is believed that he does not look kindly on those of *color blanco*"; "imprisoned for suspicion of *infidencia* [treason] during the events in Guaso in 1875."[24] The much earlier date of 1875—still during the war, no less—indicates that the list of officers may have been an old one that members themselves had to amend, and they did so fully conscious of the scrutiny under which they found themselves. Here was governmentality at work: the members did their own policing, governing themselves according to their internalized understandings of state power. They were often well aware of what roles they were supposed to be playing, and likely with hopes of avoiding more direct interventions from state officials.

What sort of public sphere, then, did the post-Zanjón reforms authorize? The institutions and organizations of Cuba's fledgling civil society provided a space, both material and discursive, that mediated relations between the Spanish colonial state and Cuban society. The public sphere provided the institutional arrangements for circulating opinions in Cuba about politics, economics, and society. Vitriolic newspaper articles, urbane *tertulias* and club meetings, and inflammatory political speeches became the media of exchange through which Cubans made sense of the changes (and the lack of change) taking place around them. Crucially, they escaped the bounds of literate bourgeois culture, which frequently modeled as the locus of public sphere activity.[25] Although these institutions existed on the island well before 1878, the capacity for increased communication grew exponentially with the post-Zanjón reforms.

In its scope and function, the invigorated public sphere brought the mixed blessing of state approval and surveillance to political discussion and dissent, an independent press, and associational life.[26] In important ways the colonial public sphere also sought to institutionalize separatism, to contain dissent within media that could be closely monitored by colonial authorities.

Seen through the prism of race, the public sphere had the potential to bring the private aspirations and obstacles of African-descended Cubans—that is, as the obstacles to their achievement—to the fore of colonial politics. It held equal power to bring long-simmering private racism and discrimination to a full boil, usually to the benefit of those of lighter color and heavier pockets. While the post-Zanjón public sphere established the rules for making claims to citizenship, equality, and freedom, those claims held special currency for individuals shedding their slave status and confronting long-standing barriers to social inclusion. Yet African-descended Cubans also had to tread more carefully in making those claims. Employing an emergent postwar racial etiquette predicated on continued and shared loyalty to the colonial apparatus, they could yield significant improvements. Making excessive demands could unleash surveillance or repression from Spanish officials who routinely equated separatism with race war. Thus the post-Zanjón reforms fulfilled the inclusionary promise of the public sphere that allowed many African-descended Cubans to situate themselves between the realm of high politics and the more mundane world of everyday life.

Anticolonial sentiments sometimes found sanctioned expression following the Ten Years' War and Guerra Chiquita, but the post-Zanjón public sphere primarily gave voice to support for Spanish rule. In part this was the outcome of conscious design by authorities; in part, Cubans themselves actively made it so. Although it may ultimately have provided a space in which separatist sentiment could ferment, Cubans operated within an idiom that continued to make rigid distinctions between loyalty and disloyalty. As ideas previously expressed and negotiated in private acquired public prominence, those better attuned to the norms and protocols of Spanish colonial politics flourished while those affiliated with Cuban separatism more routinely sought shelter away from a wary populace.

Havana: "Our History Is the History of Loyalty"

While residents of Santiago openly wrestled with the issue of eliminating the rebelliousness attributed to the east during the war, Havana's population boasted a robust civic culture with a long history of affirming Spanish rule and culture. As the military and political seat of Spanish authority, Havana also had the largest Spanish population, and though it too felt the effects of the war, sentiments of allegiance often drowned out separatist counterpoints.[27] At the beginning of the Ten Years' War, white Cubans across the island created patriotic clubs called Casinos Españoles, principally for the purposes of raising funds for military recruitment. By 1871, twenty-seven such casinos were in operation (figure 4.1). Founders constructed large and elaborate buildings to house their growing numbers, and eventually the casinos included libraries, schools, literary readings, concerts, and other performances.[28] What they did not include were Cubans of color. This was one more expression of race and loyalty that located pro-Spanish sentiment solely in the hands of white Cubans. But the casino in Havana spawned an auxiliary for African-descended Cubans—the Casino Español de la Habana de Hombres de Color—served as the primary (but not the sole) institution in the city expressly dedicated to affirming the loyalty of black and mulatto *habaneros* to Spain.

Strategically, casino members could invoke their loyalty to the crown to cushion demands. For the casino *de color,* this entailed holding the government to its postwar promises and assuring that the prescriptions of inclusion were put into practice. In 1881, they protested for equal treatment in public establishments by pressuring authorities to dictate special dispositions calling for toleration.[29] They struck a conciliatory tone that contrasted with the

FIGURE 4.1 • Casino Español, Matanzas. Courtesy of Cuban Heritage Collection, University of Miami Libraries.

uncompromising demands of former rebel leaders such as Antonio Maceo, who sought some of the same reforms. In doing so, members of the casino expected the government to reciprocate: avoiding armed conflict with the state might inspire a more generous response.

After a temporary closing, the casino reopened in 1882, ostensibly to guide Cubans of color to embrace an active role in colonial society through the association's renewed presence in Havana's burgeoning public. The casino planned an elaborate ceremony. When members gathered on the night of 11 March, they anticipated the arrival of Captain General Luis Prendergast to hear the speech by the president of the casino: Rodolfo Fernández de Trava Blanco de Lagardère. Well before the reinstatement of the casino, Lagardère had moved quickly to capitalize on the post-Zanjón reforms by founding and directing newspapers intended for an islandwide African-descended readership, among them *El Ciudadano* (The Citizen), *La América Española* (Spanish America), and *La Unión* (The Union). In addition to his leadership in Havana, Lagardère had also helped found similar casinos in Santiago de las Vegas and Santiago de los Baños.[30] His writings offer few biographical clues, but several details recur: he professed steadfast faith in God and Christianity; he was of mixed Spanish and African descent; he was extraordinarily well read in classical Western texts, as well as contemporary social and political commentary; and he consistently affirmed the principles, if not always the practice, of Spanish rule in Cuba. The captain general canceled his appearance at the casino's reopening at the last minute, and he sent in his place a high-ranking military official, the comandante general del Apostadero, along with clerks to record the full text of Lagardère's speech. It addressed the question of who the "man of color" was and what his role was in Cuba. It looked toward the future but was grounded in an interpretation of the present and past. More specifically, he saw the possibility of citizenship as reciprocating the support that African-descended Cubans had continuously offered the Spanish government: "Spain knows too well that we men of color want to continue being Spaniards. Our history is the history of loyalty."[31]

Behind Lagardère's deferential plea for the audience to indulge, as he put it, "my early age, my African origin" lay an impassioned defense of "the freedoms and interests of my poor race, at last on the eve of being declared free and citizens of these Spanish provinces." He struggled to differentiate the men of color from white men while emphasizing their shared loyalty and claims to citizenship. Racial mixture complicated the problem: although he never excluded those of full African descent from his political agenda, he acknowledged that through the veins of three hundred thousand mulattoes,

Lagardère noted, coursed "the blood of the whites. We cannot hate our Spanish or Spanish-descended fathers nor our African grandmothers." Instead of a fratricidal war, African-descended Cubans wanted "a more complete union" with white Cubans and Spaniards that entailed equality and cooperation as fellow citizens. In this direction, Lagardère argued for the Spanish government to affirm the humanity and citizenship of the "negro," "with equal rights and equal obligations as the rest of the citizens of other races." What made the "man of color" distinct from white men, then, was not aptitude, intelligence, or even necessarily blood, but rather mere appearance, and this was no reason to withhold rights and excuse obligations.

An eclectic blend of biblical and social scientific references grounded the statements that Lagardère made about race. He derived his notion of racial equality from "modern science," which taught that "man" is not free by being white or by being from a particular city, but that "man is free because he is a man. And man is also a negro." "Anthropology," on the other hand, had offered the "scientific dogma" that the blood and the humors (bile included) of the negro were richer in carbon than that of the white, proving that "colors are nothing but mere accidents." But religion also fortified arguments of racial discrimination, as Christianity "established the holy dogma of equality" and as the "yellow," "African," and "Caucasian" races emerged from the offspring of Adam and Eve. Challenging Bible-backed notions of black inferiority based on Jehovah's condemnation of the sons of Ham, Lagardère argued that, in turn, Jesus died for everyone and proclaimed "in his holy agony the liberty, equality, and fraternity among all races of the earth." Drawing from "an eminently religious, eminently Christian education for my race," he perceived African-descended Cubans as capable of taking on "the great obligations that freedom imposes." At once an exhortation to his audience members to educate themselves and a savvy demonstration of his own erudition, Lagardère's racial thinking offered ideological tools to challenge the racism that continued to structure Cuban society, all the while placing faith in a commodious empire that would uphold its promises.

In arguing that African-descended Cubans could be worthy Spanish citizens, Lagardère pointed out instances of their present, unrewarded participation in spite of the system's flaws. The ayuntamientos in Santa Clara, Trinidad, and Guantánamo counted "men of our race," he said, among their membership. In the *milicias* and *cuerpos de bomberos,* as well as in the army itself, "officials of the class of *pardos* and *morenos*" had risen to leadership. "Our dearest youth," he proclaimed, filled the offices of the Gobierno General and the classrooms of the Instituto de Segunda enseñanza . . . And just as significant was the growth of societies, clubs, and associations through which "we defend our freedoms within the circle of the laws" and which "are heard and attended when we approach the authorities."

The problem, as Lagardère saw it, lay in the inability of members of the Cortes to change Spanish laws to address the underappreciated commitment of black and mulatto Cubans. The paradox of abolitionist politicians who still owned patrocinados seemed to him at least incongruous, if not utterly hypocritical. Although he resisted immediate emancipation, Lagardère assured the audience that the patronato law needed revision. But associations and isolated ayuntamiento members, much less militia soldiers, could not alter laws. It was thus the responsibility of the Cortes and Alfonso XII to recognize that "its politics in the future will be based on the race of color, which will be at once the soldier and farmer of this dream," and work more assiduously to incorporate African-descended Cubans into colonial political life.

In his arguments for Spanish citizenship regardless of race, Lagardère backed away from notions of mutual aid and of self-improvement—the preference of indifferent conservatives—in favor of advancement grounded in Spanish patronage and participation in the institutions of Spanish colonial civil society. As opposed to loyal subjectivity reserved for exceptional individuals, Lagardère championed the need for collective endeavors that extended beyond individual sociedades. In slight contrast to single cases of black or mulatto Cubans who had used loyalty as a strategy for mobility, the casino's president saw racial equality as a collective struggle based on loyalty to Spain that demanded cross-racial participation.

When Captain General Luis Prendergast forwarded the speech to Madrid, he encouraged the overseas minister to pay heed to Lagardère's leadership among black and mulatto habaneros in "defending Spanish rights as their own and living *por España y para España* [with Spain and for Spain]." Prendergast identified Lagardère as "intimately linked to the Peninsula" and someone "whose erudition and well-being can be trusted." But Prendergast did not limit his praise to the casino and its leader. He defined Havana as the standard by which other cities should be measured for the degree of loyalty on the part of Cubans of color. He singled out Santiago as the city "where there exist people of color who are not supportive, because there the American labor movement exercises its influence." If peace, not war, had reigned in the east instead since 1868, Prendergast surmised, "it would change very much the disposition of the disaffected and would win proselytes for the Spanish element."[32] The black and mulatto separatists whom Santiago's Casino de Artesanos purged did not seem to have such a visible counterpart in Havana's more urbane meeting halls. Associations across the island treaded gingerly between affirmations of their loyalty and suspicions of their subversion.

Cienfuegos: Associational Life and Respectable Españolismo

Cienfuegos lay slightly closer to Havana, both geographically and ideologically, than to Santiago, and despite the absence of a polished and prolific personality such as Lagardère, associational life there heeded the lessons learned from similar histories of loyalty.

In 1884, the conservative newspaper of Cienfuegos, *La Lealtad* (Loyalty), and one of the city's more politically neutral newspapers, *El Crisol,* reported on "a gift from the King" to the Centro La Amistad, one of the sociedades de color active in the city. The article described a "felicitous" exchange between La Amistad and Rodolfo de Lagardère's Casino Español de Personas de Color in Havana, including congratulations to the casino for "the courtesy with which it had recently honored His Majesty the King" and thanks for "giving the gift of several works that contributed to the most rapid advancement of the industrious class of color."[33] Alfonso XII himself had given the Casino Español de Personas de Color four boxes of "instructive works" and a metal tube containing a collection of ninety-three plates from the national engraver, and the provincial governor of Havana had delivered the gift himself to Lagardère. The Havana casino appeared to be sharing its gift with affiliated associations of black and mulatto Cubans, including La Amistad, which likely deposited the engravings in its library for the benefit of its members.

The bonds of reciprocity between La Amistad and the Casino Español de Personas de Color refracted similar bonds that African-descended Cubans forged with each other and with Spain through post-Zanjón associational life. Although views of racial similarity and difference, respectively, certainly modulated those relationships, their stronger bond was shared loyalty to the colonial order. The article in *El Crisol* referred to La Amistad as "the generous *cienfueguera* society," hinting that the casino might have been repaying La Amistad for earlier financial or institutional support, just as it described as "eager the Government of His Majesty to procure the well-being and instruction of the inhabitants of this island [*Antilla*]" as a reward for their loyal subjects. The incident further revealed the degree to which associations communicated with each other for mutual support and how government officials in Havana and Madrid knew of and cultivated that allegiance.

Aside from such open manifestations of loyalty to Spanish rule, societies of color recognized that their inclusion depended on adhering to the rules of the new public sphere. Following the repression in the mid-1870s of societies centered around African-derived cultural practices, the organizations that took shape in the wake of the Pact of Zanjón carefully navigated the political currents of loyalty and disloyalty in order to claim rights to public speech and space. As evidenced by the maneuvering of the Casino de Artesanos in Santiago, many Cubans of color sought to follow the law to the letter to present themselves as faithful members of the community. Even at the most quotidian level, the new groups deployed the languages and behaviors of respectable, law-abiding colonial subjects in order to participate in the public sphere and aspire to Spanish citizenship.

Associations registered with the government by submitting a statement of their *reglamentos* (regulations) to the provincial administration for examination. This process applied to preexisting societies as well, including the Liceo—which had existed in Cienfuegos since 1847—and the Sociedad Filarmónica—which the government had suppressed in 1869.[34] Government approval did not depend on exacting scrutiny of these reglamentos; in fact, permission to inaugurate new societies often preceded the inspection of their organizing regulations. Despite being largely formulaic, these reglamentos revealed the norms and protocols that governed post-Zanjón institutional life. For the Sociedad El Progreso in Cienfuegos, its reglamento easily passed muster as much for a bureaucratic reflex as for its model organization, goals, and public self-image. On 10 June 1879, the gobernador general gave permission to "the *pardo* Masimo Coimbra" to found El Progreso, "composed of individuals of the clase de color in Cienfuegos." The society did not submit its reglamento for over a month, but the government took less than five days to approve it.[35]

Like most newly constituted organizations, El Progreso expressed its purpose in terms of mutual aid and wholesome sociability, pledging to "foment learning and morality, tightening the bonds of friendship among individuals of" its "class," with well-delineated social and educational activities. Its leadership included a president, vice-president, treasurer, secretary, board members, a librarian, and a porter. Sociedad members were often young, skilled, unmarried male workers—living in cities, they might work as mechanics, cooks, machinists, tobacco workers, and so on. El Progreso restricted its membership to men and allowed four distinct types of members: contributing, *de mérito* (those who could not pay), honorary, and corresponding. Except for honorary members, most individuals contributed six pesos to the society on entering.[36]

That money paid for the various markers of respectable sociability common among almost all associations. El Progreso proposed to open a Centro de Instrucción y Recreo in which it would conduct night classes for adults and, later on, a day school for children. Society members donated money and books for a library, which also subscribed to periodicals. On the first Sunday of each month, the centro would host a *reunión familiar* (family party) and with sufficient funds, it held dances at which *señoras* and *señoritas* of *buenas costumbres* (good habits) and morality could attend. The society's leadership policed these dances strictly: males in attendance over the age of fifteen needed to be members (sixteen was also the minimum age for bringing guests), and the reglamento promised that "indecorous ways of dancing will be punished with severity." It permitted "all types of *juegos lícitos* [legal games]," such as dominoes and chess, but not on workdays or following night classes.[37] Aware of the fine line between the gaming and dancing of civil society and those of the *mala vida,* El Progreso avoided the negative characterizations that influenced the closure of the Cocoyé Francés in Santiago.

Echoing virtually every other reglamento, El Progreso prohibited discussions that would raise *disgustos personales* (personal quarrels) or, more important, that would raise religious or political concerns. These constituted the terms of respectability and acceptable public discourse: the society and its members contracted with the state to maintain moral decency and a nominally apolitical stance. The unwritten assumption was that being apolitical equated to affirming Spanish rule. The Casino Asiático in nearby Cruces made this explicit, requiring members to "remain subject to all the laws imposed by our Spanish Government and respect in every way the mandates of the Authority."[38] It took the added step of naming Nuestra Señora de la Caridad del Cobre as its patron, as if adopting the island's principal Marian cult was devoid of political meaning.[39]

These societies organized themselves at a time when the government increasingly persecuted long-standing cabildos and *sociedades de ñáñigos* (secret societies or gangs for men of African descent), which were more closely identified with African-derived practices and traditions than with the civic culture of the Spanish empire. Government suppression eased in the 1880s, when a new associational law altered the laws of 1876 and 1877 about regulating and monitoring cabildos and *cofradías* (Catholic lay brotherhoods). It also allowed creoles to join their parents' cabildos, thereby extending the lives of the organizations that could not reproduce themselves with new African-born members.[40] The transformation came at a cost: whereas the cabildos once explicitly embraced African-derived cultural practices, linking them to Catholic and Spanish cultural forms, they now had to disavow "primitive" practices publicly. Recognition of their legitimacy had to happen on the terms of modern, "civilized" associational forms.[41]

Sharper turns from African origins occurred when some sociedades explicitly tried to cross racial lines. La Armonía, in Matanzas, had accepted members regardless of racial distinctions since 1879; La Bella Unión, in Aguacate, later proposed to accept white members; and El Abrazo, the newspaper of one Sancti Spíritus organization, stated in 1888 that it sought to unite "negro and mulatto together in ideal."[42] Societies composed primarily of African-descended Cubans nevertheless faced greater scrutiny because of popular associations between race and rebellion. Legal steps to diminish the "African" nature of societies did not eliminate the possibility that they would identify as Cuban, not Spanish, and attacks on those societies subsequently continued.

But in the post-Zanjón atmosphere of nominal toleration, that persecution tended not to take the direct and sometimes violent forms that it had in the past. If in the early nineteenth century cabildos and cofradías faced routine institutional threats that coexisted with some tentative appreciation for their monarchist intonations, a more capacious public in the 1880s and 1890s offered more consistent official support but far less tolerance for African-derived practices. Thus, authorities increasingly drew on tropes of respectability when they categorized the "African" or conspiratorial activities of African-descended societies and their individual members as dangerous or uncivilized. In 1880, for example, the provincial governor of Santa Clara notified the captain general of articles in a Remedios newspaper called El León Español denouncing the organization of a sociedad de ñáñigos and applauding the detention of the pardo Ramón Pérez Morales who had organized it. Municipal authorities made their case by amassing unfavorable opinions of Pérez from many sources. They took testimony from numerous men holding the title of Don to improve their case and numerous mulatas and morenas to lend accuracy. As Don Andrés Avelino Ruiz argued, Pérez "did not deserve buen concepto (high esteem) because he is always seen in the plaza dirty and wearing sandals." Others noted how Pérez looked young and did not wear a sombrero when he walked the streets alone late at night. In his absence of cultivated behavior, Pérez represented not only a social threat, but a political one as well. The specific questionable practices of the suspected sociedad de ñáñigos went unarticulated. As if color alone did not arouse the suspicion of authorities, a lack of respectability belied a disregard for the public ideals that the colonial state upheld, and thus forged an easy partnership with separatist sentiment. As Rebecca Scott noted, "'Spanish culture' and 'civilization' were more than euphemisms for proper behavior; they were values in themselves, in opposition to the concept of *Cuban* nationality."[43] In attempting to impose those values on Cubans, government officials fashioned a rationale for their continued surveillance in the corollary: that uncivilized and un-Spanish behavior made visible Cuban nationalist sentiments and needed to be eradicated.

Yet in terms of the impact that new associations in Cienfuegos made on governing institutions, clubs and unions did not have recourse to the new range of political and juridical means with which to influence colonial policies. Despite the inauguration of rival Liberal and Conservative political parties and limited elections, African-descended Cubans confronted a political system that still operated through long-standing patron-client relations and entrenched leadership that struggled enough to accommodate the new competing political parties. One of the few groups to petition the ayuntamiento of Cienfuegos successfully was the Gremio de Fabricantes de Tabaco (Cigar Manufacturers' Guild). A corporate group of tobacco industrialists, planters, and merchants in Cienfuegos enjoyed advantages of class and color that enhanced their clout relative to other organizations.[44] In January 1881 the gremio solicited recognition from the ayuntamiento, in addition to the provincial government.[45] In July it requested that twelve new individuals to be recognized in the municipal tax list as owners of cigar factories. In December it pleaded for control the industry "that has been exploding in this City." In response, the ayuntamiento ordered *alcaldes* of the various *barrios* to identify manufacturers by name and address in order to bring them under the gremio's control. Although the incident provides an instance of successful political action motivated by the intercession of a new association, it didn't exactly break ground in the pursuit of citizenship rights.

The scant references to asociaciones de color in the records of the Cienfuegos ayuntamiento evince a less successful record of mediation between state and society. In the midst of its bitter, protracted debate in the 1880s over racially integrating public schools, the council took the cautious step in 1884 of subsidizing the schools for boys of color at the Centros La Amistad and El Progreso.[46] These schools embodied their societies' goal of mutual aid by offering primary instruction to African-descended children who could not yet attend public schools for white children. By defraying some of the operating expenses, the ayuntamiento provided a stopgap compromise while the debate continued.

Despite the initial help, the council delayed, ignored, and bureaucratized requests for increased school assistance, especially those from sociedades de color that had not previously been funded. The director of the Colegio Santa Ana, a school for fifty indigent girls of color, attended the council meeting in February 1886. She requested seventeen pesos monthly to help pay her sole *profesora*, arguing that two schools for boys presently received subsidies whereas only one school for girls held the same privilege. The following month, the leaders of the Centro La Igualdad requested "some subsidy like the other Schools that the clase de color enjoy." The council, however, referred both matters to its Sección de Instrucción Pública for scrutiny instead of discussing and deciding the requests itself. Two months later, the [format]*sección* reported that it "cannot accede to what they request for the reasons that they cite," and, hoping to stave off future requests from other schools, the ayuntamiento denied the petitions.[47] It worked much more quickly in 1887, when the president of La Amistad petitioned for the council to declare his society's *colegio* a municipal school. The sección took less than two weeks to decide that there was no need "to make any alteration" in the status of the schools run by the sociedades de color. Two years later La Amistad made the same request to the same end.[48] Although the ayuntamiento was content to allow the sociedades de color to shoulder its educational obligations, it resisted the groups' attempts to claim political capital for performing work that the government nominally promised to complete itself.

Nevertheless, the consolidation of the public in the 1880s did not just amplify the voices of local elites; it also created the venues themselves in which old and new voices echoed and resonated. The ayuntamiento placed heavy emphasis on staging exchanges of ideas and *espectáculos públicos* (public performances). It sold lottery tickets to fund the construction of new buildings, and it installed chairs in plazas and parks, and along the city's main streets.[49] As *cienfuegueros* built theaters and annexed spaces for new clubs and associations to gather, the ayuntamiento likewise allocated resources to maintaining and creating spaces in which to foment participation, as long as participants played by the new rules of public life.

Newspapers and the Politics of Representation

So-called black newspapers, like most periodical publications sanctioned in the wake of Zanjón, occupied a less secure position than associations in the public sphere. Unless new publications—black newspapers in particular—had clear ties to the two political parties or official state institutions, few of them had extended runs. They fared slightly better when they were organs of specific sociedades de color.

Within that narrow deliberative space occurred some of the defining articulations between respectable public life and a mode of loyal subjectivity that might warrant Spanish citizenship. One of the few black newspapers whose contents are still partially known today, *El Hijo del Pueblo* began in 1885 and—like most other newspapers—cost only ten *centavos* per copy. It employed writers in more than eight different cities and towns to dispatch news and drew on the patronage of prominent individuals and *sociedades* in Remedios and Cienfuegos. Historian Pedro Deschamps Chapeaux noted how many black newspapers chafed against what he called the *integrismo* of Rodolfo de Lagardère that called on African-descended readers to maintain their loyalty to Spain.[50] *El Hijo del Pueblo* was one of the few newspapers in central Cuba that explicitly engaged in polemics with Lagardère and his Havana-based newspaper: *La España*. Nevertheless, it championed the respectable ideals of the theoretically apolitical public sphere and echoed the calls of other newspapers for educational and moral strength. Without education, for example, it warned that "we would be free in name, but slaves in reality." It challenged readers that in order to be "loyal" to their "purpose," they needed to forego politics until they were literate. It made the same call for aspiring politicians of color as well. In 1885 it asked readers, "For what do we need politicians who do not know how to read? They would obtain the vote without knowing who they're giving it to. The praise of the men of *El Hijo del Pueblo* is not destined for politicians, but for those who regenerate our social status, which is currently found in a sad state, for the conditions are not valid, nor are skin colors."[51]

African-descended women of the *sociedad* Las Hijas del Progreso forged alliances with Liberal and Conservative Party representatives alike to publish their newspaper *La Familia*, which began in 1884. They counted among their collaborators Antonio Medina y Céspedes—a poet, schoolteacher, and student of Juan Gualberto Gómez, the well-known black journalist and, in the 1880s, a Liberal Party stalwart. Like most newspapers addressed to Cubans of color, it addressed and republished articles and information from *La Amistad; El Crisol*, a Liberal daily; and *El Profesorado de Cuba*—all in Cienfuegos; *El Ejemplo*, in Sanctí Spiritus; *El Brujo* and *El Aviso*, in Sagua la Grande; and *La Aurora*, in Bayamo. The women of Las Hijas del Progreso initially had their biweekly newspaper published by the press of *La Lealtad*, the Cienfuegos Conservative Party daily. Six months after it began in 1884, *La Familia* announced that it would continue publication but had severed its ties to Las Hijas del Progreso. It remained under the editorial control of the formidable Ana Joaquina Sosa, who edited the newspaper in addition to running the Las

Hijas del Progreso school for African-descended girls. There, she oversaw a curriculum that included reading, writing, religion, grammar, arithmetic, Spanish and Cuban geography, as well as sewing, embroidery, upholstery, and crochet.

Sosa's dual management of the school and newspaper may explain the call in the issue of *La Familia* from 15 May to establish a benevolent society for children in Cienfuegos. An article publicized the idea of several cienfuegueros to establish such an organization to educate and eventually find employment for as many children as possible. In the context of a local debate about public education and school integration that had been raging for nearly five years, the proposal struck a conciliatory tone. Working in concert with the Centro de Remedios and other public institutions to advance the idea of the charitable society, Sosa and her colleagues at *La Familia* avoided the standard tactic of devising racially exclusive solutions to the problem. Although most black newspapers clearly followed the lead of societies, political parties, and other public institutions. In this instance *La Familia* itself took the initiative in attempting to shape civic life.[52]

The question of literacy had particular resonance among Cubans of color. Newspapers could have an effect on the community only to the extent that its members could read or hear the contents. Despite low literacy rates, Cubans in the nineteenth century were privy to traditions of listening to newspapers and other texts read aloud—in cigar factories, on rural estates, and likely in the meeting halls of clubs and associations.[53] In their calls for expanded educational opportunities, cienfueguero newspapers such as *La Familia* were surprisingly complimentary of the sentiments of Lagardère. "It is not enough to declare the *negro* free," he implored an audience in 1881. "It is necessary to educate, to instruct, to prepare him for freedom, for citizenship, to moralize and found families." Most African-descended Cubans, he lamented, lacked the basic prerequisites such as family and education for equal membership in Cuban society: "Without family, freedom is impossible."[54] *La Familia*'s writers agreed heartily, and they worked to strengthen these basic institutions that slavery had long maligned. Indeed, in their attention to family and education, both central to the biological and social reproduction of the population, the women writing in *La Familia* shifted the grounds of citizenship claims. If they fell short of claiming the rights of citizenship themselves, they nevertheless provided an alternative foundation to the military service often cited by men.

Mainstream newspapers likewise promoted sociedades de color nearly as frequently as they publicized others. In Las Villas in 1883, a newspaper described a conflict between the Junta Local de Patronato in Cruces and *"el moreno* Martín," a worker on the Mercedes estate. Martín had accumulated more than enough money for his manumission, but the junta had repeatedly refused to issue his *cédula personal,* the document that proved his legal freedom. The author painstakingly delineated the process by which Martín had not followed the proper procedure, thus blaming the patrocinado for the delay in receiving his papers.[55] Although the paper exonerated the Junta Local, the Junta Provincial, and the estate's owner and administrator for any wrongdoing, it did not explicitly take the side of Martín's superiors. In fact, the article offered concrete advice for patrocinados seeking to navigate the process of manumission that frequently remained unexplained by emancipation's gatekeepers. That a resident of Cruces wrote to *La Lealtad* in Cienfuegos to summarize these events only underscores the new possibilities for newspapers to educate African-descended Cubans, even patrocinados, about their new rights. Connecting rural and urban publics became especially important during *patronato* since recently freed apprentices often moved back and forth between the city and the countryside. How might a sociedad de color incorporate rural folk as upright members, and thus as loyal subjects, unless some structures on plantations and farms existed to instill practices of respectable sociability, if not patriotism (figure 4.2)? In this sense, sociedad leaders could often express the same anxieties that officials often did—often publicly, through the press—about the licentious and suspect activities of rural Cubans of color.

Urban life, however, still occupied the attention of mainstream newspapers, and the most open embrace that they gave to the African-descended population appeared in their routine reports and endorsements of the sociedades de color. The leaders of the associations provided the newspapers with synopses of their meetings and activities, and the newspapers published them, with commentary, alongside reports of the elite Sociedad Filarmónica and the Casino Español as well as the Junta de Obreros, bursting with "the desires that animate the working class to regulate wages in harmony with capital."[56] In 1883, *La Lealtad* in Cienfuegos published a sympathetic article about the rumored merging of La Amistad and El Progreso. La Amistad had made repeated efforts to fuse the two groups, despite animated disagreement among some of its members, but the proposal had received no interest from El Progreso. *La Lealtad* reported that the members of La Amistad felt snubbed for no reason: El Progreso had never actively rejected them, and the notoriety that the proposal had provoked would allow "the public to favorably judge its attitude in the future."[57] In step with the government's repression of cabildos, *La Lealtad* complained

FIGURE 4.2 • Cubans of color dancing, Havana, c. 1898. The tri-band flag does not have a clear symbolic referent but the design allows for the possibility that it is a Spanish flag. The caption described this "typical Sunday morning scene in one of the side streets of Havana" and a dance referred to as "up and down and all chassée." In *Greater America: Heroes, Battles, Camps, Dewey Islands, Cuba, Porto Rico* (New York: F. T. Neely, c. 1898). Courtesy of the Cuban Heritage Collection, University of Miami Libraries.

about the boisterous festivities that African-descended cienfuegueros held that kept their neighbors awake. A stinging article asserted that "he who invented the delightful instrument that ought to be the drum of the *negros de nación* [African-born blacks] should be in the depths of hell."[58]

The exchanges documented by newspapers in the 1880s gesture toward one more telling phenomenon about post-Zanjón racial politics. Public identification of racial status, or at least a relaxed surveillance of race, waned in the final decades of the nineteenth century in Cuba. Typically this trend has been attributed, with good reason, to the race-transcendent nationalist discourse of insurgents and postemancipation disavowals of previous potential markers of slave status.[59] Yet the emergent public sphere in the 1880s also had a significant impact on the diminishing of racial categorization in public discourse. Even as some journalists saw themselves as the vanguards of a social order that very likely maintained racial hierarchies, they relegated those distinctions to the private sphere, hidden from respectable public discussion. In shifting the line between public and private, then, they articulated a new racial etiquette that aspired to the social relations appropriate to national citizenship.

Race and the Public Sphere

To be sure, the disappearance of many judicial barriers for African-descended Cubans did not erase racial discrimination on the island. As José Piqueras explains, "Discrimination now came to manifest itself to a greater extent through the combination of norms and habits of conduct tacitly sanctioned by the white community."[60] As sociedades de color made confronting continued discrimination a priority in their public interventions, those Cubans who perpetuated discrimination faced new codes of racial etiquette: what should be said, what could no longer be said, and the effects of what was said. Proper *españolismo* came to include the careful avoidance of those divisive statements about race that elsewhere found a growing audience. Cubans who had long directed public discourse in the realm of high politics now answered to a public that educated itself about politics through the newspapers and associations that the Pact of Zanjón had encouraged.

Most ayuntamientos had typically comprised the cities' wealthiest merchants and estate owners. This composition remained well after the post-Zanjón reforms, when its members largely identified with the Conservative Party. In December 1884, the ayuntamiento held its monthly meeting at an auspicious moment in the local school calendar. This mattered because education represented a common concern within communities, and politicians seeking to curry favor with a population enjoying newly bestowed rights recognized the opportunity to affirm their support for schools publicly. Moreover, the visibly precarious conditions of many youth of color in cities was an affront to the ideals of respectability championed during the 1880s (figure 4.3) In schools for children of color in Cienfuegos, to the likely dismay of students, exams were public events to which their parents, teachers, and "all persons fond of education" were invited to observe. For the newly inaugurated schools themselves, these evenings provided an opportunity to display their accomplishments and to attract greater enrollment. The heads of the schools at La Amistad, El Progreso, and La Igualdad published warm invitations to their exams in *El Cristal* and *La Lealtad*.[61] *El Cristal* gave ample attention to private school exam invitations as an affront to the ayuntamiento. A group of private schools had invited the members of the ayuntamiento to a morning mass and a late afternoon procession of students in celebration of the feast of the Immaculate Conception. Disregarding the newspaper's call to all councils

FIGURE 4.3 • Group of Negro children playing in front of schoolhouse, c. 1898. The caption noted that the children were "members of the senior class" who graduated at age eight, and that "no further schooling for negroes is provided for by the Spanish Government." In *Greater America: Heroes, Battles, Camps, Dewey Islands, Cuba, Porto Rico* (New York: F. T. Neely, c. 1898). Courtesy of Cuban Heritage Collection, University of Miami Libraries.

in Cuba to "represent all residents of their respective Municipalities without distinction of races or religions"—the ayuntamiento members refused to attend the event and accused the school directors of obscuring the true intent of the activities.[62] With raised public expectations of the possibilities of politics, the limits of the ayuntamiento's authority had changed. *El Cristal* gave public prominence to private struggles over education, which the Spanish government had pledged to provide to its subjects. The ayuntamiento was now but one voice in an expanded conversation about race and education, and a voice answerable to challenges to even their personal opinions.

The ayuntamiento entertained a motion from the *teniente alcalde* (deputy mayor) Dámaso Pasalodos at its 15 December meeting to subsidize the Nuestra Señora de Lourdes school for African-descended girls with a monthly contribution of one ounce of gold. Pasalodos alone had recently attended the school's exams and was "left satisfied" by what he saw. One of the council's most senior members, Esteban Cacicedo, contributed the opinion: "Well I would abolish all of these schools for being unsuitable."[63]

Yet the following morning, the conservative Cienfuegos daily *La Lealtad* published a letter from Cacicedo that held the black schools in much higher regard. He lauded the exams at La Amistad and El Progreso for fulfilling "the civilizing mission that they have undertaken." Without admitting to his position on school integration or subsidization during the meeting, Cacicedo hinted in his congratulations that the private black schools provided "the system, and no other, by which the children of those classes, to those today who open themselves to such extensive horizons, [will] be, with time, worthy men in society and useful citizens of the great Spanish fatherland."[64] Thus the public served to conceal and distort sentiments that had long simmered in private. Cacicedo disguised his private disapproval of the black schools with a public statement in a newspaper.

But Cacicedo underestimated the potential of the new publics to disseminate information quickly and to pass judgment. *El Cristal* brutally attacked Cacicedo, "guided by his passions," for making the offensive comment in the council meeting.[65] One writer took pleasure in reporting the next day how Cacicedo had contradicted himself by assuming that statements in each of the venues would never be juxtaposed. Further, it questioned how *La Lealtad*—which regularly expressed favorable opinions of black societies—could publish lies from one of their loudest opponents in the ayuntamiento. *El Cristal* had the power to place the contradictory statements in full public view, and the newspaper was well positioned to challenge Cacicedo to explain how he was helping African-descended Cubans to become "useful citizens of the great Spanish fatherland" by "abolishing their schools, preventing them from learning, leaving them submerged in the ignorance that up until now has enveloped them."[66]

If Cacicedo's promise of eventual citizenship to African-descended Cubans rang hollow in light of his utterance at the ayuntamiento meeting, his complacent statement in the newspaper nonetheless reminds us that loyalty was as much the public default for white Cubans as it was for African-descended Cubans. The limits of loyalty derived in part from the private racism that still pervaded Cuban society and the unequal pressure that different individuals and different publics could exert on the shape of public discourse. As the public expanded, so too did public expressions of private opinions, including those contrary to the respectable discourse endorsed by the reforms. Increasingly, Cubans on the island and abroad saw the realization of greater political voice in an independent republic that would free Cuba from Spanish rule. In the meantime, many African-descended Cubans, in their associations and newspapers, held Spanish culture, politics, and society to its own highest standards as Cuba returned to peace. But loyalty to Spain provided a common ideological framework by which Cubans could imagine and debate Spanish citizenship.

Public debates between African-descended Cubans about political strategy and collective identification also acquired public prominence. Despite, or perhaps because of, the warm reception that Lagardère received from colonial authorities, he encountered many outspoken critics, notably among *independentistas* outside of Cuba and among other African-descended Cubans on the island who advocated a more confrontational relationship with the colonial state. Lagardère found his most vocal antagonist in Martín Morúa Delgado, the son of a freed slave and a Basque baker. Morúa was a self-educated free person of color from Matanzas province who launched a newspaper there in 1880; exiled to the United States for conspiring against the government, he became a typesetter and a reader in a tobacco factory. Returning to Cuba in 1890, he joined the Liberal Autonomist Party and became, along with Juan Gualberto Gómez, one of the two first African-descended members of the Real Sociedad Económica de Amigos del País, the esteemed institution of the creole elite. He is perhaps better known in Cuban history for his actions after independence: a member of the constitutional assembly, he became the senate president and drafted the notorious amendment in 1910 that banned the Partido Independiente de Color, the island's first black political party.[67]

After Lagardère accused Morúa Delgado of shorting a publisher forty pesos for the publication of one of his recent tracts, Morúa launched an all-out assault on Lagardère for using papers such as *El Ciudadano* to act against the unity of the *raza de color*. He centered his attack not on Lagardère's ideas but on his genealogy. He identified Lagardère's father as Don Pedro Blanco, a wealthy Catalan who lived in Havana, "dedicated to the humanitarian trade in African slaves." Having made numerous trips to Africa on behalf of what Morúa mocked as "honorable" commerce, he built a residence on the coast and befriended a king who was at war with a neighboring rival. Blanco capitalized on this conflict to acquire more slaves, and persuaded the aging king Manhas to "cede" one of his daughters to him for the sole purpose of strengthening commercial ties. Blanco named her "Rosa," moved to France, where she gave birth to Rodolfo and was subsequently married off to a Frenchman, and then moved with the child to Barcelona.

On arriving in Cuba, Morúa claimed, Rodolfo took on a variety of names; his first one—a reflection of his status as a helpless exile—was El Mandinga, a reference to an African nation that in popular lore was known for its ostentatious dress.[68] Morúa ridiculed Lagardère for having so many names and for claiming so many titles—doctor of law and philosophy at the central university of Madrid and *vizconde* de Illescas, among others. Faithful to his ancestry, Morúa argued, Lagardère should sign his name "Blanco y Manhas," not "Blanco de Lagardère." In diving further into his rival's biography, Morúa noted that Lagardère spent subsequent time in Spain and had returned to Cuba as a member of the militias, and later—after spending a short time in prison—reemerged to found the paper *El Ciudadano* and advocate for black passivity and baseless allegiance to the Spanish crown.[69]

What's striking here is less what Morúa vilified in terms of Lagardère's opinions than in how he traced the origins of Lagardère's monarchism— namely, through his ancestry. Without any corroborating historical evidence to verify the validity of Morúa's genealogy, such a dramatic yarn should be regarded with suspicion. But its cast of characters are telling: Pedro Blanco was not just any Spaniard but a slave trader, an example of the cruelty and callousness that undergirded Spain's wealth and prominence. And Lagardère's mother was herself royalty, the daughter of an African king who willingly placed her in the hands of Blanco for economic gain. In mocking the ostentation of Lagardère's public self-fashioning, Morúa's attack alluded to the figure of the *negro catedrático,* a stock character in Cuban popular theater who drew ridicule from audiences for his pretensions of wealth and education despite humble origins.

Whether or not Lagardère ever responded to Morúa's attack is unclear, but the exchange between the two men adds an additional layer to the prominence of the post-Zanjón public sphere in expressing relationships between race and political allegiance. Like Cacicedo's remarks in Cienfuegos, Lagardère's statements about race that might once have evaded public dissemination now came under public scrutiny. Occasionally, as in the case of Morúa and Lagardère, those statements bolstered claims to speak on behalf of African-descended Cubans as a unified community.

WRITING IN 1915, W.E.B. DU BOIS referred to the "cruel and bloody" war in Cuba that ended in 1878 "with the abolition of slavery" and a subsequent uprising in 1879 that "secured civil rights for Negroes."[70] He was mistaken about the date of abolition but correct about the war.[71] The story of "civil rights"—or at least civic or public rights—has its roots in the joined actions of insurgent demands and Spanish policy. What happened after that is a story of ordinary Cubans across the island transforming the nomos of loyalty. A commonly understood range of acceptable behavior in the post-Zanjón public had to be worked out through experience, and as public discourse increasingly circled around the issue of Spanish citizenship, evolving codes of conduct produced a form of loyal subjectivity to which Cubans of color could aspire. Support for independence or excessive critique of colonial rule were among the easier exclusions that Cubans made from what they wrote in newspapers and what they did within various associations. Other, more intricate considerations of race and politics also influenced the peculiar shape that colonialism gave to the public sphere. Although the policies that followed the Pact of Zanjón conferred new rights on Cubans, the distinct experiences of those of African descent in the emergent postwar public sphere reveal much about the tangled relationship between the rights of liberal citizenship and the maintenance of colonial authority in Cuba.

The words of Du Bois in 1915 might also have noted in the wake of the Ten Years' War a partial lifting, as he described it, of the veil that hung between blacks and opportunity. The post-Zanjón reforms, as José Piqueras explains, created "a civil society in relation to a political system that aimed to assure Spanish dominion but contributed at the same time to relieve the insufficiencies and oppressive character of dependence." For the thousands of African-descended Cubans shedding their legal status as slaves in particular, this new civil society, he argues, developed in tandem with "civil rights and education or access to equitable treatment." Beyond the press and associational reforms, the government took other steps to narrow racial segregation and inequalities. The Ministerio de Ultramar legalized interracial marriages in 1881. In 1885, four years after the Casino Español de la Clase de Color initially pressured authorities, the *ministerio* issued a circular stipulating that "people of color" could not be prohibited from entering and circulating in "public spaces and establishments."[72] By the 1890s, public spaces and forums allowed disaffected Cubans to advance the cause of Cuban nationalism and to organize and agitate for independence. If Cubans of color were attaining civil rights within the Spanish orbit, they did so in a political system that affirmed them as loyal subjects, even when doing so appeared to conflict with increasing talk about the rights of citizenship.

Thus although the post-Zanjón public facilitated access to the public sphere, it was not "multiracial" in the sense that public life entirely accommodated or facilitated a race-neutral society—although plenty of new associations admitted Cubans of all backgrounds. But this isn't entirely the point. The question is less one of who could or could not be an actor in the public sphere—despite the many restrictions—but rather what parts were available to the actors to play. Cubans of color who worked from the scripts of loyal subjectivity were neither improvising entirely nor being fed words. Understanding loyalty in part as a performance of governmentality is not to render it fake or meaningless. Rather, as Partha Chatterjee notes, "Governmentality can also create the ground for popular politics to endow itself with high rhetoric and moral passion."[73] Participation required adherence to Spanish norms and protocols and the general suppression of "uncivilized" African traits.[74] As it ushered in an unprecedented expansion of participation in civic life, the post-Zanjón transformations reordered social differences without necessarily constituting counterpublics, that is, publics that "contravene the rules obtaining in the world at large, being structured by alternative dispositions or protocols, making different assumptions about what can be said or what goes without saying."[75] Although African-descended Cubans often maintained, "consciously or not, an awareness of [their] subordinate status," their public institutional presence adhered to Spanish norms that conditioned loyalty. Beyond mimicry, they struggled to claim rights as respectable subjects without allowing meaningful inequalities and differences to escape public view.

FIVE

"Long Live Spain! Death to Autonomy!"
Liberalism and Slave Emancipation

Simultaneous regulation of free-colored labor and the moral and intellectual education of the freedman.

White immigration exclusively, giving preference to that made by families, and removing all obstacles in opposition to peninsular and foreign immigration.

—Excerpt from the program of the Provisional Committee of the Partido Liberal,
   1 August 1878

Either darkness had fallen on Cienfuegos unnaturally early on 20 October 1886, or none of the city's residents wanted to tell authorities who had initiated a disturbance in front of the Teatro Zorrilla that night. The *cienfuegueros* who gathered for the Partido Liberal Autonomista (Liberal or Autonomist Party) meeting at the theater as early as six o'clock included many of the black and mulatto residents from the surrounding neighborhood. Yet most people the police questioned in subsequent days claimed that it was far too dark to identify the specific individuals who produced a tumult so uncharacteristic of their respectable city.

Perhaps there were too many suspects to choose from. The Teatro Zorrilla, built a year earlier to accommodate around three hundred people, was bursting with over one thousand individuals by the time the meeting began at eight o'clock. They had come to hear the province's two newly elected Liberal deputies to the Cortes—Rafael Fernández de Castro and Miguel Figueroa—less than two weeks after a royal decree from Spain formally abolished slavery. Fernández de Castro began his speech that evening by criticizing the government in Spain, prompting an outburst of cheers and jeers. Next, he claimed that the abolition of slavery was the result of the efforts of the Liberals, which led to a second interruption, some people shouting approval, others yelling "¡Mentira!" (Lie!) and "¡Fuera a autonomía!" (Out with autonomy!).

Once guards had quieted the audience again, Fernández de Castro reiterated that Liberals had secured abolition for those Cubans who remained in bondage. Outside the theater, over fifteen hundred cienfuegueros began shouting "¡Viva España! ¡Muera a autonomía!" (Long live Spain! Death to autonomy!). Some threw sticks, rocks, and bottles at the building; someone fired a revolver repeatedly. Inside the theater, people broke chairs as audience members clambered out of doors and windows and as people outside tried to push their way into the building. Fernández de Castro and Figueroa slipped out of the theater through a side door and fled the commotion, leaving behind over 10 percent of the city's residents in the throes of disorder. A rumor circulated in newspapers in subsequent days that a black participant named Pedro Jiménez had been killed during the upheaval, and authorities spoke of "an excitement among the people of color" in the city that had sparked the conflict. One eyewitness from the meeting said that the theater and street were "completely full of people of bad appearance and for the most part people of color in shirtsleeves." A guard outside, however, insisted to investigators that the commotion had nothing to do with racial tensions, that instead "it is a question of Liberals and Conservatives."[1] How these contrasting descriptions coexisted, and what that implied about the politics of loyalty among cienfuegueros of color, are the subjects of this chapter.

Although 1886 marked the end of slavery in Cuba, historians have understandably qualified the significance of its formal legal demise. Spain's 1880 abolition of slavery in name set strict limits on the freedoms enjoyed by *patrocinados* (apprenticed former slaves) in the implementation of the *patronato* (apprenticeship period). After 1886, persistent inequalities and discrimination continued to condition the meaning of freedom. As Rebecca Scott notes, "The abolition of slavery . . . had not in itself brought respect or equal rights, and the defeat of open political revolt had not diminished ordinary Cubans' resentment of Spanish privilege and elite opportunism."[2] Excluded from most electoral lists and limited in their economic options, most former slaves—and people of color and Cubans on the whole—indeed found no lack of grievances with conditions enabled by Spanish rule. That resentment did not necessarily radicalize them, but racial subjugation foreshortened possibilities for new social formations with the end of slavery, including those that did not require the work of race as much as they had in the past.

The formal conclusion of the patronato did matter enough that politicians such as Fernández de Castro and Figueroa embraced it as a political triumph for their party and that over two thousand cienfuegueros violently disagreed. Politicians had been tinkering with the laws that regulated slavery and abolition for years, and in some respects the end of the patronato was as much a success story for a new partisan politics as it was a nonevent for many Cubans unaffected by the measure. Zooming in on Cienfuegos in this moment allows a glimpse of the extent to which these politics mattered for ordinary Cubans across the island. The disorder at the Zorrilla dramatized official and popular struggles over the meaning of formal abolition in the context of other colonial reforms. The Spanish government's authorization of political parties after the Ten Years' War gave Cubans increased representation in colonial affairs.[3] Because these reforms overlapped with gradual abolition, Spain's enhanced efforts to maintain colonial order also laid the institutional groundwork for an integrated postemancipation society. The flaws in that groundwork became evident as Cubans tested the limits of the reforms and as Liberal and Conservative politicians debated their merits. In addition, the partisan factions that had delineated the legal conclusion of gradual abolition also increasingly defined local networks of political patronage and clientelism. On 20 October 1886, cienfuegueros disrupted the Partido Liberal meeting based on an understanding of liberalism's strategies of exclusion.

Since the promulgation (and then repeal, and then promulgation and repeal again) of the Constitution of 1812, liberalism had captured the attention of Cubans. The post-Zanjón incarnation of liberalism offered no clear answers to the long-term question of liberal politics under Spanish rule, even with the institutionalization of the Liberal Party. Brazilian historian Emilia Viotti da Costa argued that liberalism can be best understood by examining its contradictions, in particular the contradictions between its ideals, slavery, and patronage.[4] Examining Cuban liberalism at the moment of emancipation through this prism reveals the frictions that had long been simmering in the consent forged between the Spanish state and most African-descended Cubans. In the late nineteenth century, Liberal politicians toured the island to seek the public support of ordinary Cubans, many of whom had little or no electoral power and may not have identified Cortes representation as a principal goal of belonging to Spain. The politicians spoke in theaters whose very spaces had become highly politicized in the wake of the post-Zanjón reforms, and they gave speeches that frequently drew upon a racialized and divisive vocabulary. The changes in the public sphere that the Partido Liberal had championed exposed the possibilities and limits that people of African descent faced in the wake of slave emancipation.[5] As a formal political event, slavery's conclusion prompted a reconsideration of the relationships between politicians and their supporters and of the terms on which those relationships operated.[6] The turmoil at the Teatro Zorrilla, and the events leading up to it, revealed the conflicts between the liberalization of the public sphere and the associational affiliations through which so many Cubans of color affirmed their loyalty to Spain.[7]

The Politics of Liberalism in the Post-Zanjón Détente

Institutional divisions between liberals and conservatives were relatively new in Cuba, a product of concessions made by the colonial government in the Pact of Zanjón. The peace settlement authorized municipal elections and the selection of twenty-four Cuban representatives to the Spanish Parliament. Initially, the main founders and supporters of the Partido Liberal were creole planters and property owners. Primarily, they sought greater control over the wealth that they generated and relief from the excessive influence of *peninsulares*. Established in July 1878, the party articulated a set of reformist positions over the course of several months, on the heels of a swift Conservative response with the formation of the Partido Unión Constitucional later that autumn.[8] Whereas propertied Spaniards and other defenders of colonial rule constituted the principal membership of the Unión Constitucional, the Partido Liberal came to attract supporters ranging from former insurgents to moderate reformers. Prominent Liberals had their economic interests at heart when they demanded the abolition of all duties on Cuban exports, further reductions of tariffs and customs fees, and more flexibility in trading with other countries, especially the United States. They sought the full extension to Cubans of the rights guaranteed under the Spanish Constitution of 1876 and the separation of political and military authority on the island. Ultimately, they sought self-government for Cuba in the control of local institutions, albeit under the continued tutelage of Spain. In 1881, the party amended its name to the Partido Liberal Autonomista, and "Autonomist" frequently stood as a synonym for "Liberal" in subsequent years.[9]

Liberals fought a near-constant battle against claims by peninsular Spaniards and members of the rival Partido Unión Constitucional that labeled them separatists in autonomists' clothing. In fact, Liberals occupied an uneasy space between separatists and supporters of Spain. Although they clashed with peninsulares and Conservatives over the degree of decision-making power to be placed in the hands of Cubans, they also recoiled from the radical solutions proposed by the *independentistas* that would threaten their dwindling economic success. Liberals such as Rafael Fernández de Castro argued that colonial rule protected Cuba from the disorder that characterized the struggling independent nations in mainland Latin America—including their racial discord. In an early speech, he warned against a Cuban strain of "the germs of disorder and revolt that have undermined the existence of the Spanish American republics, condemned to perpetual uprisings between class antagonisms, *odios de raza* [racial hatred], the despotism of caudillos, the passions of sects, and the lawless appetites of civil and military bureaucracies."[10] Liberals hoped to channel those sectarian passions into a new institutional politics. Whether that expanded the boundaries that defined the loyal subject became a principal debate within the party as much as between Conservatives and other political players.

In the face of constant harassment by peninsulares and questionable electoral results that usually kept Conservatives in control of local government, Liberals sought and invoked popular support to bolster their claim to a voice in colonial politics. In part, cultivating a popular following echoed a broader concern among deputies in the Cortes, who worried about a strained, if not hostile, relationship with Cuba's provinces. War and emancipation had created a countryside of free people whose loyalty to Spain needed confirmation. Deputy José María Carbonell expressed this sentiment in 1886 when he argued that the provinces were no less important to order than municipalities, "the foundation of Spanish nationalism." National integrity depended on conscientious attention to "the voice of the countryside, nothing less in a country eminently agricultural and in which, for that reason, rural aspirations and interests need better guarantees."[11] These sentiments provided the impetus for the *excursiones políticas,* or political tours, of the sort that Fernández de Castro and Figueroa undertook in 1886. Liberals maintained an uneasy presence in colonial politics, and they sought to reach out to ordinary Cubans to prove themselves as legitimate and faithful representatives of the Spanish government.

Among those itinerant Liberals were the men Paul Estrade calls "paradigmatic exponents of 'historical' creole autonomism." Rafael Montoro, Antonio Govín, Eliseo Giberga, and Rafael Fernández de Castro constituted the handful of party chiefs and deputies who remained powerful politicians in Cuba, even after some of them shifted allegiance during the War of Independence of 1895–1898.[12] Their public speeches, together with partisan newspapers, served as the means by which ordinary Cubans educated themselves in colonial politics. Despite calls for major changes to the relations between Spain and Cuba, the early statements of Partido Liberal leaders pledged their continued loyalty to colonial rule, setting a simultaneously oppositional and conciliatory tone. Rafael Montoro inaugurated the Partido Liberal in Cienfuegos on 22 September 1878, declaring that "the base of our politics, as many eloquent orators before me have said, can be nothing other than national unity, and the widest regimen of public freedoms." He warned of Conservatives "who want to monopolize power" and called on cienfuegueros to wage a "legal and peaceful struggle in which the triumphs cost not one tear and are of inexhaustible productivity in public benefits."[13] Antonio Govín affirmed the national unity of Spain and Cuba several days later in another meeting in Cienfuegos: "The peninsular has in Cuba his home, his heaven, his *patria*; the Cuban, at the same time, has in Spain his home, his heaven, his *patria*"; "together they are the sacred soil of the *patria*."[14] Liberals thus cut a path between presumed Conservative inertia and radical antagonism to present a unified voice for reform. In contrast to Liberal leaders in other provinces, members of the *junta* of Santa Clara Province, which included Cienfuegos, had neither rebelled during the Ten Years' War nor led earlier reformist efforts. Thus, as Montoro and Govín oversaw the election of Tomás Terry, Aurelio Rodríguez, and Laureano Muñoz as president, vice-president, and secretary, respectively, of the Liberal junta in Cienfuegos, they worried about more unpredictable leadership elsewhere and had good reason to publicize the moderate approach to post-Zanjón reformism that characterized Liberals in Cienfuegos.[15]

In its policy agenda, the Partido Liberal made top priorities of ending slavery (with compensation for slaveowners) and the establishment of the patronato. After that system took effect, Liberals championed its early termination.[16] This had its benefits from an electoral perspective. The Pact of Zanjón fixed the number of deputies to be elected to the Cortes according to the number of free men, which discounted the population of former slaves. As Montoro pointed out in his first speech to the Cortes in 1886, the Spanish government reaped significant political benefits by abolishing slavery in 1880. But the number of Cuban deputies (twenty-four) never increased after the law passed: "Now then, I ask: What is the legal condition of the *patrocinados?* Are they free men or are they slaves? Are they free men? Then correspondingly increase the number of deputies. Are they slaves? Well then you should make this declaration. I should add, however, that in the course of these eight years, the number of patrocinados has diminished notably."[17] Additional representation for Cuba offered, at most, more seats for Liberals in a crooked electoral system that almost always saw Constitucional victories. Translating that into legislative victories for Liberals relied on the questionable assumptions that freed Cuban men of color could obtain voting privileges in their communities and would be predisposed to support the party. At the very least, it augmented the Cuban bloc in the Cortes and worked toward the Autonomist aspiration of giving more Cubans a louder voice in Madrid.

Beyond political maneuvering, slave emancipation had moral, economic, and social rationales that partially resolved the signal paradox in the early nineteenth century that excluded Cubans from citizenship and representation. If the question of abolition sometimes divided the party, with slave-owners such as Fernández de Castro frustrated by the radical abolitionism of colleagues such as Miguel Figueroa, the division was sufficiently malleable for those two men to campaign together in 1886.[18] Newspapers weighed arguments for ending slavery in moral and social terms. One writer in *El Crisol,* Partido Liberal daily in Cienfuegos, characterized emancipation as a natural extension of Spanish ideas of freedom, stopping well short of linking that freedom to equality. It represented the crucial step toward bringing Cuba and Spain closer together, for "when freedom opened its gates to the people of Spain, they saw that on the distant shores there was an enslaved race, and they could do no less than proclaim the emancipation of those disgraced beings." To illustrate the affective consequences of social and national unity, the writer leaned on gendered metaphors: "The virgin slave will be protected by her lover, and the orphan will not remain unsheltered, because it will be reunited with its family."[19]

The conservative newspaper in Cienfuegos, *La Lealtad,* would have none of this. In 1883, it portrayed Liberal slaveowners and Spanish abolitionists as ignorant of Cuban realities—Spaniards for having never even visited Cuba, Liberals for their hypocrisy. The Liberal planter who sought to accelerate emancipation was the same man, a writer in *La Lealtad* argued, who calmly read political pamphlets on his porch next to "the *negrito* in chains," pausing between puffs of tobacco and cups of coffee to "order shackles put on Mateo for having broken the spurs on a fine cock the day earlier." The newspaper especially mocked the praise showered upon the Liberals by the London *Times* for their efforts to end slavery, so much more sanctimoniously than even the British had famously done that Cuban Liberals seemed "more papist than the Pope."[20] Abolition promised to deepen, not heal, political wounds.

No matter the partisan discursive battle about abolition, the transition to free labor raised new social concerns. Planters frequently invoked a labor shortage as the inevitable result of emancipation, a means of comprehending the unpredictability of postemancipation sugar production and of cloaking their desire to suppress wages. Liberals addressed this apprehension with a sustained commitment to encouraging immigration from Spain. Although migrant workers had been coming to Cuba from China and Yucatán since the middle third of the century, they did not provide the adaptive, cooperative workforce that planters and politicians desired. One of *El Crisol*'s writers argued that if the "Hispano-Cuban provinces" attracted white laborers, the population would not feel "the evils that racial heterogeneity brings with it." Chinese workers in both rural and urban Cienfuegos exemplified these evils and, to the journalist, raised doubt as to their suitability as loyal subjects: "It is such an exclusive race, so devoted to its habits and customs, that despite years of living in this country it has not been able to vary its dress or customs; its stores contain goods from its country and that they consume themselves: clothing, medicine, china . . . there is nothing from our country, for it seems that they despise it, to the extent that if they cultivate a piece of land they do not scatter seeds other than those of their own country."[21] According to the author, legal restrictions had long regulated the free migration of Spaniards to Cuba, forcing planters to use labor "that converted the countryside of this fertile land into a cemetery of the Ethiopian and Asiatic races, such that by natural law one can conclude that their introduction should always be prohibited."[22] White Spanish workers, on the other hand, would contribute to what Fernández de Castro would later call "the harmony of the Spanish family," already accustomed to the routines and practices of "Hispano-Cuban" life. In concert with other Liberal aims, the capacity and initiative of Spanish workers to cultivate wheat, cotton, cacao, and coffee would reduce Cuba's dependency on imports and foreign competition, augment foreign trade, and thus compel the government to reduce tariffs. Spanish immigration, then, complemented the most basic assumptions of Cuban liberalism as it offered a comprehensive solution to the social, political, and economic tensions of the 1880s. As colonial policy, it institutionalized racial preferences based on the assumption that the populations of African and Chinese descent constituted a degenerate force in Cuba's economy and society.

Emancipation and immigration were also on the minds of cienfuegueros, where by 1886 the effects of gradual abolition were in plain view. According to censuses, the slave population in the region (including the plantations in the city's hinterland) had dwindled from over 11,000 in 1877 to 5,447 by 1883. In the city itself, only 346 patrocinados remained in apprenticeship in 1886, compared to 1,710 two years earlier.[23] The precipitous drop had not drastically decreased the number of workers in the sugar industry. Other transformations of rural labor had a more profound effect on sugar production, especially the centralization of sugar mills and tenant cane farming.[24] The transition to freedom did offer former slaves additional mobility, and ledger books from the Santa Rosalía estate near Cienfuegos note brief, periodic departures by workers "to the city" in the months following their emancipation.[25] Canary Islanders and Galicians were arriving in larger numbers to the city and countryside, where, as Soledad estate owner Edwin Atkins noted, they "worked with the negroes in the cane fields."[26]

Planters also identified a related phenomenon that fueled their arguments about a labor shortage: the migration of African-descended workers to the Isthmus of Panama to build a canal. As patrocinados became free, some of them responded to calls for workers to leave Cienfuegos altogether for new work in a new country. The canal project drew labor from many Caribbean islands and surrounding mainland regions. The number of migrants was still small in Cuba, but a comparison to Jamaica startled Conservatives. Nearly 25,000 Jamaican workers had left to work in Panama in 1883 alone, and a proportional exodus from Cuba could have devastated the sugar economy. Locally, contractors had recruited two hundred workers to leave Cienfuegos in December 1885 on a schooner bound for the canal zone.[27] The *Diario de Cienfuegos* pleaded for awareness of the grim working conditions that awaited workers in Panama: "We hope that no more emigrants from Cuba will leave for this slaughterhouse," which promised workers "elevated wages that are perfectly illusory."[28] The North American overseer of the Soledad estate changed his perspective on migration dramatically in the course of several months. He wrote to Edwin Atkins in October 1885 that "laborers still continue to go to Panama, but at present we have more than we require"; by January 1886, he complained that "our greatest difficulty in the future I fear will be the labor question and our only remedy to pay higher wages as so many laborers have been taken to Panama and St. Jago. This meaning all the white laborers refused to go to work and the greater part of them have gone off."[29] The Cortes and the Ministerio de Ultramar had intended gradual emancipation to circumvent crises brought by sudden legal changes. But in Cienfuegos and elsewhere in Cuba, the end of the patronato and other forces generated real and imagined concerns about the future postemancipation society and economy.

Because these changes affected nonelite Cubans, the institutions of public opinion sanctioned by the Pact of Zanjón developed at an advantageous time, for they offered unprecedented potential for open discussions of political issues. Cubans of African descent faced limits on their abilities to participate in the new colonial politics. If the loyalty of free people of color had consistently been measured by their relationship to a presumed dangerous slave population, the elimination of the slave-free legal distinction only raised additional questions about their educational and civic capacities for citizenship. The challenges they faced were steep. Most lacked the material and educational resources to cultivate the respectable public personae that could mark them as loyal subjects—one of the many reasons that more radical affiliations, including the independence movement, could have held more appeal. In Cienfuegos, the Casino Español had no counterpart among residents of color, and attempts to make private opinions public continued to center on the development of other clubs, societies, and associations, and on the spaces where they could meet.

The Theatrics of Public Space and Associational Life

The process of finally extending full legal freedom to all inhabitants of the island marked an especially momentous year to test the limits of the post-Zanjón reforms. How would public life change with more Cubans of color enjoying greater mobility? What changes would occur in public demands for citizenship, since, first, the enslavement of so many subjects had long complicated efforts to include the island in national-imperial politics, and second, the ill fit between slavery and liberalism had allowed politicians in Madrid to dismiss or sideline claims to citizenship even by the island's elite? And how might definitive legal emancipation, as opposed to the gradual transition to freedom over the previous sixteen years, affect the loyalty of the Cuban population to Spanish rule? Certainly, allegiance to the state was rarely the sole or primary affiliation of individuals, and emancipation, combined with unprecedented access to public spaces, held the potential to destabilize the idealized link between public rights and loyalty to empire.

Religious and spiritual solidarities represented forms of authority that people could look to as an alternative to state power. And when Catholicism was not the religion in question, colonial officials gave rapt attention to determining the political content of institutionalized spiritual beliefs. One particular clash over associational rights in Cienfuegos sparked broad inquiry into the racial and political leanings of relatively new *centros de espiritismo*. French educator Allan Kardec (the pen name of Hippolyte Léon Denizard Rivail) explored principles of communication with spirits, and his writings caught on like wildfire in former (or remaining, in the case of Brazil) slave societies in the Americas, where some African-derived cultural practices involved communication with spirits and the dead. Spiritist centers in Cuba devoted themselves to the study of Kardec's writings but attracted a large following among Cubans of color. Clemente Pereira y Casines, the pastor of Cienfuegos's main church, halted a meeting of *espiritistas* at the Teatro Zorrilla on 31 March 1886. He appealed to the gobernador civil to deny the followers' request for official authorization. In letters to local newspapers, Pereira reminded readers that Article 11 of the Spanish Constitution proclaimed Catholicism the official state religion. It affirmed religious tolerance but forbade public displays of non-Catholic practices. Espiritismo, the pastor argued, challenged Christianity and disturbed "conscience, family, and society."[30] The *alcalde* of Cienfuegos, Juan de Campo, attempted to quell the conflict by explaining that his hands were tied: the Ley de Reuniones Públicas (Law of Public Association) from 15 July 1880 approved of meetings such as the *velada lírica-literaria* (music-literary gathering) that the espiritistas had planned.[31] Unconvinced that naming an event as something other than a religious display was a guarantee of anything, both Pereira and de Campo sought answers about what could take place in the Zorrilla.

Their queries launched a subsequent islandwide investigation of espiritismo that yielded numerous examples of meetings attended primarily by African-descended Cubans, and according to authorities, "in which they pronounce against the white race and Spanish Nationality."[32] Nevertheless, the espiritista group in Cienfuegos petitioned the captain general in Havana to revoke the suspension of their meeting at the Zorrilla based on "the legal precepts that help us." They referred to the public reunion law and to a royal decree from 1881 that extended the law to Cuba to regulate the exercise of rights proclaimed in Article 13 of the Spanish Constitution—that is, the right of every Spaniard to associate peacefully. The espiritistas had complied with the stipulation in the 1880 law requiring groups to inform local authorities in writing twenty-four hours in advance of a meeting. Such meetings were often advertised in three legally sanctioned newspapers—*La Luz de los Espacios, El Buen Deseo,* and *La Nueva Alianza*—that were "dedicated to the advertisement and defense of the doctrines of Espiritismo." A group of cienfuegueros petitioned the captain general and asked, "If in Havana and Matanzas . . . these meetings take place with the protection of the Laws, what motive, what legal reason, can exist for this city, under the protection of those same laws, not to be able to celebrate meetings of the same nature and disposition?"[33]

This question represented only a fraction of the confusion in Cuba and Spain over the limits of free association. Generally, secular groups encountered less interference from local authorities, who allowed the organization of scientific, artistic, charitable, and social groups.[34] Officials continued to monitor the proliferation of associations in terms of their potential loyalty or disloyalty to colonial rule, and Cubans of all backgrounds showed remarkable literacy and agility with the associational laws. The three weekly and monthly periodicals begun by and for black and mulatto cienfuegueros in 1886 attest to the presence of a literate, self-aware urban public.[35]

As a consequence of the associational boom, organizations and wealthy residents built new theaters. Construction finished in 1885 on the Teatro Zorrilla at the corner of Castillo and Bouyon Streets, which lay approximately four blocks west of the city's main square. It opened early in 1886 with enough space for up to three hundred people, and it competed with other medium-sized theater spaces in the city.[36] It featured public entertainment, including numerous performances by *compañías de bufo,* which offered the most popular form of public entertainment with their comic plays and vignettes (figure 5.1).[37] Bufo grew in popularity in the late nineteenth century as a form of music and theater that almost always involved blackface performance, and its coexistence with other features of civic life in theaters attests to the pervasive anxieties and preoccupations with race at the end of the century. Bufo companies performed pieces that commented on Cuban politics, with such titles as *Liberales y conservadores* and *Conflicto municipal.* As politics premiered at the Zorrilla in these comic presentations, formal political meetings tended to take place in other venues. Predictably, the Partido Unión Constitucional continued to hold its meetings at the Casino Español, the conservative pro-Spanish club, which hosted a vociferous debate on the differences between the Partido Liberal and the separatists in mid-January.[38] The Partido Liberal meetings often occurred in the Teatro Pabellón Campo, one of the city's most prominent venues.

By 1886, societies of color formed a complex network with other associations in Cienfuegos. These organizations often developed within the physical spaces that they claimed in the city. Although the spaces included centers and schools, the size and versatility of theaters gave them special prominence in public life. Only a half century earlier, Captain General Miguel Tacón worried so much about the potential for unrest in theaters that he briefly forbade applause. After the Zanjón reforms, audiences clapped at all kinds of performances. Political meetings and speeches, plays, dramatic readings, and dances by different organizations could all take place in the same theater. The Teatro Zorrilla, after all, hosted not only the Partido Liberal meeting that ended in chaos but also the espiritista meeting earlier in the year. Cienfuegos historian Victoria María Sueiro Rodríguez has argued that following the Ten Years' War, the colonial government attempted to impose a reactionary character on the activities of theaters, to transform the theater into "an instrument contrary to the aspirations of the independence of the people."[39] This was certainly the case: it was unlikely that any theater would open its doors for a

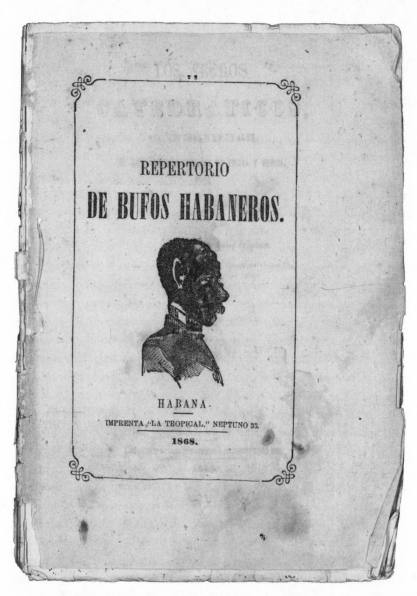

FIGURE 5.1 • Cover image of *Repertorio de bufos habaneros.* The volume features the play *Los negros catedráticos: Absurdo cómico en un acto de costumbres cubanas en prosa y verso* (The black professors: An absurd one-act comedy of Cuban customs in prose and verse), first performed at the Teatro de Villanueva, Havana, 31 May 1868. Courtesy of the Cuban Heritage Collection, University of Miami Libraries.

planning meeting for another independence war. But the political activities that did take place, including Liberal gatherings, occupied a spectrum of political ideas too broad (but not by much) to be considered universally reactionary. Public space could easily be divided along racial and ethnic lines, with many theaters converting themselves into "purely Spanish" enterprises: the Teatro Albisu, for example, almost exclusively performed Spanish *zarzuelas*. Other groups proceeded accordingly. In 1883, a theater opened exclusively for Chinese-descended cienfuegueros that housed performances by a company of Chinese actors.[40]

Sociedades de color embraced the theater milieu as well. A further indication of the post-Zanjón associational boom came in 1883, when the Conservative Cienfuegos newspaper *La Lealtad* reported that "the youth of the class of color have opened a new Center on Bouyon Street" near the Zorrilla that included a school for children.[41] This new center was on the same street as the building of the Sociedad La Amistad, one of Cienfuegos's main societies of color, whose meeting space *La Lealtad* described as sufficiently "spacious and ventilated" for residents of Cienfuegos to attend its functions.[42] The Centro La Amistad regularly held evening meetings with entertainment for men, women, and children. Activities of the Centro La Amistad ranged from magic shows by "Sr. Jiménez, El Negro Brujo" to poetry readings and plays to dances. The educational and mutual aid functions provided members with tools that the municipal government, to say nothing of the overseas ministry in Madrid, were slow to offer.

In other moments, however, members of La Amistad acted as part of a larger civic community that included Cubans of all backgrounds who expressed loyalty to the Spanish government and even to Spaniards themselves. Throughout September and October 1885, the theater at the Centro La Amistad held widely publicized benefit performances by a bufo company, "the first company of people of color that has begun to travel throughout the principal populations of the island," which had arrived in Cienfuegos for several months. It was directed by Federico Pedrosa, a well-known bufo author, a former performer, and—according to the local newspaper *El Fénix*—"a young man of color."[43] Pedrosa directed his own works for the benefits, and publicity subtly noted that white Cubans were especially welcome. The proceeds from his performances did not help the members of the company or La Amistad. Instead, they went to Spain to help "the disgraced provinces of the Peninsula," "the disgraced who suffer the consequences of cholera in the Mother Country."[44]

News of a cholera epidemic in Spain in 1885 had reached as far as rural communities, farms, and plantations around Cienfuegos, and charitable efforts flourished. Patrocinados and free workers on the Santa Rosalía sugar estate, for instance, donated small portions of their meager wages to help victims and their families.[45] Centro La Amistad's more centralized, organized, and lucrative fundraising garnered widespread praise from newspapers and municipal leaders. As much as the society's activities may have affirmed a racial identification as a patron of performers of color, their public self-fashionings did not simply assert a racially exclusive "Afro-Cuban" or "Pan-African" identity.[46] The society also staked a claim to membership in a larger colonial political community, one that might have promised more symbolic than material rewards for the loyalty of La Amistad's members, but one that benefited nonetheless from their civic and financial contributions.

A multiracial civic identity sometimes allowed for some flexibility within the general segregation of associational space, as various centros and sociedades in Cienfuegos lent out their buildings to other organizations for functions. The leadership committee of the Gremio de Obreros del Ramo de Tabaquerías—the cigar makers' union and the principal labor union in Cuba between 1878 and 1886—held a meeting on a Sunday morning in October 1885 at the Centro La Igualdad, the space held by the similarly named sociedad de color.[47] A performance of Pedrosa's Compañía de Bufos de Color moved, on very short notice, to the nearby Centro Artesano.[48] In the middle of May 1886, the Casino Gran China advertised a three-day series of "fiestas de costumbre," to which were invited "all of the *asiáticos* [Asians]," and, "on the last day, the *clase de color*."[49] However, the newspaper *El Fénix* reported that police took a *pardo* to their headquarters in late August for throwing rocks at the casino. The contested spaces revealed a fractured public sphere—or, at the very least, an interest on the part of police and journalists in highlighting racial and ethnic tensions between cienfuegueros of different backgrounds. Thus a familiar colonial dynamic of racial division could coexist with a common identification with the mother country. Even these acts could constitute sociedad members as loyal subjects with a broad vision of imperial solidarity.

By February 1886, some degree of conflict or rivalry appeared to be brewing between the Teatro Zorrilla and the Centro La Amistad. On 27 February, the *Diario de Cienfuegos* abruptly announced that "tonight [the compañía de bufos] works in the Centro La Amistad, as a result of having terminated the dates that they had with the Business of the Teatro Zorrilla."[50] Two days later, the newspaper reported that the Zorrilla would begin performances by a "new zarzuela company organizing these days," while the Compañía Bufa gave two performances over the weekend at La Amistad, "where they hope to remain for some time."[51] Weeks later, the Zorrilla boasted such large audiences that it scheduled additional performances of such works as *La mulata de rango* (The ranking mulata) and *La mala raza* (The bad race). On 17 October, just two days before the disturbance erupted at the Zorrilla, the theater hosted a meeting of the Galician-born Spaniards in Cienfuegos to explore the formation of a Sociedad de Beneficencia, a charity and mutual-aid society.[52] Although sources do not reveal details about the theatrical companies, the performances, and the audiences, the increasing polarization between the Zorrilla and La Amistad suggests that the urban population by October felt allegiances to particular theaters that delineated racial solidarities. As Cubans of color sought a presence in public spaces, associations, and forums, they confronted social impediments that tipped the resources of public opinion in favor of less marginalized groups. Their exclusion, voluntary or not, from the Zorrilla and from some of the public and political events that took place there likely amplified the controversy surrounding the Partido Liberal meeting on 20 October.

Liberalism, Now in Theaters Near You

In this environment fragmented by race, associational affiliations, and public space, Rafael Fernández de Castro and Miguel Figueroa attempted to cultivate popular loyalty to themselves and to the Partido Liberal. In 1886, the men campaigned for two of the six seats in the Cortes reserved for representatives of Santa Clara province. Throughout the year, they visited countless cities in Santa Clara and even other parts of Cuba. Although Figueroa was no less prominent than Fernández de Castro in party politics, he took a supporting role in the excursiones políticas and rarely gave speeches. Together, they appeared at centers, clubs and associations, and theaters with varying connections to the Partido Liberal, and, of course, at local party meetings themselves. By the end of 1886, they had visited Santa Clara, Sagua la Grande, Cienfuegos, Remedios, Sancti-Spíritus, Trinidad, and other small towns in the province. Fernández de Castro coined the tour an "excursión política," the first trip he had taken with Figueroa, "my unforgettable friend and *compañero.*" He had made a similar trip several years earlier with Rafael Montoro, in what constituted the most direct contact that Liberal politicians had with the Cuban populations for whom they spoke.[53] In light of the worries that Cortes deputies expressed about their tenuous ties to Cuba's provincial population, the excursión had added significance as an attempt to communicate ideas about colonial government to the public.

In pivotal moments during his tour, Fernández de Castro peppered his remarks with discourteous swipes at Conservatives that often played on racial stereotypes. During a speech in Cerro in September, he cautioned against taking for granted the Liberal presence in Spanish politics. The battle with the Partido Unión Constitucional required sustained vigilance: "Our *constitucionales* are simply and essentially the conservatives of this society; but not of the style of the conservatives of European people, rather, in the style of primitive African societies: they are the ferocious reactionaries, systematic and eternal enemies of the freedom of this land in which they have received all that they have and where they have achieved all that they are and all that they are worth."[54] The struggle against conservatism, then, did not embody high-minded political ideas as much as what Fernández de Castro saw as Cuban society's most dangerous and retrograde elements: African-descended people and their unsophisticated capacity for loyalty, which could shift as easily to "primitive African societies" as to the ferocious reactionaries in the Conservative Party. In the months preceding the formal end of slavery, he bore witness to the ideological compatibility of abolitionism and racism and communicated his political statements in the language of race. He made a weak case for the broad extension of citizenship to Cubans of color.

One week before the elections, Fernández de Castro once again appealed to racial antagonisms when he spoke in Cienfuegos on Monday, 29 March at the Teatro Pabellón Campo. He came accompanied not by Miguel Figueroa, who was in Remedios "to make good," but with Antonio Govín, the secretary of the general committee of the Partido Liberal Autonomista. The secretary did most of the talking during the meeting of two-and-one-half hours, but Fernández de Castro gave brief opening remarks. Although the *Diario de Cienfuegos* reported that he spoke "with a certain moderation," he blamed Conservatives for Cuba's problems and proceeded "to depict the class of color with the same point of view as Saco, that is, as an inferior race that was not right for Cuba. It goes without saying the effect that such words had in one part of the auditorium."[55] Fernández de Castro referred here to José Antonio Saco, the early nineteenth-century creole planter and intellectual who warned of slavery's social menace and who advocated white immigration to ensure the success of the island. Whether Fernández de Castro warranted the newspaper's comparison to Saco by underscoring previous Liberal calls for Spanish migration is debatable. Given the critical tone of the *Diario de Cienfuegos* article, however, it was likely an unflattering association and one pointing to the strong possibility that even that cienfuegueros of color had filled that "one part of the auditorium."

If Fernández de Castro's racism raised eyebrows in Cienfuegos, it had little effect on his campaign. He won the fourth-largest number of votes in the election of deputies to represent Santa Clara province in the Cortes. Candidates with the five-highest vote totals won Santa Clara's seats; Miguel Figueroa came in fifth, behind Fernández de Castro and three Unión Constitutional candidates.[56] Constitucionales won eighteen of the twenty-four Cuban seats, an imbalance that left Liberals to augment their legitimacy through appeals to public support. That Fernández de Castro and Figueroa did not conclude their excursión política after the elections suggests that winning seats in the Cortes was not their only end in crisscrossing the island.

However, the deputies interrupted their tour to make the two-week voyage back to Madrid for a momentous Cortes session in July. Fernández de Castro, Figueroa, and their colleagues tended to administrative matters including military reform in Cuba. Although the Ten Years' War and the Guerra Chiquita had ended six years earlier, Fernández de Castro still saw provincial Cuba as a breeding ground of disloyalty, of theft, and of vagrancy and unruliness. The Ministerio de Ultramar had nevertheless decreased the military presence in Cuba in the early 1880s. Those soldiers who were still on the island had ill-defined responsibilities, whereas the onerous burden of maintaining public order fell upon municipal police forces and veterans. In late July, Fernández de Castro made his case for allowing Spanish soldiers to assume partial responsibility for public order, thus increasing greatly the amount of work that this obligated the military to carry out. He singled out Cienfuegos as the city that would most benefit from such measures, not only by shifting the attention of the many local battalions and militias to public order but also by cutting costs. He even provided statistical data regarding cost-effectiveness with specific recommendations for the Ayuntamiento of Cienfuegos.[57] His political fortunes secure, he set himself to the task of making potentially unpopular decisions about the province he represented to the highest levels of colonial government.

Ending slavery, however, was the main event of the Cortes session. After six years of Liberal advocacy for ending the patronato early, most patrocinados had already obtained freedom by 1886. Political debates over abolition in Madrid and Havana had proliferated during the economic downturn of the mid-1880s, and the Spanish government, as Rebecca Scott notes, was "eager to dispense with the issue once and for all."[58] When Fernández de Castro spoke to the Congreso de Diputados in late July, he attempted to assuage recalcitrant planters and Conservatives who still opposed abolition. As Cubans, he pleaded, "we faithfully understand that in order to explain all of the vices from which social order suffers in the Antilles, they are explained by the slavery that has disturbed moral order and by the military despotism that has disturbed the order of law."[59] Free of slavery, he argued, Cuba would be more capable of managing itself economically and politically while still remaining a Spanish colony. On 30 July, after brief debate, the Senate passed a resolution to end the patronato for good.

When the royal decree ending the patronato finally came on 7 October, celebrations occurred throughout the island. Even before the formal announcement, news of the decision in Madrid inspired an upbeat reaction in Havana. On 31 August a crowd of African-descended *habaneros* gathered outside Miguel Figueroa's residence in a "testimony of gratitude." Figueroa emerged from his house, "reassigned" their good thanks to all of the deputies from the Partido Liberal, and offered the well-wishers drinks from the nearby El Louvre Restaurant.[60] On 7 October, the day of final abolition, Cubans of color took to the streets in Havana: bands and orchestras played while representatives of *cofradías* and *cabildos* from Havana and ten other cities marched toward the Parque Central. Many of them carried banners commemorating abolitionist politicians and the Sociedad Abolicionista Española. The procession ended with a large coach, flanked by four smaller horse-drawn carriages, carrying a youth who represented freedom and who wore the colors of the Spanish flag.[61] Public ceremonies elsewhere experienced less hoopla. In Santiago de Cuba, for example, the Círculo Español built a triumphal arch that stretched from its building to the main plaza, and it organized festivities on a Sunday evening that included fireworks. The Círculo planned the celebration with "a few members of the clase de color," but without much publicity. Few individuals attended, and rain showers further dampened the occasion.[62]

Residents of Cienfuegos needed no rain to muddy their enthusiasm about emancipation. They reacted with little fanfare when the city's 346 remaining patrocinados became free.[63] The only newsworthy public activities occurred the weekend earlier, when the church in the main square held a mass, sermon, and fiesta for the Virgen de Caridad (Virgin of Charity) on Saturday evening and Sunday morning. Members of the local Carabalí cabildo, whose patroness was the Virgen de Caridad, attended and carried an image of the Virgin in procession throughout the city to "the Cabildo house of the *grey carabalí* [Carabalí nation]."[64] Conservatives in Cienfuegos were less than enthusiastic to receive the news. The *Diario de Cienfuegos* ran a lackluster story that began, "Laws are made by necessity, and it is necessary to comply with them," and ended with the cautionary tale of an ill-prepared Matanzas planter whose *ingenio* had just failed when he had no replacements for his former slaves, now given to "theft, gambling, and drunkenness."[65] The final abolition of slavery, then, found no public commemoration in Cienfuegos as it did in other parts of Cuba (and, in fact, the rest of the Americas). Less than two weeks later, Fernández de Castro and Figueroa would learn the consequences of trying to stage one of their own.

"With Sticks, Stones, and Revolvers": Figueroa and Fernández de Castro at the Teatro Zorrilla

The first sign of trouble on Wednesday, 20 October appeared with the very arrival of Fernández de Castro and Figueroa at the train station in Cienfuegos at midday.[66] They came accompanied by Liberal colleagues from neighboring Sagua, Santo Domingo, Lajas, Cruces, and Palmira. Liberal sympathizers were waiting to welcome them as they proceeded to the residence of Rafael Cabrera, one of the local party officials and organizer of the meeting at the Teatro Zorrilla where they would speak that evening. Cienfuegueros of color figured prominently in the entourage, provocatively throwing kernels of corn at the houses of prominent constitucionales that they passed.

According to one investigator, the Teatro Zorrilla was a last-minute choice for the party meeting, "after having looked at other locales that did not want to cede the space, despite the owners' being affiliated in the party." By early evening, authorities noted how quickly the Zorrilla had filled with "the people of color from that barrio, having invaded the locale to the extreme of being absolutely impossible to penetrate the theater." Suspicions arose that many of the people gathered had heard "some rumor that had been delivered to them, as a consequence of the speeches given in Sagua, Santo Domingo, and Palmira." Despite the effusive protestations of darkness that witnesses invoked to excuse themselves from identifying individual instigators, nearly all of them agreed on the Conservative overtones of the initial "dark" presence: the most common descriptions of the crowd identified it as mostly constitucionales and people of color (not always distinct groups). But overall the group assembled defied easy categorization. One official offered the tepid compliment that "within the locale and despite being mostly people of color, there was a diversity of opinions." But consistent narratives of the event ended here. Nearly every account of the meeting told a different version of the basic narrative at the point when Fernández de Castro began his speech. The concern that this prompted sparked an in-depth investigation that irritated local partisan adversaries who had seized on the disorder to intensify years-long rivalries.

Local Liberal and Conservative newspapers bristled with antipathy for their political opponents. *El País,* the island-wide Liberal daily, condemned the "rude interruptions of the conservatives" throughout the "highly conciliatory and governmental sentiment" of Fernández de Castro's speech. It chastised the alcalde, Juan de Campo, who "crossed his arms" while the deputies were in physical danger, and scorned him for doing nothing in the immediate wake of the incident while "the houses in which our friends sleep were the objects of violent threats."[67] The *Diario de Cienfuegos,* on the other hand, expressed a modicum of remorse for the violence that broke out, but asserted that events were beyond the control of Conservatives *or* Liberals. "Insupportable insults, gratuitous suppositions, and at times scoffing" were bound to produce conflict and alarm, especially with "2,000 people of all classes at night."[68] It claimed that similar conditions had produced similar disorders as far away as Tapaste, Madruga, and San Antonio de los Baños. Most of all, the newspaper took offense at Fernández de Castro's claim that the Partido Liberal, not "the government of the Nation, Spain" should receive credit for the abolition of slavery: "The gratitude of the *raza de color* that has received that benefit, should be sufficient, and we do not doubt that it is Spain, the noble Spanish nation, whose glorious flag is and will always be the protective aegis of their rights, of their well-being and their progress."[69] Not only, then, had the reaction to the tumult amplified partisan bickering about who better represented the Spanish government; the terms of that debate now centered on protecting the rights of African-descended Cubans—an tacit acknowledgment of their citizenship couched in paternalistic terms. The loyalties of people of color, derived from the "protective aegis" that each party offered them, held a prominence for each party disproportionate to the political or public role that African-descended Cubans played in the region.

The overtones of patron-client maneuvering raise an important question about the willful participation of black and mulatto residents in Liberal and Conservative politics. Were the corn throwers who escorted Fernández de Castro and Figueroa from the train station, then, hired or coerced into a staged performance? Several of the people interviewed in the subsequent investigation thought so. And a curious incident in nearby Trinidad the day after the Zorrilla commotion raised further doubt about the nature of the welcome extended to the deputies. The two men were scheduled to appear in Trinidad to speak at another Partido Liberal meeting. The Autonomists in Trinidad had built a platform in the Plaza de Serrano just for the occasion, "so that they could be heard easily by the public that attended the meeting, to which they were invited the night before." *El Imparcial,* the Conservative newspaper in Trinidad, noted that "it seems that from the countryside come people, principally of color, excited to hear them." The people of color in the city already had something cooked up: "The cabildos de negros of this city descended on the train stop, carrying flowers and bouquets, with the object to welcome the autonomist orators, in the erroneous belief that to them is owed the complete extinction of the patronato. A musician, too, waited at the stop; a musician that, at the sound of the train whistle, would begin to play, with those from the cabildos prostrating themselves to receive the orators in this position." It is unlikely that so elaborate a demonstration of support was coerced or encouraged by a bribe, especially with acknowledgment that people of color could indeed maintain beliefs.

Fernández de Castro and Figueroa never appeared. They took a train back from Cienfuegos directly to Havana, where they waited until their tour could safely continue. The crowds of negros in Trinidad returned to their homes and cabildo houses disappointed because, as *El Imparcial* noted, "they believed that they were going to greet expressly authorized representatives of the National Government."[70] The Conservative author didn't seem so sure. Yet again, Liberals stood separate from popular understandings of who or what constituted the Spanish government. Conservatives in Trinidad, like those in Cienfuegos, expressed frustration that Liberals took credit for the final abolition of slavery. The added insult was that "those fine people" of African descent in Trinidad properly esteemed the Spanish government but were duped by Liberals who made a mockery of their loyalty and, the *Diario de Cienfuegos* editorialized, "abused the *derecho de reunión* [right of association]." Apparently, black and mulatto cienfuegueros had been a bit wiser.

The municipal and provincial governments expressed less interest in the competition for loyalty than in guaranteeing public order and sound associational laws. Their interrogations of locals piled on questions about associational leadership, public order, race, party affiliation, and social status. Within hours of the conflict, telegrams shot from Cienfuegos to Santa Clara to Havana and back asking for procedural clarification and promising a quick return to order. Rafael Correa, the gobernador civil of Santa Clara province, placed cardinal importance on the question of whether the numerous people in the theater violated "the use of the right of the Constitution of the State and the mentioned Law guaranteed to all citizens." With the same rapidity and with the same extensive mandate that the *orden pública* (public order) investigation of espiritismo carried, the disturbance in Cienfuegos became the subject of deep inquiry. Although authorities obsessed over the sources, origins, and instigators of the outbreak, their investigative approach focused equally on the behavior of the police and municipal authorities in promoting, maintaining, and restoring public order. Correa sent representatives to Cienfuegos to speak "with persons of distinct classes of society in Cienfuegos, as well of distinct political colors" about what happened on 20 October at the Teatro Zorrilla.[71]

In the course of two weeks, Correa and his subordinates had interrogated thirty of the city's residents, including theater guards, Partido Liberal organizers, meeting attendees, and the mayor, Juan de Campo. Correa visited the Teatro Zorrilla to count bullet holes and broken chairs. His investigation weathered a suspicious intervention when de Campo demanded new scribes and interrogators after two witnesses suggested names of possible instigators who were closely aligned with the alcalde. Witnesses observed exemplary behavior on the part of police, complimenting them for not using arms to control the uprising. Correa questioned only two African-descended residents—the mother of the black demonstrator Pedro Jiménez, and also a mulatto barber who attended the meeting—to ascertain whether or not he died from wounds suffered during the melee, as newspapers in Cuba and Spain had reported. (He lived.)

Juan de Campo himself was one of the first cienfuegueros to testify, enumerating a small disturbance in the Zorrilla and in the streets outside between 8:15 and 8:30 p.m., and a second one ten minutes later that the police could control inside the theater but not in the street. The third outburst could not be contained, he explained, because the more orderly people from inside the theater spilled into the crowd outside and those in the streets scrambled to enter the building. Chairs broke and rocks flew accordingly. Yet de Campo was quick to emphasize how quickly municipal authorities reestablished order. He claimed that many residents of the city had assisted the police in calming the unrest, but noted Manuel Rivero, a colonel in the volunteer forces, and José María Aceval in particular. Various newspapers had recently maligned the two, "treating them as rebellious, being the contrary," and de Campo wanted to acknowledge their devotion to public order. De Campo claimed that he had received word late in the evening that the home of Rafael Cabrera, where Fernández de Castro and Figueroa were staying, had been attacked "and other news of a private character" that made him "understand that the *personas de la clase de color* had risen up." Once he dispensed the Guardia Civil to the Cabrera residence, all was calm.[72]

Despite the consensus that cienfuegueros of color had been the major actors in the disturbance, Correa's commission never clarified who, if anyone, led them. Of course, interrogators never bothered to ask. They questioned

Spaniards and white island-born residents disproportionately to their involvement in the events, excluding the hundreds of black and mulatto eyewitnesses from giving their account of the events. Esteban Cacicedo, the ayuntamiento member who caused a stir in 1884 with his racist comment about La Amistad and El Progreso's schools, did not even attend the meeting, but he made a statement nevertheless. Pledging "complete impartiality," Cacicedo conceded that some people of color threw corn, but he argued that the Partido Liberal meeting should never have taken place in the first place because "its promoters really should have realized that this is a *pueblo* eminently contrary to its ideas." Moreover, he claimed, Fernández de Castro and Figueroa came preceded by the disturbing *mala fama* (rumor) of their recent dishonor, "according to the Voluntarios at the Teatro Uriarte in Sagua la Grande."[73]

Rumors of disparaging remarks about the voluntarios emerged in several of the testimonies. As one witness recalled an "insult" directed at the Spanish government at the beginning of the meeting in Cienfuegos, several more witnesses claimed that Fernández de Castro aimed his criticisms in Sagua at the military. In light of Fernández de Castro's call in July to reduce the military presence on the island, voluntarios in Sagua may have perceived Fernández de Castro as a threat to the vitality of their institution—and to the rewards of military participation. A rumor of this tenor would have struck a note among those Cubans of color who derived status, material gain, and an argument for citizenship from their military service.

The resentment generated by Fernández de Castro's past speeches that insulted people of color or that threatened military institutions emerges from the testimonies as a plausible explanation for the 20 October unrest. Joaquín Fernández, another prominent planter and businessman in Cienfuegos, placed the blame on the residents of color of the neighborhood surrounding the Teatro Zorrilla, but he also noted the presence of *comisiones forasteros* (external delegations) from Sagua. Like Cacicedo, he explained that "this population is contrary to the doctrines" of the Liberals and that "the spirits were excited" by the news of the insults toward the voluntarios and of the corn thrown at the houses of Conservative leaders.[74] Here the observers wavered: they believed that Cubans of color couldn't possibly support the Liberals because they supported the Spanish nation, which only Conservatives represented. But they also cast them as pawns in a partisan game, with little agency to support one cause or another.

Agreements like this among the witnesses were rare. Workers, planters, and city officials offered radically different interpretations of the events at the

Zorrilla. One guard claimed that the individuals from Sagua were sympathetic Liberals. One lone witness, in defiance of the famed darkness that enveloped Cienfuegos on 20 October, actually named names. Antonio Castiñeyra accused one Spaniard, Diego Riverón, of taking orders from Juan de Campo, and another—José María Aceval, who won the praise of de Campo—to denounce the Liberals in flight from the theater as traitors and insurgents. But both men denied it. Aceval claimed that he and a few of his friends had simply overheard news of the meeting the following day at the Café El Escorial. The police chief of Santa Clara tellingly closed his summary without making a formal accusation against any of the people mentioned as possible instigators of the eruption. He doubted the validity and objectivity of any individual accusation and attributed the fracas to "personal quarrels exist among those of that locality."[75]

Of all of the cienfuegueros questioned, the Liberal organizer of the 20 October meeting had the strongest obligation to convince officials to see the events as a local squabble and not a sustained threat to public order from Cubans of color. Rafael Cabrera admitted in his testimony that Liberals and Conservatives in Cienfuegos bitterly resented one another, but that he had extended a personal invitation to local Conservative leader José Pertierra to attend the meeting at the Zorrilla. He added that the violence had its origins and targets in Cienfuegos, not in broader political configurations, and that he lamented what had happened "as a citizen and loyal observer of the Law." Finally, and unlike other residents of the city, Cabrera tried to distinguish between the Liberal-Conservative feud and what he saw as a less politically charged outburst by African-descended cienfuegueros. According to the testimony, he "had recorded in his declaration that there had been alarm among the clase de color; but this was produced as a consequence of what had occurred at the Zorrilla, and was generally able to be considered as a true protest of the grave illegality committed, and under no concept as an attitude manifestly contrary to the Government nor, consequently, to *nacionalidad*."[76] Cabrera likely anticipated a double condemnation of the Partido Liberal by colonial authorities in Havana and Madrid: one for the clash with Conservatives and another for the disturbance by the population of color. To distant observers, the apparent overlap between those groups might evince a failure of both Liberal politics and liberal principles. If the Partido Liberal on the whole took credit for emancipation, its local organizer in Cienfuegos now headed off accusations that Cubans—including those recently freed—were, at best, ill-prepared to exercise their new rights and, at worst, disloyal to the Spanish state. Cabrera tried to reiterate that the post-Zanjón reforms created public spaces for making claims to inclusion in the colonial political community, not for disrupting urban life and heightening racial discord. Attesting to the loyalty of Cienfuegos's black and mulatto residents protected the principles, if not the party, of liberalism that valued the free circulation of ideas among free men.

When the Cortes met in November, Fernández de Castro had no opportunity to offer his own account of the flare-up. Liberal and Conservative deputies agreed on two matters as they discussed the events in Cienfuegos: that questions of race were subordinate to partisan issues and that there was no concrete solution to the problems that they raised. Beyond that, they disagreed vociferously on matters of fact and interpretation alike, and Fernández de Castro remained conspicuously silent. Furious Liberal deputies condemned the manner in which "voluntarios, in union with Conservatives, had determined to obstruct Autonomist propaganda." Conservative deputies, on the other hand, did not take such a clear position. They tried to portray the violence that erupted as the direct result of Fernández de Castro's inflammatory remarks, not a commotion caused by some of their own supporters. They questioned whether Cubans "have the aptitude, loyalty, and sensibility" to deserve the rights of organization and press that they had recently won as a concession in the Pact of Zanjón, but they recognized the favorable political valence of the disorder. Disloyalty to the conventions of the burgeoning public sphere had, ironically, affirmed loyalty to Spanish rule.[77]

Following their troubles in October, Fernández de Castro and Figueroa attempted one more time to spread the good news of liberalism to the people of Cienfuegos. In mid-November, four municipal guards on horseback escorted the men from the docks to the houses where each of them would sleep separately. The next day, Juan de Campo foiled their plans to hold a meeting in a storehouse on the city's northern limits when he exonerated the ayuntamiento from providing guards and security for such an isolated location. Local Liberals quickly secured the meeting rooms of the Liceo, but municipal officials again blocked the men from speaking, citing the public reunion law that required advance notice of twenty-four hours.[78] In turn, the deputies departed Cienfuegos for good, leaving the city's Conservative leaders to dominate local politics until the outbreak of the final war for independence in 1895.

At heart, Fernández de Castro's gaffes throughout his excursión política reveal a profound ignorance of local realities. As a wealthy planter from Havana province, his claim to represent the population of Santa Clara was weak at best, but representative politics on the island was not the only issue at hand. Building and strengthening a political relationship between politicians in

Madrid and subjects in provincial Cuba acquired a more important role. To this end, Fernández de Castro and other Liberal colleagues attempted a political experiment of reaching out to disfranchised Cubans with an eye toward preparing the island for self-government. In 1881, during a speech in Guanabacoa, he expressed sympathy for "cities to impede the political invasion of the State that threatens their local initiative."[79] In 1886, local initiatives in Cienfuegos had sparked an invasion of national-imperial initiatives. The racial vocabulary of liberalism and conservatism among Cuban politicians attempted to check metropolitan fears of social unrest and violent local initiatives by asserting the loyalty of African-descended Cubans.

BY FEBRUARY 1887, Rafael Fernández de Castro had ended his excursión política for good and had returned to Havana. He ensconced himself in the capital's cosmopolitan circles, heading to a theater once to take in a performance by Sarah Bernhardt and mingling with his Liberal colleagues. He gave a speech to the Círculo Autonomista that showed a tireless determination to challenge Spanish prejudices about Cuba's unpreparedness for self-rule. Yet he was surprisingly articulate about the degeneracy and disorder attributed to Cubans—informed, perhaps, by the recent memory of gunfire and flying rocks and sticks four months earlier. He faulted Spaniards for viewing Cubans as "worthless, ignorant people," those who "thought without reason and spoke without agility, that we here are 'Indians in frock-coats' or mimicking monkeys of the most depraved customs in the world." Alongside the allusion to indigenous Americans, the simian reference replicated pervasive associations in late nineteenth-century racial discourse between apes and people of African descent. Despite his faith in Cubans, he admitted that some of the island's woes were beyond his comprehension: "To give an exact idea of the social chaos in which we live, there are neither words nor concepts in the language of political men."[80]

Indeed there were no sufficient words or concepts for many people in Cienfuegos at the moment of emancipation, especially those whose turn to violence drew from their self-understandings as "political men." For them, neither the ethic of liberalism nor the ethic of patronage, in Viotti da Costa's memorable framing, offered a wholly secure approach to claiming or exercising rights. When hundreds of black and mulatto cienfuegueros swarmed the Teatro Zorrilla and its surrounding streets to shout "¡Viva España! ¡Muera a autonomía!" they expressed the social chaos of an expanding public sphere whose capacity to accommodate Cubans of color as loyal subjects met sharp limits.

In many respects, the tumult in Cienfuegos illustrates a familiar story of nineteenth-century Latin America: of liberals and conservatives vying for power in a political climate that favored clientelism over democratic participation, dramatic acts over substantive debates. On the whole, competing factions shared a number of assumptions that were plainly racist and protective of the propertied classes. In Brazil, for example, liberals and conservatives combined forces to pass electoral "reforms" in 1881 that stymied the entrance of tens of thousands of freedmen into electoral politics.[81] In Spain and Cuba, the end of slavery occasioned debates between liberals and conservatives over who better served the interests of African-descended Cubans. That both groups lamented the presence of *lo africano* in Cuban society attests to the limits of the debate. Fernández de Castro, Figueroa, and other leaders of the Partido Liberal Autonomista actively sought popular support as they traveled from town to town, but they seemed remarkably unconcerned with reconciling liberalism's inclusionary pretensions with their exclusionary practices. In their *excursiones políticas*, their reach exceeded their grasp.

At the same time, liberalism in late nineteenth-century Cuba neither conformed to models elsewhere in Latin America that repudiated the colonial past nor to the liberal vision of the Constitution of 1812.[82] Liberals constantly fought off accusations of *independentismo* as they sought legitimacy within the colonial system. They did so as Conservative propagandists tried to delegitimize Liberal claims to political authority by branding them separatist and illegitimate, as evidenced by the widespread confusion over which political entity could justifiably take responsibility for slave emancipation. Colonial officials had to adapt to rapidly changing conditions as their demands for loyalty exacted a heavy toll. And Cuban men of color left out of the political process now had more plausible claims to constitutional rights.

At the moment of formal emancipation, an autonomous, much less revolutionary, future was by no means certain to most Cubans, and they professed loyalty to Spain as various factions solicited and boasted popular support. The racist assumptions under which Fernández de Castro cultivated followers chafed against the multiracial composition of those who celebrated the Spanish government for ending slavery. The shouts outside the Zorrilla, however, differed from the "Long live the king, death to bad government!" slogan that loyal subjects in mainland Latin America invoked in earlier periods, for colonial politics now operated under different terms and new vocabularies of nationhood, government, freedom, and citizenship.[83] What Fernández de Castro's *excursión política* offered to ordinary Cubans, besides racist denunciations and exclusionary rhetoric, was an important and imperfect education in key political languages. That African-descended Cubans were becoming fluent enough to gather at political party meetings and claim fidelity to Spain testifies to the possibilities of inclusion in the post-Zanjón order. That such a declaration had to be voiced in such a confrontational context reveals its limitations.

In 1943, the renowned Cuban intellectual Jorge Mañach mused about the island's colonial past and attempted to recast the story of slave emancipation as an accomplishment of Cuban nationalism, not Spanish political maneuvering. (Nowhere did he cite the actions of patrocinados themselves in ending slavery.) In order to do so, he reclaimed Miguel Figueroa as a hero of Cuban nationalism. He recounted Figueroa's tireless efforts to establish the Liberal Party in Cuba, including an early visit to Cienfuegos to drum up support within the Casino Español. Of the tumult that occurred in 1886, Mañach blamed Spaniards for inciting the protest as a means of "political propaganda," but he did not let Figueroa off the hook, either: "And here is one of those crossroads in our inquiry when our sympathy for our hero is annulled with a subtle anguish."[84] On the whole, however, he lauded Figueroa's efforts on behalf of the raza de color, and for inspiring multiracial audiences at Liberal gatherings across the island to create "a site for pure democracy"— and end of empire hardly ever mentioned under Spanish rule.[85] Measuring the ability of such sites to transform Spanish rule became a vital gauge by which Cubans of color mapped out their political allegiances in the years after emancipation.

SIX

The Price of Integrity
Limited Loyalties in Revolution

> If the Africans didn't know what they were getting into, the Cubans didn't either.
> Most of them, I mean. What happened was that there was a revolution around
> here, a fine mess everybody fell into. Even the most cagey ones. People said "Cuba
> Libre! Down with Spain!" Then they said, "Long live the King!" What do I know?
> That was hell. The solution wasn't to be seen anywhere.
> There was only one way out, and it was war.
> —Esteban Montejo, as told to Miguel Barnet, 1966

As the rest of this book has tried to demonstrate, reports of the inevitable
death of colonial rule in Cuba have been greatly exaggerated. That Spain persisted in its control of Cuba through the 1890s was not the result of unyielding brutality or passive acceptance. Violence and inertia had their place, but
the political logic of colonialism also emphasized inequality by design, affective reciprocities between the state and its people, and, by the end of the nineteenth century, widespread confusion about whether belonging to an empire
made someone a subject, a citizen, both, or neither. Spain had more or less
maintained popular consent and contained resistance for decades after
its mainland colonies achieved independence. Esteban Montejo, the former
slave and insurgent who recounted his life story when he was 103, acknowledged both uncertainty and inevitability when he recalled the final years of
Spanish rule. Neither the "Africans" nor "Cubans" he described seemed to
have much direction or say about where they stood, but there was apparent
consensus about where they were headed.

As Cubans evaluated their political status in the period between emancipation in 1886 and the war for independence from 1895 to 1898, they faced a
crisis of integrity in the most literal sense. *Integridad nacional* (national integrity or unity) had gained momentum during the Ten Years' War as a synonym for the coherence of the Spanish empire. Spaniards and Cubans alike

invoked the concept, celebrating *integrismo* as a derivative political ideology or deriding it as a sugar-coated false unity. But the slow progress of integrating Cuban men of color as Spanish citizens with public rights caused the issue of racial discrimination to ignite passionate debate in the 1880s and 1890s. Integrity became a concept around which race and loyalty intertwined. Disagreements about how Cuban society and Spanish empire would cohere led to a proliferation of political options, rather than the contracting options that Montejo described and that many have understood to set Cuba on a course toward independence.

If at the beginning of the century fears of slave revolt convinced privileged Cubans to remain a part of the Spanish empire, what motivated their counterparts many decades later, once slavery had ended? More broadly, what value was to be found for Cubans of color in being a loyal subject if universal legal freedom had not eliminated racial inequalities or barriers to citizenship? The defeat of Spain in the 1895–1898 War of Independence would suggest that the ultimate resolution to these questions was a death blow to pro-colonial loyalty. We might better understand the war as an extension or amplification of a fragmented island in the years preceding it. In that slow disintegration, arguments for supporting Spanish rule never completely disappeared, but the proliferation of political affiliations—not all of them oriented toward independence—radically decentered loyalty. Even after the intervention of the United States and the end of the war, questions would remain as to how and if Cuba could remain whole, whether as a new nation, a former colony, or a new one.

Military Reorganization and the Decline of Loyal Service

For much of the nineteenth century, Spanish soldiers had migrated to Cuba with the frequent charge of protecting white Cubans from the African-descended population. In addition to the end of the Ten Years' War and the Guerra Chiquita, the end of slavery occasioned a reduction of the military presence on the island. "With this legislation," note historians Manuel Moreno Fraginals and José Moreno Masó, "the 'black problem' ceased to be a migratory motor for the transfer of troops although it continued being, for many years, a fundamental factor of insular politics."[1] The *ministro de ultramar* (overseas minister) remained deaf to complaints from Cuban officials that the military presence was too small to maintain order or to put down another large-scale rebellion. In Cienfuegos, for example, the surviving local volunteer regiments—the Batallón de Cazadores, the Batallón San Quintín, the Sección Caballería—barely escaped periodic efforts to disband them, and in 1885 the government even reduced officer salaries by almost 10 percent.[2]

The forces that remained on the island after the Guerra Chiquita attended to rural lawlessness. "Banditry" became an umbrella term for peasant unrest, separatist sympathies in the countryside, and small-scale anticolonial skirmishes. Island authorities were quick to link banditry to disloyalty and worried most when bandits gained the support of local populations and government officials. The 1894 kidnapping of Rafael Fernández de Castro's brother Antonio became a jarring symbol of Spain's inability to subjugate individuals who competed with its authority and to protect even its well-placed citizens.[3] Moreover, the piecemeal efforts to curb banditry became for many property owners a barometer of state legitimacy. The optimism and permissiveness that characterized select colonial policies immediately after the conclusion of the Ten Years' War and Guerra Chiquita gave way to frequent attempts by the government to cast Cubans as their own worst enemies. Within that formula, Cubans of African descent did not necessarily emerge as a more restive or threatening group than any other Cubans. Yet the onset of emancipation raised serious questions about the role that former slaves and other black and mulatto islanders would play in the island's defense. Civil and military officials had to weigh, as their predecessors had throughout the century, when to hail them as loyal subjects and when to subject them to skepticism and scrutiny.

Just as the reformist mood in the 1850s and the outbreak of the Ten Years' War promoted opportunities for free men of color in the Spanish military, slave emancipation held similar promise. Civil authorities in Havana alerted the minister of war in 1885 that the expense of maintaining a larger military presence in Cuba was nothing compared to the danger of having too few soldiers when abolition came. Foreseeing the potential for postemancipation social unrest, they proposed allowing Cuban men of color to serve in the army volunteer corps as regular members, "subject to their obligations, with the protections of all who enter into service to the Patria, that correspond to all Spanish citizens." The measure would have offered some Cubans of color—men in military service—standing equal to peninsular and creole volunteers. One official went further in emphasizing the political consequences over the military benefits: "The people of color, with greater sympathies towards us than the creole inhabitants, by their number, by their strength, and by their nature, are constantly solicited by revolutionary elements, and with more determination today than yesterday; and my purpose, in proposing to commit this to resolution, is to give to this race all the conditions of free men, raising it to the extreme . . . so by their services and by their acts, they may be

worthy of high posts or honors, opening to them the path to achieve them."
Both Cuban and Spanish authorities recognized that, beyond military defense, the measure could model broader projects for racial integration. In the
same letter, the official remarked that "the *negro* has great temperaments of
resistance, sobriety and valor but in order to develop it, and above all its in-
domitable bravura, he needs to emulate a practical example and mix with our
soldiers."[4] For civil authorities perhaps more concerned about social issues
than military leaders in Madrid, cross-racial cooperation between soldiers
of African and European descent contained an opportunity to prepare all
Cuban men for a postemancipation society, one in which military promotion
would represent only one example of equal status.

Within the military, the proposal raised mild interest but never received
approval from the crown. An official from the Ministerio de Ultramar wrote
back to the office of the captain general recommending the formation of an ad
hoc company "by battalion" in moments of unrest. The language was crystal
clear in its opacity: the more modest measure would "avoid the difficulties" that
develop when racially diverse troops mix "for various considerations that you
will understand, without enumerating them." Although the *ministerio* allowed
for the possibility of a gradual experiment of substituting Cuban soldiers of
African descent for those of Spanish ancestry, it made no pretensions of allowing such a regiment to defend the Iberian Peninsula, "for known difficulties."
Mixed troops were better suited, apparently, to laboring in Spain's remaining
overseas possessions in Asia and Africa.[5] Thus, with veiled language and criteria,
the overseas ministry nixed a proposal that would have given African-descended
men unprecedented military status within the Spanish empire.

Instead, they found their opportunities for demonstrating loyalty through
soldiering in turmoil. Beyond the sufficiently fortified capital, the labor of
soldiers often had a more measurable impact in cities and towns across the
island that added material weight to the symbolic value discussed by policy-
makers. As it has been, the case of Cienfuegos is instructive. In the absence of
an integrated volunteer army, African-descended *cienfuegueros* successfully
joined racially segregated volunteer units in the late 1880s.[6] In August 1887,
authorities in Cienfuegos responded to local pressure for public works projects and approved the creation of a Compañía de Voluntarios Ingenieros
(Volunteer Company of Engineers), which the *Diario de Cienfuegos* reported
would be "composed of the *clase de color*" and "workers" and would have "all
the privileges earned by the Cuerpos de Voluntarios."[7] Sixty-eight men joined
the unit.[8] Masimo Coimbra, the founder of the *sociedad de color* El Progreso,
was one of the original members of the company.[9]

On a Sunday afternoon in December, the Compañía de Ingenieros staged an elaborate inaugural ceremony that included presentation for review to Fidel Alonso Santocildes, the jurisdiction's military commander, speeches by Santocildes and Antonio Guimerá, the white captain of the new unit, and a parade that ended at the El Escorial Café in the center of town. The *Diario de Cienfuegos* praised the ingenieros for having "sufficient instruction and great enthusiasm" and for the music that its band played.[10] Predictably, the speeches by Guimerá and Santocildes deployed the language of loyalty that had historically reinforced reciprocities between militiamen and empire. Santocildes lauded the soldiers for passing "an unequivocal test of how much trust there is in your loyalty, and of the importance given to the cooperation of all of the elements that constitute the Spanish people, without distinction of origin or of race." Guimerá took the language a step further. Akin to Santicildes, he said that he trusted the soldiers "to hold high the just name of valor and loyalty, such proven examples of which your ancestors bequeathed to you." He conveyed that the city's Spaniards, "descendants of generous races" who had trusted soldiers of color with arms in the past, had no doubts that the ingenieros would follow in the noble tradition of military service and be "strong supporters of the national flag." But then Guimerá prophesied that possible dangers in the future would not "weaken the fulfillment of our sacred obligations as residents and citizens."[11] By identifying the soldiers as citizens, Guimerá made explicit the end to which the ingenieros would devote their service, and he staked out ground more solid than the indeterminate political rewards extended to *milicianos* in prior decades.

A little over a year after chaos erupted in Cienfuegos about the role of Cubans of color in colonial politics, Guimerá named as citizens a group of black and mulatto soldiers who almost certainly had experienced the tumult at the Teatro Zorrilla or at least its aftereffects. As many people on the island spoke increasingly about the rights of (Spanish and/or Cuban) citizenship, Guimerá focused instead its "sacred obligations." He described the ingenieros' service as the natural extension of good civic behavior by "peaceful citizens and industrious workers in times of peace." His point was relevant not only to soldiers of color. White officers also felt the sting of the government's military cutbacks. Most of them had previously held positions in companies that had been dissolved, such as the *bomberos* and the cavalry, or reduced in number, such as the artillery unit. Beneath the pomp and performance of the inaugural ceremonies lay a powerful message for all involved: that every member of the Compañía de Ingenieros was a citizen fulfilling an important civic responsibility for the benefit of Spain.

It took less than a month for local officials to begin casting doubts on the character and significance of that contribution. A counterpoint to the confident and supportive speeches published in the local paper, the internal reports that made it all the way to the war ministry in Madrid told a more ambivalent story about the efforts to cement national integrity in Cienfuegos. Santocildes chafed at a request by Guimerá to consider the company's musicians as volunteers, thus allowing more individuals to join the unit. They were not even armed, the commander reminded Guimerá, but the shift would nevertheless qualify the ingenieros for more munitions at the government's expense. On 29 December, the head of the Batallón Cazadores de San Quintín No. 4 in Cienfuegos wrote to Santocildes to recount a meeting he arranged with leaders of the Batallón de Tiradores y de Guías. The men considered the "best way for the Compañía de Ingenieros to lend [their services] or not, in the interests of all involved," for the *guardia de prevención* (patrolling duty). The guardia had long been the responsibility of the volunteers in the battalions, some of whom were wary of allowing the new company to share the task. The leaders agreed to a system in which the ingenieros "would be admitted with pleasure" into a rotation in which each of the companies would alternate guardia service. The resolution came after a heated debate about forming a single battalion composed of members of the different companies, including the ingenieros. The San Quintín captain noted that there was "a diversity of opinions" about the prospect of an integrated force. Although he himself thanked and celebrated the ingenieros "for having nourished the ranks of the institution," the separate-but-equal compromise "was in better harmony with the fractions among the whites."[12]

The ingenieros continued to observe more fractions than harmony as the dispute unfolded. Just a week after the inaugural ceremonies, the subinspector for the *voluntarios* wrote to Santocildes that having thoroughly scrutinized the outfit, "there exist some divisions among the *gente de color*." He inquired among the men out of curiosity "about friction with the white race," and they responded that the division had more to do with "the unquestionable right that the Constitution of the State concedes to them, which has recognized them in their deference to it by the highest authority on the Island." At the same time, they told the inspector that they "have not been exempt from a certain antagonism that until now has not boiled over." The subinspector warned Santocildes ominously that the day when all armed institutions felt such discontent was not too distant.[13]

Faced with competing accounts of racial conflict centered on guard duty, Santocildes sought advice from the provincial military commander in Santa

Clara and received a surprising response. On 26 December, the leader of the Batallón de Tiradores y de Guías had received an order from the commander to allow men of color into the unit for the express purpose of sharing the guardia de prevención. Thus, Santocildes focused on limiting the public fall-out over the conflict and avoiding accusations of racism. In a letter to General Manuel Sánchez Mira, he proposed meeting with the leaders of the ingenieros to "try to convince them—they have no right to said guardia but that if they want they can join the Battalion as seventh [grade members], explaining besides—there exists no antagonism between whites and [people] of color." If he was not entirely persuasive here, he would resort to placing blame not on the soldiers in any of the units but on rivalries between the white leaders of the various regiments, especially Lieutenant Isidoro Huertas, of the ingenieros, whom Santocildes referred to as a "repulsive character" and "the principal motor" of the conflict.[14]

Ultimately, the battle over the guardia de prevención ended in something of a draw. Members of the Compañía de Ingenieros earned the right to join white volunteer battalions in limited numbers and for limited purposes. Their leaders' claims of racism, however, were subject to the outright manipulations of Santocildes, who was more concerned with avoiding the appearance of racism than with the discrimination that seemed to be festering between units. Although some of the leaders of white units lost their fight to keep the volunteers racially segregated, they retained their rights to the guardia de prevención, and, just as important, they maintained the confidence of Santocildes. A second wave of young new recruits may have had little direct memory of earlier attempts to cultivate loyalty, or of the trade-off between military service and manumission during the Ten Years' War. They also joined Spanish regiments during a proliferation of war memoirs published in Cuba and abroad in which former insurgents spoke of slaves and free people who had fought in the rebellions. These accounts gained popularity and told stories that were not predicated on subordination or a well-defined place in the traditional hierarchy of colonial society. The black insurgent as a literary type, Ada Ferrer argues, was "more than just safe or unthreatening; he was also a Cuban hero and patriot."[15] The loyal subject, in contrast, lost valor among a restless population.

The Ties that Unbind: Public Leadership and Associational Life
The tumult in Cienfuegos in 1886 surrounding abolition crystallized the distinction that some Cubans of color made between support for the Spanish government and the rules of respectability governing the expression of that

support. Rafael Fernández de Castro and Miguel Figueroa became targets of a provincial urban public frustrated by the gap between the Autonomist Party's racist rhetoric and its noble claims of effecting abolition. In the long run, however, activists of African descent emphasized adherence to the decorum expected in public discourse and spaces—even as they pushed their limits by advancing political projects that variously affirmed and challenged colonialism.

This distinction in strategy came into clear view on the death of Figueroa in the summer of 1893. A new, island-wide black newspaper, *La Igualdad* (Equality), was facilitating connections and comparisons between communities of color throughout Cuba. At its helm was Juan Gualberto Gómez, the formidable journalist and activist who had spent the 1880s in exile in Madrid, was a supporter of the Liberal Party, and came to support Cuban independence.[16] In conjunction with *La Igualdad,* he established the Directorio Central de las Sociedades de la Raza de Color in 1892, a federation of approximately seventy-five sociedades on the island that increasingly took on issues of public discrimination in addition to their respectable social and cultural activities. For months articles in *La Igualdad* had been updating readers on Figueroa's declining health, and his passing in July mobilized nearly every sociedad de color to commemorate his dedication to ending slavery. Whatever stumbles he made in Cienfuegos years earlier had been forgotten. No mention appeared of the Autonomists' contradictory race rhetoric or of Figueroa's disastrous speaking engagement; in fact, *La Igualdad* praised Figueroa as an orator above all. Even the Cienfuegos sociedad El Progreso—the only one in the city affiliated with the Directorio Central—sent condolences to Figueroa's family through the newspaper and lamented the loss "to the country and to the raza de color."[17] Thus in one stroke, club members—some of whom certainly remembered the fracas at the Teatro Zorrilla—had identified both with race and country as they expressed their opinions in *La Igualdad*'s letters section.

These gestures did not go unnoticed: representatives of the sociedades played prominent roles in the elaborate funeral organized in Havana for Figueroa. They formed an honor guard around mourners and delegates from every Havana group gathered in the Plaza de Belén with their respective flags for a procession to the cemetery. In the main funeral procession, three groups immediately preceded the pallbearers. Musician Félix Cruz and his orchestra played a funeral march as girls from the schools run by El Progreso Habanero and the Centro de Cocineros marched in their uniforms. Thus the clubs that embodied respectability under Spanish rule endorsed the image of the loyal subject from which cienfuegueros had strayed seven years earlier. Setting aside the opposition to Figueroa expressed in that fracas, those commemorating Figueroa's life cemented a bond of gratitude to a man who was instrumental in the legislative demise of the patronato—and a man who emphasized repeatedly that the Spanish government had assented to one of the most persistent demands made by Cubans of color in the post-Zanjón public sphere.

Cuban politics by the 1890s offered more options than an all-or-nothing choice between Spanish colonialism and anticolonial rebellion. National independence loomed constantly as the most apparent radical alternative for the island, but other political projects beyond a national frame—be it Cuban or Spanish—and within cross-racial structures captured the imagination of Cubans as well, socialism, anarchism, annexation to the United States among them. These affiliations took various institutional forms, from loose networks of dispersed activists to formally registered associations to clandestine clubs in close contact with allies beyond the island. For Cubans of color, too, a proliferation of leadership and politics diffused support for Spanish rule. Although the Directorio Central served as an umbrella group for associations of color, it never entered into formal politics along the lines of a political party. Gómez likely knew better: anxious rumors of the creation of a black political party were common, and support among Cubans of color for the Partido Liberal Autonomista was generally favorable to the Partido Unión Constitucional.

Maintaining the conservative position embraced by the latter party was Rodolfo de Lagardère. Before emancipation, he withheld his unconditional support for the Conservatives because it was the Liberals who more aggressively advocated for an early end to the patronato. After 1886, however, that ambivalence evaporated. In a book he wrote in 1887, *La cuestión social de Cuba,* Lagardère skewered Liberal politicians who, in his view, had desecrated the ideals they championed. "That word 'equality,'" he surmised, "so oft-repeated in the program of the Antillean Liberal party, is written in sand." The leaders of the Autonomists spoke as if "the black would apparently be a guaranteed citizen," but Lagardère argued that they had no intention of opening the leadership of an autonomous Cuba to its African-descended citizens. Not only would autonomism privilege whites over nonwhites; it would revoke its support of "the magnificent ideal of the abolition of races, the abolition of castes. To the contrary, it will perpetuate crippled freedom, the right of freedom, abolished by the right of color."[18] An imperfect expression of national integrity, autonomism would defer the promised ends of Spanish sovereignty and perpetuate a racially fragmented society. In earlier speeches and writings, Lagardère expressed high hopes for Spanish liberal citizenship as a position from which to challenge discrimination. He now hinted at some skepticism, but not in the direction of upending his support for colonial rule.

Lagardère resolved the question of racial integration by waxing poetic on the nature of hybridity. Spain itself, he argued, was a multiracial society that had integrated people of "huge differences of race, of interests, of customs, of dialects, of climate and history."[19] It would have to recognize eventually that mulattoes in Cuba were but one of the diverse groups who constituted Spain. He ended his text with a rhetorical flourish affirming the role of mixed-descent individuals in the imperial world: "Yes, *mulatos, mestizos,* hybrids, we descend from European Spaniards, and as such, we are heirs to their name and their glories . . . We are [Spanish] by blood, by language, by religion, and more than anything, by the loyalty we hold for our patria. Who are our parents? What is our *patria?* Our parents are Spaniards. Our *patria* is Spain."[20] Although Lagardère's overall project was not explicitly racially exclusive, it left little space for people entirely of African descent who could not lay (hybrid) racial claim to the glories of the peninsula. And if this line of argument bears out Fernando Ortiz's assumption that nonwhite loyalty to Spain derived from mulattoes' ancestral connections to Spain, countless examples throughout this book have suggested many alternative explanations. Carmen Barcia's argument that Lagardère was a victim of interest groups and officials who fed him ideas is not far-fetched, but if Lagardère encountered criticism and skepticism from less reactionary counterparts, he was in agreement with virtually every other public figure of African descent about the need to end discrimination.[21]

Emanating from Havana in the early 1990s, however, was a strain of organizational leadership that rebuked the clientelism many associated with Lagardère and party politics. Individual leaders of color, sympathetic in varying degrees to the separatist cause, were gaining new prominence. Rafael Serra, a prominent journalist of African descent and a former tobacco worker, took advantage of the post-Zanjón reforms immediately to publicize the idea of racial harmony. In 1879 he founded *La Armonía,* a newspaper with the same name as a sociedad in Matanzas, and he founded La Liga in the early 1890s for "the intellectual advancement and the elevation of the character of the men of color born in Cuba and Puerto Rico."[22] In his writings, Serra praised insurgent leader Antonio Maceo and Juan Gualberto Gómez. Above all, he expressed affection and esteem for José Martí, the independence movement's principal leader who sought "a nation for all, and for the good of all." In a speech on 10 October 1891, he spoke to the growing frustrations of Cubans of color in terms of resistance and confrontation, calling for "the study of the origins, contrasts, bitterness and accomplishments of revolutions; those which engulf us in the examination of social themes and which are suited to the possibility of equilibrium in a people of ethnic variety."[23] Serra saw in Spanish rule an equivalent subordination that people of African descent experienced as slaves. The labor of independence, he argued, went beyond converting individuals loyal to Spain. Separatists who passively accepted Spanish rule and its reinforcement of "the arrogance, privilege, and custom of slavery" were obligated to fulfill the democratic mission of independence and "elevate and equalize men in the legal sphere."[24]

The expanded public sphere that Spanish reformers had hoped would preserve colonial order was buckling under pressure for inclusion and integration. Serra personified an alliance between journalism, activism, and associational life that expanded the range of normative political discourse., New organizational currents—and political factions that courted various constituencies—tended to flow in the direction of the independence movement. The "non-political" requirements of the post-Zanjón public had clearly fallen away, but limits existed nonetheless. Martín Morúa Delgado had to leave the island for the United States when officials in Matanzas shut down his newspaper *El Pueblo* for accusing the Spanish press of racism. Later than many others, he remained a supporter of the Autonomist Party.[25] The Directorio Central contested the regular and widespread denial of civil rights, while his newspaper, *La Igualdad,* circulated information to various cities and regions across Cuba. At the congress of the Directorio Central, organizations agreed to a common focus on education and schools, eliminating official record-keeping that was racially distinct, changing the Código Penal (Penal Code) and municipal laws when they applied harsher sanctions to Cubans of color, and soliciting the support of political parties.[26] Newspapers at this point adopted a more aggressive tone in acknowledging discrimination in Cuban society, as witnessed by the disputes in Santiago de Cuba in 1893 between the black newspaper *La Democracia* (Democracy) and the white newspaper *El Loco* (The Madman).[27]

Defying the conventions that marginalized any mention of Africa from claims to belonging—and, more broadly, to "civilization"—one organization looked to Africa as a source of inspiration. In 1892, the Unión Africana registered in Havana as an association with most of the same features as others in the post-Zanjón period: it made provisions for the establishment of schools and a system of mutual aid to cover medical expenses, for example; when mourning, for example, women were expected to wear white dresses and black capes. It also lobbied for regular ship traffic between Cuba and Africa and for the incorporation of cabildos into Cuban politics. Aware of political transformations occurring in Africa, the association petitioned in 1893 to use a blue flag with a gold star in the center—the flag of Africa, it claimed—and justified its validity by citing the treaty that Spain had signed with the International Association of the Congo in 1885. The Spanish government denied the request on the grounds that there were no foreign Africans in Cuba for the flag to represent! Instead, those individuals were recognized as Spaniards.[28] This was a categorical somersault that accomplished two feats. It attempted to imagine the Cuban political landscape as one free of retrograde African influence, and it prevented the members of the Unión Africana from embracing a source of sovereignty external to the Spanish empire. In the process, it attempted to fold Cubans of color, even those who explicitly identified with Africa, into the category of Spaniard. This had been an unfulfilled promise of the 1812 Constitution, and now, as citizenship as well as Spanishness were in reach of men of color, political projects not easily contained within the Spanish system met with resistance.

The transnational orientation of the Unión Africana extended even to its leadership, in the figure of William George Emanuel. In 1894 the organization named the Antiguan activist the "only representative of the African race before the Government" and elevated his title in 1895 to Aurora de la Esperanza, or Dawn of Hope. Emanuel sought a different approach than Gómez to creating an unifying organization for Cubans of color. Given the extensive membership of the cabildos, Emanuel built alliances that would bridge the houses' spiritual authority and the Spanish government's political authority. His efforts continued well into the final independence war. In 1896, representatives of ten different cabildos gathered, but in the midst of protests they voted to remove Emanuel from his position; a year later, the presidents of the Gangá, Mandinga, Carabalí, and Minas cabildos reorganized a scaled-back Unión Africana.[29] Clearly, Gómez's Directorio Central—and its relatively safe distance from African cultural forms—garnered the larger role in public life, but Emanuel and the Unión Africana, in their successes and failures, broadened the political landscape to include political projects that were transnational, non-national, and African.

By and large, however, organizations and their leaders avoided mentions of Africa and its cultures in their public statements, hewing closely instead to the language of civility and respectability. They also resisted associations with Haiti, although the nation and the revolution that created it remained a powerful symbol. Readers of La Igualdad had only to look to the bottom of the page on which the main articles appeared to find serialized excerpts of Bug-Jargal,

Victor Hugo's novel about the Haitian Revolution, originally published one year after France finally recognized Haiti's independence in 1825. For the editors of *La Igualdad,* this was a daring choice. Despite the many meanings of the Haitian Revolution, colonial officials and critics of black organizing tended to view the event almost exclusively as a race war, and this interpretation routinely grounded attacks against the calls for equal rights made by African-descended Cubans in newspapers, associations across the island, and the independence movement. With the translated title of *Bug-Jargal, o el negro rey* (*Bug-Jargal, or the Black King*), the novel gave readers of *La Igualdad* an account of the revolution in which Hugo compressed key events into the early, highly contingent years of insurrection and left the final outcome unspoken. Like the editorial essays and new articles in *La Igualdad,* the novel's diverse themes contained the elements of a complex political vocabulary that could express many of the positions circulating in Cuba at the time: independence, revolution, antirevolution (especially for Hugo himself), monarchism, identification with Africa or Africanness, identification with Haiti, and a struggle for rights within an empire, as well as a repudiation of those rights in favor of a new order. By leaving readers to develop their own interpretations of the meaning of Haiti, the editors offered a small corrective to the problem, which they identified in an article from 1893, that "all of the historians of Haiti are white and European."[30]

Careful avoidance of upsetting public expectations did not prohibit mass public action. Together, many associations of color facilitated island-wide demonstrations in 1894 to protest the exclusion of people of African descent from public establishments. Demonstrations that took place in Havana, Matanzas, and Cienfuegos attracted participants from surrounding rural areas. The Directorio Central spearheaded most of the organizing efforts in dialogue with various sociedades de color. Within *La Igualdad,* contributors recognized the possibility of a civil exchange with local officials and even the captain general, but only on the condition that Cubans of color adhered to the peace. Ever since Zanjón, sociedades had worked locally to secure public rights, yet collective action threatened to feed accusations of race war. One writer thus called for restraint, explicitly warning against the incivility and violence that characterized the incident in Cienfuegos in 1886. Carlos Trelles deplored the "immoderate note" that recently struck Matanzas, his home, "placing it at the level of Cienfuegos, the intransigent city that threw stones at the Cuban deputies Figueroa and Fernández de Castro." For the editors of *La Igualdad,* however, this stance diminished the gravity of the struggle at hand. It accused the Matanzas newspaper that published Trelles's letter of speaking "of the *negro* as if we still lived in barbarous, feudal times."[31] Leaders of color had to tread carefully, advancing an agenda in terms that did not violate principles of the very public they were trying to transform.

Negotiating with the Spanish government remained a principal activist strategy that occasionally achieved results. At 10:30 on the morning of 2 January 1894, Captain General Emilio Calleja called Gómez on the telephone—relatively new technology in Havana—to summon him to the captain general's palace immediately. Lengthy quotes of their conversation, likely provided by Gómez himself, appeared that afternoon in *La Igualdad*. Calleja sought both to reassure Gómez of his commitment to racial inclusion and to acknowledge recent conflicts between Cubans of color who faced continuing discrimination. He affirmed his commitment to the "exercise of rights" by "individuals of the *raza negra* [black race]" in public establishments, "rights that the Constitution and the laws granted to them, which makes them human beings identical to the rest." Gómez reminded the captain general of intransigent local authorities in Havana and Cienfuegos who continued to deny access to residents of African descent. Calleja promised in the future to correct any official "hostile to the government's resolutions," including those who Gómez intimated were conspiring to repeal the circulars from 1886 and 1887 banning racial discrimination that Calleja's measures attempted to reinforce: "I will repeal nothing! . . . I have ordered these measures because it is the natural consequence of the evolution that this society has made since slavery happily ended and there have been laws established that make all Spaniards equal, without distinction of birth, race, or colors; and although I have made these at the request of interested parties, I have made it because it seems sensible and necessary to do so." Gómez, in response, assured the captain general that the *raza de color* had no interest in confirming the suspicions of skeptics who expected retaliatory violence. Cubans of color would build their reputation with "calm and prudence": "We are interested in being seen that we are civilized, that we are moderate, that we are elements of order, that we are prepared for the life of freedom and of law, that we know how to control impatience. Others will hear the voice of despair and follow the path of violence. Ordinary tribunals will punish their misconduct immediately, and the tribune of History will whip them for the whole duration of the future."[32]

Here Gómez acknowledged the difficulties of presenting a united front for Cubans of color. Eschewing violence was one of the few lines he drew, despite his personal support for the cause of independence. Even if he questioned the pace of the evolution that Calleja cited, he still acknowledged that there was much to gain within the Spanish system. Thus he and his writers at *La Igual-*

dad would celebrate the pronouncement of universal male suffrage in Spain, and they would also sharply criticize electoral irregularities. They could scold a white association for a blackface performance and a black association for behaving too raucously. In this sense political diversity in the 1890s avoided accusations that Gómez and *La Igualdad* were in the pocket of a single cause besides the Directorio. It also gave them the flexibility to offer criticism.

Enunciations of loyal subjectivity surfaced occasionally, too. *La Igualdad* aired grievances about the use of flags, such as the suppression of a party on the Central Victoria in Yaguajay because it displayed a flag other than the Spanish one—as if bearing a different flag implied the disavowal of Spain.[33] Perhaps the most telling article of all included a complaint about how the Directorio received short shrift at a Liberal Party meeting when members tried to present a statement of its principles. Who was the party to silence them when the captain general himself had received their proposals? They had exercised "the right of petition that the humblest of citizens can exercise."[34] It was no longer subjects who were humble but citizens; in the absence of guaranteed voting rights, petitioning took their place. Colonial forms of political participation merged with expressions of liberal citizenship as they had regularly throughout the century. More than a tactic to keep all political options open, Gómez and *La Igualdad* used an idiom common to many of the diverse positions embraced by the Directorio's community. Even as pro-Spanish loyalty moved further away from the political center, the language of loyal subjectivity had become hegemonic such that multiple positions could be articulated through its political logic.

Loyalty Eroded: The War of Independence

With the outbreak of war in February 1895, virtually all negotiations between Gómez and the captains general—to say nothing of the struggles of less prominent Cubans of color—ground to a halt. In its first year, Cuba's war for independence had so unmoored the foundations of Cuban society that presumed logics of political affiliation no longer held. Louis A. Pérez Jr. has noted the paradoxical separatist support among property owners precisely as independence leaders identified property itself as a target to undermine the colonial system. Agricultural and commercial leaders who had been the most consistently committed to colonial rule had suffered from Spain's inability to maintain basic stability, if not guaranteed control. One momentous factor jeopardizing popular support came in February 1896 with the replacement of Arsenio Martínez Campos as the island's highest official with Valeriano

Weyler. No longer the ambitious young officer who recruited soldiers of color during the Ten Years' War, Weyler unleashed widespread devastation during the twenty months he was in office. He ordered the forced relocation of approximately 400,000 Cubans to centralized camps under army control. Spanish legitimacy withered as almost half of those people died in the camps. Many members of the Autonomist Party refused to stand by Spanish policies and gravitated to the insurgency some of their peers had already done.[35] The net effect of these shifting loyalties was a blow to national integrity and the relocation of the multifactional political conversation among Cubans to channels within the separatist movement. Moreover, with the accelerating decline of support for Spain, the various decrees and measures that inched toward Cuban autonomy garnered less and less attention.

As in the Ten Years' War, observers were quick to question the willful participation of Cubans of color. Because the insurgency found vital support among vast segments of the population, sizing up the nature of popular allegiance to one cause or another became a top priority among colonial and rebel leaders alike. Attention focused on central and western Cuba in particular as rebel forces began working their way west across the island with the goal of gaining control over the island's more populous and wealthy areas. A common observation among leaders was to view the presence of Cubans of color in the insurgency as the product of material scarcity or the manipulations of white patrons rather than a deliberate and intentional choice. It further confounded colonial officials when men of African descent led white men. Marcos García, the governor of Santa Clara province, wrote to military authorities about "the negro González" who was recruiting soldiers of color for rebel leader Francisco Carrillo. When José González proved instrumental in a decisive battle near the Dolores sugar estate in Abreus in 1897, Carrillo gave him command of a cannon stolen from the Spanish.[36] Thus García attributed whatever authority González held to Carrillo's questionable judgment. But when a white assistant to González presented himself to the Spanish command in Cienfuegos, García described the assistant as "an intelligent youth" who could influence the handful of other white soldiers under González. Under García's orders, the assistant then returned to the rebel camp with letters to the other soldiers that sought to undermine González's authority.[37] That it was easier for García to view González as a pawn than his white assistant exposes the deep roots of assumptions about the weak wills of Cuban soldiers of color.

As colonial authorities noted the multiracial composition of the insurgent army, they were reluctant to attribute ideological motives to the black and mulatto rebel anticipation. Some commentators warned yet again of black rebellion and race war, whereas others were more circumspect.[38] If hunger and hardship were principal factors that drove Cubans of color into the rebellion, they wondered, then perhaps racial animosity took second place to material need. Were rebel recruits just looking for a free meal? Ricardo Donoso Cortes, an early war observer from Spain, explained that there were "many Cubans, white as well as of color, who tried in vain earlier to fight for the cause of Spain; this shows that it is not the spirit of independence that inspires most of the rebels but that . . . [they are] disposed to fight by the imposition of hunger, or simply by the influence of an adventurous temper." Donoso criticized Spanish officials for being too distrustful and strict in their recruitment of irregular troops. Rebel authorities had scared, threatened, and intimidated rural Cubans into enlistment, he claimed; Spanish officials had more resources to bargain with, but they were not offering them. Donoso hoped that the collective memory of institutions of the volunteer corps and bomberos would inspire more Cubans to join the individuals, "*peninsulares* and *insulares* [Spaniards from the peninsula and the island], and of those the whites and those of color," to join the ranks of the Spanish.[39] A Matanzas sugar administrator who joined the rebellion attributed black and mulatto participation to personal allegiances to white superiors. The example of a promising young planter named Dolores who joined the insurgent ranks stirred him to ask: "What are they to think, those workers, *colonos* [contract cane farmers], *guajiros* [peasants], and negros, vassals of Señor Deudal de Dolores, who is no good, to whom they owe nothing, when they see a young man abandon his riches to enlist in the holy legion of the Liberation Army?"[40] Convinced that dire need explained popular support for the insurgency, many witnesses were slow to acknowledge that African-descended Cubans had placed loyalties to their families, communities, livelihoods—and egalitarian ideals and commitment to Cuban independence—above their fidelity to colonial rule, and that they could prioritize those affinities on a principled basis.

Or perhaps not. In the midst of a refugee crisis, of rampant illness, and of the breakdown of many social institutions, defining will in opposition to material need may unfairly prioritize one motive over the other. At the beginning of the war, and just weeks before his death, José Martí recounted a conversation on an expedition in eastern Cuba with an insurgent named Luis and Máximo Gómez, the military commander of the independence war. Martí quoted one of them reacting with incredulity, "But why do those Cubans fight against Cubans?" he asked. Not out of conviction or "an impossible affection for Spain," he surmised: "Those pigs fight like that for the pesos they're paid, one peso per day minus the food they get. They are the worst *vecinos* [residents] of the *caseríos* [villages], or those who have a fine to pay, or the vagrants who don't want to work, and a few Indians from Baitiquirí and Cajuerí."[41] By the middle of the war, it was difficult to tell the worst residents from the best ones in many areas. Never mind that Spanish supporters generally assumed that insurgents, too, came from similarly marginal social backgrounds. Usually aware that they faced the same accusations by some of their opponents, insurgent leaders associated popular loyalty with a combination of avarice, social deviance, and material desperation.

Martí was uncommon in attributing pro-Spanish support to rural areas, and in acknowledging Indians at all. The Batallones de Voluntarios that took shape in 1895 generally drew recruits from cities and in particular from the workforce of relatively recent Spanish migrants.[42] Although memories of the voluntarios during the Ten Years' War prompted early optimism among Spanish officials about the participation of ordinary Cubans in irregular troops, they provoked frustration among rebel leaders. Despite an early pronouncement by General Valeriano Weyler encouraging officers to "reanimate public spirit" by putting *los leales* (the loyal) to work in old and new volunteer regiments, volunteer recruitment and deployment were slower and less regimented than they had been in the prior insurrection.[43]

In a time of scarce resources, officers raised volunteer units with the financial support of businesses, banks, and organizations. This opportunity was not lost on Cubans of color who still identified with Spanish rule. José Bernabeu, president of the Casino Español de la Raza de Color, recruited a moderate group of soldiers in Havana, but more men of color responded to the recruiting efforts of the Conde de Sagunto, a titled Spaniard living in the city's burgeoning Vedado neighborhood. Through his efforts, the Batallón Movilizado de Color began sending hundreds of black and mulatto troops to the western and central provinces as early as 1896. They appear to have made it at least to Cruces, where Spanish troops defeated rebels dispatched there by Máximo Gómez.[44] The benefits of this military service were unclear, as were the rewards for the sponsors. As a public display of loyalty, sponsoring volunteer battalions reached a limited public at best, as wartime disruptions muted the publicity to be gained.

Spanish government attempts to recruit Cuban men of color as soldiers were not nearly as robust as they had been during the Ten Years' War. Despite military cutbacks during the previous decade, the situation for the Spanish army looked much stronger at the outbreak of the war than during the first war. The urgency of recruiting had lessened. Weyler himself regularly staged one of the most visible displays of black support. On a trip to Mariel from

Havana in November 1896, he inspected the five battalions stationed there and "accepted the offering of volunteers and bomberos." In his words, among the bomberos, "thirty of color were chosen, at the orders of an official, to form my personal escort."[45] The visibility of this group, and its physical proximity to Weyler, attracted the attention of many observers. This may have been Weyler's intent. Adelaide Rosalind Kirchner, a North American traveler, claimed that Weyler gave equal treatment to blacks and whites in the army "in order to offset the prominence the Cuban blacks have attained in the insurrection." "His body guard is composed of blacks," she noted, "and a number of the guerrillas are black; a band of which is attached to each battalion of the army, their chieftain being Benito Cerreros."[46] She referred here to one of the most notoriously violent guerrilla leaders, for whom there is little evidence of directing *guerrilleros* of color exclusively, or of leading a black unit, and the association subtly linked the black soldiers to the worst of Spanish brutality.[47]

Weyler made sure that Cubans would see his bodyguards during the dwindling regularity of public ceremonies in cities. U.S. war journalist Stephen Bonsal noticed Weyler's black bodyguards in the context of an elaborate ceremony in "the loyal city of Santa Clara." After lengthy speeches by city leaders, Weyler began his procession from the cemetery outside the city to the main plaza, "escorted by a squadron of cavalry and followed on foot by about fifty men of his black escort." Despite all of the pageantry, the strength and support that the event intended to convey showed signs of fatigue. A weary Weyler watched the military parade, but "as the last of the black *bomberos* went limping by," he immediately dismounted his horse and went inside.[48] Public commemorations like these grew rarer as the war progressed, drawing feeble audiences for Weyler's showy escort—or foreign visitors stationed in cities. Yet for the man who actively recruited black soldiers during the Ten Years' War, the personal escort spoke to a longer history of military engagement that complicated the frequent accusations by supporters of Spain that the insurgency was, at heart, a race war.

Whatever their motivations, ordinary Cubans were organized into guerrillas in cities and the countryside to accompany Spanish columns. Usually understood as an urban phenomenon, guerrillas also formed in plenty of small towns on the island, and, as Spanish troops diffused into rural areas, they recruited from rural estates as well. Guerrillas organized in San Antonio de los Baños frequently found themselves dispatched to rural estates to attack rebel camps.[49] The humble backgrounds of most of the volunteers became one of their most salient features. Insurgent officer Bernabé Boza described the guerrillas as being composed mostly of "white and colored Cubans" and only a few Spaniards, presumably recent immigrants "who were familiar with the country."[50] Perhaps the best evidence of a racially mixed Spanish effort comes obliquely from the maneuvering of one cunning rebel. Ricardo Batrell, a black soldier in the Liberation Army's western invasion, recounted in his memoir a mission near the end of the war to find cattle for the infantry. Near Jovellanos, outside the city of Matanzas, Batrell and a small group of soldiers took five Spanish guerrilleros prisoner and wore their clothes in order to pass into town without raising suspicion. The sight of black guerrilleros was apparently common enough that Batrell's comrades could pass for enemy soldiers simply by donning Spanish gear.[51]

Detailed information about the composition of the guerrillas is rare, but a lieutenant colonel's report from Matanzas in 1896 offers a few clues about who enlisted. Charged in April with recruiting a battalion composed of somewhere between eight hundred and one thousand "white and colored volunteers," Adolfo Álvarez Almendariz had recruited three hundred men by the end of May. The only list of individual recruits identifies the twenty-seven men, ranging in age from eighteen to forty, who gathered at the Aguedita sugar estate on 14 May. The guerrillas contained more than a few Spaniards: thirteen of them, including three of the four officers, were from various areas in Spain. The roster did not identify recruits by race, although a curious pattern of repeating surnames emerges among nine of the non-Spanish members. Despite the conventions of taking the surname of both the father and mother, codified in the Spanish Civil Code of 1889, many Cubans of color struggled to adapt to this system when their parentage was unknown or when they or their parents had no surnames under slavery and had taken the surname of their owner. Michael Zeuske has identified the record-keeping practice of using *sin otro apellido* (without another surname). Ángel Barbón Barbón, Agustín Barbón Barbón, Candelario Delgado Delgado, Juan Pinillos Pinillos, and five other guerrilleros are all listed with both a father and mother identified by first name. It is certainly possible that both parents happened to have the same surname, and that one-third of a guerrilla formed on a sugar estate happened to experience this phenomenon. A more likely possibility—though still highly speculative—is that these nine non-Spaniards were of African descent, having only one surname but repeating it—with both parents having taken the surname of their common master.[52]

If Spaniards figured more prominently in the guerrillas than Boza acknowledged, why would he minimize their presence and simultaneously highlight guerrilleros of color, especially when the rebels themselves claimed substantial black support for the cause of independence? The answer lies in Boza's characterization of the guerrilleros as dangerous and marginal types. He claimed that the Spanish government deliberately avoided recruiting "honorable men" and instead targeted murderers, thieves, and pickpockets, and prisoners. Crimes such as arson and forgery, in his opinion, constituted "the best letter of recommendation" for admission into the guerrilla.[53] This military strategy was not, for Boza, a desperate measure forged in crisis. Instead, it exposed the very foundations of Spanish rule: the kinds of behavior that counted as valor and honor; the values that people identified with the Spanish flag and soldier's uniform; the credentials that qualified Spain to be a "civilized nation" in contrast to the values honored by the rebels. For Boza, the criminal and corrupt Cubans of color who joined guerrillas did so because they recognized aspects of themselves in the leadership and execution of the counterinsurgency. This stinging portrayal cleared the way for Boza to praise the black leadership of the liberation army as a more esteemed group of individuals. In contrast to the "exaggerations and quixotic" denigrating characterizations of the multiracial insurgency, the image Boza conveyed was of "enlightened, enthusiastic, and active" men who were not bound by Spanish conventions.[54]

Evidence of widespread creation of segregated black and mulatto units fighting for Spain is rare—again, in part because of the race-blind record-keeping of local officials (at least in military registers).[55] Manuel Corral, a Spanish volunteer, recalled that the black soldiers he encountered were always rebels. Yet he did note that among the volunteer units organized in and around Cienfuegos, the only racially segregated battalion was the Batallón Tiradores de las Lomas, "composed in its near totality of Chinese." He praised it more for its patriotism and the low costs of maintaining it than for the services its members lent to the war effort. The battalion's vigilance of the military hospital in the city, however, proved a task more significant than Corral recognized given wartime conditions.[56] The cuerpos de bomberos frequently fortified cities and towns, and in 1896, Weyler organized three hundred bomberos under a black colonel to fight in the western provinces, specifically against Maceo.[57] Maceo was developing plans to take Candelaria, a town in the west and a key Spanish fortification along the railroad. When he heard that many of the troops defending Candelaria were of African descent, he veered from his normal practice and ordered all enemy combatants of color to be killed with machetes after victory.[58]

This episode of targeted killings represents one of the highest estimates of the price of integrity. What may be lost in the attention to loyal subjectivity is a keener sense of the repressive forces that most Cubans of African descent confronted regularly in their lives, and not just during wartime. It downplays the idea that supporting Spanish rule—or at least the *perception* of supporting Spain—could be a life-or-death decision. If loyalty constituted the normative subject position in Cuban society, the violence inflicted on the disloyal—rebel and runaway slaves and insurgents, especially—could appear more conspicuous to war observers, either in the interests of making an example or making a martyr. Loyalty, too, had its costs, most apparent during military conflicts to be sure, but in noncrisis moments as well. Each side of the conflict had its traitors on the other side, and neither side monopolized brutality. Aside from loyalty concerns were warfare traditions; that is, actions of Maceo's troops appear to have had parallels in other conflicts: pro-Spanish Cubans forced to dig their own graves, beheaded, fingernails pulled out.[59]

By the middle of 1897, Spanish forces reported numerous desertions. Reasons for desertion were likely as varied as the deserters themselves; nonetheless, the increasing advantage of the insurgents over the Spanish troops precipitated a gradual exodus to the Liberation Army. Manuel Corral described how his unit, camped in Arimao one night in October with nothing to consume but coffee, heard news that the *guerrilleros movilizados* in nearby Cumanayagua who accompanied them "showed that they served no one, [and] many of them proceeded to enemy lines."[60] Elsewhere in Santa Clara province, a cavalry unit in Remedios posted a notice for the capture of a guerrillero from Caibarién named Luis Abreu, "of unknown parents, native of Africa."[61] Mateo Sarría, described as "color negro" and the son of "la *morena* Nicolasa Sarría," deserted the Guerrilla de San Fernando in Cienfuegos on 14 July.

With a rebel victory becoming an increasingly probable outcome at the end of 1897, the Spanish government made a last-minute and unprecedented conciliatory move. In November, two royal decrees established full equality of political rights for residents of Cuba and Puerto Rico in accordance with the Spanish electoral law of 1890, which guaranteed universal male suffrage. Autonomism, once a movement eyed with official suspicion and synchronized to the machinations of a single political party, now reigned as a new politics of empire. Elections were scheduled for the following March. The momentum of the new Autonomist government ground to a halt just one month later when the United States entered the war. On 22 April 1898, William McKinley gave orders for a naval blockade.

At last, Cuban men of all colors received the full political equality that had motivated them, and their predecessors, to remain loyal subjects in recent decades. Certainly the U.S. invasion curtailed many of the possibilities of this moment, but general fatigue from the war, multiple conversions of Liberals and even Conservatives to the cause of independence, and the perceived illegitimacy of the Spanish government by much of the island also foreclosed the potential that autonomy held. Yet this did not necessarily cause the death of the loyal subject. Even those who could no longer imagine why anyone would still be ever faithful nonetheless valued loyal subjectivity, even as the object of that loyalty changed, as did the terms on which it operated.

Seeing through Loyalty

As Ada Ferrer has noted, the entrance of the United States into the conflict compelled vast numbers of men to join the rebel forces. Not least of those new supporters were Spaniards: soldiers, officers, and civilians alike.[62] This shift dealt a critical blow to any popular support the Spanish government might still claim. Whatever national integrity meant as an idea or a practice had lost virtually all meaning in the final months of the war, and its demise came at a steep price. There were thousands of deaths among the Spanish and Cubans involved, productive endeavors in disarray, unmoored social relations, and a new imperial presence. The end of the war obscured the ends of empire that many Spaniards and Cubans had pursued over the previous decades. Cuba by 1898 was an island of dislocations: bodily, in the goriest and most visceral image of wartime violence (recall the fingernails ripped off of pro-Spanish Cuban soldiers); socially, as families, communities, and many post-Zanjón associations did not survive the war intact; and politically, as alliances shattered and forged between various "sides" bore little resemblance to their earlier forms. With no preexisting visions of how all of these pieces might now fit together, Cubans, Spaniards, and North Americans struggled in the final months before and after the war to reconcile old and new connections between political allegiances and the other solidarities that gave their lives meaning.

In spite of obstacles, Cubans began to make sense out of the mayhem. Ricardo Batrell found that there was "truly a Cuban community" as city crowds cheered entering liberation forces in 1899: "There were no worries or any races. Everyone was joyful and full of brotherly love."[63] Indeed, celebrating independence from Spain figured as perhaps the easiest political change to process, and triumphal arches, parades, and music rang in a new, albeit ambiguous, order. There were also holdouts. Two days before the signing of the armistice, the leaders of the Cienfuegos brigade had taken to the street in protest. They accused public authorities of imposing peace on Spain despite the continued vigilance of the "intact and determined" Spanish army in the city.[64] Despite their celebration of the new or stubborn defense of the old, Cubans had no choice but to reconsider their relationships to the states to which they risked their lives.

The end of the war for Cuban independence had also been the beginning of the conflict for U.S. soldiers and the masses of supporters they left behind. Wartime mobilization raised questions about the political aspirations of the nation and government, and who might claim the rights of its citizenship based on fulfilling the obligations of military service. Across the country were advocates for sending black soldiers from the United States to fight in Cuba. Booker T. Washington figured among those who recognized a rare opportunity for African Americans to demonstrate their loyalty to the nation. And indeed, loyalty figured as one of the most common themes among the black soldiers who wrote letters to newspapers in the United States about their experiences in Cuba. Over three thousand black soldiers had converged on Tampa in early May 1898 to await embarkation to Cuba, and George Prioleau, a chaplain in the Ninth Cavalry, reflected on his upcoming mission in a letter to the *Cleveland Gazette*. As black troops left communities in the United States ravaged by poverty and violence to free Cubans from Spanish brutality, he had to ask: "Is America any better than Spain?" Despite his ambivalence about the promise of national citizenship, he insisted on the allegiance of the race: "Yet the Negro is loyal to his country's flag. O! he is a noble creature, loyal and true . . . Forgetting that he is ostracized, his race considered as dumb as driven cattle, yet, as loyal and true men, he answers the call to arms and with blinding tears in his eyes and sobs he goes forth." Prioleau's hope was that black regiments would return home "and begin again to fight the battle of American prejudice."[65] "When I fall I intend to draw my last breath for the old flag under which I was born," wrote Simon Brown of the Twenty-Third Kansas infantry to the "Citizens of Oswego." In recognition of a common racial bond, Brown was also ready to die for "the poor Cubans as well": "I am convinced that these people are of our Negro race, although they cannot speak the English language, but they have the complexion of our race."[66] In the meantime, many soldiers who fought in "colored regiments" hoped that their actions would be rewarded with inclusion in the regular U.S. Army. The war thus brought into focus the transnational dimension of loyalty as political practice. In a comparative sense, people of color invoked their allegiance to their respective nations where they resided in order to attain similar goals of political inclusion; in a connective sense, a recognition of shared African descent or blackness generated by encounters such as the war in 1898 nodded to allegiances that transcended national boundaries and might ground alternative projects for collective progress.

The fact that U.S. intervention extended the United States beyond its borders met with diverse responses by black soldiers. For some of them, loyalty and patriotism had their limits, especially when, as a member of the Tenth Cavalry asserted, "Cuba was a paradise." "There is not one soldier in the camp," he argued, "who would not rather go to Cuba than remain in any part of the South."[67] They saw other opportunities in Cuba and mused about abandoning the United States and seeking new lives in a new Cuba: a "Negro republic," imagined W. C. Payne, "because the greater portion of the insurgents are Negroes and they are politically ambitious."[68] In this possibility, some recognized the strength of transnational loyalties. In Santiago, wrote W. C. Warmsley, a surgeon in the Ninth Infantry, "the professional colored man would be idolized." He cited "the businessmen (colored) of Santiago" who expressed a desire to share their national independence with "one million colored men of education from the States. The colored here, unlike those in the states, are loyal to each other and honest to a fault. They will support a colored man in whatever business he undertakes."[69] The combined strength of Cubans and North Americans of African descent, wrote M. W. Dadler to *The Freeman* in Indianapolis, would "show to the world that true patriotism is in the minds of the sons of Ham."[70] Capitalizing on such true patriotism had been the goals of every power involved in the conflict. Debates about the meaning of race to that devotion had been far from resolved when Spain surrendered in August. Even as loyalty to Spain dissipated, the power of the idea of loyalty continued to give perspective to new conditions of citizenship and patriotism.

Perspectives on Spain in the United States changed as the contours of intervention came into view. Spaniards had claimed the moral high ground in the war by casting insurgents as barbaric and uncivilized, which they reinforced by linking the insurgency to race war. By the end of the war, they found themselves on the losing side of the battle between civilization and barbarism. This characterization echoed that of Antonio Maceo during the Ten Years' War, but it had now gained internationally recognized importance. Building on routine reports of Spanish tyranny—"Butcher" Weyler, the reconcentration, an iron grip on an enticing market, and the destruction of the uss *Maine*—North American observers linked Spain to the unspeakable brutality of the general. The power of the U.S. state to suppress that brutality became a powerful image. Political cartoons in U.S. newspapers regularly represented Cuba or Cubans through an easily recognized depiction of subordination: a child, a woman, and, quite often, a black child or woman. In a period when African Americans, too, appeared in cartoons as apes, one *Philadelphia Inquirer* image portrayed "the Great Weyler Ape," not as an untamed savage beast running amok but as one caged and safely viewable (see figure 6.1). As a "great addition to our museum," Weyler signified a dominated and contained strain of Spanish barbarism.

So, too, did Weyler's personal executioner. The Greater America Exposition that took place in Omaha in 1899 featured a Cuban Village that included "Valentine" (probably a poor translation of Valentín or Valentino), billed as Weyler's hangman responsible for hundreds of executions. On a daily basis he gave performances that reenacted executions (with his chair and garrote brought from Cuba). Fairgoers could take in the spectacle from safe distance, and they could take home stereographs of Valentine and his chair. In the comfort of their parlors, they could gaze at Valentine's black savagery in the service of Spain, content in knowing that his killing days were behind him.[71] It was on the foundation of images like those that Major-General James Wilson reminisced in 1912 that he knew in 1898 that Spain was "powerless to carry on the war in civilized fashion," not because of material shortcomings but because of the impoverished condition that "her rapacity and misrule for four hundred years" had created on the island.[72] That he came to attribute this same lack of "civilization" to Cubans as well speaks to the heavy lifting that concept did at the time. In Wilson's and many other imaginings, Cuba remained linked to Spain, though through a common lack of civilization rather than a formal colonial relationship.

How did Spaniards make sense of this new realignment? The evolution of the great Spanish Liberal statesman Francisco Pí y Margall offers a glimpse into the malleability of Spanish racial and political discourse. A champion of Iberian federalism, he had long supported autonomy for Cuba, and his arguments as early as the 1850s made a strong case for abolishing slavery as an application of "the lessons of Santo Domingo" and a necessary step in preserving Cuba as part of the Spanish empire.[73] With slavery abolished, Pí y Margall took a different approach to balancing Cuban autonomy with continued support for Spain. By the 1890s he spoke of Cuba's relationship to Spain in gendered terms—that Cuba was "already of age" and no longer in need of Spain's fatherly protection. His advocacy for Cuban independence during the war distinguished him among his political peers, and so did his advocacy for conceiving of a "Latin race" whose imagined community would preserve commercial ties between Spain and its former American colonies.[74] He joined a

Would make an excellent addition to our museum.—Philadelphia Inquirer.

No Spanish governor-general of Cuba was ever so thoroughly hated and detested as Weyler. The above picture, representing him as an ape, is probably the most expressive form in which public contempt for him could have been shown.

FIGURE 6.1 • Cartoon of "The Great Weyler Ape," 1898. The caption reads, "Would make an excellent addition to our museum." Originally published in the *Philadelphia Inquirer*.

small chorus of Spanish writers who placed a history of global imperial dominance and fantastic wealth in the service of rendering the Spanish world civilized. Pseudoscientific arguments about Anglo-Saxon superiority lurked in the shadows, motivating these arguments, and after the war for independence of 1898, the implications for Spaniards were none too subtle. Reflecting in 1900 on what the Spaniards came to call *El Desastre* (The Disaster), Spanish journalist Joaquín Costa acknowledged the failures of old social categories and called for a new Spanish *raza* "as a counterweight to the Saxon race, to maintain the moral equilibrium in the infinite game of history."[75]

That the game had changed was still difficult for some Cubans to accept. In August 1898, as Cubans watched with distress as Spain and the United States negotiated peace without representation from the Liberation Army, Rodolfo de Lagardère took time to write to a Spanish lieutenant colonel. If any person in this book could justifiably represent a Spanish "loyalist," it was Lagardère. He wrote to remind the officer of the historic contributions of people of African descent to the Spanish empire. "I'm sure you know better than anyone the virtuous history of loyalty of the long-suffering black race," Lagardère wrote. Citing nearly one hundred years of independence movements against Spanish rule in Latin America, his words of praise were for "our conduct in Chile, in Buenos Aires, in San Juan, in Cartagena, in the past and in the current war, as well our decision to take up arms when the maintenance of order has demanded it." He also requested, "in reward for our services," that the services of Cubans of African descent be acknowledged in a public forum. Lagardère wanted assurance that dispatches would be sent to Madrid to document "that we were fine Spanish soldiers and that this, with complete, free, and honest authority, is agreed to, in recognition of *nuestra fidelidad jamás desmentida* [our never-betrayed loyalty] during this century of so many revolts."[76] As he saw it, Cubans of color had been as ever-faithful to Spain over the long haul as the island as a whole, and this was no time to betray that fidelity. He pinpointed, in the broadest terms possible, the significance of African-descended peoples' historical allegiance to Spain: it had been a central element of Spanish rule in its American colonies that demanded public recognition, and the disintegration of national integrity threatened to devalue this remarkable contribution.

But what, one wonders, was Lagardère thinking? Hadn't he also witnessed during that same century countless disappointing examples of Spain's limited and broken promises to the "long-suffering black race"? The evidence amassed in this book has intended to widen our political imagination to understand how even those broken promises could be accommodated by a subjective mode—not necessarily a fixed identity—that maintained faith in Spanish colonialism. In his classic formulation of exit, voice, and loyalty, Albert Hirschman postulated that "loyalty is at its most functional when it looks most irrational."[77] Of course, this depends on who's doing the looking. Lagardère only appears irrational from the perspective that his attachments to Spain were unwarranted and counterintuitive (a free upgrade from "irrational") and that he should have been supporting the cause of *Cuba libre*—that it was in his interests to do so. Even allowing that his support of Spain now put him in the minority, and that the historical value of loyalty needed better reconciliation with the state of Cuba at the end of the war, the assumption that his embrace of "exit" was prolonged flattens a position that many Cubans of color had long inhabited. Especially during a month when the supporters of the Cuban independence movement realized their clear subjection to a new imperial power, neither adherence to Spain nor to Cuban nationalism entirely fulfilled Hirschman's dictum that "loyalty holds exit at bay and activates voice."[78]

SPAIN'S DEFEAT AND THE CONCLUSION of the war confounded expectations on all sides of the conflict. For insurgents, U.S. intervention had compromised their vision of national independence. Spaniards were left to discern meaning in El Desastre. And while the U.S. military government had identified and secured the support of the island's "best men"—"the propertied, the educated, the white," in the words Louis A. Pérez Jr., including longtime supporters of Spain—it faced an uphill battle to convince most Cubans of its legitimacy.[79] If the political landscape of the early 1890s had been characterized by fracture, war had only exacerbated—rather than reconciled—competing factions and ideas.

In a moment when the war's outcome muffled many Cuban voices, then, the work that race performed satisfied few. The independence movement's commitment to ending racial difference and discrimination represented, at this point, the strongest critique of the concept itself, but one imperiled by changing circumstances; Spanish optimism about a unified Latin race held only limited appeal on the island; and assertions of Anglo-Saxon superiority hardly held any appeal at all. How those fluent in the language of Cuban nationalism would, and could, challenge racism after Spanish rule depended in part on how Cubans assessed the changes and continuities between their Spanish imperialist past and the new imperialist presence of the United States.

After experiencing an expansion of political options leading up to the war, Cubans now faced the task of narrowing them down and defining national integrity anew. And so citizens of an independent Cuba, constrained by U.S. intervention and intent on preserving inclusionary goals of *Cuba libre,* ultimately rendered loyalty to Spain anachronistic, irrational, and increasingly, but not entirely, invisible.

Subject Citizens and the Tragedy of Loyalty

Three years after winning independence from Spanish rule, Cubans gathered in Havana in 1901 for the island's first Constitutional Convention. The U.S. occupation government had sanctioned restricted elections for convention delegates one year earlier, and military authorities now anxiously monitored the proceedings.[1] As debates revolved around universal male suffrage, William George Emmanuel—the Antiguan activist who had led the Unión Africana in Havana during the 1890s—wrote a flurry of letters to President William McKinley and other U.S. officials that spring. He protested the possible enfranchisement of Cubans of color on the grounds that "the African natives, against their will, [were] being forced into Cuban Nationality" and that they received more rights during slavery, as subjects of the Spanish crown, than they were likely to receive in an independent Cuba.[2] Emmanuel was less concerned with the damaging effects of universal male citizenship rights on Cuban politics than on Cuban men of color themselves. To the north, ongoing African American disfranchisement loomed as a chilling example of what postwar national reconciliation could effect.[3] In the end, Emmanuel's pleas went unanswered, and the Cuban Constitutional Convention extended voting rights, with a few restrictions, to all Cuban men. With the inauguration of the Cuban Republic the following year, a system of representative government conferred rights of citizenship without making race a criterion, something that the architects of Spanish rule had inched toward in the final decades of colonial rule but had never allowed to flourish.

On the first day of 1899, U.S. soldiers stood watch as Adolfo Jiménez Castellanos, Spain's last captain general, was escorted from his palace to the Bay of Havana, where he set sail to complete repatriation efforts on the island and then to return to Spain (see figure C.1). As General John Ruller Brooke assumed control of the island, it was clear that Cubans would not enjoy the unencumbered sovereignty they had earned in the course of a grueling war. So why would Emmanuel, a steadfast advocate for Cubans of color, try to compromise that national vision even further? His skepticism about national citizenship, acknowledgment of rights conferred through imperial subject-hood, and insistence that "African natives" had no instinctive draw to either one might seem anachronistic today, when citizenship and suffrage remain the locus of so many (but certainly not all) aspirations of democratic political community. This book has provided a genealogy of those ideas as they unfolded in practice, in various forms, throughout the final decades of the Spanish empire in Cuba. It explains how arguments like Emmanuel's drew on a rich history of experiences and experiments with reciprocal relationships between Cubans of African descent and the Spanish government. Such reciprocities could be paternalistic, rewarding, exploitive, affective, and, above all, partial. But behind the continuity implied by the motto "Ever Faithful" was a dynamic process that transformed the way that Cubans came to politics.

The ontogeny of two parallel strategies for political inclusion under colonial rule comes into view through the actions of African-descended Cubans and shifts in Spanish colonial policy. Military participation, whether in a militia or in service during wartime, alternately afforded black and mulatto men social status, freedom from slavery, and grounds for claiming citizenship in what evolved as Spain's national empire.[4] And as the institutions of the public sphere emerged in full force, associational life provided Cubans of color with an opportunity to participate and organize through associations, political parties, and newspapers. The reach of loyal subjectivity extended into the Cuban Republic, even though Cubans in the new political and cultural environment actively forgot what Rodolfo de Lagardère referred to in 1898 as "the virtuous history of loyalty."

Most Cubans disavowed that history after 1898. Intent on defending and advancing a national project always under threat of U.S. manipulation, Cubans discussed alternatives to nationalism perhaps less than they had before independence. Understanding that process calls for a careful excavation of what Steven Feierman has called invisible history: the result of a process by which "colonized social forms came to be cut off from coherence—from the meaningful orientation of social action in historically rooted patterns."[5] What becomes visible in exploring Cuba's invisible history is a closer relationship between forms of political personhood constituted under Spanish rule and after Cuban independence. As is clear from the history of race and loyalty during the nineteenth century, modes of colonial subjectivity and citizenship were not just sequential but simultaneous. The same can be said for the Cuban Republic: to the extent that Cuba still endured the vicissitudes of empire after 1898, most Cubans figured as both subjects and citizens.

FIGURE C.1 • Captain General Adolfo Jiménez Castellanos being escorted from the captain general's palace to return to Spain, 1 January 1899. Courtesy of Houghton Library, Harvard University.

At a quick glance, U.S. occupiers seem to have been the first (after those who fought for independence) to minimize and demonize the memory of Spain in Cuba. William George Emmanuel, was rare in his search for things positive about Spanish colonial rule. However, the racial politics of the vision of Cuban independence forged since 1868 should also be remembered in that forgetting. The overlap of Emmanuel's statements with those of Cubans from earlier decades, such as Lagardère, suggests that the suppression and fragmentation of the history of loyalty was not exclusively the product of North American intervention. Indeed, the fabric of Cuban nationalism itself worked to conceal that narrative.

Concrete shifts in Cuba had occurred throughout the island with the war's denouement, prompting an uneven process of extricating Spanish authority. In contrast to the countryside, cities had remained Spanish strongholds for much of the war. *Ayuntamientos* counted numerous but dwindling pro-colonial members in their ranks. Thus, as the war ended, colonial officials and local governments awkwardly and begrudgingly cleared the way for a new political order. The captain general issued a circular that called on ayuntamientos to gather up the Spanish flags and royal portraits from civil and military institutions so that they could be shipped back to Spain.[6] Residents of Havana later forced the city's mayor to ban the display of the Spanish flag or emblem on any building, including the meeting houses of unions, mutual aid societies, and veterans' organizations. As the statue of Isabel II came down from its lofty pedestal on Havana's Paseo del Prado, municipal leaders in Santiago de Cuba—on the opposite end of the island—called on ayuntamientos throughout Cuba to contribute funds for a statue of Antonio Maceo, the revered insurgent general of African descent.[7] Although the victory of *Cuba libre* ushered in a new order, its institutionalization was by no means obvious, predictable, or guaranteed, especially in the shadow of the North American presence. Liquidating the material culture of Spanish colonialism was a clear enough task. Erasing or displacing memories of loyalty to Spanish rule would not be so easy.

For journalist and independence activist Rafael Serra, the harsh experience of war had obliterated any nostalgia for Spanish rule. Between 1895 and 1898, Serra routinely publicized the successes of Cubans of color in the independence effort and helped to create a pantheon of national martyrs and heroes. If the sides were clearly delineated during the armed conflict itself, the conclusion of the war left Serra, like many Cubans, frustrated and confused about the island's future as a free and sovereign nation. "Neither Spanish nor Yankee" became Serra's postwar motto. He recognized the uncanny similarities between the rhetoric of Spanish officials who branded the independence movement as "a revolt of blacks," as he wrote in 1899, commanded by "discontent farmers," and statements such as one in the New York *Herald* warning that "Cuba Libre signifies another Black Republic. We do not want something of that disposition so close. Haiti is already enough."[8]

The dismaying idea that "two or three rich Americans would be the economic owners of Cuba" accompanied Serra's worries that U.S. imperial power would nullify the independence movement's egalitarian promises of citizenship. As early as 1897, he predicted a battle over universal male suffrage—a portent of the Constitutional Convention debates of 1901. Influential in the reconfiguration of Cuban sovereignty, Serra feared, would be African Americans from the southern United States. The U.S. government might encourage the emigration of African Americans "in order to stimulate patriotism, exploit their loyalty, and set them like an attack dog against everything that may not be blind obedience to the arrogant gods of Yankee paganism." Confronting limited job opportunities and the ominous threat of lynching, Serra allowed that African Americans might also be favorably disposed to seeking new lives in Cuba. This apprehension might have been well founded. Serra concluded that "the difference in language, the superiority of education of the American black, and many other circumstances will come to impoverish the condition of the also miserable Cuban black."[9] Equally appalling for Serra was that the military intervention of the United States in the summer of 1898 diminished the status of the Cuban Liberation Army, which the occupation government dissolved after the peace negotiations. Cubans of African descent, who occupied prominent positions in the army, stood to lose the most. With the reconstitution of the Cuban army, the United States invalidated the multiracial leadership of the Liberation Army and insisted on an all-white officer corps. With the strongest evidence he could muster, Serra combated statements that the "element of color" neither gained from nor contributed to the war.

His ambivalence extended to Spanish rule and to Cuban leaders. He acknowledged that even "the government of Spain grasped how much the blacks gained by having contributed with their arms and blood to the Ten Years' War. If that was with Spain, must we fall in error to consider Cubans inferior in generosity to the cruel Spanish governments?"[10] Serra included in his collection of writings from 1907 a report by a commission formed after a meeting between Liberal President Tomás Estrada Palma and Generoso Campos Marquetti, president of the association of veterans of color. The commission charged that the artillery corps "decisively" excluded Cubans of African descent from its officer ranks. In the Guardia Rural, officers delayed and ignored the hiring and promotion of *hombres de color*. In police hiring, officers harassed black and mulatto applicants with so many unfavorable investigations that very few of them could become patrolmen or policemen. In the few exceptional cases of black or mulatto superiors, the police presented a "wicked pretext" for their ultimate exclusion. Serra questioned the fact that for many years, even the southern United States had black police officers, and now white policemen from the United States had found employment in Cuba.

These exclusions affronted one of the greatest achievements of the nationalist insurgency. The movement's antiracist ideal, and model for subsequent cross-racial politics, found its most visible practice in the diverse composition of the Liberation Army's leadership and ranks. Segregating and discriminating military institutions robbed Cubans of one of their most powerful symbols of independence. Virtually powerless to change the new policies themselves, Cubans worked in the 1900s to preserve the memory of that achievement of racial cooperation. Monuments, homages, and banquets commemorated black and mulatto veterans, martyrs, and heroes of the war and forced their audiences to confront publicly the social significance of the multiracial and antiracist elements of Cuban nationalism.[11] In addressing this specific issue, the military loyalties that linked people of African descent to the Spanish crown as late as 1898 served little purpose for Cubans in the Republic looking to the past for explanation, orientation, or inspiration. For one thing, North American occupiers offered terms of inclusion for Cubans of African descent that were similar to those of Spain: conditional inclusion in public life and little chance of officer status in the regular military. Simply put, there was little comparative advantage to invoking Spanish military participation over the contributions of insurgents who as early as 1868 claimed the title of *ciudadano cubano* (Cuban citizen).

More important, the racial lines drawn in new military institutions formed part of a larger conflict over representing the nation. The image of racial cooperation was now eclipsed by an alternative depiction of Cuban nationhood emphasizing, in Ada Ferrer's words, the "prominence of educated white leaders, commonalities with American achievements, and the modern, civilized status of the would-be nation." This was not a new war of images, but its resurgence during U.S. intervention "helped overdetermine the outcome."[12] Cubans, those of African descent in particular, had to plan their public interventions strategically, and the military loyalties of the independence effort made a more compelling case for commemorating Cuban citizenship than those of Spanish colonial rule. In this environment, every act of remembrance signaled a victory in a battle over *cubanismo* that was tipping in favor of a severely limited vision of racial justice and inclusion.

The stakes of this battle were not lost on Rafael Serra, nor were its consequences. Writing from New York in 1901, he recognized that conditions for most Cubans of color had not dramatically changed from the time of Spanish rule. But he explained the continuity between colony and Republic by citing the intransigence of nationalist leaders to address racial inequalities. When cubanismo existed under Spanish rule, in his view, it

> openly opposed itself against the enjoyment of civil rights that the government of the monarchy decreed in favor of blacks. But then they told us: suffer a little now, because any disagreement between Cubans can ruin the redemptive work for which we have come together. The black conceded. The war erupted. The blacks had to suffer injustices of emigration and injustices in the battlefield and here, like before, they said: suffer a little now,

because any disagreement between Cubans can ruin the redemptive work for which we have come together. The war ended. Spaniards and Cubans embraced, [Rafael] Montoro and Martí kissed, and they leave the blacks in nearly the same condition as during Spanish rule. But still they say: suffer a little now, because what happens here is because of the Yankees, and any disagreement between Cubans can ruin the redemptive work for which we have come together, and we now ought to be arm in arm and with a single heart, to work so that these Yankee lynchers go and leave us.[13]

Serra was almost always openly critical of the United States: of lynching, disfranchisement, and antimiscegenation laws within its borders, and of its presence in Cuba for the many reasons previously discussed. But he was not ready to concede that the new imperialist presence exclusively explained racism and produced inequalities. In Serra's view, colonialism—whether Spanish or North American—provided Cuban leaders with convenient opportunities for scapegoating. The real problem lay in the inherent inability the adherents of Cuban nationalism to address racial problems in a serious way. As Louis A. Pérez Jr. has noted, "The imperative of nation thus foreclosed the invocation of race, presumably by whites and blacks, under the aegis of racial equality. 'Equality' between the races within racist structures, however, promised to institutionalize racism."[14] In their struggle to complete the "redemptive work" of cubanismo, Cuban leaders had to strike a balance between making claims to sovereignty in the shadow of United States imperialism and leveling the inequities that had survived after independence. To Rafael Serra, asserting the imperative of nation and attending to racist structures were identical processes, and the inability of those leaders to share that vision and act on it led to a polity with differential access to citizenship and the continued subjugation of Cubans of color.

In many respects, the Cuban Republic did reproduce many of the problems of the Spanish colony. The idea of *Cuba libre* confronted limits as United States intervention denied Cubans the national sovereignty, self-determination, and independence they had never fully attained under Spain. Despite shifts in the meaning of race and the achievements of the independence movement, inequalities and discrimination still existed. Such social inequities guaranteed that many Cubans of African descent would not enjoy the same rewards for their labor or the same access to the rights of citizenship as those enjoyed by white Cubans.[15]

In general terms, the colonial legacy in Latin America has made its inhabitants, as Steve Stern has argued, "less rooted in the quest to treat the past as closed and sealed" and instead "free to see it as open, surprising, and therefore contestable."[16] In what he calls the "tricks of time," he shows how some Latin Americans have invoked the colonial past to challenge persistent postcolonial inequalities. Yet, the similarities between the colony and the Republic in Cuba did not seem to inspire the inventive responses that Stern highlights. Cubans largely sought to forget about the colony and allegiances to the former imperial power in the interests of asserting a national identity within the context of the new colonial domination by the United States. For Cubans of African descent, this meant abandoning a history of loyalty that some now saw as contributing to the same continuities they struggled to change.

Very few commentators of African descent, then, thought with the history of loyalty, overlooking a narrative with as many layers of counterrevolution in the nineteenth century as layers of revolution that Cubans came to celebrate in the twentieth century. In that earlier history, strategic ascriptions loyalty subjectivity singled out potentially rebellious populations and attempted to integrate them as devoted subjects. As a concept of social organization, it could connect people—in a colonial polity and through a public sphere—in a continuous process of identification and differentiation.[17] Colonial loyalty became an odd idea in a political culture in which U.S. imperialism attempted to stifle and distort even the memory of the struggle for independence. Many Cubans of African descent in the Republic sought to make a new history, one that might occasionally carefully draw from the colonial past if only to illustrate resistance to it. They preferred other tricks of time, and worked so that the history of loyalty indeed remain "closed and sealed" in order to remember a revolutionary past and to imagine a revolutionary future.

Nevertheless, aspects of loyal subjectivity informed struggles for citizenship rights in the Cuban Republic. Cubans of color identified "two principal modes of imagining citizenship," as Alejandra Bronfman notes: claims based on military service and those tied to "civic virtue, [which] sought equal status through education and participation in associational life."[18] Nor did vertical relationships between political leaders and race-based associations disappear; members of black associations regularly relied on patronage from well-placed politicians for resources.[19] Even the language used to comprehend the presence of the United States clung closely to paternalistic ideas about gratitude, even as they delineated anticolonial possibilities.[20] Although the specific history of loyalty to Spanish rule faded from view, the political subjectivities that it generated conditioned the participation of Cubans of color in Republican politics as well as its affective structures of power. Whether or not activists understood themselves to be performing radically different or similar politics to those of their colonial predecessors, they embodied a process of surrogacy in which earlier memories, consciously or not, improvised from—as Joseph Roach puts it—"representations by those whom they imagined into existence as their definitive opposites."[21]

If the story of colonial loyalty ended tragically after independence, it helps to remember the ambivalence and unresolved ends implicit in the tragic mode.[22] Both race-based claims to inclusion in the Spanish empire and the race-transcendent citizenship of Cuban independence emerged out of flawed, incomplete, and uneven processes. "Colonial legacy" might not adequately characterize this ambivalent (tragic) relationship. A more generative understanding of the connection between colonial formations to anti- and postcolonial aspirations might draw from the work of David Scott, who asks: "Does anticolonialism depend upon a certain way of telling the story about the past, present, and future? . . . Or to put it slightly differently: Does the political point of anticolonialism depend on constructing colonialism as a particular kind of conceptual and ideological object? Does the moral point of anticolonialism depend on constructing colonialism as a particular kind of obstacle to be overcome?"[23] One could easily ask the same of antiracism. These questions underscore the importance of the colonial past to reimagining Cuba's historical struggles against foreign power and racial discrimination. Prospects for pessimism abound: does it diminish the heroism and moral force of antiracism and anticolonialism to retell the story of Spanish rule as one of popular support, even as it continued to limit political membership—as subjects or citizens—through deeply entrenched ideologies of racial difference and hierarchy? In many respects, the history of loyalty in the nineteenth century foregrounds the uphill battles faced by those who fought for independence and for a race-free nation. Instead of encouraging nostalgia for the colonial past, a new vision of Spanish colonialism might identify across the imperial-national divide allied but not identical struggles. Recalling Spanish political ideology as both national and imperial, colonial formations within the Cuban nation receive their due; national legacies within neocolonial Cuba open up new ways of thinking about citizenship and subjecthood, and the racial presumptions implicit in each.

What makes empire such a persistent political form? Quite often, the forces of state and capital that give it strength and meaning appear unstoppable, if not because of deeply entrenched inequalities that concentrate power in the few, then because those forces appear to transcend human agency altogether. They chug along, absorbing resources and eclipsing viable alternative visions. Yet examples of people at all levels of power mounting challenges to empire are to be found throughout history, quite visibly so in the history of Cuba, the African diaspora, and Latin America as a whole. If the agency of those individuals has been a motor of anti-imperialism, we must acknowledge and account for its obverse: the actions of people who have strengthened imperial formations through their active consent, willful participation, and benign neglect. This book is intended as a contribution to the intellectual project of making sense of that power. But it is not a celebration of it. Nor should the endurance of empire make the past seem unchanging or to make the fight to broaden the political imagination futile. Proponents of that view might consider a parallel to the history of racial ideology. Emphasizing the persistence of race obscures the historically contingent ways that individuals have reproduced and revised it to adapt to changing worlds.[24] Although this effect may explain why race remains as crucially linked to imperial as to national forms of political community, it should also strike a better balance between persistence and change. It is little wonder, then, that Cubans in the nineteenth century—as citizens and subjects, slave and free—arrived at diverse answers to these same questions. Many, if not most of them, expressed their political ideas through the vocabularies of race and loyalty, keenly aware of the possibilities for change that they contained.

Obviously, 1898 did not mark the end of imperialism in Cuba. Nor did the replacement of Spanish influence by almost six decades of a weighty United States presence simply reproduce or perpetuate imperial practices developed over four hundred years—in other words, making empire permanent on the island. If the independence movements to which Rodolfo de Lagardère wistfully referred throughout his career did not represent the definitive end of the Spanish empire—contrary to arguments that they initiated the "modern" period in Latin American history—Cuban independence likewise brought ambivalent ends to Spanish rule, not least because of the hierarchies and inequalities it sustained left enduring legacies. But the continuities of racial discrimination in Cuba contained within them constantly changing ideological frames, with mutating praxes of subordination as well as novel tactics for contesting them. That the rhetoric of United States domination, quite differently from Spanish tradition, routinely disavowed the label of empire, quite different from Spanish tradition, attests to the multiplicity of goals, methods, and limits of imperial power. Empire, no matter how many challengers and supporters it has endured, has—and continues to have—a great many ends.

Unless otherwise noted, translations of Spanish-language quotations are my own.

Preface

1. For a more detailed history of the building, see Emilio Reug de Leuchsenring, *La Casa de Gobierno o Palacio Municipal de la Habana* (Havana: n.p., 1961).

2. The Cuban poet Nancy Morejón vividly links the building to the history of colonial violence in her poem "Negro" of 1986: "Your hair,/for some,/Was the devil's work from hell;/But the hummingbird/Built its nest there, unheeding,/When you were hanging at the end of the gallows,/In front of the Governor Generals' Palace./They did say that the dust of the road/Made you disloyal and purplish." *Looking Within/Mirar adentro: Selected Poems/Poemas escogidos, 1954–2000*, ed. Juanamaría Cordones-Cook (Detroit: Wayne State University Press, 2003), 167.

3. Fernando Ortiz, *Martí y las razas* (Havana: Publicaciones de la Comisión nacional organizadora de los actos y ediciones del centenario y del monumento de Martí, 1953), 6. Published in English as "Cuba, Martí, and the Race Problem," *Phylon* 3:3 (1942): 253–276.

4. On Martínez Campos, see José Ibáñez Marín, *Monumento al General Martínez Campos* (Madrid: Establecimiento Tipográfico "El Trabajo," 1906); Antonio Navarro Martín, *Glorias de España: Opúsculo sobre la pacificación de Cuba* (Mexico City: Imprenta Poliglota de Carlos Ramiro, 1878); and T. Ochando, *El general Martínez Campos en Cuba* (Madrid: Imprenta de Fortanet, 1878).

5. Ortiz, *Martí y las razas,* 7.

6. Ortiz, *Martí y las razas,* 27.

7. See, for example, Kathryn Burns, "Gender and the Politics of *Mestizaje:* The Convent of Santa Clara in Cuzco, Peru," *Hispanic American Historical Review* 78:1 (1998): 5–44; and María Elena Martínez, *Genealogical Fictions: Limpieza de Sangre, Religion, and Gender in Colonial Mexico* (Stanford: Stanford University Press, 2008), chap. 6.

INTRODUCTION *A Faithful Account*

1. Marial Iglesias Utset, *Las metáforas del cambio en la vida cotidiana: Cuba, 1898–1902* (Havana: Ediciones Unión, 2003), 28.

2. Jeremy Adelman gives up-front attention to these contingencies in *Sovereignty*

and *Revolution in the Iberian* Atlantic (Princeton: Princeton University Press, 2006). Although Cuba is not included in the analysis, its example only amplifies his broad arguments.

3. Simón Bolívar, "Contestación de un Americano meridional a un caballero de esta isla," Kingston (6 September 1815), accessed 9 June 2012, http://es.wikisource.org/wiki/Carta_de_Jamaica.

4. John Lynch, *Latin American Revolutions, 1808–1826: Old and New World Origins* (Norman: University of Oklahoma Press, 1994), 19.

5. José A. Piqueras, "La siempre fiel Isla de Cuba, o la lealtad interesada," *Historia Mexicana* 58:1 (2008): 427–486; Dominique Goncalvès, *Le planteur et le roi: L'aristocratie havanaise et la couronne d'Espagne (1763–1838)* (Madrid: Casa de Velázquez, 2008); José Cayuela Fernández, *Bahía de ultramar: España y Cuba en el siglo XIX: El control de las relaciones coloniales* (Mexico City: Siglo Veintiuno Editores, 1993); Allan Kuethe, "La fidelidad cubana durante la edad de las revoluciones," *Anuario de Estudios Americanos* 55:1 (1998): 209–220.

6. Jorge I. Domínguez, "Loyalists, Race, and Disunity during the Spanish American Wars of Independence: A Grumpy Reading," *Latin American Studies Association Forum* 41 (2010): 9.

7. John Leddy Phelan, *The People and the King: The Comunero Revolution in Colombia, 1781* (Madison: University of Wisconsin Press, 1978); AJR Russell-Wood, "'Acts of Grace': Portuguese Monarchs and Their Subjects of African Descent in Eighteenth-Century Brazil," *Journal of Latin American Studies* 32:2 (May 2000): 307–332; Kirsten Schultz, *Tropical Versailles: Empire, Monarchy, and the Portuguese Royal Court of Rio de Janeiro, 1808–1821* (New York: Routledge, 2001).

8. Eric Van Young, *The Other Rebellion: Popular Violence, Ideology, and the Mexican Struggle for Independence, 1810–1821* (Stanford: Stanford University Press, 2001), 518. On "popular messianism," see 463–466; on loyalist clerics, see 230–238.

9. Rebecca Earle, "Creole Patriotism and the Myth of the 'Loyal Indian,'" *Past and Present* 172 (August 2001): 125–145.

10. David Garrett, *Shadows of Empire: The Indian Nobility of Cuzco, 1750–1825* (New York: Cambridge University Press, 2005); Cecilia Méndez, *The Plebeian Republic: The Huanta Rebellion and the Making of the Peruvian State, 1820–1850* (Durham, N.C.: Duke University Press, 2005).

11. Renée Soulodre-La France, "Los esclavos de su Magestad: Slave Protest and Politics in Late Colonial New Granada," in *Slaves, Subjects, and Subversives: Blacks in Colonial Latin America*, ed. Jane G. Landers and Barry M. Robinson (Albuquerque: University of New Mexico Press, 2006), 175–208; Marixa Lasso, *Myths of Harmony: Race and Republicanism during the Age of Revolution, Colombia, 1795–1831* (Pittsburgh: University of Pittsburgh Press, 2007), 20. See also Aline Helg, *Liberty and Equality in Caribbean Colombia, 1770–1835* (Chapel Hill: University of North Carolina Press, 2004), 131–134.

12. Schultz, *Tropical Versailles*, 165–176.

13. Peter Blanchard, *Under the Flags of Freedom: Slave Soldiers and the Wars of Independence in Spanish South America* (Pittsburgh: University of Pittsburgh Press, 2008), 17–36, 64–85, 93–94, 169–170; Marcela Echeverri, "Popular Royalists, Empire, and Politics in Southwestern New Granada, 1809–1819," *Hispanic American Historical Review* 91, no. 2 (2011): 237–269.

14. See, most recently, Matt D. Childs, *The 1812 Aponte Rebellion in Cuba and the Struggle against Atlantic Slavery* (Chapel Hill: University of North Carolina Press, 2006), chap. 3; and Jane G. Landers, *Atlantic Creoles in the Age of Revolutions* (Cambridge: Harvard University Press, 2010), chaps. 4 and 6.

15. José Luciano Franco, *Las minas de Santiago del Prado y la rebelión de los cobreros, 1530–1800* (Havana: Editorial de Ciencias Sociales, 1975); María Elena Díaz, *The Virgin, the King, and the Royal Slaves of El Cobre: Negotiating Freedom in Colonial Cuba, 1670–1780* (Stanford: Stanford University Press, 2000); Childs, *The 1812 Aponte Rebellion in Cuba and the Struggle against Atlantic Slavery,* chap. 5.

16. Katia M. de Queirós Mattoso, *To Be a Slave in Brazil, 1550–1888* (New Brunswick: Rutgers University Press, 1988), 89.

17. Giorgio Marotti, *Black Characters in the Brazilian Novel* (Los Angeles: Center for Afro-American Studies, UCLA, 1987), 391–393.

18. Kirk Savage, *Standing Soldiers, Kneeling Slaves: Race, War, and Monument in Nineteenth-Century America* (Princeton, N.J.: Princeton University Press, 1997); Micki McElya, *Clinging to Mammy: The Faithful Slave in Twentieth-Century America* (Cambridge: Harvard University Press, 2007).

19. In researching the African-descended subjects at the heart of this study, one of the more disappointing results has been the scarce evidence of the political ideologies whose origins predate the Middle Passage—for example, how ideas about monarchism in the Iberian world and in west and central Africa might have inflected each other. For some inviting leads, see John K. Thornton, "'I Am the Subject of the King of Congo': African Political Ideology and the Haitian Revolution," *Journal of World History* 4:2 (1993): 181–214; and David H. Brown, "Black Royalty: New Social Frameworks and Remodeled Iconographies in Nineteenth-Century Havana," in *Santería Enthroned: Art, Ritual, and Innovation in an Afro-Cuban Religion* (Chicago: University of Chicago Press, 2003), 46.

20. Statement from Havana's ingenio owners to the king, 19 January 1790, in Gloria García Rodríguez, *La esclavitud desde la esclavitud: La visión de los siervos* (Mexico City: Centro de Investigación Científica "Ing. Jorge L. Tamayo," 1996), 79.

21. Sibylle Fischer, *Modernity Disavowed: Haiti and the Cultures of Slavery in the Age of Revolution* (Durham, N.C.: Duke University Press, 2004), 117.

22. J. Lorand Matory, *Black Atlantic Religion: Tradition, Transnationalism, and Matriarchy in the Afro-Brazilian Candomblé* (Princeton: Princeton University Press, 2005), 35, 2. For Matory's explanation of invoking "transnationalism" in periods before the ascendancy of the nation-state, see 8–10.

23. See, for example, Mintz and Price, *The Birth of African-American Culture: An Anthropological Perspective* (Boston: Beacon Press, 1992 [1976]); Andrew Apter, "On African Origins: Creolization and Connaissance in Haitian Vodou," *American Ethnologist* 29 (2002): 233–260; and Vincent Brown, *The Reaper's Garden: Death and Power in the World of Atlantic Slavery* (Cambridge: Harvard University Press, 2008).

24. Steven Hahn, *The Political Worlds of Slavery and Freedom* (Cambridge: Harvard University Press, 2009), xvii. Hahn's *A Nation under our Feet: Black Political Struggles in the Rural South from Slavery to the Great Migration* (Cambridge: Harvard University Press, 2005) takes up this interpretive challenge in comprehensive and breathtaking detail.

25. John Thornton explores the question of black royalism among rebel slaves in the Haitian Revolution in "'I am a Subject of the King of Congo,'" 182, esp. n. 3.

26. The Tunisian Jewish anticolonial writer Albert Memmi wrote in 1957, in the thick of British and French decolonization conflicts, "The colonized does not seek merely to enrich himself with the colonizer's virtues. In the name of what he hopes to become, he sets his mind on impoverishing himself, tearing himself away from his true self . . . As soon as the colonist adopts those values, he similarly adopts his own condemnation." *The Colonizer and the Colonized* (Boston: Beacon Press, 1991 [1957], 121). Ranajit Guha describes a "cult of loyalism" in India under British rule that could be "activated to induce collaboration." *Domination without Hegemony: History and Power in Colonial India* (Cambridge: Harvard University Press, 1997), 42.

27. Ejemplar No. 2 de *El Habanero,* cited in José Luciano Franco, *Plácido: Una polémica que tiene cien años y otros ensayos* (Havana: Ediciones Unión, 1964), 72. The original language is "Quiera o no quiera Fernando, sea cual fuere la opinión de sus vasallos en la Isla de Cuba, la revolución de aquel país es inevitable."

28. Frederick Cooper, *Colonialism in Question: Theory, Knowledge, History* (Berkeley: University of California Press, 2005), 200.

29. Ada Ferrer, *Insurgent Cuba: Race, Nation, and Revolution, 1868–1898* (Chapel Hill: University of North Carolina Press, 1999); Jorge Ibarra, *Ideología mambisa* (Havana: Instituto Cubano del Libro, 1967), and *Patria, etnia y nación* (Havana: Editorial de Ciencias Sociales, 2007); Francisco Pérez Guzmán, *La guerra en la Habana: Desde Enero de 1896 hasta el combate de San Pedro* (Havana: Editorial de Ciencias Sociales, 1974).

30. Josep M. Fradera, *Colonias para después de un imperio* (Barcelona: Ediciones Bellaterra, 2005); Christopher Schmidt-Nowara, *The Conquest of History: Spanish Colonialism and National Histories in the Nineteenth Century* (Pittsburgh: University of Pittsburgh Press, 2006).

31. James King, "The Colored Castes and American Representation in the Cortes of Cádiz," *Hispanic American Historical Review* 33:1 (February 1953): 33–64; Tamar Herzog, *Defining Nations: Immigrants and Citizens in Early Modern Spain and Spanish America* (New Haven, C.T.: Yale University Press, 2004).

32. Many contemporary theories of subjectivity emphasize the constitution of the "modern" subject, and my use of the term "subject" is not intended to assert the inherently modern nature of colonialism—or not—as recent authors have. I also acknowledge the possible anachronism in this use: "in the nineteenth century," according to a recent study, "*subjectivity* referred to an essential individuality, the consciousness of one's perceived states," implying "a kind of affective domination." João Biehl, Byron Good, and Arthur Kleinman, eds., "Introduction: Rethinking Subjectivity," in *Subjectivity: Ethnographic Investigations* (Berkeley: University of California Press, 2007), 5. If anything, my use offers a gentle nudge to recall nominally "pre-modern" understandings of "subject" that may not be so distinct from modern ones. See Cooper, *Colonialism in Question,* chap. 5; and David Scott, *Conscripts of Modernity: The Tragedy of Colonial Enlightenment* (Durham, N.C.: Duke University Press, 2004), chap. 3.

33. Jeremy Adelman, "Introduction: The Problem of Persistence in Latin American History," in *Colonial Legacies: The Problem of Persistence in Latin American History,* ed. Jeremy Adelman (New York: Routledge, 1999), 1–13. See, for example, François-

Xavier Guerra, *Modernidad e independencias: Ensayos sobre las revoluciones hispánicas* (Madrid: Editorial MAPFRE, 1992); Ivana Frasquet, ed., *Bastillas, cetros y blasones: La independencia en Iberoamérica* (Madrid: Editorial MAPFRE, 2006); Jordana Dym, *From Sovereign Villages to National States: City, State, and Federation in Central America, 1759–1839* (Albuquerque: University of New Mexico Press, 2006); Karen Caplan, *Indigenous Citizens: Local Liberalism in Early National Oaxaca and Yucatán* (Stanford: Stanford University Press, 2010); Peter Guardino, *The Time of Liberty: Popular Political Culture in Oaxaca, 1750–1850* (Durham, N.C.: Duke University Press, 2005); Sarah C. Chambers, *From Subjects to Citizens: Honor, Gender, and Politics in Arequipa, Peru, 1780–1854* (University Park: Pennsylvania State University Press, 1999); Brooke Larson, *Trials of Nation Making: Liberalism, Race, and Ethnicity in the Andes, 1810–1910* (Cambridge: Cambridge University Press, 2004); and Cecilia Méndez, *The Plebeian Republic*.

34. Adelman, *Sovereignty and Revolution in the Iberian Atlantic*, 397.

35. Rebecca J. Scott, "Slavery and the Law in Atlantic Perspective: Jurisdiction, Jurisprudence, and Justice," *Law and History Review* 29 (2011): 921. See also Andrew B. Fisher and Matthew D. O'Hara, "Introduction: Racial Identities and Their Interpreters in Colonial Latin America," in *Imperial Subjects: Race and Identity in Colonial Latin America*, ed. Fisher and O'Hara (Durham, N.C.: Duke University Press, 2009), 1–37.

36. Manuel Chust and Ivana Frasquet, eds., *Los* colores *de las independencias iberoamericanas: Liberalismo, etnia y raza* (Madrid: CSIC, 2009); Uday Singh Mehta, *Liberalism and Empire: A Study in Nineteenth-Century British Liberal Thought* (Chicago: University of Chicago Press, 1999); Thomas C. Holt, *The Problem of Freedom: Race, Labor, and Politics in Jamaica and Britain, 1832–1938* (Baltimore: Johns Hopkins University Press, 1993), 3–9; Daniel Gorman, *Imperial Citizenship: Empire and the Question of Belonging* (Manchester and New York: Palgrave, 2006), chaps. 1 and 7; Sukanya Banerjee, *Becoming Imperial Citizens: Indians in the Late-Victorian Empire* (Durham, N.C.: Duke University Press, 2010); David Kazanjian, *The Colonizing Trick: National Culture and Imperial Citizenship in Early America* (Minneapolis: University of Minnesota Press, 2003); Amit S. Rai, *Rule of Sympathy: Sentiment, Race, and Power, 1750–1850* (New York: Palgrave Macmillan, 2002); Gregory Mann, *Native Sons: West African Veterans and France in the Twentieth Century* (Durham, N.C.: Duke University Press, 2006).

37. Walter Johnson, "On Agency," *Journal of Social History* 37:1 (2003): 113–124.

38. Joanne Rappaport and Tom Cummins, *Beyond the Lettered City: Indigenous Literacies in the Andes* (Durham, N.C.: Duke University Press, 2012), chap. 5.

39. Kathryn Burns, *Into the Archive: Writing and Power in Colonial Peru* (Durham, N.C.: Duke University Press, 2010), 146.

40. See, for example, Philip Howard, *Changing History: Afro-Cuban Cabildos and Societies of Color in the Nineteenth Century* (Baton Rouge: Louisiana State University Press, 1998).

41. James C. Scott, *Domination and the Arts of Resistance: Hidden Transcripts* (New Haven, C.T.: Yale University Press, 1990), chap. 3.

42. Ann Laura Stoler, *Along the Archival Grain: Epistemic Anxieties and Colonial Common Sense* (Princeton: Princeton University Press, 2009), 2. See also Stoler, "Colonial

Archives and the Arts of Governance: On the Content in the Form," *Archival Science* 2 (2002): 87–109.

43. Carole Pateman, *The Problem of Political Obligation: A Critical Analysis of Liberal Theory* (Chichester, England: John Wiley and Sons, 1979). See also Simon Keller, "Making Nonsense of Loyalty to Country," in *New Waves in Political Philosophy,* ed. Boudewijn de Bruin and Christopher F. Zinn (New York: Palgrave Macmillan, 2009); Alberto Calsamiglia, *Cuestiones de lealtad: Límites de liberalismo. Corrupción, nacionalismo y multiculturalismo* (Barcelona: Paidós, 2000); George P. Fletcher, *Loyalty: An Essay on the Morality of Relationships* (New York: Oxford University Press, 1993); and Alasdair MacIntyre, *Is Patriotism a Virtue?* (Lawrence: University of Kansas Press, 1984). Albert O. Hirschman acknowledged that loyal behavior retains "an enormous dose of reasoned calculation" but gave slight definitional priority to "such primordial human groupings such as family, tribe, church, and state." See Hirschman, *Exit, Voice, and Loyalty: Responses to Decline in Firms, Organizations, and States* (Cambridge: Harvard University Press, 1970), 79, 76.

44. Scholarly literature on honor in Latin American history is extensive. See, for example, Lyman L. Johnson and Sonya Lipsett-Rivera, eds., *The Faces of Honor: Sex, Shame, and Violence in Colonial Latin America* (Albuquerque: University of New Mexico Press, 1998); and Sueann Caulfield, Sarah C. Chambers, and Lara Putnam, eds. *Honor, Status, and Law in Modern Latin America* (Durham, N.C.: Duke University Press, 2005).

45. Hirschman, *Exit, Voice, and Loyalty,* 78.

46. Adelman, *Sovereignty and Revolution in the Iberian Atlantic,* 185–194.

47. Ranajit Guha's description of colonial India helps to situate these practices within the model of hegemony put forth by Antonio Gramsci: "Loyalism is not content simply with situating itself in the structure of domination and subordination and providing an ideological justification for consent. It is demonstrative by its very nature: it speaks up because it wants to be noticed." *Domination without Hegemony,* 45.

48. Works benefiting from attention to the Cienfuegos archive, and to the city more generally, include Orlando García Martínez, "La Brigada de Cienfuegos: Un análisis social de su formación," in *Espacios, silencios y los sentidos de la libertad: Cuba entre 1878 y 1912,* ed. Fernando Martínez Heredia, Rebecca J. Scott, and Orlando García Martínez (Havana: Ediciones Unión, 2001), "Estudio de la economía cienfueguera desde la fundación de la colonia Fernandina de Jagua hasta mediados del siglo XIX," and *Esclavitud y colonización en Cienfuegos, 1819–1879;* Naranjo Orovio, "El temor a la 'africanización': Colonización blanca y nuevas poblaciones en Cuba (el caso de Cienfuegos)," in *Las Antillas en la era de las luces y la revolución,* ed. José A. Piqueras (Madrid: Siglo XXI, 2005), 85–121; Iglesias García, "La concentración azucarera y la comarca de Cienfuegos," in *Espacios, silencios, y los sentidos de la libertad: Cuba entre 1878 y 1912,* 85–107; Lilia Martín Brito, *El desarrollo urbano de Cienfuegos en el siglo XIX* (Oviedo: Universidad de Oviedo, Servicio de Publicaciones, 1998); Rebecca J. Scott, *Degrees of Freedom: Louisiana and Cuba after Slavery* (Cambridge: Harvard University Press, 2006), "Race, Labor, and Citizenship in Cuba: A View from the Sugar District of Cienfuegos, 1886–1909," *Hispanic American Historical Review* 78:4 (November 1998): 687–728, and "The Provincial Archive as a Place of Memory: Confronting Oral and Written Sources on the Role of Former Slaves in the Cuban War of Independence (1895–98)," *New West Indian*

Guide/Nieuwe West-Indische Gids 76 (2002): 191–209.; Rebecca J. Scott and Michael Zeuske, "Property in Writing, Property on the Ground: Pigs, Horses, Land, and Citizenship in the Aftermath of Slavery, Cuba, 1880–1909," *Comparative Studies in Society and History* 44 (2002): 669–699; and Zeuske, "'Los negros hicimos la independencia': Aspectos de la movilización afrocubana en un hinterland cubano. Cienfuegos entre colonia y República," in *Espacios, silencios, y los sentidos de la libertad*, 193–234, and *Sklavereien, Emanzipationen und atlantische Weltgeschichte: Essays über Mikrogeschichten, Sklaven, Globalisierungen und Rassismus* (Leipzig: Leipziger Universitätsverlag, 2006). A thorough description of the archive, written by its former director, Orlando García Martínez, appears in Louis A. Pérez and Rebecca J. Scott, *The Archives of Cuba/Los archivos de Cuba* (Pittsburgh: University of Pittsburgh Press, 2003), 94–104.

49. The political and ethical stakes of this practice receive thoughtful treatment in Micol Seigel, *Uneven Encounters: Making Race and Nation in Brazil and the United States* (Durham, N.C.: Duke University Press, 2009), xvii–xviii.

50. I thank Larissa Brewer-Yarcia and Ann Twinam for helping me think through this question. Twinam generously shared portions of her forthcoming book, *Erasing American "Defects": Pardos, Mulatos, and the Quest for Whiteness* (Stanford, CA: Stanford University Press).

51. These fine distinctions are explained clearly by María Elena Martínez in *Genealogical Fictions: Limpieza de Sangre, Religion, and Gender in Colonial Mexico* (Stanford: Stanford University Press, 2008).

52. Bianca Premo, *Children of the Father King: Youth, Authority, and Legal Minority in Colonial Lima* (Chapel Hill: University of North Carolina Press, 2005); Alejandro Cañeque, *The King's Living Image: The Culture and Politics of Viceregal Power in Colonial Mexico* (New York: Routledge, 2004).

53. Recent attention to popular support for British colonial rule in North America has made clear that such allegiance was neither the sole product of material and pragmatic concerns of ordinary people nor the privileged musings of an invested intellectual and political class. See, for example, Maya Jasanoff, *Liberty's Exiles: American Loyalists in the Revolutionary World* (New York: Knopf, 2011); and Brendan McConville, *The King's Three Faces: The Rise and Fall of Royal America, 1688–1776* (Chapel Hill: Omohundro Institute of Early American History and Culture, University of North Carolina Press, 2006). The literature on black loyalists in the British North America is extensive. See Sylvia R. Frey, *Water from the Rock: Black Resistance in a Revolutionary Age* (Princeton: Princeton University Press, 1991); Peter M. Voelz, *Slave and Soldier: The Military Impact of Blacks in the Colonial Americas* (New York: Garland, 1993); James W. St. G. Walker, *The Black Loyalists: The Search for a Promised Land in Nova Scotia and Sierra Leone, 1783–1870* (New York: Africana/Dalhousie University Press, 1976); and Ellen Gibson Wilson, *The Loyal Blacks* (New York: Capricorn Books, 1976). Elsewhere in the British colonial world, see Roger Norman Buckley, *The British Army in the West Indies: Society and the Military in the Revolutionary Age* (Gainesville: University Press of Florida, 1998); and Brian Dyde, *The Empty Sleeve: The Story of the West India Regiments of the British Army* (Saint John's, Antigua: Hansib Publishing, 1997).

54. Cooper, *Colonialism in Question*, 67–70.

Epigraph source: Adolfo de Castro, ed., *Cortes de Cádiz: Complementos de las sesiones verificadas en la isla de León y en Cádiz*, 2 vols. (Madrid: Imprenta de Prudencio Pérez de Velasco, 1913), 1:178.

1. Regency decree, León, 14 February 1810, Archivo General de Indias, Seville, Sección Ultramar (hereafter, AGI, SU), 795, cited in Timothy Anna, "Spain and the Breakdown of the Imperial Ethos: The Problem of Equality," *Hispanic American Historical Review* 62:2 (May 1982): 257.

2. Manuel José Quintana, *Quintana: Memoria del Cádiz de las Cortes,* ed. Fernando Durán López (Cádiz: Universidad de Cádiz, 1996), 196.

3. Ramón Solís, *El Cádiz de las Cortes: La vida en la ciudad en los años 1810 a 1813* (Madrid: Alianza Editorial, 1969), 88–90, 456–460. Of the 178 signers of the constitution, 51 were American delegates. Brian Hamnett, "Constitutional Theory and Political Reality: Liberalism, Traditionalism, and the Spanish Cortes, 1810–1814," *Journal of Modern History* 49:1 (March 1977): D1086.

4. José María Rodríguez to Gracia y Justícia, 13 February 1812, AGI, SU, legajo 153, número 6.

5. These tensions are explored in detail in Christopher Schmidt-Nowara, *The Conquest of History: Spanish Colonialism and National Histories in the Nineteenth Century* (Pittsburgh: University of Pittsburgh Press, 2006); and Jesús Raúl Navarro García, *Entre esclavos y constituciones: El colonialismo liberal de 1837 en Cuba* (Seville: CSIC, 1991). See also Uday Mehta, *Liberalism and Empire: A Study in Nineteenth-Century British Liberal Thought* (Chicago: University of Chicago Press, 1999); and Jennifer Pitts, *A Turn to Empire: The Rise of Imperial Liberalism in Britain and France* (Princeton: Princeton University Press, 2005).

6. Jeremy Adelman, *Sovereignty and Revolution in the Iberian Atlantic* (Princeton: Princeton University Press, 2006).

7. Levi Marrero, *Cuba: Economía y sociedad,* vol. 10: *Azúcar, ilustración y conciencia,* 15 vols. (Madrid: Editorial Playor, 1986), 32. A more generous take by Jorge Domínguez suggests that "nationalization of decisionmaking had effectively taken place within the colonial context," referring to the creole elite's economic interests and the repression of the slave population. Domínguez, *Insurrection or Loyalty: The Breakdown of the Spanish American Empire* (Cambridge MA: Harvard University Press, 1980), 250–251. On the conflicts within the Cuban elite, see Allan J. Kuethe, "La fidelidad cubana durante la edad de las revoluciones," *Anuario de Estudios Americanos* 55:1 (1998): 209–220; and José A. Piqueras Arenas, "Leales en la época de insurrección: La élite criolla cubana entre 1810 y 1814," in *Visiones y revisiones de la independencia americana,* ed. Izaskun Álvarez Cuartero y Julio Sánchez Gómez (Salamanca: Ediciones Universidad de Salamanca, 2003), 183–206.

8. John Lynch, "Introduction," in *Latin American Revolutions, 1808–1826: Old and New World Origins,* (Norman: University of Oklahoma Press, 1994), 19. See also Jaime E. Rodríguez O., *The Independence of Spanish America* (Cambridge: Cambridge University Press, 1998), 195, 244; and José A. Piqueras, "La siempre fiel Isla de Cuba, o la lealtad interesada," *Historia Mexicana* 58:1 (2008): 427–486.

9. Anthony Pagden, *Lords of All the World: Ideologies of Empire in Spain, Britain, and France, c. 1500–c.1800* (New Haven, C.T.: Yale University Press, 1995), chap. 5; and

Bianca Premo, *Children of the Father King: Youth, Authority, and Legal Minority in Colonial Lima* (Chapel Hill: University of North Carolina Press, 2005.

10. Henry Kamen, *Imagining Spain: Historical Myth and National Identity* (New Haven, C.T.: Yale University Press, 2008), 21.

11. Tamar Herzog, *Defining Nations: Immigrants and Citizens in Early Modern Spain and Spanish America* (New Haven, Conn.: Yale University Press, 2003), 54 and 71, quoting Pedro Fernández Navarrete, *Conservación de monarquías y discursos políticos*, ed. Michael D. Gordon (Madrid: Instituto de Estudios Fiscales, 1982 [1792]), 126.

12. Josep M. Fradera, "Raza y ciudadanía: El factor racial en la delimitación de los derechos políticos de los americanos," in *Gobernar colonias* (Barcelona: Ediciones Península, 1999), 51–69.

13. Allan J. Kuethe, *Cuba, 1753–1815: Crown, Military, and Society* (Knoxville: University of Tennessee Press, 1986), 155–156.

14. Real orden of 22 January 1810, transcribed in Miguel Méndez to ?, 18 August 1817, Archivo Histórico Nacional, Sección Estado (hereafter, AHN, SE), leg. 6367, expediente 35, núm. 2.

15. Olga Portuondo Zúñiga, *Cuba: Constitución y liberalismo (1808–1841)*, 2 vols. (Santiago de Cuba: Editorial Oriente, 2008), 1:25.

16. James King, "The Colored Castes and American Representation in the Cortes of Cádiz," *Hispanic American Historical Review* 33:1 (February 1953): 33–64.

17. *Diario de sesiones de las Cortes generales y extraordinarias,* 15 vols. (Madrid: Imprenta de J. A. García, 1870–1871), session of 29 August 1811, 3:1723.

18. *Diario de sesiones de las Cortes generales y extraordinarias,* session of 31 August 1811, 3: 1735.

19. "Documentos que atañen 1a Representación de 20 de julio de 1811," in *Obras de don Francisco de Arango y Parreño*, 2 vols. (Havana: Ministerio de Educación, 1952), 2:224.

20. "Documentos que atañen 1a Representación de 20 de julio de 1811," in *Obras de don Francisco de Arango y Parreño*, 2:226.

21. *Diario de sesiones de las Cortes generales y extraordinarias,* session of 11 April 1811, 2:812.

22. Dale Tomich, "The Wealth of Empire: Francisco Arango y Parreño, Political Economy, and the Second Slavery in Cuba," *Comparative Studies in Society and History* 45:1 (2003): 6.

23. Francisco Arango y Parreño, "Representación de la ciudad de la Habana a las Cortes, el 20 de julio de 1811, con motivo de las proposiciones hechas por Don José Miguel Guridi y Alcocer y Don Agustín de Argüelles, sobre el tráfico y esclavitud de los negros," in *Obras de don Francisco de Arango y Parreño*, 2:145–187.

24. Manuel Moreno Fraginals, *Cuba/España, España/Cuba: Historia común* (Barcelona: Grijalbo Mondadori, 1995), 187.

25. Figures cited from Franklin W. Knight, *Slave Society in Cuba during the Nineteenth Century* (Madison: University of Wisconsin Press, 1970), 22.

26. *Diario de sesiones de las Cortes generales y extraordinarias,* session of 4 September, 3:1760.

27. *Diario de sesiones de las Cortes generales y extraordinarias,* session of 5 September 1811, 3:1775.

28. *Diario de sesiones de las Cortes generales y extraordinarias,* session of 4 September 1811, 3:1768.

29. *Diario de sesiones de las Cortes generales y extraordinarias,* session of 5 September 1811, 3:1776.

30. *Diario de sesiones de las Cortes generales y extraordinarias,* session of 6 September 1811, 3:1788.

31. *Diario de sesiones de las Cortes generales y extraordinarias,* session of 6 September 1811, 3:1789.

32. *Diario de sesiones de las Cortes generales y extraordinarias,* session of 6 September 1811, 3:1798.

33. Uday Mehta, "Liberal Strategies of Exclusion," in *Tensions of Empire: Colonial Cultures in a Bourgeois World,* ed. Frederick Cooper and Ann Laura Stoler (Berkeley: University of California Press, 1997), 59–86.

34. Andrés de Jáuregui to the Ayuntamiento de la Habana, 3 October 1811, Archivo Nacional de Cuba, Fondo Gobierno Superior Civil (hereafter, ANC, GSC), leg. 1100, exp. 40589.

35. Andrés de Jáuregui to the Ayuntamiento de la Habana, 4 November 1811, ANC, GSC, leg. 1100, exp. 40589.

36. Andrés de Jáuregui to the Ayuntamiento de la Habana, 2 April 1811, ANC DR, Fondo Donativos y Remisiones (hereafter DR), leg. 561, núm. 8.

37. Francisco Sedano to the Marqués de Someruelos, 17 March 1811, AGI, Sección Papeles de Cuba (hereafter SC), leg. 1640, núm. 22.

38. Someruelos to Pedro Caballos, 25 May 1804, AHN, SE, leg. 6366, caja 2, núm. 78. On the circulation of news about Haiti in Cuba, see Ada Ferrer, "Cuba en la sombra de Haití: Noticias, sociedad y esclavitud," in María Dolores González-Ripoll et al., *El rumor de Haití en Cuba: Temor, raza y rebeldía, 1789–1844* (Madrid: Consejo Superior de Investigaciones Científicas, 2004), 179–231,

39. Francisco Sedano to Someruelos, 3 February 1811, AGI SC, leg. 1640, núm. 6.

40. "Papel sobre los negros esclavos por un religioso de la Isla de Cuba con ocasión de los debates habidos en las Cortes extraordinarias Españolas de 2 de abril de 1811," Biblioteca Nacional "José Martí," Havana, Colección Cubana, Colección Manuscrito Vidal Morales y Morales (hereafter, BNJM, CM Morales), tomo 97, núm, 107.

41. Broadsheet signed by Ignacio de la Pezuela in Cádiz, 2 May 1812, Houghton Library, Harvard University, José Escoto Papers (hereafter HL, JE, BMS Span, box 862, folder 4.

42. Sedano to Someruelos, 9 January 1812, AGI, SC, leg. 1640, núm. 119.

43. "Representación de Andrés de Jáuregui con motivo del levantamiento de esclavos ocurrido en el ingenio Peñas Altas," 31 May 1812, BNJM, CM Morales, núm. 83.

44. On the *gracias al sacar,* see Ann Twinam, *Public Lives, Private Secrets: Honor, Gender, Sexuality, and Illegitimacy in Colonial Spanish America* (Stanford: Stanford University Press, 1999).

45. Manuel Marcial, pardo natural de Stgo. de Cuba, solicita se le agracie a él y descendencia con el carácter de ciudadano y en clase de blanco, 1813, AGI, SC, leg. 153, núm. 46.

46. "Donativos hechos en manos del Sor. Gobernador de esta Plaza para subvenir a los gastos del Partido contra Negros Cimarrones," 14 April 1816, Archivo Provincial de Santiago de Cuba, Fondo Gobierno Provincial (hereafter APSC, GP), leg. 554, núm. 3.

47. Albert O. Hirschman, *Exit, Voice, and Loyalty: Responses to Decline in Firms, Organizations, and States* (Cambridge: Harvard University Press, 1970), chap. 7.

48. Antonio de Castro to the captain general, 23 January 1811, AGI, SC, leg. 1766, núm. 38.

49. Matt D. Childs, *The 1812 Aponte Rebellion in Cuba and the Struggle against Atlantic Slavery* (Chapel Hill: University of North Carolina Press, 2006), 174.

50. On these developments, see Mario Rodríguez, *The Cádiz Experiment in Central America, 1808–1826* (Berkeley: University of California Press, 1978); Jorge María García Laguardia, "Centroamérica en Cádiz: Orígenes y destino del primer Proyecto constitucional y la primera Declaración de Derechos del Hombre de Guatemala," in *La Constitución de Cádiz de 1812: Hacia los orígenes del constitucionalismo iberoamericano y latino*, ed. Asdrúbal Aguiar Aranguren (Caracas: Universidad Católica Andres Bello, 2004), 193–221; Jordana Dym, "Enseñanza en los jeroglíficos y emblemas": Igualdad y lealtad en Guatemala por Fernando VII (1810)," *Secuencia, Numero Conmemorativo* (Mexico) (2008): 75–99; Peter Guardino, *The Time of Liberty: Popular Political Culture in Oaxaca, 1750–1850* (Durham, N.C.: Duke University Press, 2005); and Charles F. Walker, *Smoldering Ashes: Cuzco and the Creation of Republican Peru, 1780–1840* (Durham, N.C.: Duke University Press, 1999).

51. Real orden de 1 March 1814, ANC, Fondo Reales ordenes y cédulas (hereafter ROC), leg. 50, exp. 77.

52. "Expediente sobre que al Pueblo de Jiguaní se le [illegible] en villa y ponga un Juez de Letras con otras cosas," 16 May 1818, AGI, SU, leg. 32, núm. 15. The underscored word is in the original.

53. Pedro Alcántara de Acosta to the Real Audiencia, 6 August 1814, AGI, SU, leg. 32, núm. 15.

54. Petition from Juán Miguel Randón and José Antonio del Toro to the Real Audiencia, 30 May 1816, AGI, SU, leg. 32, núm. 15.

55. Real orden de 11 January 1821, ANC, ROC, leg. 62, exp. 21.

56. Andrés de Jáuregui to the Ayuntamiento de la Habana, 23 April, 31 May, and 27 November 1812, ANC, GSC, leg. 1100, exp. 40589.

57. Comunica las medidas adoptadas para impedir la entrada en la isla de negros que no fuesen bozales y especialmente de esclavos que hubiesen vivido en paises extranjeros, 27 January 1800, AHN, SE, leg. 6366 parte 1 exp. 2.

58. Someruelos to Pedro Cevallos, 6 September 1803, AHN, SE, leg. 6366, caja 1, núm. 56. See also Gabriel Debien, "Les colons de Saint-Domingue réfugiés à Cuba (1793–1815)," *Revista de Indias* 54 (1953): 559–605.

59. "Acuso recibo de la Real Orden prohibiendo la permanencia en Cuba de los emigrados franceses procedentes de Santo Domingo," 14 June 1804, AHN, SE, leg. 6366, caja 2, núm. 81.

60. Peter Blanchard, *Under the Flags of Freedom: Slave Soldiers and the Wars of Independence in Spanish South America* (Pittsburgh: University of Pittsburgh Press, 2008), 133; Sarah C. Chambers and Lisa Norling, "Choosing to Be a Subject: Loyalist Women in the Revolutionary Atlantic World," *Journal of Women's History* 20:1 (2008): 40.

61. Records of loyalty oaths by French and Spanish Americans arriving in Cuba between 1808 and 1812 can be found in "Juramentos de fidelidad de franceses," AGI, SC, leg. 1766.

62. Representación el oficio Real Honorado Don Pedro Alcántara de Acosta, 15 March 1817, AHN, SE, leg. 6367, carpeta 1, exp. 25.

63. Comisión de D. Andrés de Zayas y D. Francisco Chacón sobre aumento de la población blanca, 1816, BNJM, CM Morales, tomo 80, núm. 13.

64. Similar developments in Puerto Rico are discussed in Raquel Rosario Rivera, *La Real Cédula de Gracias de 1815 y sus primeros efectos en Puerto Rico* (San Juan, P.R.: First Book Publications, 1995).

65. Representación el oficio Real Honorado Don Pedro Alcántara de Acosta, 15 March 1817, AHN, SE, leg. 6367, carpeta 1, exp. 25.

66. Comunicación del Brigadier Sr. José Ricardo O'Farrill al Intendente, 11 September 1818, ANC, Fondo Asuntos Políticos (hereafter AP), leg. 125, exp. 7.

67. Representación el oficio Real Honorado Don Pedro Alcántara de Acosta, 15 March 1817AHN, SE, leg. 6367, exp. 25.

68. Julio LeRiverend, *Historia económica de Cuba* (Havana: Editorial Nacional de Cuba, 1983), chap. 10; Levi Marrero, *Cuba: Economía y sociedad: Azucar, ilustración y conciencia (1763–1868)*, tomo 9 vol. 10: Azúcar, ilustración y conciencia (1763–1868), 15 vols. (Madrid: Editorial Playor, 1986), 211–247.

69. E. Castiñeyra y Rangel, *Historia local de Cienfuegos* (Havana: Cultural, 1932), 19–20.

70. Consuelo Naranjo Orovio, "La amenaza haitiana, un miedo interesado: Poder y fomento de la población blanca en Cuba," in *El rumor de Haití en Cuba*, 129–131.

71. Pablo L. Rousseau and Pablo Díaz de Villegas, *Memoria descriptiva, histórica y biográfica de Cienfuegos* (Havana: "El Siglo XX," 1920), 43.

72. Luis J. Bustamante y Fernandez, *La comarca de Jagua hasta la fundación de la Colonia Fernandina de Jagua (1819)* (Havana: Imprenta "El Siglo XX," 1948), 34.

73. Marrero, *Cuba: Economía y sociedad*, 9:231–232.

74. Rousseau and Díaz de Villegas, *Memoria descriptiva, histórica y biográfica de Cienfuegos*, 55.

75. Enrique Edo y Llop, *Memoria histórica de Cienfuegos y su jurisdicción*, 2nd ed. (Cienfuegos: J. Andreu, 1888), 28.

76. Edo y Llop, *Memoria histórica de Cienfuegos y su jurisdicción*, 30–31. The Yuquinos may have derived their name from the yucca cultivated by new arrivals to the region on less desirable land than that claimed by earlier settlers. See Rousseau and Díaz de Villegas, *Memoria descriptiva, histórica y biográfica de Cienfuegos*, 58.

77. Rousseau and Díaz de Villegas, *Memoria descriptiva*, 71.

78. Rousseau and Díaz de Villegas, *Memoria descriptiva*, 47.

79. Rousseau and Díaz de Villegas, *Memoria descriptiva*, 43.

80. Edo y Llop, *Memoria histórica de Cienfuegos y su jurisdicción*, 21.

81. Orlando García Martínez, "Estudio de la economía cienfueguera desde la fundación de la colonia Fernandina de Jagua hasta mediados del siglo XIX," *Islas* 55/56 (September 1976–April 1977): 116–169; Carmen Guerra Díaz and Isabel Jiménez Lastre, "La industria azucarera cienfueguera en el siglo XIX: Notas históricas para su estudio," *Islas* 91 (September–December 1988): 42–76.

82. Rousseau and Díaz de Villegas, *Memoria descriptiva*, 71.

83. 1827 census information appears in *Cuba, resumen del censo de población de la Isla de Cuba a fin del año de 1841* (Havana: Imprenta del Gobierno, 1842); and *Cuadro*

estadístico de la siempre fiel Isla de Cuba . . . 1846 (Havana: Imprenta del Gobierno, 1847). The totals for 1846 census are: 16,211 white inhabitants, 3,997 free people of color, and 7,789 slaves.

84. Edo y Llop, *Memoria histórica de Cienfuegos y su jurisdicción*, 57.

85. Jacobo dela Pezuela, *Historia de la Isla de Cuba*, 4 vols. (Madrid: C. Bailly-Baillière, 1878), 4:86–89.

86. Francisco Dionisio Vives to the Secretario del Estado, 12 June 1823, AHN, Estado, leg. 6368, caja 1, núm. 2.

87. Father Félix Varela, "Primer proyecto cubano de abolición de la esclavitud," in Hortensia Pichardo, ed., *Documentos para la historia de Cuba*, 4th ed., 4 vols (Havana: Editorial de Ciencias Sociales, 1976–1980), 267–275.

88. *Diario de sesiones de las Cortes Constituyentes, 1836–1837* (Madrid: Imprenta de J. A. García, 1870), I: "Apéndice al número 40," 2. See also William Spence Robertson, "The Recognition of the Spanish Colonies by the Motherland," *Hispanic American Historical Review* 1:1 (1918): 70–91.

89. Manuel Lorenzo, *Manifiesto del general Don Manuel Lorenzo a la nación española* (Cádiz: Campe, 1837), 42.

90. Lorenzo, *Manifiesto del general Don Manuel Lorenzo a la nación española*, 70–71.

91. Lorenzo, *Manifiesto del general Don Manuel Lorenzo a la nación española*, 10.

92. Domingo Figarola-Caneda, *José Antonio Saco: Documentos para su vida* (Havana: Imprenta El Siglo XX, 1921), 173.

93. José Antonio Saco, *Examen analítico del informe de la comisión especial nombrada por las Cortes (sobre la exclusión de los actuales y futuros diputados de ultramar, y sobre la necesidad de regir aquellos países por leyes especiales)* (Madrid: Oficina de D. Tomás Jordan, 1837), 11. See also Eduardo Torres-Cuevas, *Félix Varela: Los orígenes de la ciencia y con-ciencia cubanas* (Havana: Editorial de Ciencias Sociales, 1995).

94. Saco, *Examen analítico del informe de la comisión especial nombrada por las Cortes*, 10.

95. Saidiya V. Hartman, *Scenes of Subjection: Terror, Slavery, and Self-Making in Nineteenth-Century America* (New York: Oxford University Press, 1997), 122.

96. Rousseau and Díaz, *Memoria descriptiva* 79.

97. The archival file containing Estrada's investigation includes the pamphlet itself. ANC, Fondo Comisión Militar (hereafter CM), leg. 18, núm. 10.

98. Karl Marx, *Revolution in Spain* (Westport, Conn.: Greenwood Press, 1975 [1854]), 73.

99. Louis de Clouet to the Consejo de Indias, 3 July 1824 and 29 April 1845, AHN, Sección Ultramar (herafter SU) leg. 5510.

100. John Leddy Phelan, "Authority and Flexibility in the Spanish Imperial Bureaucracy," *Administrative Science Quarterly* 5 (1960): 47–65; Ann Laura Stoler, "On Degrees of Imperial Sovereignty," *Public Culture* 18:1 (Winter 2006): 125–146; Lauren Benton, *Law and Colonial Cultures: Legal Regimes in World History, 1400–1900* (New York: Cambridge University Press, 2001).

101. This phenomenon may not be an unintended side effect of liberal theory. See James R. Martel, *Love Is a Sweet Chain: Desire, Autonomy, and Friendship in Liberal Political Theory* (New York: Routledge, 2001).

Epigraph source: Juan Francisco Manzano, *The Life and Poems of a Cuban Slave,* ed. Edward J. Mullen (Hamden, Conn.: Archon Books, 1981 [1840]), 105.

1. Alexander von Humboldt, *Ensayo político sobre la Isla de Cuba,* introduction by Fernando Ortiz (Havana: Talleres del Archivo Nacional, 1960 [1826]), 290, 294, 282.

2. James C. Scott, *Domination and the Arts of Resistance: Hidden Transcripts* (New Haven, C.T.: Yale University Press, 1990), 18, 70, 96, chap. 1 and 4. See esp. 96–103 on popular monarchism.

3. My thinking here draws inspiration from Saba Mahmood, *Politics of Piety: The Islamic Revival and the Feminist Subject* (Berkeley: University of California Press, 2005).

4. See, for example, Walter Johnson, "On Agency," *Journal of Social History* 37, no. 1 (2003), 113–124.

5. Gertrudis Gómez de Avellaneda y Arteaga, *Sab* (Havana: Instituto del Libro Cubano, 1973 [1841]), 243.

6. José Zacarías González del Valle, *La vida literaria en Cuba (1836–1840)* (Havana: Publicaciones de la Secretaria de Educación, 1938), 152.

7. Sibylle Fischer, *Modernity Disavowed: Haiti and the Cultures of Slavery in the Age of Revolution* (Durham, N.C.: Duke University Press, 2004), 119.

8. Judith Butler, *The Psychic Life of Power: Theories in Subjection* (Stanford: Stanford University Press, 1997), 2.

9. Sebastián de Covarrubias, *Tesoro de la lengua castellana o española,* ed. Martin de Riquer (Barcelona: Editorial Alta Fulla, 1987 [1611]).

10. Sección de Educación de la Sociedad Patriótica de la Habana, *Instrucciones morales y sociales para el uso de los niños* (Havana: Oficina del Gobierno y Capitanía General por S.M., 1824), 37.

11. *Diario de la Marina,* 25 August 1853 and 16 January 1853, respectively.

12. Honorable status for men may have derived from earning titles, but Cuba's complicated social matrix might temper associations of honor with racial exclusivity, as suggested in an 1806 from a newspaper. It concerns a man's aspirations for obtaining a title associated not with a locale in Spain but with a minor Cuban town:

"¿Te casas? ¿Tienes dinero?	Are you getting married? Do you have money?
No, mas tiénelo Donata	No, but Donata has some
Que es parda y yo Caballero;	She is *parda* and I a Gentleman;
Y con mi sangre y su plata	And with my blood and her silver
Soy Marqués del Matadero.	I'll be the Marqués of Matadero.
A UN MATRIMONIO IGUAL	"TO AN EQUAL MARRIAGE."

J. M. de Andueza, *Isla de Cuba pintoresca, histórica, política, literaria, mercantil e industrial* (Madrid: Boix, 1841), 115.

13. Dominique Goncalvès, *Le planteur et le roi: L'aristocratie havanaise et la couronne d'Espagne (1763–1838)* (Madrid: Casa de Velázquez, 2008), 284–293.

14. Carole Leal Curiel, *El discurso de la fidelidad: Construcción social del espacio como símbolo del poder regional (Venezuela, Siglo XVIII)* (Caracas: Biblioteca de la Academia Nacional de la Historia, 1990).

15. This generalization should not suggest that women could not be political subjects. See Sarah C. Chambers and Lisa Norling, "Choosing to Be a Subject: Loyalist

Women in the Revolutionary Atlantic World," *Journal of Women's History* 20:1 (2008): 39–62.

16. "Expediente suscitado por la Junta encargada de la Casa de Maternidad de la Habana solicitando arbitrios para atender a los piadosos objetos de su instituto," 31 August 1833, AHN, SE, leg. 4603, exp. 4.

17. María de las Mercedes, Condesa de Merlín, *Los esclavos en las colonias españolas* (Madrid: Impr. de Alegría y Charlain, 1841), 76.

18. Cirilo Villaverde, *Cecilia Valdés or el Angel Hill,* trans. Helen Lane (New York: Oxford University Press, 2005), 173.

19. In his play *El conde Alarcos,* José Jacinto Milanés, in parallel fashion, used the figure of a plebeian Cuban instead of a lettered elite to criticize Tacón and even question the infallibility of the king. See José María Aguilera Manzano, "La entronización de la literatura en la construcción de la 'cultura cubana,' 1823–1845," in *Cuba: De colonia a república,* ed. Martín Rodrigo y Alharilla (Madrid: Biblioteca Nueva, 2006), 55. For the play itself, see *Obras de Don José Jacino Milanés,* 2nd ed. (New York: Juan F. Trow y Compañía, 1865), 113–152.

20. Ignacio González Olivares, *Observaciones sobre la esclavitud en la Isla de Cuba* (Madrid: A. de San Martín y Agustín Jubera, 1865), 75.

21. Agustín Rossell, *Opúsculo que trata de materias muy interesantes para la Isla de Cuba* (Madrid: Imprenta de M. Minuesa, 1860), 8.

22. *Diario de la Marina,* 31 December 1847, 3.

23. *Diario de la Marina,* 2 December 1853. The newspaper made explicit comparisons to Mexico (10 November 1853) and Chile (23 November 1853).

24. José Antonio Saco, *La situación política de Cuba y su remedio* (Paris: Impr. De E. Thunot, 1851), 6.

25. Saco, *La situación política de Cuba y su remedio,* 20.

26. Saco, *La situación política de Cuba y su remedio,* 36.

27. Gómez de Avellaneda, *Sab,* 257–258.

28. On slaves' notions of rights and politics, see Gloria García, "A propósito de La Escalera: El esclavo como sujeto político," *Boletín del Archivo Nacional de Cuba* 12 (2000): 1–13; and Alejandro de la Fuente, "Slavery and the Creation of Legal Rights in Cuba: *Coartación* and *Papel,*" *Hispanic American Historical Review* 87:4 (2007): 659–692.

29. Evelyn Powell Jennings, "Paths to Freedom: Imperial Defense and Manumission in Havana, 1762–1800," in *Paths to Freedom: Manumission in the Atlantic World,* ed. Rosemary Brana-Shute and Randy J. Sparks (Columbia: University of South Carolina Press, 2009), 121–141.

30. Maria Elena Díaz, *The Virgin, the King, and the Royal Slaves of El Cobre: Negotiating Freedom in Colonial Cuba, 1670–1780* (Stanford: Stanford University Press, 2000); José Luciano Franco, *Las minas de Santiago del Prado y la rebelión de los cobreros, 1530–1800* (Havana: Editorial de Ciencias Sociales, 1975). However, with the edict of 1800 that freed them and the waning of communal landholding initiated during Spain's liberal experiment, cobreros received individual land titles unaccompanied by individual citizenship. This signaled a changing relationship to the state, as the freed people watched much of their land transfer to new white settlers. On a broader canvas, these conflicts between colonial privileges and liberal rights resonated

throughout Spanish America, particularly among the many indigenous communities who enjoyed similar protections and privileges.

31. Lara Putnam, Sarah C. Chambers, and Sueann Caulfield, "Introduction: Transformations in Honor, Status, and Law over the Long Nineteenth Century," in *Honor, Status, and Law in Modern Latin America*, ed. Putnam, Chambers, and Caulfield (Durham, N.C.: Duke University Press, 2005), 3. Recall from chapter 1 that Article 22 of the Constitution of 1812, which allowed the possibility of citizenship to free men of color who could prove "merits and services," required those men to have wives.

32. Cuba, *Cuba, resumen del censo de población de la Isla de Cuba a fin del año de 1841* (Havana: Imprenta del Gobierno, 1842).

33. Cirilo Villaverde, *Cecilia Valdés or el Angel Hill*, 122.

34. Sarah C. Chambers and Lisa Norling, "Choosing to Be a Subject," 50. On "loyalist" exiles in San Antonio de los Baños, see Julian Vivanco, *Crónicas históricas de San Antonio Abad de los Baños* (Havana: Editorial El Sol, 1955), 16–17 and 492.

35. José Luciano Franco, *El Gobierno Colonial de Cuba y la independencia de Venezuela* (Havana: Casa de las Américas, 1970), chap. 3.

36. Eduardo Torres-Cuevas, *Historia de la masonería cubana: Seis ensayos* (Havana: Imagen Contemporánea, 2004), 48–50. See also Francisco Ponte Domínguez, *La masonería en la independencia de Cuba*. Victor M. Uribe-Urán notes that mainland Latin American Masonic networks had links to France and Britain more than Spain. "The Birth of a Public Sphere in Latin America during the Age of Revolution," *Comparative Studies in Society and History* 42:2 (2000): 453.

37. Declaración de José Salmonte, cited as Archivo Nacional de Cuba, Historia, "1a pieza de la causa instruida por la conspiración de los Soles de Bolívar, Rollo de Guanajay," fols. 30, in Roque Garrigó, *Historia documentada de la conspiración de los Soles y rayos de Bolívar* (Havana: Imprenta "Siglo XX," 1929), 167. Cited on 180.

38. Garrigó, *Historia documentada de la conspiración de los Soles y rayos de Bolívar*, 171, 179.

39. Garrigó, *Historia documentada de la conspiración de los Soles y rayos de Bolívar*, 179–180.

40. "Certificación relativo del sumario de conspiración que le actua en la Habana y principio en 2 de agosto de 1823," AHN, SE, leg. 6367, exp. 51.

41. On Bolívar and pardocracy, see Aline Helg, *Liberty and Equality in Caribbean Colombia, 1770–1835* (Chapel Hill: University of North Carolina Press, 2004), 165–167, 195–196; and John Lynch, *Simón Bolívar: A Life* (New Haven: Yale University Press, 2006), 290–291.

42. Marixa Lasso, *Myths of Harmony: Race and Republicanism during the Age of Revolution, Colombia 1795–1831* (Pittsburgh: University of Pittsburgh Press, 2007), 153, 22.

43. "Testimonio de incidentes o ramo separado del sumario de conspiración actuado en la Habana en lo conferente al Brig. Dr. Francisco Correa, natural y vecino de esta ciudad, por el tral. del Sr. Alcalde 3 constitución Don Juan Agustín de Ferrety," 22 August 1823, AHN, SE, leg. 6367, exp. 51, núm. 3.

44. "Declaración del negro Tomás, de nación gangá, esclavo de D. Miguel de Oro," in Garrigó, *Historia documentada de la conspiración de los Soles y rayos de Bolívar*, 165.

45. Francisco Dionisio Vives to Secretario de Ultramar, 12 June 1823, AHN, SE, leg. 6368, caja 1, núm. 2.

46. Declaration of Bruno Aristegui, 26 August 1823, AHN, SE, leg. 6367, exp. 51, núm. 3.

47. Ignacio García Osuna, the *alcalde ordinario primero* (justice of the peace) of the cabildo of Guanabacoa, was swiftly detained on the orders of Vives when his connection to the Soles y Rayos became clear, but twelve years later he had apparently rebounded and was elected as alcalde. Participation in the conspiracy for some, then, did not permanently alienate them from colonial politics. Gerardo Castellanos, *Relicario histórico: Frutos coloniales y de la vieja Guanabacoa* (Havana: Editorial Librería Selecta, 1948), 414–416.

48. Joaquín Balmaseda, a free pardo, was the only nonwhite detainee. Franco, *El Gobierno Colonial de Cuba y la independencia de Venezuela*, 94.

49. Coterminous proindependence uprisings that shook cities beyond Havana in 1823 suggest varying degrees of connection to the Soles y Rayos movement. The Yuquinos uprising in Cienfuegos and tumults in Nuevitas and Trinidad embraced rhetoric and iconography that resemble, within a wide margin of error, that of Soles y Rayos; an uprising led by los Cadenarios in Puerto Príncipe appears to be distinct from the movement of Lemus and his followers. See Garrigó, *Historia documentada de la conspiración de los Soles y rayos de Bolívar*, 183–198. Carlos Trelles y Govín claims that of 174 of the 602 individuals implicated in the conspiracy were from Matanzas. See Carlos Trelles, *Matanzas en la independencia de Cuba* (Havana: Imprenta Avisador Comercial, 1928), 10.

50. Francisco Dionisio Vives to secretario del despacho de guerra, 17 December 1823, AHN, SE, leg. 6367, exp. 54, núm. 1.

51. Franco, *El Gobierno Colonial de Cuba y la independencia de Venezuela*, 94.

52. Andueza, *Isla de Cuba pintoresca, histórica, política, literaria, mercantil e industrial*, 112. See also Juan José Sánchez Baena, *El terror de los tiranos: La imprenta en la centuria que cambió Cuba (1763–1868)* (Castellón: Publicacions de la Universitat Jaume I, 2009).

53. Victor M. Uribe-Urán, "The Birth of a Public Sphere in Latin America during the Age of Revolution," 453.

54. Manuel Moreno Fraginals, *Cuba/España, España/Cuba: Historia común* (Madrid: Grijalbo Mondadori, 1995), 195.

55. Izaskun Álvarez Cuartero, *Memorias de la ilustración: Las Sociedades Económicas de Amigos del País en Cuba (1783–1832)* (Madrid: Real Sociedad Bascongada de Amigos del País Delegación en Cortes, 2000). On censors, see José Antonio Saco, *Carta de un patriota: O sea Clamor de los Cubanos* (Cádiz: n.p., 1835); 8–9, and Larry R. Jensen, *Children of Colonial Despotism: Press, Politics, and Culture in Cuba, 1790–1840* (Tampa: University of South Florida Press, 1988), 29–30, 70. On segregating education, see Justo Reyes, *Consideraciones sobre la educación doméstica y instrucción pública en la Isla de Cuba* (Havana: Imprenta del gobierno, capitanía general y real Sociedad patriótica por S.M., 1832), 83–84.

56. *Memoria de la Sección de historia de la Real Sociedad Patriótica de la Habana*, 2 vols. (Havana: Imprenta de las viudas de Arazoza y Soler, 1830), 1:40.

57. Benedict Anderson, *Imagined Communities: Reflections on the Origin and Spread of Nationalism*, 2nd ed. (London: Verso, 1991 [1983]), 1–9, 47–66.

58. Someruelos to Pedro Ceballos, 25 May 1804, AHN, SE, leg. 6366, caja 2, núm. 78.

59. Miguel Tacón to secretario de estado, 31 December 1835, AHN, SE, leg. 4603, exp. 47.

60. See Kirsten Schultz, *Tropical Versailles: Empire, Monarchy, and the Portuguese Royal Court in Rio de Janeiro, 1808–1821* (New York: Routledge, 2001).

61. *Lealtad cubana. Alegoría: En loor de nuestros amados monarcas* (Havana: Oficina del Gobierno y Capitanía general por S.M., 1833).

62. Miguel Tacón to Secretario de Estado, 7 November 1835, BNJM, CM Tacón, núm. 23.

63. Andueza, *Isla de Cuba pintoresca, histórica, política, literaria, mercantil e industrial,* 104.

64. Richard Henry Dana, *To Cuba and Back: A Vacation Voyage* (Boston: Houghton, Mifflin, 1859), 233–234. The opera anecdote is originally cited in Ivan A. Schulman, "Reflections on Cuba and Its Antislavery Literature," SECOLAS *Annals* 7 (1976): 66n4.

65. Juan Bernardo O'Gaván, *Observaciones sobre la suerte de los negros del África, considerados en su propia patria y trasplantados a las Antillas españolas: y reclamación contra el tratado celebrado con los ingleses el año de 1817* (Madrid: Imprenta Universal, 1821), 5, 9.

66. C. Stanley Urban, "The Africanization of Cuba Scare, 1853–1855," *Hispanic American Historical Review* 37:1 (1957): 29–45.

67. *Cuba desde 1850 á 1875: Colección de informes, memorias, proyectos y antecedentes sobre el gobierno de la Isla de Cuba, relativos al citado período que ha reunido por comisión del gobierno D. Carlos de Sedano y Cruzat (Ex-diputado a Cortes)* (Madrid: Imprenta Nacional, 1873), 295.

68. Fernando Ortiz, *La antigua fiesta afrocubana del "Día de Reyes"* (Havana: Ministerio de Relaciones Exteriores, 1960 [1925]); Roberto González Echevarría, *Cuban Fiestas* (New Haven, C.T.: Yale University Press, 2010), chap. 3. On the cabildos, see Pedro Deschamps Chapeaux, *El negro en la economía habanera del siglo XIX* (Havana: UNEAC, 1971), 31–46.

69. Gloria García Rodríguez, *Conspiraciones y revueltas: La actividad política de los negros en Cuba (1790–1845)* (Santiago de Cuba: Editorial Oriente, 2003), 111–112, 116–117.

70. Francisco García del Sierro (Regente de la Audiencia de Puerto Príncipe) to Captain General Leopoldo O'Donnell, 1 November 1843, ANC, Fondo Gobierno Superior Civil (hereafter GSC), leg. 367, exp. 19877.

71. Philip A. Howard, *Changing History: Afro-Cuban Cabildos and Societies of Color in the Nineteenth Century* (Baton Rouge: Louisiana State University Press, 1998), 96–97.

72. On this phenomenon more broadly, see Michael Taussig, *Mimesis and Alterity: A Particular History of the Senses* (New York: Routledge, 1992).

73. Antonio de las Barras y Prado, *La Habana a mediados del siglo XIX* (Madrid: Imprenta de la Ciudad Lineal, 1926), 122. *Tango* referred to African dances generally or to groups of dancers. See John Charles Chasteen, *National Rhythms, African Roots: The Deep History of Latin American Popular Dance* (Albuquerque: University of New Mexico Press, 2004), 26.

74. Barras y Prado, *La Habana a mediados del siglo XIX,* 133.

75. David H. Brown, "Black Royalty: New Social Frameworks and Remodeled Iconographies in Nineteenth-Century Havana," in *Santería Enthroned: Art, Ritual,*

and Innovation in an Afro-Cuban Religion (Chicago: University of Chicago Press, 2003), 35.

76. Brown, "Black Royalty," 46, 47. Swedish traveler Frederika Bremer also observed cabildo activity in 1851. See *The Homes of the New World: Impressions of America,* trans. Mary Howitt, 2 vols. (New York: Harper Brothers, 1853), 2:379–383.

77. "El capataz de cabildo Mariano Mora solicitando ocupar el lugar de capataz imperante de los tangos de congos," HL JE, BMS Span 502 (943, *Introducción de negros bozales,* 1819–1869), folder 8.

78. "Instrucción para el gobierno del Teniente de Infanteria de la Habana Don Manuel de Chenard Comandante de la parida destinada por este Gobierno para la persecución de negros cimarrones y la cual debera arreglarse," 1816, Archivo Histórico Provincial de Santiago de Cuba, Fondo Gobierno Provincial (hereafter AHPSC, GP), leg. 554, exp. 1.

79. Rita Llanes Miqueli, *Víctimas del año del cuero* (Havana: Editorial de Ciencias Sociales, 1984), 28.

80. "Expediente sobre las causes que influyen en el frecuente suicidio de los esclavos y medidas que son de adoptarse para evitarlos," 15 December 1846, ANC, AP, leg. 141, núm. 12.

81. "Cesación de la Comisión Regia de la Colonia de Jagua en el ejercicio de sus atribuciones, 19 de octubre de 1833," AHN, SU, leg. 5842 núm. 39.

82. Orlando García Martínez, *Esclavitud y colonización en Cienfuegos, 1819–1879* (Cienfuegos: Ediciones Mecenas, 2008), 57.

83. Leopoldo O'Donnell, *Cuadro estadístico de la siempre fiel Isla de Cuba . . . 1846* (Havana: Imprenta del Gobierno, 1847); Enrique Edo y Llop, *Memoria histórica de Ciefuegos y su jurisdicción,* 2nd. ed. (Cienfuegos: J. Andreu, 1888), 229–230.

84. On the office of the síndico, see de la Fuente, "Slavery and the Creation of Legal Rights in Cuba"; and García Martínez, *Esclavitud y colonización en Cienfuegos,* 51–52.

85. José Quijano to Cecilio Ayllon, governor of Matanzas, 6 July 1824, BNJM, CM José Augusto Escoto (hereafter Escoto), núm. 118.

86. "Expediente sobre sublevación de negros en Cienfuegos," 19 November 1840, ANC, AP, leg. 136, núm. 6.

87. Matthias Perl, "Las estructuras de comunicación de los esclavos negros en Cuba en el siglo XIX," *Islas* 77–79 (1984): 43–59.

88. Florentino Morales Hernández, *Breve panorama de la esclavitud en la jurisdicción de Cienfuegos* (Cienfuegos: Museo Provincial de Cienfuegos, 1987), 25.

89. The books titled *Actas Capitulares* record the minutes from ayuntamiento meetings throughout the century. Gabriel Montel, José Gregorio Díaz de Villegas, and Manuel Suárez del Villar—all from planter families—were selected by the ayuntamiento to investigate and report: 9 September 1864, libro 8, Archivo Provincial de Cienfuegos, Actas Capitulares (hereafter APC, AC). Edo y Llop, *Memoria histórica de Cienfuegos,* 255–257.

90. Ayuntamiento de Cienfuegos, *Ordenanzas municipales de la villa de Cienfuegos* (Cienfuegos: Imprenta de D. Eduardo Feixas, 1856), 10.

91. *El Telégrafo,* 31 July 1865.

92. Florentino Morales Hernández, *Apuntes históricos sobre el desarrollo de la cultura en Cienfuegos* (Cienfuegos: n.p. 1958), 9. Short-lived newspapers proliferated in Cienfuegos in the city's early years. *La Hoja Económica,* whose content rarely strayed

from trade and shipping news, ended a lengthy run in 1860; it was replaced by *El Telégrafo* as the city's most prominent newspaper, despite its Liberal, reformist bent. *El Fomento* enjoyed a four-year run in the late 1850s; when it reappeared in the early 1860s under the editorship of Antonio Hurtado del Valle, a local poet given to campaigning for Cuban independence, the Spanish authorities began to watch it carefully, which they continued even after a Conservative editor took over. In 1866, Hurtado del Valle began another newspaper, *El Comercio*. On the outbreak of insurgency in 1868, the government allowed for the creation of a military newspaper, *El Pabellón Nacional*, at the same time that it shut down *El Telégrafo*, *El Comercio*, and *El Damují*, a separatist weekly that Hurtado del Valle published five or six times that year. To set the tone of acceptable publications, the government in 1870 established the *Diario de Cienfuegos*, a staunch defender of Spanish policies and colonial rule, which continued publication until 1898.

93. *El Telégrafo*, 8 August 1865, 3.

94. Florentino Morales Hernández, *Breve panorama de la esclavitud en la jurisdicción de Cienfuegos* (Cienfuegos: Museo Provincial de Cienfuegos, 1987), 33–34.

95. Robert L. Paquette, *Sugar Is Made with Blood: The Conspiracy of La Escalera and the Conflict between Empires over Slavery in Cuba* (Middletown, C.T.: Wesleyan University Press, 1988), 101.

96. Juan Francisco Manzano, *The Life and Poems of a Cuban Slave*, ed. Edward J. Mullen (Hamden, C.T.: Archon Books, 1981 [1840]), 102.

97. Sonia Labrador Rodríguez, "Nicolás Guillén y sus antecesores: La 'poesía blanca' de los poetas negros del siglo XIX," in *Homenaje a Nicolás Guillén* (Veracruz: Colección Cuadernos, Instituto de Investigaciones Lingüístico-Literarias, Universidad Veracruzana, 2006), 231–247

98. Francisco Calcagno, *Poetas de color. [Plácido, Manzano, Rodríguez, Echemendía, Silveira, Medina.]* (Havana: Imprenta militar de la v. de Soler y compañía, 1878), 47–48.

99. Calcagno, *Poetas de color,* 51–52.

100. Fischer, *Modernity Disavowed,* chap. 3, discusses the "discourse of the abject" surrounding Plácido and makes a compelling case for his affinities for both Spanish monarchism and constitutional rights.

101. Calcagno, *Poetas de color,* 7. See also Daisy Cue Fernández, *Plácido: El poeta conspirador* (Santiago de Cuba: Editorial Oriente, 2007).

102. Matt Childs, *The 1812 Aponte Rebellion in Cuba and the Struggle against Atlantic Slavery* (Chapel Hill: University of North Carolina Press, 2006), 91.

103. Díaz, *The Virgin, the King, and the Royal Slaves of El Cobre,* 89–90.

104. Herbert S. Klein, "The Colored Militia of Cuba: 1568–1868," *Caribbean Studies* 6:2 (1966): 18.

105. Sherry Johnson, *The Social Transformation of Eighteenth-Century Cuba* (Gainesville: University Press of Florida, 2000), 11.

106. *Reglamento provisional para los cuerpos de milicia nacional local de la Habana y su distrito* (Havana: Oficina de Arazoza y Soler, impresores del Gobierno constitucional, 1821), 11.

107. Ministro de la Guerra to the capitan ceneral, 12 September 1818, ANC, AP, leg. 125, núm. 8.

108. Klein, "The Colored Militia of Cuba," 22.

109. Francisco Marín Villafuerte, *Historia de Trinidad* (Havana: Jesús Montero, 1945), 148.

110. Francisco Oribarri to comandante general de provincia, 14 October 1833, AHPSC, GP, leg. 632.

111. See Matt Childs, *The 1812 Aponte Rebellion in Cuba and the Struggle against Atlantic Slavery*, chap. 3.

112. Declaration of loyalty by Havana's pardo and militiamen, 1823, ANC, CM, leg. 60, núm. 2, fols. 208–210, published in Michele Reid-Vazquez, "Empire, Loyalty, and Race: Militiamen of Color in Nineteenth-Century Cuba," in *Documenting Latin America: Gender, Race, and Empire*, 2 vols., ed. Erin E. O'Connor and Leo J. Garafolo (Boston: Prentice Hall, 2011), 1:260–264.

113. See Jane Landers, *Atlantic Creoles in the Age of Revolutions* (Cambridge: Harvard University Press, 2011), 170–174.

114. "Informe que a la comisión regia da la sección de guerra y marina de ella sobre alteraciones en los gastos que hacen las Milicias de Infantería y caballería de la Isla, con el fin de establecer las económicas que propone, porque a su concepto pueden hacerse, sin nada perjudicarse," 27 August 1839, HL, JE, ms Span, 843, folder 3.

115. Real orden of 4 December 1839, ANC, AP, leg. 40, núm. 31.

116. On fuero rights, see Landers, *Atlantic Creoles in the Age of Revolutions*, 50; Childs, *The 1812 Aponte Rebellion in Cuba and the Struggle against Atlantic Slavery*, 83–86; Ben Vinson III, *Bearing Arms for His Majesty: The Free Colored Militia in Colonial Mexico* (Stanford: Stanford University Press, 2001), 173–174; and Joseph P. Sánchez, "African Freedmen and the Fuero Militar: A Historical Overview of Pardo and Moreno Militiamen in the Late Spanish Empire," *Colonial Latin American Historical Review* 3 (1994): 165–184.

117. Joaquín Navarro, Joaquín Pompa, and Tomás Cardona to Miguel Tacón, 3 April 1843, AHPSC, PI, leg. 356, exp. 16.

118. *Diario de la Habana*, 11 February 1844, in AHN, SU, leg. 5460, exp. 48.

119. Leopoldo O'Donnell to the governor of Matanzas, 26 March 1844, HL, JE, msSpan no. 701, folder 7.

120. Justo Zaragoza, *Las insurrecciones en Cuba*, 2 vols. (Madrid: Imprenta de Miguel G. Hernández, 1872–1873), 1:536; Klein, "The Colored Militia of Cuba," 24.

121. Llanes Miqueli, *Víctimas del año del cuero*, 4.

122. Walter Benjamin, "Critique of Violence," in *Walter Benjamin: Selected Writings*, vol. 1: *1913–1926*, ed. Marcus Bullock and Michael W. Jennings (Cambridge: Harvard University Press, 1996), 249.

123. See for example Walterio Carbonell, "Plácido, ¿Conspirador?" *Revolución y cultura* 2 (1987): 53–57.

124. Paquette, *Sugar Is Made with Blood*, 4, 265. Pedro Deschamps Chapeaux's pioneering study of the militias ends in 1844, "marking the end of almost two and a half centuries of the presence of the African and his creole descendants in the military history of colonial Cuba." *Los batallones de pardos y morenos libres* (Havana: Instituto Cubano del Libro, 1976), 90.

125. José Ahumada y Centurión, *Memoria histórico político de la Isla de Cuba* (Habana: Librería e Imprenta de A. Pego, 1874), 255; Verena Martínez-Alier, *Marriage,*

Class, and Colour in Nineteenth-Century Cuba: A Study of Racial Attitudes and Sexual Values in a Slave Society (Cambridge: Cambridge University Press, 1974), 26–41.

126. Ramiro Guerra y Sánchez, *Manual de historia de Cuba (Económica, Social y Política)* (Havana: Cultural, 1938), 508.

127. *Cuba desde 1850 á 1875*, 178; Dana, *To Cuba and Back*, 246.

128. Mariano Torrente, *Política ultramarina que abraza todos los puntos referentes a las relaciones de España con los Estados Unidos, con Inglaterra y las Antillas, y señaladamente con la Isla de Santo Domingo* (Madrid: Compañía General de Impresos y Libros del Reino, 1854), 113–114.

129. Guerra y Sánchez, *Manual de historia de Cuba*, 508.

130. On the enlistment and activities of the milicias de color, see, for example, "Expediente formado para el alistamiento de las Milicias de color de la jurisdicción de Cienfuegos," 1859, ANC, GSC, leg. 1267, exp. 49798. On *cimarrones*, see "Expediente relativo a los cimarrones existentes en Cienfuegos," 1 February 1858, ANC, GSC, leg. 1630, exp. 82060.

131. "Expediente promovido para llevar a efecto al alistamiento forzoso de pardos y morenos con objeto de cubrir las bajas que hay en las Milicias de color por no ser suficientes los alistados voluntariamente, 28 junio 1859," ANC, GSC, 1268, exp 49859.

132. Manuel Arrayá to teniente gobernador de Cienfuegos, 30 September 1859, "Distintos documentos sobre milicias de color, Años 1858–1860," ANC, GSC, leg. 1267, exp. 49799.

133. "Tenencia de Gobierno de Cienfuegos. Expediente formado para el alistamiento de las Milicias de color de esta jurisdicción," 5 August 1859, ANC, GSC, leg. 1267, exp. 49798. The reglamento carefully delineated conditions that qualified individuals to be excused from militia duty. Age, height, and health were the most obvious variables, but free people could also substitute others in their place, remain in the service of the Cuerpos de Bomberos (fire brigades) if they were already so engaged, and invoke obligations of household authority to escape militia obligation. Providing for one's wife and children was insufficient justification, but draftees could receive an exemption if they were caring for orphans who could not be apprenticed, if they were the only children of an infirm parent, or if all of their other brothers were in militias.

134. The name Ayllo derived from the Yorùbá term Òyó, which alongside the more common designation "lucumí," identified more precise origins and a likely link to the Oyo Empire.

135. See, for example, de la Fuente, "Slavery and the Creation of Legal Rights in Cuba"; and Bianca Premo, "An Equity against the Law: Slave Rights and Creole Jurisprudence in Spanish America," *Slavery and Abolition* 32:4 (2011): 495–451.

136. Pedro Deschamps Chapeaux, *El negro en la economía habanera del siglo XIX* (Havana: Unión de Escritores y Artistas de Cuba, 1971), 61.

137. Raymond Carr, "Liberalism and Reaction, 1833–1931," in *Spain: A History,* ed. Raymond Carr (New York: Oxford University Press, 2000), 214.

138. "Dos circulares de la regencia de la Audiencia Pretorial de la Habana dirigidas al Alcalde Mayor de Holguín relativos a una recoleta organizada en la isla para auxiliar al gobierno español en la Guerra contra el imperio de Marruecos . . . ," 20 January and 10 March 1860, ANC, DR, leg. F83, exp. 21.

139. Diego Sevilla Andrés, *África en la política española del siglo XIX* (Madrid: Consejo Superior de Investigaciones Científicas, 1960), 84–87.

140. "Documento acerca del proyecto de D. Martín de Arredondo y Oléa de formar un batallón de Voluntarios de pardos y morenos libres que pasasen a tomar parte en la Guerra de África, recaudación de recursos al efecto y ofrecimientos de servidos," 24 February 1860, ANC, AP, leg. 53, exp. 1.

141. S. C. Ukpabi, "West Indian Troops and the Defence of British West Africa in the Nineteenth Century," *African Studies Review* 17:1 (April 1974): 133–150. On Fernando Po, see Ibrahim Sundiata, *From Slaving to Neoslavery: The Bight of Biafra and Fernando Po in the Era of Prohibition, 1827–1930* (Madison: University of Wisconsin Press, 1996).

142. Eugenio Alonso y Sanjurjo, *Apuntes sobre los proyectos de abolición de la esclavitud en las Islas de Cuba y Puerto Rico* (Madrid: Imprenta del Biblioteca de Instrucción y Recreo, 1874), 59.

143. Homi Bhabha, "Of Mimicry and Man: The Ambivalence of Colonial Discourse," in *The Location of Culture* (New York: Routledge, 1994), 85–92.

144. José de la Luz y Caballero, "Aforísmos," in Eduardo Torres-Cuevas, ed., *Historia el pensamiento cubano,* ed. (Havana: Editorial de Ciencias Sociales, 2006), vol. 1, pt. 2, 117.

CHAPTER 3 *The Will to Freedom*

Epigraph source: José Martí, "El presidio político en Cuba," in *Obras completas,* 27 vols. (Havana: Editorial Nacional de Cuba, 1963–66), 1:49.

1. José Abreu Cardet, *Introducción a las armas: La Guerra de 1868 en Cuba* (Havana: Editorial de Ciencias Sociales, 2005), 128.

2. Ada Ferrer, *Insurgent Cuba: Race, Nation, and Revolution, 1868–1898* (Chapel Hill: University of North Carolina Press, 1999), chap. 1.

3. Antonio Caballero to the ministro de ultramar, 30 August 1869, AHN, SU, leg. 4933, 2a parte, exp. 234.

4. Manuel Moreno Fraginals, *Cuba/España, España/Cuba: Historia común* (Barcelona: Grijalbo Mondadori, 1995), 273–274.

5. Octavio Avelino Delgado, "The Spanish Army in Cuba, 1868–1898: An Institutional Study," 2 vols. (Ph.D. dissertation, Columbia University, 1980), 1:264. Militia officers were often supernumerary or off-duty army officers.

6. Free-colored militias in Cienfuegos, for example, destroyed enemy camps in outlying areas in the early years of the war. See "Cienfuegos," *La Quincena,* 15 October 1869.

7. "Voluntarios de color," *La Quincena,* 15 April 1869.

8. Dulce to the ministro de ultramar, 8 February 1869, AHN, SU, leg. 4933 exp. 3.

9. Emilio A. Souleré, *Historia de la insurrección en Cuba* (Barcelona: Est. Tip de Juan Pons, 1879), 53–54. Captain General Francisco Lersundi suspended Fernández Cavada as vice-consul.

10. Entries for 17 February and 9 April 1869, APC, AC, libro 12.

11. Camps y Feliu, Fernando de, *Españoles e insurrectos: Recuerdos de la Guerra de Cuba,* 2nd ed. (Havana: Imprenta de A. Álvarez y Cia., 1890), 25.

12. Jill Lane, *Blackface Cuba, 1840–1895* (Philadelphia: University of Pennsylvania Press, 2005), 143.

13. Carles Llorens and Clàudia Pujol, *La Guerra de Cuba* (Barcelona: Pòrtic, 2000), 107.

14. Antonio Pirala y Criado, *Anales de la guerra de Cuba,* 3 vols. (Madrid: F. González Rojas, 1895–1898), 1:402–404, 591.

15. *Rasgos biográficos del Excmo. Sr. Gral. D. Eusebio Puello y Castro y exposición que meses antes de morir* (Havana: Imprenta militar de viuda de Soler y Cía, 1872), 8. See also Carlos Esteban Deive, *Honor y gloria: Los dominicanos en las guerras de independencia de Cuba,* 137–155; and Ramiro Guerra y Sánchez, *Guerra de los 10 años,* 2 vols. (Havana: Editorial de Ciencias Sociales, 1972), 287, 294–295, 298, 407.

16. Francisco J. Ponte Domínguez, *Historia de la Guerra de los diez años* (Havana: Imprenta El siglo XX, 1958), 100. Ponte described Puello as a *moreno*. Rolando Rodríguez refers to Puello as a "Dominican mulatto in search of celebrity." *Cuba: La forja de una nación,* 2 vols. (Madrid: Caja Madrid, 1999), 1:276.

17. *Rasgos biográficos del Excmo. Sr. Gral. D. Eusebio Puello y Castro,* 4–7.

18. Ponte Domínguez, *Historia de la Guerra de los diez años,* 261–262.

19. Pirala, *Anales de la guerra de Cuba,* 1:592, 702, 741.

20. *Rasgos biográficos del Excmo. Sr. Gral. D. Eusebio Puello y Castro,* 12.

21. Pirala, *Anales de la guerra de Cuba,* 1:592.

22. Antonio Maceo, *Ideología política: Cartas y otros documentos,* 2 vols. (Havana: Editorial de Ciencias Sociales, 1998), 1:64–65. Ada Ferrer gives careful treatment to Maceo's response, and his role in the insurgency more broadly, in *Insurgent Cuba,* 57–67, passim.

23. F. de Laiglesia, "El General Puello," *La Ilustración de Madrid,* 12 February 1870, 14. On Spanish efforts to reimagine the colonial relationship during the Ten Years' War, see Christopher Schmidt-Nowara, *Empire and Antislavery: Spain, Cuba, and Puerto Rico, 1833–1874* (Pittsburgh: University of Pittsburgh Press, 1999), 108–116; and "'Spanish' Cuba: Race and Class in Spanish and Cuban Antislavery Ideology, 1861–1868," *Cuban Studies* 25 (1995): 101–122.

24. José de la Gándara, *Anexión y guerra de Santo Domingo por el general Gándara* (Madrid: Imprenta de "El Correo Militar," 1884), 2:93–94. See also 2:66, 81. One study suggests that Puello was only a field marshal and the two men met and fought alongside each other. See Gabriel Cardona and Juan Carlos Losada, *Weyler: Nuestro hombre en la Habana* (Barcelona: Planeta, 1997), 29, 32n19, 33.

25. On the reconcentration, see John Lawrence Tone, *War and Genocide in Cuba, 1895–1898* (Chapel Hill: University of North Carolina Press, 2006), chap. 14; and Francisco Pérez Guzmán, *Herida profunda* (Havana: Ediciones Unión, 1998).

26. Valeriano Weyler, *Memorias de un general: De caballero cadete a general en jefe,* ed. María Teresa Weyler (Barcelona: Ediciones Destino, 2004), 64, 66, 69. The same encounter is described in Abreu Cardet, *Introducción a las armas,* 182–183, citing "Ponencia de Ultramar. Cuba," Archivo Histórico Militar, Segovia, leg. 3, núm. 6. The battle at El Salado enabled the Spanish to enter and retake the city of Bayamo from the insurgents.

27. Weyler, *Memorias de un general,* 74–75.

28. On the complicated relationships between fraternal and paternalistic soldier relations, see Graham Dawson, *Soldier Heroes: British Adventure, Empire, and the Imagining of Masculinities* (New York: Routledge, 1994), chaps. 1–3; James M. McPher-

son, *For Cause and Comrades: Why Men Fought in the Civil War* (New York: Oxford University Press, 1997), chap. 6; Mary A. Renda, *Taking Haiti: Military Occupation and the Culture of U.S. Imperialism* (Chapel Hill: University of North Carolina Press, 2001), 62–74, 89–130; Mimi Sheller, "Sword-Bearing Citizens: Militarism and Manhood in Nineteenth-Century Haiti," *Plantation Society in the Americas* 4, nos. 2–3 (1997): 233–278; and Mrinalani Sinha, *Colonial Masculinity: The 'Manly Englishman' and the "Effeminate Bengali' in the Late Nineteenth Century* (Manchester: Manchester University Press, 1995).

29. I draw here on the insights of David Scott in *Conscripts of Modernity: The Tragedy of Colonial Enlightenment* (Durham, N.C.: Duke University Press, 2004).

30. Antonio Caballero to the ministro de ultramar, 25 April 1870, AHN, SU, leg. 4933, 2a parte, exp. 324.

31. Antonio Caballero to the ministro de ultramar, 11 May 1870, AHN, SU, leg. 4933, 2a parte, exp. 338. The "provincial laws" here may refer to the discretion granted to the captain-general. See Franklin W. Knight, *Slave Society in Cuba during the Nineteenth Century* (Madison: University of Wisconsin Press, 1970), 172.

32. Souleré, *Historia de la insurrección en Cuba*, 294.

33. Speech by Ortiz de Zárate, 10 June 1870, *Diario de sesiones de las Cortes Constituyentes,* tomo XIII (Madrid: Imprenta de J. A. García, 1870–1871), 8757.

34. Manuel Ruiz Zorrilla, *Sobre el cumplimiento de la Ley Preparatoria (de Julio de 1870) para la abolición de la esclavitud en las Antillas españolas* (Madrid: Secretaría de la Sociedad Abolicionista Española, 1872), 19.

35. Arthur Corwin, *Spain and the Abolition of Slavery in Cuba* (Austin: University of Texas Press, 1967), 280.

36. *La Iberia*, núm. 4188, quoted in *La abolición de la esclavitud y el proyecto del Señor Moret* (Madrid: Est. Tip. De T. Fortanet, 1870), 21–22.

37. *El Sufragio Universal*, núm 99–101, quoted in *La abolición de la esclavitud y el proyecto del Señor Moret*, 52–53.

38. *El Puente de Alcolea*, núm. 481, quoted in *La abolición de la esclavitud y el proyecto del Señor Moret*, 66.

39. *La Voz del Derecho*, núms. 43, 45, and 46, quoted in *La abolición de la esclavitud y el proyecto del Señor Moret*, 109.

40. DAM to *Diario de Barcelona*, 24 August 1869, quoted in Souleré, *Historia de la insurrección en Cuba*, 138.

41. Gil Gelpi y Ferro, *Situación de España y de sus posesiones de Ultramar, su verdadero peligro y el único medio de conjurarlo* (Madrid: Imprenta Santiago Aguado, 1871), 74, 80–81.

42. "Bando apercibiendo con la ejecución a quienes subleven esclavos, atenten a la propiedad o ayuden al enemigo," 9 November 1868, in Fernando Portuondo del Prado and Hortensia Pichardo Viñals, eds., *Carlos Manuel de Céspedes: Escritos* 3 vols. (Havana: Editorial de Ciencias Sociales, 1982), 1:123. On calls for obligatory service, see 3:113.

43. "Orden del día prohibiendo admitir en el ejército libertador a esclavos no autorizados por sus dueños," 29 October 1868, in *Carlos Manuel de Céspedes: Escritos*, 1:117.

44. "Sumaria instruida en averiguación de los servicios presados por el moreno esclavo de la Compañía Guillermo Bell," 30 August 1870, ANC, AP, leg. 62, exp. 5.

45. "Expediente instruido en averiguación de la procedencia o captura y servicios que ha prestado en este Batallón el moreno José Caimares agregado a la 1a Compañía del mismo en calidad de camillero," 17 October 1870, ANC, AP, leg. 62, exp. 21.

46. "Expediente instruido en averiguación de los servicios prestados al Gobierno de la nación por el negro Alejandro Néstor," 15 November 1870, ANC, AP, leg. 62, exp. 33.

47. Grover Flint, *Marching with Gomez: A War Correspondent's Field Note-Book Kept during Four Months with the Cuban Army,* introduction by John Fiske (Boston: Lamson, Wolffe, and Co., 1898), 153.

48. "Expediente instruido en averiguación de los servicios prestados y conducta observada durante esta campaña por el moreno Ignacio Calixto de la propiedad de D. Félix Duruti," 29 December 1870, ANC, AP, leg. 2, exp. 6.

49. "Expediente instruido en averiguación de la procedencia del moreno de la 1a Compañía Eustaquio Adelín, punto y fecha donde se presentó o fue aprehendido, dueño a quien pertenece y servicios que ha prestado," 17 October 1870, ANC, AP, leg. 62 exp. 23 .

50. "Comunicación del Gobierno Político y Militar de Matanzas dirigida al Capitán General sobre la libertad del moreno Luciano Sosa, esclavo de Antonio María Cabrera, por los servicios prestados a las columnas del ejército español," 14 November 1870, ANC, AP, leg. 62, exp. 29.

51. "Expediente promovido para justificar los servicios del negro Manuel Olivares, esclavo del que se dice ser cabecilla de la rebelión Ramón Rubio," 30 August 1870, ANC, AP, leg. 62, exp. 9.

52. "Expediente instruido en averiguación de la procedencia y servicios prestados en este Batallón del Moreno agregado a la 4a Compañía del mismo Andrés Aguilera, como asimismo su dueño y si ha sido aprehendido o presentado," 15 October 1870, ANC, AP, leg. 62, exp. 19 .

53. See, for example, "Sumaria instruida en averiguación de los servicios prestados por el negro de la 5a Compa. Santiago Morell," 30 August 1870, and "Sumaria instruida en averiguación de los servicios prestados por el esclavo de la 6a Compa. Valeriano Pinacha," 30 August 1870, ANC, AP, leg. 62, exps. 8 and 10 respectively.

54. See, for example, "Expediente instruido en averiguación de los servicios presados al Gobierno de la nación por el negro Alejandro Néstor," 15 November 1870, ANC, AP, leg. 62, exp. 33.

55. "Expediente instruido en averiguación de los servicios que ha prestado al Gobierno de la nación el negro esclavo Vicente del Castillo," 15 November 1870, ANC, AP, leg. 62, exp. 31 .

56. "Expediente instruido en averiguación de los servicios prestados por el negro esclavo Zacarios Priol al Gobierno de la Nación Española durante la insurrección de la Isla de Cuba," 15 November 1870, ANC, AP, leg. 62, exp. 34.

57. "Declaración del esclavo negro Felipe San José, in Expediente instruido en averiguación de los servicios prestados al Gobierno de la nación por los esclavos Felipe y Santiago San José," 15 November 1870, ANC, AP, leg. 62, exp. 36.

58. "Expediente instruido en averiguación de los servicios prestados en campaña por el moreno Antonio Abad Criollo esclavo de D. Antonio Llamosas, y por los cuales pueda o no tener derecho a su libertad," 27 November 1870, ANC, AP, leg. 62, exp. 46.

59. "Expediente promovido por doña Juana y doña Luisa del Castillo que piden indemnización por el negro Felipe declarando libre," 10 November 1870, ANC, AP, leg. 62, exp. 28.

60. Antonio C. N. Gallenga, *The Pearl of the Antilles* (London: Chapman and Hall, 1873), 96.

61. Denise Helly, ed. *The Cuba Commission Report: A Hidden History of the Chinese in Cuba* (Baltimore: Johns Hopkins University Press, 1993), 58.

62. On the presence of the Chinese in the insurgent forces, see Juan Jiménez Pastrana, *Los chinos en las luchas por la liberación cubana* (Havana: Editorial de Ciencias Sociales, 1983); Antonio Chuffat Latour, *Apunte histórico de los chinos en Cuba* (Havana: Molina, 1927); and Gonzalo de Quesada, *Los chinos y la revolución cubana* (Havana: Ucar, García, 1946).

63. Helly, *The Cuba Commission Report*, 93–94.

64. José Abreu Cardet, *Las fronteras de la guerra: Mujeres, soldados y regionalismo en el 68* (Santiago de Cuba: Editorial Oriente, 2007), 14–18.

65. Guidelines for Cuba's eighteenth-century militias included an artillery regiment of royal slaves, likely bozales, in Havana with similar domestic duties for the slave women who lived in the garrison with slave men. These arrangements did not offer routes to legal freedom. See Jane Landers, "Transforming Bondsmen into Vassals: Arming Slaves in Colonial Spanish America," in Christopher Leslie Brown and Philip D. Morgan, eds., *Arming Slaves: From Classical Times to the Modern Age* (New Haven, C.T.: Yale University Press, 2006), 127.

66. "Expediente promovido por la morena Juana Sariol solicitando su libertad por servicios prestados," 7 September 1874, ANC, AP, leg. 69, núm. 49.

67. "Expediente de manumisión de la esclava Manuela Betancourt por servicios prestados a nuestras tropas," 29 March 1875, ANC, AP, leg. 70, núm. 32.

68. Expediente de manumisión de la esclava Manuela Betancourt por servicios prestados a nuestras tropas, 29 March 1875, ANC, AP, leg. 70 núm 32.

69. Declarations of Anastasio Betancourt and Pedro Carranza, 14 July 1872, , ANC, AP, leg. 67, núm. 22.

70. Eduardo Viqueira to Anastasio Suárez, 8 September 1872, ANC, AP, leg. 67, núm. 22.

71. Antonio José Nápoles Fajardo, *El sitio de Holguín: Relación histórica precedida de una mirada retrospectiva del estado de la ciudad y su jurisdicción desde el año de 1861 hasta últimos de febrero de 1869* (Havana: Imprenta militar de la viuda de Soler, 1869), 49.

72. Michael Zeuske, "Two Stories of Gender and Slave Emancipation in Cienfuegos and Santa Clara, Central Cuba: A Microhistorical Approach to the Atlantic World," in *Gender and Slave Emancipation in the Atlantic World*, ed. Pamela Scully and Diana Paton (Durham, N.C.: Duke University Press, 2005), 182.

73. Entry for 6 February 1874, APC, AP, libro 17.

74. Entry for 7 November 1874, APC, AP, libro 17.

75. Souleré, *Historia de la insurrección en Cuba*, 687.

76. The documents relating to this second wave of recruitment can be found in Servicio Histórico Militar, Madrid, Fondo Capitanía General de Cuba (hereafter, SHM, CGC), caja 37, leg. 22, núm. gral. 2634, carpeta 22.17.

77. Enrique Edo y Llop, *Memoria histórica de Cienfuegos*, 2nd ed. (Cienfuegos: J. Andreu, 1888), 414–415.

78. Edo y Llop, *Memoria histórica de Cienfuegos,* 424–425. Edo y Llop estimates that 10 percent of those populations left to join.

79. Gabriel Pellicer to the captain general, 8 March 1874; Pellicer to the captain general, 20 March 1874; José de Merás to gobernador superior político, Havana, 3 April 1874; Pellicer to the captain general, 8 April 1874; all in SHM, SU, caja 27, leg. 22 núm. gral. 2634, carpete 72.5.

80. Slaveowners had paid a seventy-five-cent tax on each working-age slave, and a decree on 13 June 1873 imposed a provisional additional twenty-five-cent tax. "Sobre que los esclabos coartados entreguen el precio de tasación en billetes y en la sucesivo," AHN, SU, leg. 97, exp. 94. In contrast to the drain on productive resources that planters experienced, Alfonso W. Quiroz has argued that Cuba's middle class suffered more from the financial costs of loyalty—namely, the taxes levied by Spain to pay for its increased military spending. See "Loyalist Overkill: The Socioeconomic Costs of 'Repressing' the Separatist Insurrection in Cuba, 1868–1878," *Hispanic American Historical Review* 78:2 (May 1998): 261–306.

81. See the entries for Juan de Dios Quesada in "Libro No. 1 de los negros, Santa Rosalía" and "Libro No. 3," APC, Personal collection of Orlando García Martínez.

82. Expediente promovido por Ramón Gangá pidiendo libertad o traslación, 8 April 1874, ANC, AP, leg. 69 núm. 13.

83. José Gutiérrez de la Concha, *Memoria sobre la Guerra de la Isla de Cuba y sobre su estado político y económico desde abril de 1874 hasta marzo de 1875* (Madrid: Est. Tip. E R. Labajos, 1875), 62–63, 112. Gutiérrez de la Concha also proposed amnesty for free men of color who joined the insurgency, as well as slaves, whose fear of returning to their owners made them reluctant to present themselves. *Memoria sobre la Guerra de la Isla de Cuba,* 102.

84. Entry for 8 February 1875, APC, AC, libro 18.

85. *Disposiciones dictadas por el Excmo. Sr. Capitán General en 7 de febrero de 1874 publicadas en la Gaceta oficial* (Havana: Imp. Del Gobierno y Capitanía General, 1874), 16.

86. Arthur Corwin, comparing government figures on emancipation and census records, surmises that the Moret Law accounts for about one half of the 135,000-person decline of the slave population during the war. However, he also lists only 301 slaves freed for "serving the Spanish Flag" between 1870 and 1875. Corwin, *Spain and the Abolition of Slavery in Cuba,* 245–246, 294. Rebecca Scott cites an 1878 estimate of the slave population's decline between 1870 and 1877, which claims that only 658 slaves received their freedom through Article 3. Rebecca J. Scott, *Slave Emancipation in Cuba: The Transition to Free Labor, 1860–1899* (Princeton: Princeton University Press, 1985), 72, table 9.

87. Frank Tannenbaum, *Slave and Citizen: The Negro in the Americas* (New York: Knopf, 1946), 97. On moral personality, see also 82, 93, 100, 115.

88. Peter M. Beattie, *The Tribute of Blood: Army, Honor, Race, and Nation in Brazil, 1864–1945* (Durham, N.C.: Duke University Press, 2001), 280.

CHAPTER 4 *Publicizing Loyalty*
Epigraph source: Rodolfo de Lagardère, *La cuestión social de Cuba: Cuba no es Venecia,* tomo 1 (Havana: La Universal de Ruiz y Hermano, 1887), 18.

1. On the Guerra Chiquita, see Ada Ferrer, *Insurgent Cuba: Race, Nation, and Revolution, 1868–1898* (Chapel Hill: University of North Carolina Press, 1999), chap. 3; and Francisco Pérez Guzmán and Rodolfo Sarracino, *La Guerra Chiquita: Una experiencia necesaria* (Havana: Editorial Letras Cubanas, 1982).

2. On the *patronato*, see Rebecca J. Scott, *Slave Emancipation in Cuba: The Transition to Free Labor, 1860–1899* (Princeton: Princeton University Press, 1985), chap. 6.

3. Iterations of this policy had been in place since the late eighteenth century, but General Ramón Blanco reaffirmed it after the Ten Years' War.

4. Los Cubanos de Color to the Comandancia General, "Antecedentes de personas que contribuyeron al movimiento insurreccional. Proclamas de cabecillas," 26 October 1879, AGI, Sección Diversos (hereafter SD), leg. 7, ramo 2, núm. 12.

5. Jürgen Habermas, *The Structural Transformation of the Public Sphere: An Inquiry into a Category of Bourgeois Society,* trans. Thomas Burger (Cambridge, M.A.: MIT Press, 1989 [1962]).

6. Benedict Anderson, *Imagined Communities: Reflections on the Origin and Spread of Nationalism,* 2nd ed. (London: Verso, 1991 [1983]), chap. 4.

7. Geoff Eley,"Nations, Publics, and Political Cultures: Placing Habermas in the Nineteenth Century," in *Culture/Power/History: A Reader in Contemporary Social Theory,* ed. Nicholas B. Dirks, Geoff Eley, and Sherry B. Ortner (Princeton: Princeton University Press, 1994), 298, 299.

8. Acta de "El Rosario" acuerdo del levantamiento, 6 October 1868, in *Carlos Manuel de Céspedes: Escritos,* eds. Fernando Portuondo del Prado and Hortensia Pichardo Viñals, 3 vols. (Havana: Editorial de Ciencias Sociales, 1982), 1:104.

9. Enrique Collazo, *Desde Yara hasta el Zanjón* (Havana: Instituto del Libro, 1967), chap. 6; Louis A. Pérez Jr., *Cuba between Empires, 1878–1902* (Pittsburgh: University of Pittsburgh Press, 1983), chap. 1.

10. In the administrative reorganization of the island, Cienfuegos became included in the province of Santa Clara, whose capital was the city of the same name. The region of Cienfuegos, still formally the Fernandino de Jagua colony, remained divided into discrete municipalities (Cruces, Camarones, Palmira, Santa Isabel de las Lajas, Cartagena, Abreus, and Rodas) with their own *ayuntamientos* and their district seat in Cienfuegos. Violeta Rovira González, *Cienfuegos desde el Pacto del Zanjón hasta 1902* (Cienfuegos: Consejo Científico de la Sección de Investigaciones Históricas del PCC Provincial Cienfuegos, n.d.), 5. Rebecca J. Scott uses "the Cienfuegos region" to delineate the outlying agricultural areas surrounding the city itself that the agricultural census of 1877–1878 identified: "Race, Labor, and Citizenship in Cuba: A View from the Sugar District of Cienfuegos, 1886–1909, *Hispanic American Historical Review* 78:4 (November 1998), 690n11. See also "Noticia de las fincas azucareras en producción que existían en toda la Isla de Cuba al comenzar el presupuesto de 1877–1878 . . ." *Revista Económica* [Havana] (7 June 1878): 7–24.

11. José A. Piqueras, "Sociedad civil, política y dominio colonial en Cuba (1878–1895)," *Studia histórica, Historia contemporánea* [Salamanca] 15 (1997): 108.

12. Municipal elections had existed prior to 1878, but in Cienfuegos, at least, *electores* were almost entirely planters and merchants. A list from 1872 of taxpaying electores of age identifies one hundred men with "Don" preceding each name,

suggesting in that era the absence of African-descended participants. *Diario de Cienfuegos,* 23 December 1872, 3.

13. Cited in Carmen Victoria Montejo Arrechea, *Sociedades de Instrucción y Recreo de pardos y morenos que existieron en Cuba colonial: Período 1878–1898* (Veracruz: Instituto Veracruzano de Cultura, 1994), 41.

14. "Protesta de fidelidad y adhesión de los artesanos de la clase de color de Santiago de Cuba," 11 October 1879, AHN, SU, leg. 4760, exp. 69.

15. María del Carmen Barcia argues that casinos españoles de color, like the Casino de Artesanos and other loyalist organizations, were products of political clientelism. *Capas populares y modernidad en Cuba (1878–1930)* (Havana: La Fuente Viva, 2005), 113–116.

16. Junta Directiva del Casino de artesanos (Juan Casamayor, Lino Caraballo, Antonio Serrano, Nicasio Escobar, Juan Bautista Jaime, Eusebio Caraballo, Pablo Rimbau, Juan Díaz, Pedro Beola) to Gómez, 26 October 1879, AGI, SD, leg. 7, ramo 2, núm. 17.

17. "Varios socios del Casino de Santiago de Cuba en queja contra la Directiva de esa Sociedad," 11 July 1883, AHPSC, GP, leg. 2655, núm. 11.

18. Emilio Bacardí y Moreau, *Crónicas de Santiago de Cuba,* 2nd ed., 10 vols. (Madrid: Gráficas Breogán, 1973), 6:253.

19. "Manifestaciones de lealtad," *La Bandera Español,* 3 September 1879, reprinted in Bacardí y Moreau, *Crónicas de Santiago de Cuba,* 6:265.

20. Trata de elecciones del cabildo de Cocoyé y supresión del mismo, 8 April 1878. AHPSC, GP, leg. 2383, exp. 2.

21. Bacardí y Moreau, *Crónicas de Santiago de Cuba,* 6:327. Bacardí notes that the government played a role in the divisiveness, embracing "the well known maxim of Machiavelli: divide and conquer."

22. Adolfo Jiménez Castellanos, *Sistema para combatir las insurrecciones en Cuba* (Madrid: Est. Tip. Calle de la Reina, núm. 8, bajo, 1883), 97–98.

23. On military reforms in the early 1880s, see Octavio Avelino Delgado, "The Spanish Army in Cuba, 1868–1898: An Institutional Study," 2 vols. (Ph.D. dissertation, Columbia University, 1980), 94–96.

24. "Relación Trata conceptuada de los individuos pardos que componen la Directiva del 'Casino Popular de Artesanos' de Guantánamo," 16 October 1879, AHPSC, GP, leg. 2655, exp. 2.

25. Contemporary scholarly understandings of the public sphere derive in large part from Jürgen H. Habermas, *The Structural Transformation of the Public Sphere,* trans. Thomas Burger (Cambridge, M.A.: MIT Press, 1989). See also Victor M. Uribe-Uran, "The Birth of a Public Sphere in Latin America during the Age of Revolution," *Comparative Studies in Society and History* (2000): 425–457.

26. For a rich discussion of the public sphere in Cuba in the early nineteenth century, see Marikay McCabe, "Commercial and Legal Topographies of Nineteenth-Century Havana, Cuba" (Ph.D. dissertation, Columbia University, 2002).

27. Joan Casanovas, *Bread, or Bullets! Urban Labor and Spanish Colonialism, 1850–1898* (Pittsburgh: University of Pittsburgh Press, 1998), 66.

28. José Joaquín Ribó, *Historia de los voluntarios cubanos,* 2 vols. (Madrid: Imprenta de T. Fortanet, 1876), 1:573.

29. Verena Stolke, *Racismo y sexualidad en la Cuba colonial* (Madrid: Alianza Editorial, 1992), 79.

30. Martín Morúa Delgado, *Obras Completas,* (Havana: Publicaciones de la Comisión Nacional de Centenario de Don Martín Morúa Delgado, 1957), 3:24.

31. "Discurso pronunciado por el Sr. Rodolfo de Lagardère en la noche del 11 de Marzo de 1882 en la reinaguración del Casino Español de color de la Habana," AHN, SU), leg. 4884, exp. 142. Discussion and quotations in the paragraphs that follow are also from this source.

32. El gobernador general de la Isla de Cuba to Sr. ministro de ultramar, 15 March 1882, AHN, SU, leg. 4884, exp. 140.

33. "Un regalo al Rey," *El Crisol,* 17 August 1884, 3.

34. Rafael Rodríguez Altunaga, *Las Villas: Biografía de una provincia* (Havana: Imprenta "El Siglo XX," 1955), 196–197.

35. The early years of El Progreso are recounted in "Se nos engarga," *La Lealtad,* 8 August 1883.

36. Later reglamentos of El Progreso kept to these same principles. See the one covering the years 1888–1893 in APC, Fondo Registro de Asociaciones, Fondo 4 (Colonial), leg. 1, exp. 14.

37. On El Progreso's school, see "Escuela de 'El Progreso,' *El Crisol,* 5 January 1884; "Siga el Progreso," *El Crisol,* 30 January 1884; and "Centro 'El Progreso,'" 18 February 1884. On dances and performances organized by El Progreso, see "Otra velada," *El Crisol,* 16 January 1884, and "Centro 'El Progreso,'" *El Crisol* 9 June 1884.

38. "Expediente promovido por el Gobernador de Santa Clara sobre el Reglamento del Casino asiático de las 'Cruces,'" 21 May 1879, AHN, SU, leg. 4884, exp. 10046.

39. On the historic links between the Virgen del Cobre and the Spanish crown, see María Elena Díaz, *The Virgin, the King, and the Royal Slaves of El Cobre: Negotiating Freedom in Colonial Cuba, 1670–1780* (Stanford: Stanford University Press, 2000).

40. Philip A. Howard, *Changing History: Afro-Cuban Cabildos and Societies of Color in the Nineteenth Century* (Baton Rouge: Louisiana State University Press, 1998), 150.

41. On recognition and the public sphere, see Nancy Fraser, "Rethinking the Public Sphere: A Contribution to a Critique of Actually Existing Democracy," in *Habermas and the Public Sphere,* ed. Craig Calhoun (Cambridge, M.A.: MIT Press, 1992), 109–142; and Seyla Benhabib, *The Claims of Culture: Equality and Diversity in the Global Era* (Princeton: Princeton University Press, 2002), chap. 3.

42. Orum, "The Politics of Color," 25. Translation Orum's.

43. Scott, *Slave Emancipation in Cuba,* 66.

44. Joan Casanovas, *Bread, or Bullets! Urban Labor and Spanish Colonialism in Cuba, 1850–1898,* 135–136.

45. Entry for 10 January 1884, APC, AC, libro 24.

46. Entry for 15 December 1884, APC, AC, libro 29.

47. Entries for 19 February, 22 March, and 17 May 1886, APC, AC, libro 30.

48. Entries for 24 January and 7 February 1887, 9 August 1889, APC, AC, libros 31 and 33.

49. Entry for 15 March 1880, APC, AC, libro 23.

50. Deschamps did so, however, with a distinct eye toward celebrating those journalists of color who eventually figured prominently as insurgents in the final war for independence that erupted in 1895. Pedro Deschamps Chapeaux, *El negro en el periodismo cubano en el siglo XIX: Ensayo bibliográfico* (Havana: Ediciones Revolución, 1963).

51. *El Hijo del Pueblo*, 15 May 1885, in Deschamps Chapeaux, *El negro en el periodismo cubano en el siglo XIX*, 72.

52. *La Familia*, 15 May 1884, cited in Deschamps Chapeaux, *El negro en el periodismo cubano en el siglo XIX*, 49.

53. Fernando Ortiz, *Cuban Counterpoint: Tobacco and Sugar* (Durham, N.C.: Duke University Press, 1995 [1947]), 89–92. Bárbara Pérez was a slave on the Pérez Galdós plantation whose mistress taught her to read. She went to live in Arimao, a peripheral town to Cienfuegos, and would read the newspaper aloud to residents. Rebecca J. Scott, "Small-Scale Dynamics of Large-Scale Processes," *American Historical Review* 105, no. 2 (April 2000): 475–477.

54. "Discurso pronunciado por el sr. Rodolfo E. Lagardère en la noche del 11 de Marzo de 1882 en la reinaguración del Casino Español de color de la Habana," AHN, SU, leg. 4884, exp. 142.

55. "Comunicado," *La Lealtad*, 17 July 1883.

56. "Se nos remite," *La Lealtad*, 20 August 1883.

57. "Se nos encarga," *La Lealtad*, 8 August 1883.

58. "Los timbales," *La Lealtad*, 7 July 1884.

59. Ada Ferrer, "The Silence of Patriots: Race and Nationalism in Martí's Cuba," in *José Martí's "Our America": From National to Hemispheric Cultural Studies*, ed. Jeffrey Belnap and Raúl Fernández (Durham, N.C.: Duke University Press, 1998), 228–249; Scott, *Slave Emancipation in Cuba*, 227–228.

60. José A. Piqueras, *Sociedad civil y poder en Cuba: Colonia y poscolonia* (Madrid: Siglo XXI, 2005), 177.

61. *El Cristal*, 11 December 1884. The invitations came from Carlos Fernández y Velasco, director of the Escuela San José at the Centro La Amistad; Pedro Tellería, director of the Escuela Elemental de Color at the Centro El Progreso; and Pedro de Zerquera, director of the Escuela de niños perteneciente al Centro de Instrucción y Recreo La Igualdad.

62. "Digno de censura," *El Cristal*, 12 December 1884.

63. "En el Ayuntamiento," *El Cristal*, 16 December 1884.

64. "'Así estamos,'" *El Cristal*, 17 December 1884.

65. "En el Ayuntamiento," *El Cristal*, 16 December 1884.

66. "'Así estamos,'" *El Cristal*, 17 December 1884.

67. Aline Helg, *Our Rightful Share: The Afro-Cuban Struggle for Equality, 1886–1912* (Chapel Hill: University of North Carolina Press, 1995), 32.

68. David H. Brown, *Santería Enthroned: Art, Ritual, and Innovation in an Afro-Cuban Religion* (Chicago: University of Chicago Press, 2003), 49.

69. Martín Morúa Delgado, *Obras completas* (Havana: Publicaciones de la Comisión Nacional del Centenario de Martin Morúa Delgado, 1957), 3:11–44.

70. W.E.B Du Bois, *The Negro* (Philadelphia: University of Pennsylvania Press, 2001 [1915]), 163.

71. The Cortes passed a Law of Abolition in 1880 that initiated an apprenticeship period whose gradual plan for emancipation ended two years ahead of schedule, in 1886.

72. José A. Piqueras, "Sociedad civil, política y dominio colonial en Cuba (1878–1895)," *Studia histórica, Historia contemporánea* [Salamanca] 15 (1997): 94.

73. Partha Chatterjee, *Lineages of Political Society: Studies in Postcolonial Democracy* (New York: Columbia University Press, 2011), 147.

74. Brian Cowan makes an analogous argument with respect to women and the public sphere in eighteenth-century England. "What Was Masculine about the Public Sphere? Gender and the Coffeehouse Milieu in Post-Restoration England," *History Workshop Journal* 51 (2001): 127–157.

75. Michael Warner, *Publics and Counterpublics* (New York: Zone, 2002), 56. Craig Calhoun criticizes arguments about counterpublics for emphasizing subalterns' willful invention of counterdiscourses over their often violent expulsion from publics. Craig Calhoun, *The Roots of Radicalism: Tradition, the Public Sphere, and Early Nineteenth-Century Social Movements.* (Chicago: University of Chicago Press, 2012).

CHAPTER 5 *"Long Live Spain!"*

Epigraph source: "Programa propuesto por la Junta Provisional en 1 de Agosto de 1878 y aprobado por la Junta General en 3 de Agosto del propio año," in Hortensia Pichardo, ed., *Documentos para la historia de Cuba,* 4th ed., 4 vols. (Havana: Editorial de Ciencias Sociales, 1977–1980), 1:410.

1. Extensive documentation of this event can be found in two complementary archival files: "Reunión autonomista en Cienfuegos," AHN, SU, leg. 4896 parte 10, exp. 174, and "Expediente promovido por telegrama del Gobierno Civil de Santa Clara, dando cuenta del incidente ocurrido en Cienfuegos con motivo de una reunión política celebrada el día 20 de Octubre," ANC, AP, leg. 81, exp. 13 . A narrative of the event appears in Enrique Edo y Llop, *Memoria histórica de Cienfuegos y su jurisdicción,* 2nd ed. (Cienfuegos: J. Andreu, 1888), 640–642. This episode has also been discussed briefly in several previous studies: Ada Ferrer, *Insurgent Cuba: Race, Nation, and Revolution, 1868–1898* (Chapel Hill: University of North Carolina Press, 1999), 233 n78; and Rebecca J. Scott, "Race, Labor, and Citizenship in Cuba: The View from the Sugar District of Cienfuegos, 1886–1909," *Hispanic American Historical Review* 78:4 (November 1998): 703–704; and again in Rebecca J. Scott, *Degrees of Freedom: Louisiana and Cuba after Slavery* (Cambridge: Harvard University Press, 2005), 124–125.

2. Scott, *Degrees of Freedom,* 123.

3. The Liberal and Conservative parties were the major, but not first or only, parties on the island. The Partido Reformista formed in 1865 in the 1860s attempted to advance the agenda of reform-minded creoles, leading to the establishment of a Junta de Información in 1867 to investigate conditions on the island. The Partido Democrático also appeared during the post-Zanjón period but did not garner the support to elect a representative to the Cortes. In the 1890s, several more political parties formed, including a new Partido Reformista.

4. Emilia Viotti da Costa, *The Brazilian Empire: Myths and Histories* (Chicago: University of Chicago Press, 1985), 55.

5. See Elsa Barkley Brown, "Negotiating and Transforming the Public Sphere: African American Political Life in the Transition from Slavery to Freedom," *Public Culture* 7 (1994): 267–302; and C. K. Doreski, "Reading Riot: 'A Study in Race Relations and a Race Riot in 1919,'" in *Writing America Black: Race Rhetoric in the Public Sphere* (Cambridge: Cambridge University Press, 1998), 25–58.

6. On the symbolic significance of emancipation in a wider context, see Gad Heuman, "Riots and Resistance in the Caribbean at the Moment of Freedom," *Slavery and Abolition* 21 (September 2000): 135–149.

7. Debates about monarchism and slave emancipation in Brazil have produced instructive disagreements that inform this investigation. See George Reid Andrews, *Blacks and Whites in São Paulo, Brazil, 1888–1988* (Madison: University of Wisconsin Press, 1991), 43–45; and Barbara Weinstein, "The Decline of the Progressive Planter and the Rise of Subaltern Agency: Shifting Narratives of Slave Emancipation in Brazil," in *Reclaiming the Political in Latin American History: Essays from the North,* ed. Gilbert M. Joseph (Durham, N.C.: Duke University Press, 2001), 94–95.

8. On the Partido Unión Constitucional, see Inés Roldán de Montaud, *La restauración en Cuba: El fracaso de un proceso reformista* (Madrid: CSIC, 2001), chaps. 3 and 6.

9. On Cuban Liberals, see Marta Bizcarrondo and Antonio Elorza, *Cuba/España: El dilema autonomista, 1878–1898* (Madrid: Editorial Colibrí, 2001); Mildred de la Torre, *El autonomismo en Cuba, 1878–1898* (Havana: Editorial de Ciencias Sociales, 1997); Paul Estrade, "El autonomismo criollo y la nación cubana (antes y después del 98)," in *Imágenes e imaginarios nacionales en el ultramar español,* ed. Consuelo Naranjo Orovio and Carlos Serrano (Madrid: CSIC / Casa de Velázquez, 1999), 155–170; Luis Miguel García Mora, "La fuerza de la palabra: El autonomismo en Cuba en el último tercio del siglo XIX," *Revista de Indias* 61:223 (September–December 2001): 715–748, and "Tras la revolución, las reformas: El partido liberal cubano y los proyectos reformistas tras la paz del Zanjón," in *Cuba la perla de las Antillas,* eds. Consuelo Naranjo Orovio and Tomás Mallo Gutiérrez (Madrid/Aranjuez: Doce Calles–CSIC, 1994), 197–212; and Louis A. Pérez Jr., "Liberalism in Cuba: Between Reaction and Revolution, 1878–1898," in *Liberals, Politics, and Power: State Formation in Nineteenth-Century Latin America,* eds. Vincent C. Peloso and Barbara A. Tenenbaum (Athens: University of Georgia Press, 1997), 259–277.

10. Rafael Fernández de Castro, *Para la historia de Cuba. I. Trabajos políticos* (Havana: La Propaganda Literaria, 1899), xxv.

11. Spain, Cortes, *Diario de Sesiones: Senado* (Madrid: Imp. de los hijos de J. A. García, 1887), 9 July 1886, 2:1002.

12. Estrade, "El autonomismo criollo y la nación cubana," 157. Fernández de Castro, in fact, served during those years as gobernador civil of Havana province.

13. Rafael Montoro, "Discurso pronunciado en Cienfuegos el 22 de septiembre de 1878, al constituirse el partido Liberal," in *Obras,* 3 vols. (Havana: Cultural, 1952), 1:3, 6–7.

14. Antonio Govín, *Discursos* (Havana: Burgay y Cía., 1955), 5, originally published in *El Triunfo,* 28 September 1878, and cited in Estrade, "El autonomismo criollo y la nación cubana," 158.

15. De la Torre, *El autonomismo en Cuba,* 49–50. Municipal government generally remained under the control of *constitucionales,* although Santa Clara, Santiago de

Cuba, and Puerto Príncipe routinely had Liberal majorities. A. de las Casas, *Cartas al pueblo americano (sobre Cuba y las Repúblicas Latino-Americanas)*, 3rd ed. (Buenos Aires: Est. Tip. El Correo Español, 1897), 53.

16. On the *patronato*, see Rebecca J. Scott, *Slave Emancipation in Cuba: The Transition to Free Labor, 1860–1899* (Princeton: Princeton University Press, 1985), chap. 6.

17. Montoro, "Primer discurso en las Cortes," in *Obras* 1:144–145.

18. De la Torre, *El autonomismo en Cuba*, 101.

19. "La Libertad," *El Crisol*, 28 May 1884.

20. "Más papistas que el Papa," *La Lealtad*, 23 August 1883.

21. "Inmigración blanca," *El Crisol*, 18 February 1884.

22. "Población blanca," *El Crisol*, 8 July 1884.

23. Violeta Rovira González, *Cienfuegos desde el Pacto del Zanjón hasta 1902* (Cienfuegos: Partido Comunista Cubana de Cienfuegos, 1983), 8–9. For Santa Clara province as a whole, patrocinados numbered around 23,000 (or 31 percent of the population) in 1883 and 13,000 (or 13 percent of the population) by 1885. Scott, *Slave Emancipation in Cuba*, 193–194.

24. Fe Iglesias García, "La concentración azucarera y la comarca de Cienfuegos," in *Espacios, silencios y los sentidos de la libertad: Cuba entre 1878 y 1912*, ed. Fernando Martínez Heredia, Rebecca J. Scott, and Orlando F. García Martínez (Havana: Ediciones Unión, 2001), 85–107.

25. "Libro No. 1 de los negros, Santa Rosalía," APC, OGM.

26. Edwin F. Atkins, *Sixty Years in Cuba: Reminiscences of Edwin F. Atkins* (Cambridge: Riverside Press, 1926), 39.

27. Edo y Llop, *Memoria histórica de Cienfuegos y su jurisdicción*, 627.

28. "Lo que pasa en el Canal," *Diario de Cienfuegos*, 4 January 1886. Imilci Balboa Navarro compares the rhetoric and reality of labor shortage in *Los brazos necesarios: Inmigración, colonización y trabajo libre en Cuba, 1878–1898* (Valencia: Fundación Instituto de Historia Social, 2000), chap. 6.

29. J. S. Murray to Edwin F. Atkins, 13 October 1885 and 19 January 1886, respectively, in Massachusetts Historical Society, Edwin F. Atkins Papers vol. 2, box 1.

30. Clemente Pereira to the editor of *Diario de Cienfuegos*, 31 March 1886, Archivo del Catedral de Cienfuegos, "Expediente contra la celebración de una velada espiritista, que se suspendió por orden telegráfica del Exmo. Sr. Gob. Gral., en el acto de comenzarse," Archivo Parroquial de la Ciudad de Cienfuegos (hereafter, APCC), exp. 13.

31. Juan de Campo to Clemente Pereira, 31 March 1886, APCC, exp. 13.

32. Francisco de Acosta y Albear to the gobernador general de la isla, 28 August 1886, AHN, SU, leg. 4835, exp. 62.

33. Multiple authors to the gobernador general de la Isla de Cuba, 3 April 1886, AHN, SU, leg. 4835, exp. 62.

34. Carmen Victoria Montejo Arrechea, *Sociedades de Instrucción y Recreo de pardos y morenos que existieron en Cuba colonial: Período 1878–1898* (Veracruz: Instituto Veracruzano de Cultura, 1993), 50–51.

35. The mutual aid society Nuestra Señora de los Desamparados began *La Caridad;* the San Cayetano mutual aid society published *El Socorro;* and two individuals— P. Carell and Francisco Acosta y Monduy—published *El Hijo del Pueblo* and *El Látigo*. Edo y Llop, *Memoria histórica de Cienfuegos y su jurisdicción*, 635–636.

36. Rafael Rodríguez Altunaga, *Las Villas: Biografía de una provincia* (Havana: Imprenta "El Siglo XX," 1955), 284–285.

37. On *teatro bufo*, see Jill Lane, *Blackface Cuba, 1840–1895* (Philadelphia: University of Pennsylvania Press, 2005), esp. chap. 5.

38. "Camino de la Autonomía," *Diario de Cienfuegos*, 18 January 1886.

39. Victoria María Sueiro Rodríguez, "Apuntes sobre la vida teatral cienfueguera del siglo XIX," *Ariel: La Revista Cultural de Cienfuegos* 2:1 (1999): 28.

40. A second theater opened in 1885 after the *ayuntamiento* first rejected a petition from Pastor Pelayo, a Chinese resident, to open a theater in a part of town in which municipal ordinances banned wooden buildings. Edo y Llop, *Memoria histórica de Cienfuegos y su jurisdicción*, 626–627.

41. "Un nuevo centro," *La Lealtad*, 3 September 1883. The article applauded the group for making the effort "to educate itself and improve its social status."

42. "Función," *La Lealtad*, 18 August 1883.

43. "Compañía de bufos de color," *El Fénix*, 24 August 1885.

44. See "Función benéfica," 19 September 1885, and "Funciones," 28 September 1885, in *El Fénix*.

45. See the contributions made from the accounts of various men and women in "Libro No. 1 de los negros, Santa Rosalía," Archivo Provincial de Cienfuegos, OGM.

46. Philip Howard offers a contrasting perspective in *Changing History: Afro-Cuban Cabildos and Societies of Color in the Nineteenth Century* (Baton Rouge: Louisiana State University Press, 1998).

47. "Gremio de Tabaqueros," *El Fénix*, 3 October 1885.

48. "Bufos de Pedrosa," *El Fénix,* 7 September 1885.

49. "Casino 'Gran China,' Calle de San Fernando—Casa de Montalvo," 15 May 1886, and "Policia," 31 August 1886, both in the *Diario de Cienfuegos*.

50. "Los Bufos," *Diario de Cienfuegos*, 27 February 1886.

51. "Teatro Zorrilla" and "Teatro 'La Amistad,'" *Diario de Cienfuegos*, 1 March 1886.

52. "Los suevos," *Diario de Cienfuegos*, 12 October 1886.

53. Fernández de Castro, *Para la historia de Cuba*, xvii.

54. "Discurso pronunciado en la noche del 4 de Septiembre de 1886 en 'La Caridad' del Cerro," in Fernández de Castro, *Para la historia de Cuba*, 89.

55. "Meeting autonomista," *Diario de Cienfuegos*, 30 March 1886.

56. "Resultado de las elecciones," *Diario de Cienfuegos*, 5 April 1886. The three Constitutional Union candidates—Julio Apezteguía, Martín Zozaya, and José F. Vergez—each received 243 votes; Fernández de Castro received 95, Miguel Figueroa received 93.

57. *Diario de sesiones: Senado* (Madrid: Imp. de los hijos de J. A. García, 1887), 29 July 1886, 2:973.

58. Scott, *Slave Emancipation in Cuba*, 196.

59. "Discurso pronunciado en el Congreso de los Diputados el día 27 de Julio de 1886, en el debate sobre el presupuesto de Cuba," in Fernández de Castro, *Para la historia de Cuba*, 48.

60. Bizcarrondo and Elorza, *Cuba/España*, 227, quoting Elías Entralgo, *La liberación étnica de Cuba* (Havana: Universidad de la Habana, 1953), 101–113.

61. María del Carmen Barcia Zequeira, "La historia profunda: La sociedad civil del 98," *Temas* 12–13 (October 1997–March 1998): 32.

62. Emilio Bacardí y Moreau, *Crónicas de Santiago de Cuba,* 10 vols. (Madrid: Gráficas Breogán, 1973), 7:177.

63. In May, the lottery had reduced the number of remaining patrocinados from 942 to 436. By October, ninety of them had already been freed. Edo y Llop, *Memoria histórica de Cienfuegos y su jurisdicción,* 635. For the province as a whole, approximately 13,000 patrocinados remained in 1885. Scott, *Degrees of Freedom,* 114.

64. "Aviso religioso," 2 October 1886, and "Fiestas religiosas," 4 October 1886, both in *Diario de Cienfuegos.* Note that the term *grey* instead of *nación* inflected the reference to the cabildo with religious overtones.

65. "Cumplase el Ley," *Diario de Cienfuegos,* 9 August 1886.

66. For this summary of Fernández de Castro's and Figueroa's visit, I rely on the introductory summary that preceded the lengthy investigations that make up the *expedientes* (files) found in Madrid and Havana. See Rafael Correa to the Gobernador Superior, 26 October 1886, AHN, SU, leg. 4896 parte 10, exp. 174.

67. "El motín de Cienfuegos," *El País,* 24 October 1886, quoted in its entirety in "Procedimientos de 'El País,'" *Diario de Cienfuegos,* 25 October 1886.

68. "Lo que era de esperar," *Diario de Cienfuegos,* 21 October 1886.

69. "Sépanlo todos," *Diario de Cienfuegos,* 22 October 1886.

70. "Oradores autonomistas," *El Imparcial,* 22 October 1886, quoted in its entirety in "La propaganda en Trinidad," *Diario de Cienfuegos,* 25 October 1886.

71. Rafael Correa to the gobernador superior, 26 October 1886, in "Reunión autonomista en Cienfuegos," AHN, SU, leg. 4896, parte 10, exp. 174.

72. Testimony of Juan del Campo, 31 October 1886, ANC, AP, leg. 81, exp. 13. Enrique Edo y Llop suggests that African-descended people constituted a rival group at Cabrera's house in opposition to that which was harassing Fernández de Castro and Figueroa. Edo y Llop, *Memoria histórica de Cienfuegos y su jurisdicción,* 641.

73. Testimony of Esteban Cacicedo, 23 October 1886, ANC, AP, leg. 81, exp. 13 .

74. Testimony of Joaquín Fernández, 23 October 1886, ANC, AP, leg. 81, exp. 13.

75. Luis González to the gobernador civil, 1 November 1886, "Reunión autonomista en Cienfuegos," AHN, SU, leg. 4896 parte 10, exp. 174.

76. Testimony of Rafael Cabrera, 26 October 1886, ANC, AP, leg. 81, exp. 13 .

77. Spain, Cortes, *Diario de Sesiones: Senado,* 24 November 1886, 3:1179–1182.

78. Edo y Llop, *Memoria histórica de Cienfuegos y su jurisdicción,* 641–642.

79. Fernández de Castro, "Discurso pronunciado el día 31 de Abril de 1881, en el meeting celebrado por los autonomistas de Guanabacoa en el 'Salón de las Ilusiones,'" in Fernández de Castro, *Para la historia de Cuba,* 4.

80. "En el Círculo Autonomista, Discurso pronunciado en la noche de 18 de Febrero de 1887," in Rafael Fernández de Castro, *Clamores de libertad* (Havana: Editorial Cuba, 1936), 48, 53. See also Bizcarrondo and Elorza, *Cuba/España,* 248–253.

81. Richard Graham, *Patronage and Politics in Nineteenth-Century Brazil* (Stanford: Stanford University Press, 1990), chap. 7.

82. See Charles Hale, *Mexican Liberalism in the Age of Mora, 1821–1853* (New Haven, C.T.: Yale University Press, 1968); and Mark Thurner, *From Two Republics to One Divided: Contradictions of Postcolonial Nationmaking in Andean Peru* (Durham, N.C.: Duke University Press, 1997), chap. 5.

83. Eric Hobsbawm locates a linguistic change in the concept of *nación* in the edition from 1884 of the *Diccionario de la Real Academia Española*. Although earlier editions had defined *nación* as "the aggregate of the inhabitants of a province," the term came to encompass "a State or political body which recognizes a supreme centre of common government." Hobsbawm identifies this shift linking *nación* to *gobierno* as a foundational moment in the development of modern nationalism. *Nations and Nationalism since 1780: Programme, Myth, Reality*, 2nd. ed. (Cambridge: Cambridge University Press, 1992). 14–15. Recall that the monarch as a political icon had diminished in significance by the late nineteenth century: from 1874 to 1885, a young king ruled without an heir, and a queen regent assumed power in 1885, followed by two more children. Hugh Thomas, *Cuba, or The Pursuit of Freedom*, 2nd ed. (New York: DaCapo Press, 1998), 298.

84. Jorge Mañach, *Miguel Figueroa, 1851–1893: discurso leído . . . el 6 de julio de 1943, en conmemoración del cincuentenario de su muerte* (Havana: Imprenta El Siglo XX, 1943), 17.

85. Mañach, *Miguel Figueroa*, 26.

CHAPTER 6   *The Price of Integrity*
Epigraph source: Miguel Barnet, *Biografía de un cimarrón* (Barcelona: Ediciones Ariel, 1968), 149.

1. Manuel Moreno Fraginals and José J. Moreno Masó, *Guerra, migración y muerte (El ejército español en Cuba como vía migratoria)* (Barcelona: Ediciones Júcar, 1993), 114.

2. See correspondence from the mid-1880s in Subinspección General de Voluntarios de Cuba, 3004-175, SHM, CGC, Organización de fuerzas, Cienfuegos (1877–1895), caja 175. On salary reductions, see Octavio Avelino Delgado, "The Spanish Army in Cuba, 1868–1898: An Institutional Study," 2 vols. (Ph.D. dissertation, Columbia University, 1980)," 1:95.

3. On banditry, see Ada Ferrer, *Insurgent Cuba: Race, Nation, and Revolution, 1868–1898* (Chapel Hill: University of North Carolina Press, 1999), 109–110, 179. On Antonio Fernández de Castro, see and Louis A. Pérez, Jr., *Lords of the Mountain: Social Banditry and Peasant Protest in Cuba, 1878–1918* (Pittsburgh: University of Pittsburgh Press, 1989), 32.

4. [Illegible] Fajardo to ministerio de guerra, 25 May 1885, "Consultando la admisión de Voluntarios de Color en los Cuerpos de este Ejército, sin obligación de servir en la Península," SHM, CGC, caja 122, leg. 72, núm. 1447.

5. Ministerio de Ultramar to the capitan general, 28 August 1885, SHM, CGC, caja 122, leg. 72, núm. 1447.

6. Not all Cuerpos de Bomberos were dissolved in Cuba. Telisfonte Gallego García reported in 1892 that "in reduced numbers," the Cuerpo de Bomberos still existed as a type of reserve force for the regular army, as did the *milicias disciplinadas,* which he described as "dissolved today." Telisfonte Gallego García, *Cuba por fuera*, 2nd ed. (Havana: La Propaganda Literaria, 1892), 230.

7. "Una compañía más," *Diario de Cienfuegos*, 13 August 1887.

8. "Lista nominal de los individuos con que se cuenta en la fecha para la organización de la espresada Compañía," 23 August, 1887, SHM, CGC, caja 175. Half of the soldiers were natives of Cienfuegos, whereas most of the others hailed from Trinidad or Santa Clara. Nearly half of them had already performed some kind of military service, either

as musicians in the white volunteer units, or, most commonly, in the city's recently dissolved Cuerpo de Bomberos. Most of the men were unmarried, and their full-time professions encompassed a wide range of skilled trades: carpenters, shoemakers, tobacco workers, barbers, tailors, cooks, painters, shoe smiths, bakers, and masons.

9. "Una compañía más," *Diario de Cienfuegos*, 13 August 1887.

10. "Presentación," *Diario de Cienfuegos*, 5 December 1887.

11. A copy of Guimerá's speech can be found in SHM, CGC, caja 175.

12. Lesmis de Saro to Santocildes, 29 December 1887. SHM, CGC, caja 175.

13. General Subinspector de Voluntarios to Fidel A. de Santocildes, 11 December 1887, SHM, CGC, caja175.

14. Santocildes to Manuel Sánchez Mira, 4 January 1888, SHM, CGC, caja 175.

15. Ferrer, *Insurgent Cuba*, 118.

16. For Gómez, resistance to Cuban independence hit close to home. He recounted in a 1913 speech at the Ateneo y Círculo de la Habana the skepticism of his father, born a slave, about the independence movement, though not out of affective ties to the empire. "He was very Cuban," noted Gómez, but had a "mortal fear of Spain." He told his son each time Gómez went to prison "Son, I'm telling you! It's not possible with these people! What you want is crazy, and you can't cause more calamities and misfortunes." José Manuel Pérez Cabrera, *La juventud de Juan Gualberto Gómez* (Havana: El Siglo XX, 1945), 12–13.

17. "En honor de Figueroa," *La Igualdad*, 8 July 1893. El Progreso is the only Cienfuegos sociedad listed in the *Anexo* of Oilda Hevia Lanier, *El Directorio Central de las Sociedades Negras de Cuba* (Havana: Editorial de Ciencias Sociales, 1996), 63.

18. Rodolfo de Lagardère, *La cuestión social de Cuba: Cuba no es Venecia* (Havana: La Universal de Ruiz y Hermano, 1887), 17–19, 29.

19. Lagardère, *La cuestión social de Cuba*, 41.

20. Lagardère, *La cuestión social de Cuba*, 50.

21. María del Carmen Barcia, *Élites y grupos de presión: Cuba, 1868–1898* (Havana: Editorial de Ciencias Sociales, 1998), 164–166.

22. Rafael Serra, *Ensayos políticos* (New York: Imprenta Porvenir, 1892), 124.

23. Serra, *Ensayos políticos*, 1892, 91.

24. Serra, *Ensayos políticos*, 2nd ser. (New York: Imprenta de P .J. Díaz, 1896), 164.

25. Hevia Lanier, *El Directorio Central de las Sociedades negras de Cuba*, 11.

26. See Hevia Lanier, *El Directorio Central de las Sociedades negras de Cuba*, 45–46.

27. Emilio Bacardí y Moreau, *Crónicas de Santiago de Cuba*, 2nd ed., 10 vols. (Madrid: Gráficas Breogán, 1973), 7:429.

28. Fernando Ortiz, *Ensayos etnográficos* (Havana: Editorial de Ciencias Sociales, 1984), 26.

29. Ortiz, *Ensayos etnográficos*, 27. Ortiz knew Emanuel personally and noted that his efforts to unite Cubans of color through their cabildos continued until 1910.

30. "Lo que pasó en Haití," *La Igualdad*, 25 May 1893. On *Bug-Jargal*, see Chris Bongie, "Introduction," in Victor Hugo, *Bug-Jargal*, ed. and trans. Chris Bongie (Peterborough, Ontario: Broadview Editions, 2004), 9–47.

31. *La Igualdad*, 20 January 1894.

32. "El General Calleja," *La Igualdad*, 2 January 1894.

33. "Al alcalde de Yaguajay," *La Igualdad*, 29 July 1894.

34. "Conste así," *La Igualdad,* 4 February 1894.

35. Louis A. Pérez Jr., *Cuba between Empires, 1878–1902* (Pittsburgh: University of Pittsburgh Press, 1983), 124–132.

36. Fernando Gómez, *La insurrección por dentro: Apuntes para la historia,* 2nd ed. (Madrid: Biblioteca de La Irradiación, 1900), 230.

37. Marcos García to General [illegible], 24 March 1898, Correspondencia, Gobernador Civil de la Provincia de Santa Clara y Gobernador de la Región Oriental de la Provincia de Santiago de Cuba, 1897–1898, SHM, CGC, no. 2535, leg. 14, caja 23. García's letter spells the surname both as "Gonzales" and "González" (accent added).

38. On racialized Spanish propaganda regarding the insurgents, see Aline Helg, *Our Rightful Share: The Afro-Cuban Struggle for Equality, 1886–1912* (Chapel Hill: University of North Carolina Press, 1995), 80–83.

39. Ricardo Donoso Cortes, *Cuba española: El problema de la guerra* (Madrid: n.p., 1896), 65–66, 71.

40. Eduardo Rosell y Malpica, *Diario del Teniente Coronel Eduardo Rosell y Malpica (1895–1897),* 2 vols. (Havana: Imprenta "El Siglo XX," 1949), 20.

41. José Martí, Diario, 23 April 1895, in *Obras completas,* 27 vols. (Havana: Editorial Nacional de Cuba, 1963–1966), 19:222.

42. Juan Andrés Blanco and Coralia Alonso Valdés, *Presencia castellana en el "Ejército Libertador Cubana" (1895–1898)* (UNED Zamora, Spain: Junta de Castilla y León, Consejería de Educación y Cultura, 1996), 126.

43. "Circular manuscrita dirigida a los Sres. Generales de Cuerpo de Ejército, División y Brigada, Jefes de Columnas y Comandantes Militares," 10 February 1896, ANC, DR, leg. 257, exp. 12.

44. Correspondence to and from the Batallón Urbano de Color can be found in SHM, CGC, caja 1382. Regional official newspapers, such as the *Boletín Oficial de la Provincia de Santa Clara,* regularly reported desertions of soldiers in the Spanish army. On its actions in Cruces, see Bacardí y Moreau, *Crónicas de Santiago de Cuba,* 8:114. On Bernabeu, see Helg, *Our Rightful Share,* 84.

45. Valeriano Weyler, *Memorias de un general: De caballero cadete a general en jefe,* ed. María Teresa Weyler (Barcelona: Ediciones Destino, 2004), 221.

46. Adelaide Rosalind Kirchner, *Flag for Cuba: Pen Sketches of a Recent Trip across the Gulf of Mexico to the Island of Cuba* (New York: Mershon Company, 1897), 125.

47. Richard Harding Davis, *Cuba in War Time* (New York: R. H. Russell, 1898), 105–112.

48. Stephen Bonsal, *The Real Condition of Cuba Today* (New York: Harper and Brothers, 1897), 31.

49. Julián Vivanco, *Crónicas históricas de San Antonio Abad de los Baños,* 19 vols. (Havana: Editorial El Sol, 1955), 6:180.

50. Bernabé Boza, *Diario de la guerra desde Baire hasta la intervención americana,* 2 vols. (Havana: Librería Cervantes, 1924), 1:105.

51. Ricardo Batrell Oviedo, *Para la historia: Apuntes autobiográficos de la vida de Ricardo Batrell Oviedo* (Havana: Seoane y Álvarez, 1912), 149.

52. Michael Zeuske, "Hidden Markers, Open Secrets: On Naming, Race-Marking, and Race-Making in Cuba," *New West Indian Guide/Nieuwe West-Indische Gids* 76:3–4 (2002): 211–242.

53. Boza, *Diario de la guerra desde Baire hasta la intervención americana*, 1:105.

54. Boza, *Diario de la guerra desde Baire hasta la intervención americana*, 1:105.

55. This quality bears a striking resemblance to the lack of racial attributions in the records of the separatist army, consistent with their raceless conception of Cuban nationalism. See Rebecca J. Scott, "The Provincial Archive as a Place of Memory: Confronting Oral and Written Sources on the Role of Former Slaves in the Cuban War of Independence (1895–98)," *New West Indian Guide/Nieuwe West-Indische Gids* 76 (2002): 196.

56. Corral, *¡El desastre! Memorias de un voluntario en la campaña de Cuba* (Barcelona: Impr. Alejandro Martínez, 1899), 169–170.

57. Valeriano Weyler, *Mi mando en Cuba*, 5 vols. (Madrid: Imprenta de Felipe González Rojas, 1910–1911), 2:41–42.

58. Philip S. Foner, *The Spanish-Cuban-American War and the Birth of American Imperialism, 1895–1902*, 2 vols. (New York: Monthly Review Press, 1972), 1:75. I am grateful to David Carlson for bringing this incident to my attention.

59. John Lawrence Tone, *War and Genocide in Cuba, 1895–1898* (Chapel Hill: University of North Carolina Press, 2006), 147–148.

60. Corral, *¡El desastre!*, 142–143.

61. *Boletín oficial de la provincia de Santa Clara*, 30 April 1897, 4, in APC Fondo Ayuntamiento de Layas, Leg. 1 Exp. 52.

62. Ferrer, *Insurgent Cuba*, 184.

63. Batrell Oviedo, *Para la historia*,193.

64. Carlos Serrano, *Final del imperio: España 1895–1898* (Madrid: Siglo XXI, 1984), 185.

65. George W. Prioleau to the *Gazette* [Cleveland], 13 May 1898, in Willard B. Gatewood Jr., *"Smoked Yankees" and the Struggle for Empire: Letters from Negro Soldiers, 1898–1902* (Urbana: University of Illinois Press, 1971), 28–29.

66. Simon Brown in the *Parsons Weekly Blade*, 22 October 1898, in Gatewood, *"Smoked Yankees" and the Struggle for Empire*, 193.

67. Unknown to *Illinois Record*, 12 November 1898, in Gatewood, *"Smoked Yankees" and the Struggle for Empire*, 89.

68. W. C. Payne to the *Colored American* [Washington, D.C.], 13 August 1898, in Gatewood, *"Smoked Yankees" and the Struggle for Empire*, 54.

69. W. C. Warmsley to the *Bee* [Washington, D.C.], 17 June 1899, in Gatewood, *"Smoked Yankees" and the Struggle for Empire*, 232.

70. M. W. Saddler to the *Freeman* [Indianapolis], 27 August 1898, in Gatewood, *"Smoked Yankees" and the Struggle for Empire*, 57.

71. Bonnie Miller, *From Liberation to Conquest: The Visual and Popular Cultures of the Spanish-American War of 1898* (Amherst: University of Massachusetts Press, 2011), 244. On stereographs and fairs, see James Gilbert, *Whose Fair? Experience, Memory, and the History of the Great St. Louis Exposition* (Chicago: University of Chicago Press, 2009).

72. James H. Wilson, *Under the Old Flag*, 2 vols. (New York: D. Appleton and Co., 1912), 2:410.

73. Juan M. Dihigo y Mestre, *Pí y Margall y la revolución cubana* (Havana: Imprenta El Siglo XX, 1928), 7. From chap. 2, libro 2, of *Reacción y revolución* (1854), cited in José Conangla Fontanilles, *Cuba y Pí y Margall* (Havana: Editorial Lex, 1947), 164.

74. Conangla Fontanilles, *Cuba y Pí y Margall,* 172.

75. Gumersindo de Azcárate, *Educación y enseñanza según Costa,* 69, quoted in Frederick B. Pike, *Hispanismo, 1898–1936: Spanish Conservatives and Liberals and Their Relationships with Spanish America* (South Bend, I.N.: University of Notre Dame Press, 1971), 57.

76. Rodolfo de Lagardère to Luis Fontana, 25 August 1898, SHM, CGC, caja 1383.

77. Albert O. Hirschman, *Exit, Voice, and Loyalty: Responses to Decline in Firms, Organizations, and States* (Cambridge: Harvard University Press, 1970), 81.

78. Hirschman, *Exit, Voice, and Loyalty,* 78.

79. Louis A. Pérez Jr., *Cuba and the United States: Ties of Singular Intimacy* (Athens: University of Georgia Press, 1990), 103.

CONCLUSION *Subject Citizens*

1. On the Constitutional Convention of 1901, see Alejandro de la Fuente, *A Nation for All: Race, Inequality, and Politics in Twentieth-Century Cuba* (Chapel Hill: University of North Carolina Press, 2001), 56–59. Four earlier constitutions had been promulgated during the independence struggle, in Guáimaro (1869), Baraguá (1878), Jimaguayú (1895), and La Yara (1897). See José L. Escasena, *La evolución de la legalidad en Cuba* (Havana: Editorial de Ciencias Sociales, 1990), 92–94.

2. William George Emanuel to William McKinley, 15 February 1901, file 2499, entry 5, United States National Archives, Records of the Bureau of Insular Affairs, Record Group, 350.

3. The effects of national "reconciliation" on black suffrage and disfranchisement are discussed in David W. Blight, *Race and Reunion: The Civil War in American Memory* (Cambridge, M.A.: Harvard University Press, 2002), 45–46, 59–60, 271–272.

4. That this has been my focus throughout the book does not intend to leave the impression that the experiences of Cubans of color, or Cubans as an unstable whole, or most people in general, were and have been fully captured by the logic of state power.

5. Steven Feierman, "Colonizers, Scholars, and the Creation of Invisible Histories," in *Beyond the Cultural Turn: New Directions in the Study of Society and Culture,* ed. Victoria E. Bonnell and Lynn Hunt (Berkeley: University of California Press, 1999), 186. See also Michel-Rolph Trouillot, *Silencing the Past: Power and the Production of History* (Boston: Beacon Press, 1995).

6. Entry for 4 November 1898, Archivo Provincial de Cienfuegos, Actas Capitulares (hereafter, APC, AC), libro 42. The captain general issued the circular on 22 October.

7. Entry for 7 January 1899, APC, AC, libro 42; see also Marial Iglesias Utset, *Las metáforas del cambio en la vida cotidiana: Cuba, 1898–1902* (Havana: Ediciones Unión, 2003), chap. 1.

8. Rafael Serra, "Ni español ni yankee" and "Confirmando su derrota," in *Ensayos políticos* (New York: Imprenta de A. W. Howes, 1899), 116–125.

9. Rafael Serra, *Para blancos y negros: Ensayos políticos, sociales y económicos* (Havana: Imprenta El Score, 1907), 188–189.

10. Serra, *Ensayos políticos,* 1899, 212.

11. De la Fuente, *A Nation for All,* 35–39; Iglesias Utset, "Las metáforas del cambio en la vida cotidiana," chap. 5.

12. Ferrer, *Insurgent Cuba*, 200.

13. Rafael Serra, *Para blancos y negros*, 92–93. This passage is taken from a letter from Serra to Juan Sardiñas y Villa, 26 January 1901, which was subsequently published in the Havana newspaper *El Pueblo Libre*.

14. Pérez, *On Becoming Cuban*, 91.

15. This analysis is not intended to deny or underestimate the areas in which Cubans of African descent improved their circumstances in the Republic, which are spelled out by Alejandro de la Fuente in *A Nation for All*, pt. 1.

16. Steve J. Stern, "The Tricks of Time: Colonial Legacies and Historical Sensibilities in Latin America," in *Colonial Legacies: The Problem of Persistence in Latin American History*, ed. Jeremy Adelman (New York: Routledge, 1999), 173.

17. See Amit Rai, *Rule of Sympathy: Sentiment, Race, and Power, 1750–1850* (New York: Palgrave Macmillan, 2002).

18. Alejandra Bronfman, *Measures of Equality: Social Science, Citizenship, and Race in Cuba, 1902–1940* (Chapel Hill: University of North Carolina, Press, 2004), 12. On citizenship and race in Cuba, see González García, *La otra ciudadanía: Tres ensayos sobre ciudadanía y repúbica* (Havana: Editorial de Ciencias Sociales, 2004), 56–87.

19. Melina Pappademos, *Black Political Activism and the Cuban Republic* (Chapel Hill: University of North Carolina Press, 2011), 12.

20. Louis A. Pérez Jr., "Incurring a Debt of Gratitude: 1898 and the Moral Sources of United States Hegemony in Cuba," *American Historical Review* 104 (1999): 356–398.

21. Joseph Roach, *Cities of the Dead: Circum-Atlantic Performance* (New York: Columbia University Press, 1996), 6.

22. David Scott, *Conscripts of Modernity: The Tragedy of Colonial Enlightenment* (Durham, N.C.: Duke University Press, 2004), chap. 4.

23. Scott, *Conscripts of Modernity*, 7.

24. These ideas have been thoughtfully expressed in Thomas Holt, *The Problem of Race in the Twenty-First Century* (Cambridge: Harvard University Press, 2000); and Barbara Jeanne Fields, "Slavery, Race, and Ideology in the United States of America," *New Left Review* 81 (May/June 1990): 95–118.

Archival Manuscripts

Boston, Massachusetts
  Massachusetts Historical Society (MHS)
    Edwin F. Atkins Family Papers (EA)

Cambridge, Massachusetts
  Houghton Library, Harvard University (HL)
    José Escoto Collection (JE)

Cienfuegos, Cuba
  Archivo Parroquial de la Ciudad de Cienfuegos (APCC)
  Archivo Provincial de Cienfuegos (APC)
    Actas Capitulares (AC)
    Ayuntamiento de Lajas (AL)
    Fondo Registro de Asociaciones (RA)
    Personal Collection of Orlando García Martínez (OGM)

Havana, Cuba
  Archivo Nacional de Cuba (ANC)
    Adquisiciones (ADQ)
    Asuntos Políticos (AP)
    Comisión Militar (CM)
    Consejo de Administración (CA)
    Donativos y Remisiones (DR)
    Gobierno General (GG)
    Gobierno Superior Civil (GSC)
    Miscelánea de Libros (ML)
    Reales ordenes y cédulas (ROC)
    Revolución de 1895 (REV)
  Biblioteca Nacional "José Martí" (BNJM), Colección Cubana, Colecciónes Manu-
    scritas (CM)
  José Augusto Escoto
  Julio Lobo
  Vidal Morales y Morales
  Manuel Pérez Beato

Néstor Ponce de León
Miguel Tacón

Madrid, Spain
  Archivo Histórico Nacional (AHN)
    Sección de Estado (SE)
    Sección de Ultramar (SU)
  Biblioteca Nacional (BNM)
  Fundación Antonio Maura (FAM)
  Real Academia de Historia (RAH)
  Servicio Histórico Militar (SHM)
    Capitanía General de Cuba (GCG)
    Sección Ultramar, Cuba (SUC)

Santiago de Cuba, Cuba
  Archivo Histórico Municipal Santiago de Cuba (AHMSC)
    Actas Capitulares (AC)
  Archivo Histórico Provincial de Santiago de Cuba (AHPSC)
    Gobierno Provincial (GP)
    Juzgado de Primera Instancia de Santiago de Cuba (PI)

Seville, Spain
  Archivo General de Indias (AGI)
    Sección Cuba (SC)
    Sección Diversos (SD)
    Sección Estado (SE)
    Sección Polavieja (SP)
    Sección Ultramar (SU)

Washington, D.C.
  United States National Archives, Washington, D.C. (USNA)

Periodicals
La Bandera Español, Havana
Boletín Oficial, Havana
Boletín Oficial de la Provincia de Santa Clara, Santa Clara
Diario de Barcelona, Barcelona
Diario de Cienfuegos, Cienfuegos
Diario de la Marina, Havana
El Apuntador, Cienfuegos
El Ciudadano, Havana
El Crisol, Cienfuegos
El Fénix, Cienfuegos
El Fomento, Cienfuegos
El Habanero, Philadelphia

El Hijo del Pueblo, Havana
El Imparcial, Cienfuegos
El León Español, Remedios
El Negro Bueno, Cienfuegos
El País, Havana
El Pueblo Libre, Havana
El Puente de Alcolea, Madrid
El Sufragio Universal, Madrid
El Telégrafo, Cienfuegos
Gaceta de la Habana, Havana
Gaceta de Madrid, Madrid
La América Española. Havana
La Fraternidad, Havana
La Hoja Económica, Cienfuegos
La Iberia, Madrid
La Igualdad, Havana
La Lealtad, Cienfuegos
La Quincena, Cienfuegos
La Unión, Havana
La Voz del Derecho, Madrid

Books and Articles

Abreu Cardet, José. *Introducción a las armas: La Guerra de 1868 en Cuba.* Havana: Editorial de Ciencias Sociales, 2005.

———. *La furia de los nietos: Guerra y familia en Cuba.* Guantánamo: Editorial El Mar y la Montaña, 2003.

———. *Las fronteras de la guerra: Mujeres, soldados y regionalismo en el 68.* Santiago de Cuba: Editorial Oriente, 2007.

Adelman, Jeremy, ed. *Colonial Legacies: The Problem of Persistence in Latin American History.* New York: Routledge, 1999.

———. *Sovereignty and Revolution in the Iberian Atlantic.* Princeton, N.J.: Princeton University Press, 2006.

Aguiar Aranguren, Asdrúbal, ed. *La Constitución de Cádiz de 1812: Hacia los orígenes del constitucionalismo iberoamericano y latino.* Caracas: Universidad Católica Andrés Bello, 2004.

Aguilera Manzano, José María. "La entronización de la literatura en la construcción de la 'cultura cubana,' 1823–1845." In *Cuba: De colonia a república,* 53–68. Ed. Martín Rodrigo y Alharilla. Madrid: Biblioteca Nueva, 2006.

Aguirre, Sergio. *Historia de Cuba.* 2 vols. Havana: Editorial Pedagógica, 1966.

Ahumada y Centurión, José. *Memoria histórico político de la Isla de Cuba.* Habana: Librería e Imprenta de A. Pego, 1874.

Alberto, Paulina. *Terms of Inclusion: Black Intellectuals in Twentieth-Century Brazil.* Chapel Hill: University of North Carolina Press, 2011.

Álbum de la Trocha: Breve reseña de una excursión feliz desde Cienfuegos a San Fernando, recorriendo la línea militar por cuatro periodistas. Havana: Imprenta y Papelería "La Universal" de Ruiz y Hermano, 1897.

Alonso Baquer, Miguel. "El ejército español y las operaciones militares en Cuba (1868: la campaña de Martínez Campos)." In *1895: La guerra en Cuba y la España de la restauración,* 297–318. Ed. Emilio de Diego. Madrid: Editorial Complutense, 1996.

Alonso y Sanjurjo, Eugenio. *Apuntes sobre los proyectos de abolición de la esclavitud en las Islas de Cuba y Puerto Rico.* Madrid: Imprenta de la Biblioteca de Instrucción y Recreo, 1874.

Althusser, Louis. "Ideology and Ideological State Apparatuses." In *Lenin and Philosophy, and Other Essays,* 121–176. Trans. Ben Brewster. New York: Monthly Review Press, 1971.

Álvarez Cuartero, Izaskun. *Memorias de la ilustración: Las Sociedades Económicas de Amigos del País en Cuba (1783–1832).* Madrid: Real Sociedad Bascongada de Amigos del País Delegación en Cortes, 2000.

Álvarez Cuartero, Izaskun, and Julio Sánchez Gómez, ed. *Visiones y revisiones de la independencia americana.* Salamanca: Ediciones Universidad de Salamanca, 2003.

Amores Carredano, Juan B. *Cuba y España, 1868–1898: El final de un sueño.* Pamplona: Ediciones Universidad de Navarra, 1998.

Anderson, Benedict. *Imagined Communities: Reflections on the Origin and Spread of Nationalism.* 2nd ed. London: Verso, 1991 [1983].

Andrews, George Reid. *Afro-Latin America, 1800–2000.* New York: Oxford University Press, 2004.

———. *Blacks and Whites in São Paulo, Brazil, 1888–1988.* Madison: University of Wisconsin Press, 1991.

Andueza, J. M. de. *Isla de Cuba pintoresca, histórica, política, literaria, mercantil e industrial.* Madrid: Boix, 1841.

Anna, Timothy. "Spain and the Breakdown of the Imperial Ethos: The Problem of Equality." *Hispanic American Historical Review* 62:2 (May 1982): 254–272.

Appleton's English-Spanish and Spanish-English Dictionary, 4th ed. New York: Appleton-Century-Crofts, Inc., 1956 [1903]), 73.

Apter, Andrew. "On African Origins: Creolization and *Connaissance* in Haitian Vodou." *American Ethnologist* 29 (2002): 233–260.

Arango y Parreño, Francisco. *Obras de don Francisco de Arango y Parreño,* 2 vols. Havana: Ministerio de Educación, 1952.

Arendt, Hanna. *Willing.* New York: Harcourt Brace Jovanovich, 1978.

Armas, Ramón de. *La revolución pospuesta.* Havana: Editorial de Ciencias Sociales, 1975.

Atkins, Edwin F. *Sixty Years in Cuba: Reminiscences of Edwin F. Atkins.* Cambridge: Riverside Press, 1926.

Ayuntamiento de Cienfuegos. *Ordenanzas municipales de la ciudad de Cienfuegos.* Cienfuegos: Imprenta de "Diario de Cienfuegos," 1896.

———. *Ordenanzas municipales de la villa de Cienfuegos.* Cienfuegos: Imprenta de D. Eduardo Feixas, 1856.

Azoy Andrés, Antonio. *Colección de causas criminales.* Matanzas: Imprenta del Ferrocarril, 1868.

Bacardí y Moreau, Emilio. *Crónicas de Santiago de Cuba.* 2nd ed. 10 vols. Madrid: Gráficas Breogán, 1973.

Baker, Houston A., Jr. "Critical Memory and the Black Public Sphere." *Public Culture* 7 (1994): 7–33.

Balboa Navarro, Imilci. *La protesta rural en Cuba: Resistencia cotidiana, bandolerismo y revolución (1898–1902)*. Madrid: CSIC, 2003.

———. *Los brazos necesarios: Inmigración, colonización y trabajo libre en Cuba, 1878–1898*. Valencia: Fundación Instituto de Historia Social, 2000.

Banerjee, Sukanya. *Becoming Imperial Citizens: Indians in the Late-Victorian Empire*. Durham, N.C.: Duke University Press, 2010.

Barcia Paz, Manuel. "Rebeliones de esclavos, rebeliones de 'libres de color': Una comparación entre Bahía y la Habana-Matanzas, 1795–1844." In *Trabajo libre y coactivo en sociedades de plantación*, 345–368. Ed. José A. Piqueras. Madrid: Siglo XXI, 2009.

———. "Revolts amongst Enslaved Africans in Nineteenth-Century Cuba: A New Look at an Old Problem." *Journal of Caribbean History* 39:2 (2005): 173–200.

Barcia Zequeira, María del Carmen. *Capas populares y modernidad en Cuba (1878–1930)*. Havana: La Fuente Viva, 2005.

———. *Élites y grupos de presión: Cuba, 1868–1898*. Havana: Editorial de Ciencias Sociales, 1998.

———. "La historia profunda: La sociedad civil del 98." *Temas* 12–13 (October 1997–March 1998): 27–33.

———. *Los ilustres apellidos: Negros en la Habana colonial*. Havana: Ediciones Bolona, 2009.

———. *Una sociedad en crisis: La Habana a finales del siglo XIX*. Havana: Editorial de Ciencias Sociales, 2000.

Barkey, Karen. *Empire of Difference: The Ottomans in Comparative Perspective*. Cambridge: Cambridge University Press, 2008.

Barnet, Miguel. *Biografía de un cimarrón*. Barcelona: Ediciones Ariel, 1968 [1966].

Barras y Prado, Antonio de las. *La Habana a mediados del siglo XIX*. Madrid: Imprenta de la Ciudad Lineal, 1926.

Barroeta Scheidnagel, Santiago. *Los sucesos de Cienfuegos: La situación actual de la Isla de Cuba*. New York: n.p., 1897.

Bas y Cortós, Vicente. *Cartas al Rey acerca de la Isla de Cuba*. Havana: Libr. de Abraido y la Cruz Verde, 1871.

Batrell Oviedo, Ricardo. *Para la historia: Apuntes autobiográficos de la vida de Ricardo Batrell Oviedo*. Havana: Seoane y Álvarez, 1912.

Bauman, Zigmunt. *In Search of Politics*. Stanford: Stanford University Press, 1999.

Beattie, Peter M. *The Tribute of Blood: Army, Honor, Race, and Nation in Brazil, 1864–1945*. Durham, N.C.: Duke University Press, 2001.

Beck, Earl. "The Martínez Campos Government of 1879: Spain's Last Chance in Cuba." *Hispanic American Historical Review* 56:2 (May 1976): 268–289.

Benhabib, Seyla. *The Claims of Culture: Equality and Diversity in the Global Era*. Princeton, N.J.: Princeton University Press, 2002.

Benítez-Rojo, Antonio. *The Repeating Island: The Caribbean and the Postmodern Perspective*. Trans. James Maraniss. Durham, N.C.: Duke University Press, 1992.

Benjamin, Walter. "Critique of Violence." In *Walter Benjamin: Selected Writings*. Vol. 1: *1913–1926*, 1:236–252. Ed. Marcus Bullock and Michael W. Jennings. 4 vols. Cambridge: Harvard University Press, 1996.

Bennett, Herman L. *Colonial Blackness: A History of Afro-Mexico*. Bloomington: Indiana University Press, 2009.

Benton, Lauren. *Law and Colonial Cultures: Legal Regimes in World History, 1400–1900*. New York: Cambridge University Press, 2001.

Bergad, Laird W. *Cuban Rural Society in the Nineteenth Century: The Social and Economic History of Monoculture in Matanzas*. Princeton, N.J.: Princeton University Press, 1990.

Bergad, Laird W., Fe Iglesias García, and María del Carmen Barcia. *The Cuban Slave Market, 1790–1880*. Cambridge: Cambridge University Press, 1995.

Berlin, Ira. *Many Thousands Gone: The First Two Centuries of Slavery in North America*. Cambridge: Harvard University Press, 2000.

Berlin, Isaiah. *The Proper Study of Mankind: An Anthology of Essays*. Ed. Henry Hardy and Roger Hausheer. New York: Farrar, Straus and Giroux, 1998.

Bhabha, Homi. "Of Mimicry and Man: The Ambivalence of Colonial Discourse." In *The Location of Culture*, 85–92. New York: Routledge, 1994.

Biehl, João, Byron Good, and Arthur Kleinman, eds. *Subjectivity: Ethnographic Investigations*. Berkeley: University of California Press, 2007.

Bilby, Kenneth. "Swearing by the Past, Swearing to the Future: Sacred Oaths, Alliances, and Treaties among the Guianese and Jamaican Maroons." *Ethnohistory* 44 (1997): 655—689.

Bizcarrondo, Marta, and Antonio Elorza. *Cuba/España: El dilema autonomista, 1878–1898*. Madrid: Editorial Colibrí, 2001.

Blanchard, Peter. *Under the Flags of Freedom: Slave Soldiers and the Wars of Independence in Spanish South America*. Pittsburgh: University of Pittsburgh Press, 2008.

Blanco, Juan Andrés, and Coralia Alonso Valdés. *Presencia castellana en el "Ejército Libertador Cubana" (1895–1898)*. UNED Zamora, Spain: Junta de Castilla y León, Consejería de Educación y Cultura, 1996.

Blight, David W. *Race and Reunion: The Civil War in American Memory*. Cambridge, Mass.: Harvard University Press, 2002.

Bonsal, Stephen. *The Real Condition of Cuba Today*. New York: Harper and Brothers, 1897.

Bowen, Wayne H., and José E. Álvarez, eds. *A Military History of Modern Spain: From the Napoleonic Era to the International War on Terror*. Westport, Conn.: Praeger, 2007.

Bowie, Katherine A. *Rituals of National Loyalty: An Anthropology of the State and the Village Scout Movement in Thailand*. New York: Columbia University Press, 1997.

Boza, Bernabé. *Diario de la guerra desde Baire hasta la intervención americana*. 2 vols. Havana: Librería Cervantes, 1924.

Bremer, Frederika. *The Homes of the New World: Impressions of America*. Trans. Mary Howitt. 2 vols. New York: Harper Brothers, 1853.

Bronfman, Alejandra M. *Measures of Equality: Social Science, Citizenship, and Race in Cuba, 1902–1940*. Chapel Hill: University of North Carolina, Press, 2004.

Brown, Christopher, and Philip D. Morgan, eds. *Arming Slaves: From Classical Times to the Modern Age*. New Haven, C.T.: Yale University Press, 2006.

Brown, David H. "Black Royalty: New Social Frameworks and Remodeled Iconographies in Nineteenth-Century Havana" In *Santería Enthroned: Art, Ritual, and Innovation in an Afro-Cuban Religion*, 25–61. Chicago: University of Chicago Press, 2003.

Brown, Elsa Barkley. "Negotiating and Transforming the Public Sphere: African American Political Life in the Transition from Slavery to Freedom." *Public Culture* 7 (1994): 267–302.

Brown, Vincent. *The Reaper's Garden: Death and Power in the World of Atlantic Slavery*. Cambridge: Harvard University Press, 2008.

Buckley, Roger Norman. *The British Army in the West Indies: Society and the Military in the Revolutionary Age*. Gainesville: University Press of Florida, 1998.

Burdiel, Isabel. "Myths of Failure, Myths of Success: New Perspectives on Nineteenth-Century Spanish Liberalism." *Journal of Modern History* 70:4 (1998): 892–912.

Burns, Kathryn J. *Into the Archive: Writing and Power in Colonial Peru*. Durham, N.C.: Duke University Press, 2010.

———. "Gender and the Politics of *Mestizaje:* The Convent of Santa Clara in Cuzco, Peru." *Hispanic American Historical Review* 78:1 (1998): 5–44.

Bustamante, Luis J. *Diccionario biográfico cienfueguero*. Cienfuegos: Impr. R. Bustamante, 1931.

———. *La comarca de Jagua hasta la fundación de la Colonia Fernandina de Jagua (1819)*. Havana: Imprenta "El Siglo XX," 1948.

Butler, Judith. *The Psychic Life of Power: Theories in Subjection*. Stanford: Stanford University Press, 1997.

———. "Restaging the Universal: Hegemony and the Limits of Formalism." In *Contingency, Hegemony, Universality: Contemporary Dialogues on the Left*, 11–43. Ed. Judith Butler, Ernesto Laclau, and Slavoj Žižek. London: Verso, 2000.

Cabrera, Francisco de A. *Razón y fuerza: Narración militar y de costumbres cubanas*. 3rd ed. Madrid: Impr. a cargo de Felipe Marqués, 1893.

Calcagno, Francisco. *Diccionario biográfico cubano*. New York: N. Ponce de León, 1878.

———. *Poetas de color. [Plácido, Manzano, Rodríguez, Echemendía, Silveira, Medina.]* Havana: Imprenta militar de la v. de Soler y compañía, 1878.

Calhoun, Craig. *The Roots of Radicalism: Tradition, the Public Sphere, and Early Nineteenth-Century Social Movements*. Chicago: University of Chicago Press, 2012.

Calsamiglia, Alberto. *Cuestiones de lealtad: Límites de liberalismo. Corrupción, nacionalismo y multiculturalismo*. Barcelona: Paidós, 2000.

Camps y Feliu, Fernando de. *Españoles e insurrectos: Recuerdos de la Guerra de Cuba*. 2nd ed. Havana: Imprenta de A. Álvarez y Cía., 1890.

Cañeque, Alejandro. *The King's Living Image: The Culture and Politics of Viceregal Power in Colonial Mexico*. New York: Routledge, 2004.

Caplan, Karen. *Indigenous Citizens: Local Liberalism in Early National Oaxaca and Yucatán*. Stanford: Stanford University Press, 2010.

Carbonell, Walterio. "Plácido, ¿Conspirador?" *Revolución y cultura* 2 (1987): 53–57.

Cardona, Gabriel, and Juan Carlos Losada. *Weyler: Nuestro hombre en la Habana*. Barcelona: Planeta, 1997.

Carr, Raymond. "Liberalism and Reaction, 1833–1931." In *Spain: A History*, 205–242. Ed. Raymond Carr. New York: Oxford University Press, 2000.

Casanovas, Joan. *Bread, or Bullets! Urban Labor and Spanish Colonialism in Cuba, 1850–1898*. Pittsburgh: University of Pittsburgh Press, 1998.

Castellanos, Gerardo. *Relicario histórico: Frutos coloniales y de la vieja Guanabacoa*. Havana: Editorial Librería Selecta, 1948.

Castiñeyra y Rangel, E. *Historia local de Cienfuegos*. Havana: Cultural, 1932.

Castro Arroyo, María de los Ángeles. "La lealtad anticolonial: Ramón Power en las Cortes de Cádiz." In *Las Antillas en la era de las luces y la revolución*, 277–300. Ed. José A. Piqueras. Madrid: Siglo XXI, 2005.

Caulfield, Sueann, Sarah C. Chambers, and Lara Putnam, "Introduction: Transformations in Honor, Status, and Law over the Long Nineteenth Century." In *Honor, Status, and Law in Modern Latin America*, 1–24. Ed. Putnam, Chambers, and Caulfield. Durham, N.C.: Duke University Press, 2005.

Cayuela Fernández, José. *Bahía de ultramar: España y Cuba en el siglo XIX: El control de las relaciones coloniales*. Mexico City: Siglo Veintiuno Editores, 1993.

———. "Los capitanes generales ante la cuestión de la esclavitud." In *Esclavitud y derechos humanos*, 415–454. Ed. Francisco de Paula Solano Pérez Lila and Agustín Guimerá Ravina. Madrid: CSIC, 1990.

Céspedes, Carlos Manuel de. *Carlos Manuel de Céspedes: Escritos*. Ed. Fernando Portuondo del Prado and Hortensia Pichardo Viñals. 3 vols. Havana: Editorial de Ciencias Sociales, 1982.

Chain, Carlos. *Formación de la nación cubana*. Havana: Ediciones Granma, 1968.

Chakrabarty, Dipesh. *Provincializing Europe: Postcolonial Thought and Historical Difference*. Princeton, N.J.: Princeton University Press, 2000.

Chambers, Sarah C. *From Subjects to Citizens: Honor, Gender, and Politics in Arequipa, Peru, 1780–1854*. University Park: Pennsylvania State University Press, 1999.

Chambers, Sarah C., and Lisa Norling. "Choosing to Be a Subject: Loyalist Women in the Revolutionary Atlantic World." *Journal of Women's History* 20:1 (2008): 39–62.

Chasteen, John Charles. *National Rhythms, African Roots: The Deep History of Latin American Popular Dance*. Albuquerque: University of New Mexico Press, 2004.

Chatterjee, Partha. *Lineages of Political Society: Studies in Postcolonial Democracy*. New York: Columbia University Press, 2011.

Childs, Matt D. *The 1812 Aponte Rebellion in Cuba and the Struggle against Atlantic Slavery*. Chapel Hill: University of North Carolina Press, 2006.

Chuffat Latour, Antonio. *Apunte histórico de los chinos en Cuba*. Havana: Molina, 1927.

Chust, Manuel, and Ivana Frasquet, eds. *Los colores de las independencias iberoamericanas: Liberalismo, etnia y raza*. Madrid: CSIC, 2009.

Clark, Kathleen Ann. *Defining Moments: African American Commemoration and Political Culture in the South, 1863–1913*. Chapel Hill: University of North Carolina Press, 2005.

Colectivo de Autores Franceses y Cubanos. *La historia y el oficio de historiador*. Havana: Editorial de Ciencias Sociales, 1996.

Collazo, Enrique. *Desde Yara hasta el Zanjón*. Havana: Instituto del Libro, 1967.

Conangla Fontanilles, José. *Cuba y Pí y Margall*. Havana: Editorial Lex, 1947.

Conroy, David W. *In Public Houses: Drink and the Revolution of Authority in Colonial Massachusetts*. Chapel Hill: University of North Carolina Press, 1995.

Cooper, Frederick. *Colonialism in Question: Theory, Knowledge, History*. Berkeley: University of California Press, 2005.

Cordoví Núñez, Yoel. *Liberalismo, crisis e independencia en Cuba, 1880–1914*. Havana: Editorial de Ciencias Sociales, 2003.

Corral, Manuel *¡El desastre! Memorias de un voluntario en la campaña de Cuba.* Barcelona: Impr. Alejandro Martínez, 1899.

Correspondencia reservada del Capitán General Don Miguel Tacón con el gobierno de Madrid, 1834–1838. Ed. Juan Pérez de la Riva. Havana: Biblioteca Nacional José Martí, 1963.

Corrigan, Philip, and Derek Sayer. *The Great Arch: English State Formation as Cultural Revolution.* London: Blackwell, 1985.

Cortes de Cádiz: Complementos de las sesiones verificadas en la Isla de León y en Cádiz. Ed. Adolfo de Castro. 2 vols. Madrid: Imprenta de Prudencio Pérez de Velasco, 1913.

Corwin, Arthur. *Spain and the Abolition of Slavery in Cuba.* Austin: University of Texas Press, 1967.

Covarrubias, Sebastián de. *Tesoro de la lengua castellana o española.* Ed. Martín de Riquer. Barcelona: Editorial Alta Fulla, 1987 [1611].

Cowan, Brian. "What Was Masculine about the Public Sphere? Gender and the Coffeehouse Milieu in Post-Restoration England." *History Workshop Journal* 51 (2001): 127–157.

Cuba. *Cuadro estadístico de la siempre fiel Isla de Cuba . . . 1846.* Havana: Imprenta del Gobierno, 1847.

———. *Cuba, resumen del censo de población de la Isla de Cuba a fin del año de 1841.* Havana: Imprenta del Gobierno, 1842.

Cuba desde 1850 á 1875: Colección de informes, memorias, proyectos y antecedentes sobre el gobierno de la Isla de Cuba, relativos al citado período que ha reunido por comisión del gobierno D. Carlos de Sedano y Cruzat (Ex-diputado a Cortes). Madrid: Imprenta Nacional, 1873.

Cué Fernández, Daisy. *Plácido: El poeta conspirador.* Santiago de Cuba: Editorial Oriente, 2007.

Cunha Reis, Manuel Basilio da, José Suárez Argudín, and Luciano Fernández Perdones. *Memoria general o sea resumen de las razones justificativas del proyecto de inmigración de brazos libres africanos.* Madrid: Imprenta de Manuel de Rojas, 1861.

Da Costa e Silva, Alberto. "Portraits of African Royalty in Brazil." In *Identity in the Shadow of Slavery,* 129–136. Ed. Paul E. Lovejoy. London: Continuum, 2000.

Dana, Richard Henry. *To Cuba and Back: A Vacation Voyage.* Boston: Houghton, Mifflin, 1859.

Davis, David Brion. *The Problem of Slavery in the Age of Revolution, 1770–1823.* Ithaca: Cornell University Press, 1975.

Davis, Richard Harding. *Cuba in War Time.* New York: R. H. Russell, 1898.

Dawson, Graham. *Soldier Heroes: British Adventure, Empire, and the Imagining of Masculinities.* New York: Routledge, 1994.

Deas, Malcolm. "The Man on Foot: Conscription and the Nation-State in Nineteenth-Century Latin America." *Studies in the Formation of the Nation State in Latin America,* 77–93. Ed. James Dunkerly. London: Institute of Latin American Studies, 2002.

Debien, Gabriel. "Les colons de Saint-Domingue réfugiés à Cuba (1793–1815)." *Revista de Indias* 54 (1953): 559–605.

Deive, Carlos Esteban. *Honor y gloria: Los dominicanos en las guerras de independencia de Cuba.* Santo Domingo: Fundación García Arévalo, 2011.

De la Fuente, Alejandro. *Havana and the Atlantic in the Sixteenth Century.* With the collaboration of César García del Pino and Bernardo Iglesias Delgado. Chapel Hill: University of North Carolina Press, 2008.

———. *A Nation for All: Race, Inequality, and Politics in Twentieth-Century Cuba.* Chapel Hill: University of North Carolina Press, 2001.

———. "Slavery and the Creation of Legal Rights in Cuba: *Coartación* and *Papel.*" *Hispanic American Historical Review* 87:4 (2007): 659–692.

De las Casas, A. *Cartas al pueblo americano (sobre Cuba y las Repúblicas Latino-Americanas.* 3rd ed. Buenos Aires: Est. Tip. El Correo Español, 1897.

De la Torre, Mildred. *El autonomismo en Cuba, 1878–1898.* Havana: Editorial de Ciencias Sociales, 1997.

Delgado, Octavio Avelino. "The Spanish Army in Cuba, 1868–1898: An Institutional Study." 2 vols. Ph.D. dissertation, Columbia University, 1980.

Del Valle, Adrián. *Historia documentada de la conspiración de la Gran Legión del Águila Negra.* Havana: Siglo XX, 1930.

Derby, Lauren. *The Dictator's Seduction: Politics and the Popular Imagination in the Era of Trujillo.* Durham, N.C.: Duke University Press, 2009.

Deschamps Chapeaux, Pedro. *El negro en la economía habanera del siglo XIX.* Havana: Instituto Cubano del Libro, 1971.

———. *El negro en el periodismo cubano en el siglo XIX: Ensayo bibliográfico.* Havana: Ediciones Revolución, 1963.

———. *Los batallones de pardos y morenos libres.* Havana: Instituto Cubano del Libro, 1970.

———. *Rafael Serra y Montalvo: Obrero incansable de nuestra independencia.* Havana: UNEAC, 1975.

Deschamps Chapeaux, Pedro, and Juan Pérez de la Riva. *Contribución a la historia de la gente sin historia.* Havana: Editorial de Ciencias Sociales, 1974.

Diario de sesiones de las Cortes constituyentes . . . 15 vols. Madrid: Imprenta de J.A. García, 1870–1871.

Diario de sesiones de las Cortes generales y extraordinarias. 9 vols. Madrid: Imprenta de J. A. García, 1870–1874.

Díaz, María Elena. *The Virgin, the King, and the Royal Slaves of El Cobre: Negotiating Freedom in Colonial Cuba, 1670–1780.* Stanford: Stanford University Press, 2000.

Díaz Martínez, Yolanda. "El lado oscuro de las luces: Violencia y criminalidad entre 1823 y 1845." In *Voces de la sociedad cubana: Economía, política e ideología, 1790–1862,* 145–184. Ed. Mildred de la Torre Molina. Havana: Editorial de Ciencias Sociales, 2007.

———. *Vida y avatares de los hombres de contienda.* Havana: Editora Política, 2004.

Díaz-Quiñones, Arcadio. "Fernando Ortiz y Allan Kardec: Espiritismo y transculturación." *Catauro: Revista cubana de antropología* 1:0 (1999): 14–31.

Dihigo y Mestre, Juan M. *Pí y Margall y la revolución cubana.* Havana: Imprenta El Siglo XX, 1928.

Disposiciones dictadas por el Excmo. Sr. Capitán General en 7 de febrero de 1874 publicadas en la Gaceta oficial. Havana: Imp. Del Gobierno y Capitanía General, 1874.

Domínguez, Jorge I. *Insurrection or Loyalty: The Breakdown of the Spanish American Empire.* Cambridge: Harvard University Press, 1980.

———. "Loyalists, Race, and Disunity during the Spanish American Wars of Independence: A Grumpy Reading." *Latin American Studies Association Forum* 41 (2010): 8–9.

Donoso Cortes, Ricardo. *Cuba española: El problema de la guerra*. Madrid: n.p., 1896.

Doreski, C. K. "Reading Riot: 'A Study in Race Relations and a Race Riot in 1919.'" *Writing America Black: Race Rhetoric in the Public Sphere*, 25–58. Cambridge: Cambridge University Press, 1998.

Dubois, Laurent. *A Colony of Citizens: Revolution and Slave Emancipation in the French Caribbean, 1787–1804*. Chapel Hill: University of North Carolina Press, 2004.

———. "An Enslaved Enlightenment: Rethinking the Intellectual History of the French Atlantic." *Social History* 31 (2006): 1–14.

———. "Our Three Colors: The King, the Republic, and the Political Culture of Slave Revolution in Saint-Domingue," *Historical Reflections* 29 (2003): 83–102.

Du Bois, W.E.B *The Negro*. Philadelphia: University of Pennsylvania Press, 2001 [1915].

Duharte Jiménez, Rafael. *El negro en la sociedad colonial*. Santiago de Cuba: Editorial Oriente, 1988.

Dunkerly, James, ed. *Studies in the Formation of the Nation State in Latin America*. London: Institute of Latin American Studies, 2002.

Duquette, Elizabeth. *Loyal Subjects: Bonds of Nation, Race, and Allegiance in Nineteenth-Century America*. New Brunswick: Rutgers University Press, 2010.

Dyde, Brian. *The Empty Sleeve: The Story of the West India Regiments of the British Army*. Saint John's, Antigua: Hansib Publishing, 1997.

Dym, Jordana. "'Enseñanza en los jeroglíficos y emblemas': Igualdad y lealtad en Guatemala por Fernando VII (1810)." *Secuencia, Numero Conmemorativo* (Mexico) (2008): 75–99.

———. *From Sovereign Villages to National States: City, State, and Federation in Central America, 1759–1839*. Albuquerque: University of New Mexico Press, 2006.

Earle, Rebecca. "Creole Patriotism and the Myth of the 'Loyal Indian.'" *Past and Present* 172 (August 2001): 125–145.

Echeverri, Marcela. "Popular Royalists, Empire, and Politics in Southwestern New Granada, 1809–1819." *Hispanic American Historical Review* 91, no. 2 (2011): 237–269.

Edo y Llop, Enrique. *Memoria histórica de Cienfuegos y su jurisdicción*. 2nd ed. Cienfuegos: J. Andreu, 1888.

Eguren, Gustavo. *La fidelísima Habana*. Havana: Editorial Letras Cubanas, 1986.

Eley, Geoff. "Nations, Publics, and Political Cultures: Placing Habermas in the Nineteenth Century." In *Culture/Power/History: A Reader in Contemporary Social Theory*, 297–335. Ed. Nicholas B. Dirks, Geoff Eley, and Sherry B. Ortner. Princeton, N.J.: Princeton University Press, 1994:

Entralgo, Elías. *La liberación étnica de Cuba*. Havana: Universidad de la Habana, 1953.

Escasena, José L. *La evolución de la legalidad en Cuba*. Havana: Editorial de Ciencias Sociales, 1990.

Estrade, Paul. "El autonomismo criollo y la nación cubana (antes y después del 98)." In *Imágenes e imaginarios nacionales en el ultramar español*, 155–170. Ed. Consuelo Naranjo Orovio and Carlos Serrano. Madrid: CSIC / Casa de Velázquez, 1999.

Evans, G.N.D, ed. *Allegiance in America: The Case of the Loyalists*. Menlo Park, Calif. .: Addison Wesley, 1969.

Ezponda, Eduardo. *La mulata: Estudio fisiológico, social y jurídico.* Madrid: Imprenta de Fortanet, 1878.

Feierman, Steven. "Colonizers, Scholars, and the Creation of Invisible Histories," In *Beyond the Cultural Turn: New Directions in the Study of Society and Culture,* 182–216. Ed. Victoria E. Bonnell and Lynn Hunt. Berkeley: University of California Press, 1999.

Fermoselle, Rafael. *Política y color en Cuba: La guerrita de 1912.* Montevideo: Editorial Géminis, 1974.

Fernández, Damian J. *Cuba and the Politics of Passion.* Austin: University of Texas Press, 2000.

Fernández de Castro, Rafael. *Clamores de libertad.* Havana: Editorial Cuba, 1936.

———. *Para la historia de Cuba. I. Trabajos políticos.* Havana: La Propaganda Literaria, 1899.

Fernández Robaina, Tomás. *Crítica bibliográfica y sociedad.* Havana: Editorial de Ciencias Sociales, 2011.

———. *El negro en Cuba, 1902–1958: Apuntes para la historia de la lucha contra la discriminación racial.* Havana: Editorial de Ciencias Sociales, 1990.

Ferrer, Ada. "Cuba, 1898: Rethinking Race, Nation, and Empire." *Radical History Review* 73 (1999): 22–46.

———. *Insurgent Cuba: Race, Nation, and Revolution, 1868–1898.* Chapel Hill: University of North Carolina Press, 1999.

———. "The Silence of Patriots: Race and Nationalism in Martí's Cuba." In *José Martí's "Our America": From National to Hemispheric Cultural Studies,* 228–249. Ed. Jeffrey Belnap and Raúl Fernández. Durham, N.C.: Duke University Press, 1998.

———. "Speaking of Haiti: Slavery and Freedom in Cuban Slave Testimony." In *The World of the Haitian Revolution,* 223–247. Ed. David Geggus and Norman Fiering. Bloomington: Indiana University Press, 2009.

Fields, Barbara Jeanne. "Slavery, Race, and Ideology in the United States of America." *New Left Review* 181 (May/June 1990): 95–118.

Figarola-Caneda, Domingo. *José Antonio Saco: Documentos para su vida.* Havana: Imprenta El Siglo XX, 1921.

Figueredo, Fernando. *La revolución de Yara.* 2 vols. Havana: Instituto del Libro, 1969.

Fischer, Sibylle. *Modernity Disavowed: Haiti and the Cultures of Slavery in the Age of Revolution.* Durham, N.C.: Duke University Press, 2004.

Fisher, Andrew B., and Matthew D. O'Hara, eds. *Imperial Subjects: Race and Identity in Colonial Latin America.* Durham, N.C.: Duke University Press, 2009.

Flathman, Richard F. *Willful Liberalism: Voluntarism and Individuality in Political Theory and Practice.* Ithaca: Cornell University Press, 1992.

Fletcher, George P. *Loyalty: An Essay on the Morality of Relationships.* New York: Oxford University Press, 1993.

Flint, Grover. *Marching with Gomez: A War Correspondent's Field Note-Book Kept during Four Months with the Cuban Army.* Introduction by John Fiske. Boston: Lamson, Wolffe, and Co., 1898.

Foner, Philip S. *The Spanish-Cuban-American War and the Birth of American Imperialism, 1895–1902.* 2 vols. New York: Monthly Review Press, 1972.

Forment, Carlos. *Democracy in Latin America, 1760–1900.* Vol. 1: *Civic Selfhood and Public Life in Mexico and Peru.* Chicago: University of Chicago Press, 2003.

Fradera, Josep María. *Colonias para después de un imperio*. Barcelona: Ediciones Bellaterra, 2005.

——. "Raza y ciudadanía: El factor racial en la delimitación de los derechos políticos de los americanos." In *Gobernar colonias*, 51–69. Barcelona: Ediciones Península, 1999.

Franco, José Luciano. *El gobierno colonial de Cuba y la independencia de Venezuela*. Havana: Casa de las Américas, 1970.

——. "La conspiración de Morales." In *Ensayos históricos*, 93–100. Havana: Editorial de Ciencias Sociales, 1974.

——. *La presencia negra en el Nuevo Mundo*. Havana: Casa de las Américas, 1968.

——. *Las minas de Santiago del Prado y la rebelión de los cobreros, 1530–1800*. Havana: Editorial de Ciencias Sociales, 1975.

——. *Plácido: Una polémica que tiene cien años y otros ensayos*. Havana: Ediciones Unión, 1964.

Frank, Jason. *Constituent Moments: Enacting the People in Postrevolutionary America*. Durham, N.C.: Duke University Press, 2010.

Fraser, Nancy. "Rethinking the Public Sphere: A Contribution to a Critique of Actually Existing Democracy." In *Habermas and the Public Sphere: A Contribution to a Critique of Actually Existing Democracy*. 109–142. Ed. Craig Calhoun. Cambridge, Mass.: MIT Press, 1992.

Frasquet, Ivana, ed., *Bastillas, cetros y blasones: La independencia en Iberoamérica*. Madrid: Editorial MAPFRE, 2006.

Fredrickson, George M. *Racism: A Short History*. Princeton, N.J.: Princeton University Press, 2002.

Frey, Sylvia R. *Water from the Rock: Black Resistance in a Revolutionary Age*. Princeton, N.J.: Princeton University Press, 1991.

Gallego García, Telisfonte. *Cuba por fuera*. 2nd. ed. Havana: La Propaganda Literaria, 1892.

Gallenga, Antonio C. N. *The Pearl of the Antilles*. London: Chapman and Hall, 1873.

Gándara y Navarro, José de la. *Anexión y guerra de Santo Domingo por el general Gándara*. 2 vols. Madrid: Imprenta de "El Correo Militar," 1884.

García Álvarez, Alejandro, and Consuelo Naranjo Orovio. "Cubanos y españoles después del 98: De la confrontación a la convivencia pacífica." *Revista de Indias* 212 (1998): 101–129.

García de Arboleya, José. *Manual de la Isla de Cuba: Compendio de su historia, geografía, estadística y administración*. 2nd ed. Havana: Imprenta del Tiempo, 1859.

García Martínez, Orlando. *Esclavitud y colonización en Cienfuegos, 1819–1879*. Cienfuegos: Ediciones Mecenas, 2008.

——. "Estudio de la economía cienfueguera desde la fundación de la colonia Fernandina de Jagua hasta mediados del siglo XIX." *Islas* 55/56 (September 1976–April 1977): 117–170.

——. "La Brigada de Cienfuegos: Un análisis social de su formación." In *Espacios, silencios y los sentidos de la libertad: Cuba entre 1878 y 1912*, 163–192. Ed. Fernando Martínez Heredia, Rebecca J. Scott, and Orlando García Martínez. Havana: Ediciones Unión, 2001.

García Mora, Luis Miguel. "La fuerza de la palabra: El autonomismo en Cuba en el último tercio del siglo XIX." *Revista de Indias* 61:223 (September-December 2001): 715–748.

———. "Tras la revolución, las reformas: El partido liberal cubano y los proyectos reformistas tras la paz del Zanjón." In *Cuba la perla de las Antillas,* 197–212. Ed. Consuelo Naranjo Orovio and Tomás Mallo Gutiérrez. Madrid/Aranjuez: Doce Calles–CSIC, 1994.

García Morales, Francisco. *Guía de gobierno y policía de la Isla de Cuba: Compendio de las atribuciones gubernativas de los alcaldes tenientes y alcaldes del barrio con un prontuario alfabético de la legislación vigente sobre política y orden público.* Havana: La Propaganda Literaria, 1881.

García Rodríguez, Gloria. "A propósito de La Escalera: El esclavo como sujeto político." *Boletín del Archivo Nacional de Cuba* 12 (2000): 1–13.

———. *Conspiraciones y revueltas: La actividad política de los negros en Cuba (1790–1845).* Santiago de Cuba: Editorial Oriente, 2003.

———. *La esclavitud desde la esclavitud: La visión de los siervos.* Mexico City: Centro de Investigación Científica "Ing. Jorge L. Tamayo," 1996.

Garrett, David T. *Shadows of Empire: The Indian Nobility of Cusco, 1750–1825.* Cambridge: Cambridge University Press, 2005.

Garrigó, Roque E. *Historia documentada de la Conspiración de Soles y Rayos de Bolívar.* Havana: Imprenta El Siglo XX, 1929.

Gatewood, Willard B., Jr. *"Smoked Yankees" and the Struggle for Empire: Letters from Negro Soldiers, 1898–1902.* Urbana: University of Illinois Press, 1971.

Gelpi y Ferro, Gil. *Situación de España y de sus posesiones de Ultramar, su verdadero peligro y el único medio de conjurarlo.* Madrid: Imprenta Santiago Aguado, 1871.

Gendzel, Glen. "Political Culture: Genealogy of a Concept." *Journal of Interdisciplinary History* 28 (1997): 225–251.

Genovese, Eugene D. *Roll, Jordan, Roll: The World the Slaves Made.* New York: Vintage Books, 1972.

Gilbert, James. *Whose Fair? Experience, Memory, and the History of the Great St. Louis Exposition.* Chicago: University of Chicago Press, 2009.

Goldberg, David Theo. *The Racial State.* London: Blackwell, 2002.

Gómez, Fernando. *La insurrección por dentro: Apuntes para la historia.* 2nd ed. Madrid: Biblioteca de La Irradiación, 1900.

Gómez, Juan Gualberto. *Por Cuba libre.* Havana: Editorial de Ciencias Sociales, 1974.

Gómez de Avellaneda y Arteaga, Gertrudis. *Sab.* Havana: Instituto del Libro Cubano, 1973 [1841].

Goncalvès, Dominique. *Le planteur et le roi: L'aristocratie havanaise et la couronne d'Espagne (1763–1838).* Madrid: Casa de Velázquez, 2008.

González Alonso, Benjamin. "La fórmula 'obedézcase, pero no se cumpla' en el derecho castellano de baja edad media." *Anuario de Historia del Derecho Español* 50 (1980): 469–487.

González del Valle, José Zacarías. *La vida literaria en Cuba (1836–1840).* Havana: Publicaciones de la Secretaría de Educación, 1938.

González Echevarría, Roberto. *Cuban Fiestas.* New Haven, Conn.: Yale University Press, 2010.

González Olivares, Ignacio. *Observaciones sobre la esclavitud en la Isla de Cuba.* Madrid: A. de San Martín y Agustín Jubera, 1865.

González-Ripoll, María Dolores. "Entre la adhesión y el exilio: Trayectoria de dos cubanos en una España segmentada (1808–1837)." In *Las Antillas en la era de las Luces y la Revolución,* 343–362. Ed. José A. Piqueras. Madrid: Siglo XXI, 2005.

———. "Hacia el ciudadano útil: Filantropía e ilustración en la Casa de Beneficencia de la Habana." *Cuadernos Americanos, Nueva Época* 80:2 (2000): 81–91.

González-Ripoll, María Dolores, Consuelo Naranjo, Ada Ferrer, Gloria García, and Josef Opartný, *El rumor de Haití en Cuba: Temor, raza y rebeldía, 1789–1844.* Madrid: CSIC, 2004.

Gorman, Daniel. *Imperial Citizenship: Empire and the Question of Belonging.* New York: Palgrave, 2006.

Govín, Antonio. *Discursos.* Havana: Burgay y Cía., 1955.

Graham, Richard. *Patronage and Politics in Nineteenth-Century Brazil.* Stanford: Stanford University Press, 1990.

Gruzinski, Serge. *The Mestizo Mind: The Intellectual Dynamics of Colonization and Globalization.* Trans. Deke Dusinberre. New York: Routledge, 2002.

Guardino, Peter. *The Time of Liberty: Popular Political Culture in Oaxaca, 1750–1850.* Durham, N.C.: Duke University Press, 2005.

Guerra, François-Xavier. "Lógicas y ritmos de las revoluciones hispánicas." In *Revoluciones hispánicas, independencias americanas y liberalismo español,* 13–46. Ed. François-Xavier Guerra. Madrid: Editorial Complutense, 1995.

———. *Modernidad e independencias: Ensayos sobre las revoluciones hispánicas.* Madrid: MAPFRE, 1992.

Guerra, François-Xavier, Annick Lempérière, et al. *Los espacios públicos en Iberoamérica: Ambigüedades y problemas, Siglos XVIII–XIX.* México City: Centro Francés de Estudios Mexicanos y Centroamericanos / Fondo de Cultura Económica, 1998.

Guerra Díaz, Carmen "Sobre la crisis esclavista en la antigua región de Cienfuegos." *Islas* 85 (September–December 1986): 133–148.

Guerra Díaz, Carmen, and Isabel Jiménez Lastre. "La industria azucarera cienfueguera en el siglo XIX: Notas históricas para su estudio." *Islas* 91 (September–December 1988): 42–76.

Guerra y Sánchez, Ramiro. *Guerra de los 10 años.* 2 vols. Havana: Editorial de Ciencias Sociales, 1972.

———. *Historia de la nación cubana.* 10 vols. Havana: Editorial Historia de la Nación Cubana, 1952.

———. *Manual de historia de Cuba (Económica, Social y Política).* Havana: Cultural, 1938.

Guha, Ranajit. *Domination without Hegemony: History and Power in Colonial India.* Cambridge: Harvard University Press, 1997.

———. "The Prose of Counter-Insurgency." In *Selected Subaltern Studies,* 45–84. Ed. Ranajit Guha and Gayatri Chakravorty Spivak. New York: Oxford University Press, 1988.

Gupta, Partha Sarathi, and Anirudh Deshpande, eds.*The British Raj and Its Indian Armed Forces, 1857—1939.* New Delhi: Oxford University Press, 2002.

Gutiérrez de la Concha, José. *Memoria sobre la Guerra de la Isla de Cuba y sobre su estado político y económico desde abril de 1874 hasta marzo de 1875.* Madrid: Est. Tip. E R. Labajos, 1875.

Habermas, Jürgen H. *The Structural Transformation of the Public Sphere.* Trans. Thomas Burger. Cambridge, Mass.: MIT Press, 1989 [1962].

Hahn, Steven. *A Nation under Our Feet: Black Political Struggles in the Rural South from Slavery to the Great Migration.* Cambridge: Harvard University Press, 2005.

———. *The Political Worlds of Slavery and Freedom.* Cambridge: Harvard University Press, 2009.

Hale, Charles. *Mexican Liberalism in the Age of Mora, 1821–1853.* New Haven, Conn.: Yale University Press, 1968.

Hall, Stuart. "Cultural Identity and Diaspora." In *Colonial Discourse and Post-colonial Theory: A Reader,* 392–401. Ed. Patrick Williams and Laura Chrisman. London: Harvester Wheatsheaf, 1994.

Hamnett, Brian. "Constitutional Theory and Political Reality: Liberalism, Traditionalism, and the Spanish Cortes, 1810–1814." *Journal of Modern History* 49:1 (March 1977): D1071–D1110.

Hanger, Kimberly. "Free Blacks in Spanish New Orleans." In *Against the Odds: Free Blacks in the Slave Societies of the Americas,* 44–64. Ed. Jane G. Landers. London: Frank Cass, 1996.

Hartman, Saidiya V. *Scenes of Subjection: Terror, Slavery, and Self-Making in Nineteenth-Century America.* New York: Oxford University Press, 1997.

Helg, Aline. *Liberty and Equality in Caribbean Colombia, 1770–1835.* Chapel Hill: University of North Carolina Press, 2004.

———. *Our Rightful Share: The Afro-Cuban Struggle for Equality, 1886–1912.* Chapel Hill: University of North Carolina Press, 1995.

Helly, Denise, ed. *The Cuba Commission Report: A Hidden History of the Chinese in Cuba.* Baltimore: Johns Hopkins University Press, 1993.

Herzog, Tamar. "Citizenship and Empire: The Meaning of Spanishness in the Eighteenth Century." In *Privileges and Rights of Citizenship: Law and the Juridical Construction of Civil Society,* 147–167. Berkeley: University of California Press, 2002.

———. *Defining Nations: Immigrants and Citizens in Early Modern Spain and Spanish America.* New Haven, Conn.: Yale University Press, 2003.

Heuman, Gad. "Riots and Resistance in the Caribbean at the Moment of Freedom." *Slavery and Abolition* 21 (September 2000): 135–149.

Hevia Lanier, Oilda. *El Directorio Central de las Sociedades negras de Cuba.* Havana: Editorial de Ciencias Sociales, 1996.

Hirschman, Albert O. *Exit, Voice, and Loyalty: Responses to Decline in Firms, Organizations, and States.* Cambridge: Harvard University Press, 1970.

Hobsbawm, Eric. *The Age of Revolution: 1789–1848.* New York: Vintage, 1996 [1962].

———. *Nations and Nationalism since 1780: Programme, Myth, Reality.* 2nd ed. Cambridge: Cambridge University Press, 1992.

Hobson, J. A. *Imperialism: A Study.* Ann Arbor: University of Michigan Press, 1965 [1938].

Holt, Thomas C. "Marking: Race, Race-making, and the Writing of History." *American Historical Review* 100:1 (February 1995): 1–20.

———. *The Problem of Freedom: Race, Labor, and Politics in Jamaica and Britain, 1832–1938*. Baltimore: Johns Hopkins University Press, 1993.

———. *The Problem of Race in the Twenty-First Century*. Cambridge: Harvard University Press, 2000.

Howard, Philip A. *Changing History: Afro-Cuban Cabildos and Societies of Color in the Nineteenth Century*. Baton Rouge: Louisiana State University Press, 1998.

Hugo, Victor. *Bug-Jargal*. Ed. and trans. Chris Bongie. Peterborough, Ontario: Broadview Editions, 2004, [1826].

Humboldt, Alexander von. *Ensayo político sobre la Isla de Cuba*. Introduction by Fernando Ortiz. Havana: Talleres del Archivo Nacional, 1960 [1826].

Ibáñez Marín, José. *Monumento al General Martínez Campos*. Madrid: Establecimiento Tipográfico "El Trabajo," 1906.

Ibarra, Jorge. "El final de la Guerra de los Diez Años." *Revista Bimestre Cubana* 84 (2001): 59–85.

———. *Ideología mambisa*. Havana: Instituto Cubano del Libro, 1967.

———. *Patria, etnia y nación*. Havana: Editorial de Ciencias Sociales, 2007.

Iglesias García, Fe. "La concentración azucarera y la comarca de Cienfuegos." In *Espacios, silencios y los sentidos de la libertad: Cuba entre 1878 y 1912*, 85–107. Ed. Fernando Martínez Heredia, Rebecca J. Scott, and Orlando F. García Martínez. Havana: Ediciones Unión, 2001.

Iglesias Utset, Marial. *Las metáforas del cambio en la vida cotidiana: Cuba, 1898–1902*. Havana: Ediciones Unión, 2003.

Instituto de Historia de Cuba. *Historia de Cuba. La colonia: Evolución socioeconómica y formación nacional: de las orígenes hasta 1867*. Ed. María del Carmen Barcia, Gloria García, and Eduardo Torres-Cuevas. Havana: Editora Política, 1992.

James, C.L.R. *The Black Jacobins: Toussaint L'Ouverture and the San Domingo Revolution*. 2nd. ed. New York: Vintage, 1989.

Jasanoff, Maya. *Liberty's Exiles: American Loyalists in the Revolutionary World*. New York: Knopf / Harper Press, 2011.

Jennings, Evelyn Powell. "Paths to Freedom: Imperial Defense and Manumission in Havana, 1762–1800." In *Paths to Freedom: Manumission in the Atlantic World*. 121–141. Ed. Rosemary Brana-Shute and Randy J. Sparks. Columbia: University of South Carolina Press, 2009.

Jensen, Larry R. *Children of Colonial Despotism: Press, Politics, and Culture in Cuba*. Tampa: University Presses of Florida / University of South Florida Press, 1988.

Jiménez Castellanos, Adolfo. *Sistema para combatir las insurrecciones en Cuba*. Madrid: Est. Tip. Calle de la Reina, núm. 8, bajo, 1883.

Jiménez Pastrana, Juan. *Los chinos en las luchas por la liberación cubana*. Havana: Editorial de Ciencias Sociales, 1983.

Johnson, Lyman L. and Sonya Lipsett-Rivera, eds. *The Faces of Honor: Sex, Shame, and Violence in Colonial Latin America*. Albuquerque: University of New Mexico Press, 1998.

Johnson, Sara E. *The Fear of French Negroes: Transcolonial Collaboration in the Revolutionary Atlantic*. Berkeley: University of California Press, 2012.

Johnson, Sherry. *The Social Transformation of Eighteenth-Century Cuba*. Gainesville: University Press of Florida, 2001.

Johnson, Walter. "On Agency." *Journal of Social History* 37:1 (2003): 113–124.

Kamen, Henry. *Imagining Spain: Historical Myth and National Identity*. New Haven, Conn.: Yale University Press, 2008.

Kazanjian, David. *The Colonizing Trick: National Culture and Imperial Citizenship in Early America*. Minneapolis: University of Minnesota Press, 2003.

Keller, Simon. "Making Nonsense of Loyalty to Country." In *New Waves in Political Philosophy*. 87–104. Ed. Boudewijn de Bruin and Christopher F. Zurn. New York: Palgrave Macmillan, 2009.

Kerr-Ritchie, Jeffrey. *Rites of August First: Emancipation Day in the Black Atlantic World*. Baton Rouge: Louisiana State University Press, 2007.

Kiddy, Elizabeth W. "Kings, Queens, and Judges: Hierarchy in Lay Religious Brotherhoods of Blacks, 1750–1830." In *Africa and the Americas: Interconnections during the Slave Trade*, 95–126. Ed. José C. Curto and Renée Soulodre-La France. Trenton: Africa World Press, 2004.

King, James F. "The Colored Castes and American Representation in the Cortes of Cádiz." *Hispanic American Historical Review* 33:1 (February 1953): 33–64.

Kirchner, Adelaide Rosalind. *Flag for Cuba: Pen Sketches of a Recent Trip across the Gulf of Mexico to the Island of Cuba*. New York: Mershon Company, 1897.

Klein, Herbert S. "The Colored Militia of Cuba: 1568–1868," *Caribbean Studies* 6:2 (1966): 17–27.

———. *Slavery in the Americas: A Comparative Study of Virginia and Cuba*. Chicago: University of Chicago Press, 1967.

Knight, Alan. "Is Political Culture Good to Think?" In *Political Cultures in the Andes, 1750—1950*, 25–57. Ed. Nils Jacobsen and Cristóbal Aljovín de Losada. Durham, N.C.: Duke University Press, 2005.

Knight, Franklin W. "Cuba." In *Neither Slave nor Free: The Freedman of African Descent in the Slave Societies of the New World*, 278–308. Ed. David William Cohen and Jack P. Greene. Baltimore: Johns Hopkins University Press, 1972.

———. *Slave Society in Cuba during the Nineteenth Century*. Madison: University of Wisconsin Press, 1970.

Kornweibel, Theodore, Jr. *"Investigate Everything": Federal Efforts to Compel Black Loyalty during World War I*. Bloomington: Indiana University Press, 2002.

Koselleck, Reinhart. *Futures Past: On the Semantics of Historical Time*. Trans. Keith Tribe. New York: Columbia University Press, 2004.

———. *The Practice of Conceptual History: Timing History, Spacing Concepts*. Trans. Todd Samuel Presner and Others. Stanford: Stanford University Press, 2002.

Koss, Joan D. "El porque de los cultos religiosos: El caso del espiritismo en Puerto Rico." *Revista de Ciencias Sociales* 16:1 (1972): 61–72.

Kuethe, Allan J. *Cuba, 1753–1815: Crown, Military, and Society*. Knoxville: University of Tennessee Press, 1986.

———. "La fidelidad cubana durante la edad de las revoluciones." *Anuario de Estudios Americanos* 55:1 (1998): 209–220.

Kutzinski, Vera M. *Sugar's Secrets: Race and the Erotics of Cuban Nationalism*. Charlottesville: University of Virginia Press, 1993.

La abolición de la esclavitud y el proyecto del Señor Moret. Madrid: Est. Tip. de T. Fortanet, 1870.

Labrador Rodríguez, Sonia. "Nicolás Guillén y sus antecesores: La 'poesía blanca' de los poetas negros del siglo XIX." In *Homenaje a Nicolás Guillén*, 231–247. Veracruz: Colección Cuadernos, Instituto de Investigaciones Lingüístico-Literarias, Universidad Veracruzana, 2006.

Laclau, Ernest, and Chantal Mouffe. *Hegemony and Socialist Strategy: Towards a Radical Democratic Politics*. 2nd ed. London: Verso, 2001.

Lagardère, Rodolfo de. *Blancos y negros*. Havana: Imprenta La Universal, 1889.

———. *La cuestión social de Cuba: Cuba no es Venecia*. Havana: La Universal de Ruiz y Hermano, 1887.

———. *Marinos y pequeñeces*. Havana: La Propagandista, 1901.

Landers, Jane G. *Atlantic Creoles in the Age of Revolutions*. Cambridge: Harvard University Press, 2011.

———. *Black Society in Spanish Florida*. Urbana: University of Illinois Press, 1999.

Landers, Jane G., and Barry M. Robinson, eds. *Slaves, Subjects, and Subversives: Blacks in Colonial Latin America*. Albuquerque: University of New Mexico Press, 2006.

Lane, Jill. *Blackface Cuba, 1840–1895*. Philadelphia: University of Pennsylvania Press, 2005.

———. "Smoking *Habaneras*, or A Cuban Struggle with Racial Demons." *Social Text* 104 (2010): 11–38.

La Rosa Corzo, Gabino. *Runaway Slave Settlements in Cuba: Resistance and Repression*. Trans. Mary Todd. Chapel Hill: University of North Carolina Press, 2003.

Larson, Brooke. *Trials of Nation Making: Liberalism, Race, and Ethnicity in the Andes, 1810–1910*. Cambridge: Cambridge University Press, 2004.

Lasso, Marixa. *Myths of Harmony: Race and Republicanism during the Age of Revolution, Colombia 1795–1831*. Pittsburgh: University of Pittsburgh Press, 2007.

La turbulencia del reposo: Cuba, 1878–1895. Colectivo de autores. Havana: Editorial de Ciencias Sociales, 2005.

Leal Curiel, Carole. *El discurso de la fidelidad: Construcción social del espacio como símbolo del poder regional (Venezuela, Siglo XVIII)*. Caracas: Biblioteca de la Academia Nacional de la Historia, 1990.

Leal, Rine. *Teatro bufo: Antología*. 2 vols. Havana: Editorial Arte y Literatura, 1975.

Lealtad cubana. Alegoría: En loor de nuestros amados monarcas. Havana: Oficina del Gobierno y Capitanía general por S.M., 1833.

Lealtad y heroísmo de la Isla de Puerto Rico. 1797–1897. Puerto Rico: Impr. de A. Lynn é Hijos de Pérez Morris, 1897.

León Rosabal, Blancamar. *La voz del Mambí: Imagen y mito*. Havana: Editorial de Ciencias Sociales, 1997.

LeRiverend, Julio. *Historia económica de Cuba*. Havana: Editorial Nacional de Cuba, 1965.

Lewis, Laura. *Hall of Mirrors: Power, Witchcraft, and Caste in Colonial Mexico*. Durham, N.C.: Duke University Press, 2003.

Llanes Miqueli, Rita. *Víctimas del año del cuero*. Havana: Editorial de Ciencias Sociales, 1984.

Llorens, Carles, and Clàudia Pujol. *La Guerra de Cuba*. Barcelona: Pòrtic, 2000.

Lomnitz, Claudio. "Nationalism as a Practical System: Benedict Anderson's Theory of Nationalism from the Vantage Point of Spanish America." In *The Other Mirror: Grand Theory through the Lens of Latin America, 329–359*. Ed. Miguel Ángel Centeno and Fernando López-Alves. Princeton, N.J.: Princeton University Press, 2001.

Lorenzo, Manuel. *Manifiesto del general Don Manuel Lorenzo a la nación española*. Cádiz: Campe, 1837.

Loyola, Óscar. "La alternativa histórica de un 98 no consumado." *Temas* 12–13 (1998): 19–26.

Lucena Salmoral, Manuel. *Los códigos negros de la América española*. Alcalá: Ediciones UNESCO / Universidad Alcalá, 1996.

Lynch, John, ed. *Latin American Revolutions, 1808–1826: Old and New World Origins*. Norman: University of Oklahoma Press, 1994.

———. *Simón Bolívar: A Life*. New Haven: Yale University Press, 2006.

MacIntyre, Alasdair. *Is Patriotism a Virtue?* Lawrence: University of Kansas Press, 1984.

Mahmood, Saba. *Politics of Piety: The Islamic Revival and the Feminist Subject*. Berkeley: University of California Press, 2005.

Mallon, Florencia. "The Promise and Dilemma of Subaltern Studies: Perspectives from Latin American History." *American Historical Review* 99 (1994): 1491–1515.

Malveaux, Julianna, and Reginna A. Green, eds. *The Paradox of Loyalty: An African American Response to the War on Terrorism*. Foreword by Cornel West. Chicago: Third World Press, 2002.

Mañach, Jorge. *Miguel Figueroa, 1851–1893: discurso leído . . . el 6 de julio de 1943, en conmemoración del cincuentenario de su muerte*. Havana: Imprenta El Siglo XX, 1943.

Mann, Gregory. *Native Sons: West African Veterans and France in the Twentieth Century*. Durham, N.C.: Duke University Press, 2006.

Manzano, Juan Francisco. *The Life and Poems of a Cuban Slave*. Ed. Edward J. Mullen. Hamden, Conn.: Archon Books, 1981 [1840].

Marchena Fernández, Juan. *Ejército y milicias en el mundo colonial Americano*. Madrid: Editorial MAPFRE, 1992.

———. *Oficiales y soldados en el ejército de América*. Seville: Escuela de Estudios Hispano-Americanos, 1983.

Marín Villafuerte, Francisco. *Historia de Trinidad*. Havana: Jesús Montero, 1945.

Markell, Patchen. *Bound by Recognition*. Princeton, N.J.: Princeton University Press, 2003.

Marotti, Giorgio. *Black Characters in the Brazilian Novel*. Los Angeles: Center for Afro-American Studies, UCLA, 1987.

Marrero, Levi. *Cuba: Economía y sociedad*. 15 vols. Madrid: Editorial Playor, 1986.

Martel, James R. *Love Is a Sweet Chain: Desire, Autonomy, and Friendship in Liberal Political Theory*. New York: Routledge, 2001.

Martí, José. *Obras completas*. 27 vols. Havana: Editorial Nacional de Cuba, 1963–1966.

———. *Selected Works*. Trans. Esther Allen. New York: Penguin 2002.

Martín Brito, Lilia. *El desarrollo urbano de Cienfuegos en el siglo XIX*. Oviedo: Universidad de Oviedo, Servicio de Publicaciones, 1998.

Martínez, María Elena. *Genealogical Fictions: Limpieza de Sangre, Religion, and Gender in Colonial Mexico*. Stanford: Stanford University Press, 2008.

Martínez-Alier, Verena. *Marriage, Class, and Colour in Nineteenth-Century Cuba: A Study of Racial Attitudes and Sexual Values in a Slave Society.* Cambridge: Cambridge University Press, 1974.

Martínez-Fernández, Luis. *Protestantism and Political Conflict in the Nineteenth-Century Hispanic Caribbean.* New Brunswick: Rutgers University Press, 2002.

Martínez Heredia, Fernando. "Nationalism, Races, and Classes in the Revolution of 1895 and the Cuban First Republic." *Cuban Studies* 33 (2002): 95–123.

Marx, Karl. *Revolution in Spain.* Westport, Conn.: Greenwood Press, 1975 [1854].

Matory, J. Lorand. *Black Atlantic Religion: Tradition, Transnationalism, and Matriarchy in the Afro-Brazilian Candomblé.* Princeton, N.J.: Princeton University Press, 2005.

Mattoso, Katia M. de Queirós. *To Be a Slave in Brazil, 1550–1888.* New Brunswick: Rutgers University Press, 1988.

McCabe, Marikay. "Commercial and Legal Topographies of Nineteenth-Century Havana, Cuba." Ph.D. dissertation, Columbia University, 2002.

McConville, Brendan. *The King's Three Faces: The Rise and Fall of Royal America.* Chapel Hill: University of North Carolina Press, 2006.

McElya, Micki. *Clinging to Mammy: The Faithful Slave in Twentieth-Century America.* Cambridge: Harvard University Press, 2007.

McMichael, Andrew. *Atlantic Loyalties: Americans in Spanish West Florida, 1785–1810.* Athens: University of Georgia Press, 2008.

McPherson, James M. *For Cause and Comrades: Why Men Fought in the Civil War.* New York: Oxford University Press, 1997.

Mehta, Uday S. *Liberalism and Empire: A Study in Nineteenth-Century British Liberal Thought.* Chicago: University of Chicago Press, 1999.

———. "Liberal Strategies of Exclusion." In *Tensions of Empire: Colonial Cultures in a Bourgeois World,* 59–86. Ed. Frederick Cooper and Ann Laura Stoler. Berkeley: University of California Press, 1997.

Memmi, Albert. *The Colonizer and the Colonized.* Introduction by Jean-Paul Sartre. Boston: Beacon Press, 1991 [1957].

Memoria de la sección de historia de la Real Sociedad Patriótica de la Habana. 2 vols. Havana: Imprenta de las viudas de Arazoza y Soler, 1830.

Méndez, Cecilia. *The Plebeian Republic: The Huanta Rebellion and the Making of the Peruvian State, 1820–1850.* Durham, N.C.: Duke University Press, 2005.

Merlín, María de las Mercedes, Condesa de. *Los esclavos en las colonias españolas.* Madrid: Impr. de Alegría y Charlain, 1841.

Metcalf, Alida C. *Go-Betweens and the Colonization of Brazil, 1500–1600.* Austin: University of Texas Press, 2005.

Milanés, José Jacinto. *Obras de Don José Jacinto Milanés.* 2nd ed. New York: Juan F. Trow y Compañía, 1865.

Miller, Bonnie M. *From Liberation to Conquest: The Visual and Popular Cultures of the Spanish-American War of 1898.* Amherst: University of Massachusetts Press, 2011.

Mintz, Sidney W. "Panglosses and Pollyannas; or Whose Reality are We Talking About?" In *The Meaning of Freedom: Economics, Politics, and Culture after Slavery,* 245–256. Ed. Frank McGlynn and Seymour Drescher. Pittsburgh: University of Pittsburgh Press, 1992.

———. "Slave Life on Caribbean Sugar Plantations: Some Unanswered Questions." In *Slave Cultures and the Cultures of Slavery*, 12–22. Ed. Stephan Palmié. Knoxville: University of Tennessee Press, 1995.

Mintz, Sidney W., and Richard Price. *The Birth of African-American Culture: An Anthropological Perspective*. Boston: Beacon Press, 1992 [1976].

Montejo Arrechea, Carmen Victoria. *Sociedades de Instrucción y Recreo de pardos y morenos que existieron en Cuba colonial: Período 1878–1898*. Veracruz: Instituto Veracruzano de Cultura, 1993.

Montoro, Rafael. *Obras*. 3 vols. .Havana: Cultural, 1952.

Morales Hernández, Florentino. *Apuntes históricos sobre el desarrollo de la cultura en Cienfuegos*. Cienfuegos: n.p. 1958.

———. *Breve panorama de la esclavitud en la jurisdicción de Cienfuegos*. Cienfuegos: Museo Provincial de Cienfuegos, 1987.

Morán, Elizabeth. "Visions of a Nineteenth-Century Cuba: Images of Blacks in the Work of Victor Patricio de Landaluze." In *Comparative Perspectives on Afro-Latin America*, 114–132. Ed. Kwame Dixon and John Burdick. Gainesville: University Press of Florida, 2012.

Morejón, Nancy. *Looking Within/Mirar adentro: Selected Poems/Poemas escogidos, 1954–2000*. Ed. Juanamaría Cordones-Cook. Detroit: Wayne State University Press, 2003.

Moreno, F. *Cuba y su gente (Apuntes para la historia)*. Madrid: Est. Tip. de Enrique Teodoro, 1887.

Moreno Fraginals, Manuel. *Cuba/España, España/Cuba: Historia común*. Barcelona: Grijalbo Mondadori, 1995.

———. *El ingenio: Complejo económico social cubano del azúcar*. 3 vols. Havana: Editorial de Ciencias Sociales, 1978.

———. *La historia como arma y otros estudios sobre esclavos, ingenios y plantaciones*. Barcelona: Grijalbo, Editorial Crítica, 1983.

Moreno Fraginals, Manuel R., and José J. Moreno Masó. *Guerra, migración y muerte (El ejército español en Cuba como vía migratoria)*. Barcelona: Ediciones Júcar, 1993.

Morúa Delgado, Martín. *Obras completas*. Notes by Alberto Baeza Flores. Havana: Publicaciones de la Comisión Nacional de Centenario de Don Martín Morúa Delgado, 1957.

Murphy, Keith M., and Jason Throop, eds. *Toward an Anthropology of the Will*. Stanford: Stanford University Press, 2010.

Nápoles Fajardo, Antonio José. *El sitio de Holguín: Relación histórica precedida de una mirada retrospectiva del estado de la ciudad y su jurisdicción desde el año de 1861 hasta últimos de febrero de 1869*. Havana: Imprenta militar de la viuda de Soler, 1869.

Naranjo Orovio, Consuelo. "El temor a la 'africanización': Colonización blanca y nuevas poblaciones en Cuba (el caso de Cienfuegos)." In *Las Antillas en la era de las luces y la revolución*, 85–121. Ed. José A. Piqueras. Madrid: Siglo XXI, 2005.

———. "Immigration, 'Race,' and Nation in Cuba in the Second Half of the 19th Century." *Ibero-Amerikanisches Archiv* 24 (1998): 303–326.

———. "La amenaza haitiana, un miedo interesado: Poder y fomento de la población blanca en Cuba." In *El rumor de Haití en Cuba: Temor, raza y rebeldía, 1789–1844*, 129–131. Madrid: Consejo Superior de Investigaciones Científicas, 2004.

Nash, Gary B. *The Forgotten Fifth: African Americans in the Age of Revolution.* Cambridge: Harvard University Press, 2006.

Navarrete, Pedro Fernández. *Conservación de monarquías y discursos políticos.* Ed. Michael D. Gordon. Madrid: Instituto de Estudios Fiscales, 1982 [1792].

Navarro García, Jesús Raúl. *Entre esclavos y constituciones: El colonialismo liberal de 1837 en Cuba.* Seville: CSIC, 1991.

Navarro García, Luis. "La última campaña del general Martínez Campos: Cuba, 1895." *Anuario de estudios americanos* 58:1 (2001): 185–208.

Navarro Martín, Antonio. *Glorias de España: Opúsculo sobre la pacificación de Cuba.* Mexico City: Imprenta Poliglota de Carlos Ramiro, 1878.

"Noticia de las fincas azucareras en producción que existían en toda la Isla de Cuba al comenzar el presupuesto de 1877–1878 . . ." *Revista Económica* [Havana] (7 June 1878): 7–24.

Noticias estadísticas de la Isla de Cuba en 1862. Havana: Imprenta del Gobierno, Capitanía General y Real Hacienda por S.M., 1864.

Ochando, T. *El general Martínez Campos en Cuba.* Madrid: Imprenta de Fortanet, 1878.

O'Gaván, Juan Bernardo. *Observaciones sobre la suerte de los negros del África, considerados en su propia patria, y trasplantados a las Antillas españolas: Y reclamación contra el tratado celebrado con los ingleses el año de 1817.* Madrid: Imprenta del Universal, 1821.

Opatrný, Joseph. *Antecedentes históricos de la formación de la nación cubana.* Prague: Universidad Carolina, 1986.

Ortiz, Fernando. *Cuban Counterpoint: Tobacco and Sugar.* Durham, N.C.: Duke University Press, 1995 [1940].

———. *Ensayos etnográficos.* Havana: Editorial de Ciencias Sociales, 1984.

———. *La antigua fiesta afrocubana del "Día de Reyes."* Havana: Ministerio de Relaciones Exteriores, 1960 [1925].

———. *Los negros curros.* Havana: Editorial de Ciencias Sociales, 1986.

———. *Los negros esclavos.* Havana: Editorial de Ciencias Sociales, 1975 [1916].

———. *Martí y las razas.* Havana: Publicaciones de la Comisión nacional organizadora de los actos y ediciones del centenario y del monumento de Martí, 1953. Published in English as "Cuba, Martí, and the Race Problem," *Phylon* 3:3 (1942): 253–276.

———. *Nuevo catauro de cubanismos.* Havana: Editorial de Ciencias Sociales, 1985.

Ortner, Sherry B., *Anthropology and Social Theory: Culture, Power, and the Acting Subject.* Durham, N.C.: Duke University Press, 2006.

Orum, Thomas T. "The Politics of Color: The Racial Dimension of Cuban Politics during the Early Republican Years, 1900–1912." Ph.D. dissertation, New York University, 1975.

Pagden, Anthony. *Lords of All the World: Ideologies of Empire in Spain, Britain, and France, c. 1500–c.1800.* New Haven, Conn.: Yale University Press, 1995.

Palmié, Stephan. *Wizards and Scientists: Explorations in Afro-Cuban Modernity and Tradition.* Durham, N.C.: Duke University Press, 2002.

Pappademos, Melina. *Black Political Activism and the Cuban Republic.* Chapel Hill: University of North Carolina Press, 2011.

Paquette, Robert W. *Sugar Is Made with Blood: The Conspiracy of La Escalera and the Conflict between Empires over Slavery in Cuba.* Middletown, Conn.: Wesleyan University Press, 1988.

Pateman, Carole. *The Problem of Political Obligation: A Critical Analysis of Liberal Theory.* Chichester, England: John Wiley and Sons, 1979.

Perera Díaz, Aisnara, and María de los Ángeles Meriño Fuentes. *La cesión de patronato: Una estrategia familiar en la emancipación de los esclavos en Cuba (1870–1880).* Havana: Editorial Unicornio, 2009.

———. *Para librarse de lazos, antes Buena familia que Buenos brazos: Apuntes sobre la manumisión en Cuba (1880–1881).* Santiago de Cuba: Editorial Oriente, 2009.

———. "Between Baseball and Bullfighting: The Quest for Nationality in Cuba, 1868–1898." *Journal of American History* 81 (1994): 493–517.

———. *Cuba and the United States: Ties of Singular Intimacy.* Athens: University of Georgia Press, 1990.

———. *Cuba between Empires, 1878–1902.* Pittsburgh: University of Pittsburgh Press, 1983.

———. "Incurring a Debt of Gratitude: 1898 and the Moral Sources of United States Hegemony in Cuba." *American Historical Review* 104 (1999): 356–398.

———. "Liberalism in Cuba: Between Reaction and Revolution, 1878–1898." In *Liberals, Politics, and Power: State Formation in Nineteenth-Century Latin America,* 259–277. Ed. Vincent C. Peloso and Barbara A. Tenenbaum. Athens: University of Georgia Press, 1997.

———. *Lords of the Mountain: Social Banditry and Peasant Protest in Cuba, 1878–1918.* Pittsburgh: University of Pittsburgh Press, 1989.

Pérez, Louis A, Jr. *On Becoming Cuban: Identity, Nationality, and Culture.* Chapel Hill: University of North Carolina Press, 1999.

———. "Politics, Peasants, and People of Color: The 1912 'Race War' in Cuba Reconsidered." *Hispanic American Historical Review* 66:3 (1986): 509–539.

———, ed. *Slaves, Sugar, and Colonial Society: Travel Accounts of Cuba, 1801–1899.* Wilmington, Del.: Scholarly Resources, Inc., 1992.

———. *The War of 1898: The United States and Cuba in History and Historiography.* Chapel Hill: University of North Carolina Press, 1999.

———. *Winds of Change: Hurricanes and the Transformation of Nineteenth-Century Cuba.* Chapel Hill: University of North Carolina Press, 2001.

Pérez, Louis A., Jr., and Rebecca J. Scott. *The Archives of Cuba / Los archivos de Cuba.* Pittsburgh: University of Pittsburgh Press, 2003.

Pérez Cabrera, José Manuel. *La juventud de Juan Gualberto Gómez.* Havana: El Siglo XX, 1945.

Pérez de la Riva, Juan. *El barracón y otros ensayos.* Havana: Editorial de Ciencias Sociales, 1975.

Pérez Guzmán, Francisco. *Bolívar y la independencia de Cuba.* Havana: Editorial Letras Cubanas, 1988.

———. *Herida profunda.* Havana: Ediciones Unión, 1998.

———. *La guerra en la Habana: Desde Enero de 1896 hasta el combate de San Pedro.* Havana: Editorial de Ciencias Sociales, 1974.

Pérez Guzmán, Francisco, and Rodolfo Sarracino. *La Guerra Chiquita: Una experiencia necesaria.* Havana: Editorial Letras Cubanas, 1982.

Perl, Matthias. "Las estructuras de comunicación de los esclavos negros en Cuba en el siglo XIX." *Islas* 77–79 (1984): 43–59.

Pezuela y Lobo, Jacobo de la. *Diccionario geográfico, estadístico, histórico de la Isla de Cuba*. 4 vols. Madrid: Imprenta del Establecimiento de Mellado, 1863.

———. *Historia de la Isla de Cuba*. 4 vols. Madrid: C. Bailly-Baillière, 1878.

Phelan, John Leddy. "Authority and Flexibility in the Spanish Imperial Bureaucracy." *Administrative Science Quarterly* 5 (1960): 47–65.

———. *The People and the King: The Comunero Revolution in Colombia, 1781*. Madison: University of Wisconsin Press, 1978.

Pichardo, Hortensia, ed. *Documentos para la historia de Cuba*. 4th ed. 4 vols. Havana: Editorial de Ciencias Sociales, 1976–1980.

Pike, Frederick B. *Hispanismo, 1898–1936: Spanish Conservatives and Liberals and Their Relationships with Spanish America*. South Bend, Ind.: University of Notre Dame Press, 1971.

Piqueras, José A. "La siempre fiel Isla de Cuba, o la lealtad interesada." *Historia Mexicana* 58:1 (2008): 427–486.

———. "Leales en la época de insurrección: La élite criolla cubana entre 1810 y 1814." In *Visiones y revisiones de la independencia americana*, 183–206. Ed. Izaskun Álvarez Cuartero and Julio Sánchez Gómez. Salamanca: Ediciones Universidad de Salamanca, 2003 .

———. "Sociedad civil, política y dominio colonial en Cuba (1878–1895)." *Studia histórica, Historia contemporánea* [Salamanca] 15 (1997): 93–114.

———. *Sociedad civil y poder en Cuba: Colonia y poscolonia*. Madrid: Siglo XXI, 2005.

Pirala y Criado, Antonio. *Anales de la guerra de Cuba*. 3 vols. Madrid: F. González Rojas, 1895–1898.

Pitts, Jennifer. *A Turn to Empire: The Rise of Imperial Liberalism in Britain and France*. Princeton, N.J.: Princeton University Press, 2005.

Ponte Domínguez, Francisco J. *Historia de la Guerra de los diez años*. Havana: Imprenta El siglo XX, 1958.

———. *La masonería en la independencia de Cuba (1809–1869)*. Havana: Editorial "Modas Magazine," 1944.

Porrua, Antonio. *Cuba española: Apuntes para un estudio de política antillana por Antonio Porrua presidente de la Juventud Constitucional de Cienfuegos*. Cienfuegos: Imprenta de Valero, 1895.

Portuondo Zúñiga, Olga. *Cuba: Constitución y liberalismo (1808–1841)*. 2 vols. Santiago de Cuba: Editorial Oriente, 2008.

———. *Entre esclavos y libres de Cuba colonial*. Santiago de Cuba: Editorial Oriente, 2003.

Prados-Torreira, Teresa. *Mambisas: Rebel Women in Nineteenth-Century Cuba*. Gainesville: University Press of Florida, 2005.

Premo, Bianca. *Children of the Father King: Youth, Authority, and Legal Minority in Colonial Lima*. Chapel Hill: University of North Carolina Press, 2005.

———. "An Equity against the Law: Slave Rights and Creole Jurisprudence in Spanish America." *Slavery and Abolition* 32:4 (2011): 495–451.

Procopio de Camargo, Candido. *Aspectos sociológicos del espiritismo en São Paulo*. Freiburg/Bogotá: Oficina Internacional de Investigaciones Sociales de FERES, 1961.

Quesada, Gonzalo de. *Los chinos y la revolución cubana*. Havana: Ucar, García, 1946.

Quintana, Manuel José. *Quintana: Memoria del Cádiz de las Cortes.* Ed. Fernando Durán López. Cádiz: Universidad de Cádiz, 1996.

Quiroz, Alfonso W. "Loyalist Overkill: The Socioeconomic Costs of 'Repressing' the Separatist Insurrection in Cuba, 1868–1878." *Hispanic American Historical Review* 78:2 (1998): 261–305.

Rael, Patrick. *Black Identity and Black Protest in the Antebellum North.* Chapel Hill: University of North Carolina Press, 2002.

Rai, Amit. *Rule of Sympathy: Sentiment, Race, and Power, 1750–1850.* New York: Palgrave Macmillan, 2002.

Ramos, José Antonio. *El traidor: La leyenda de las estrellas. La recurva.* Havana: La Verónica, 1941.

Ramos, Julio. *Divergent Modernities: Culture and Politics in Nineteenth-Century Latin America.* Durham, N.C.: Duke University Press, 2001.

———. "La ley es otra: Literatura y constitución de la persona jurídica." *Revista de Crítica Literaria Latinoamericana* 20 (1994): 305–335.

Rancière, Jacques. *On the Shores of Politics.* Trans. Liz Heron. London: Verso, 2007.

———. "Politics, Identification, and Subjectivization." *October* 61 (1992): 58–64.

Rappaport, Joanne, and Tom Cummins. *Beyond the Lettered City: Indigenous Literacies in the Andes.* Durham, N.C.: Duke University Press, 2012.

Rasgos biográficos del Excmo. Sr. Gral. D. Eusebio Puello y Castro y exposición que meses antes de morir. Havana: Imprenta militar de viuda de Soler y Cía, 1872.

Reglamento de la Sociedad "El Recreo de Palmira." Cienfuegos: Imprenta "El Comercio," 1880.

Reglamento para establecer en esta municipalidad de la Habana las cartas de seguridad y protección. Havana: Imprenta Fraternal de los Díaz de Castro, impresores del Consulado y del Ayuntamiento por S.M., 1823.

Reglamento provisional para los cuerpos de milicia nacional local de la Habana y su distrito. Havana: Oficina de Arazoza y Soler, impresores del Gobierno constitucional, 1821.

Reid-Vazquez, Michele. "Empire, Loyalty, and Race: Militiamen of Color in Nineteenth-Century Cuba." In *Documenting Latin America: Gender, Race, and Empire,* 1:260–264. 2 vols. Ed. Erin E. O'Connor and Leo J. Garafolo. Boston: Prentice Hall, 2011.

———. *The Year of the Lash: Free People of Color in Cuba and the Nineteenth-Century Atlantic World.* Athens: University of Georgia Press, 2011.

Reis, João José. *Slave Rebellion in Brazil: The Muslim Uprising of 1835 in Bahia.* Trans. Arthur Brakel. Baltimore: Johns Hopkins University Press, 1993.

Renda, Mary A. *Taking Haiti: Military Occupation and the Culture of U.S. Imperialism.* Chapel Hill: University of North Carolina Press, 2001.

Reyes, Justo. *Consideraciones sobre la educación doméstica y instrucción pública en la Isla de Cuba.* Havana: Imprenta del gobierno, capitanía general y real Sociedad patriótica por S.M., 1832.

Riaño San Marful, Pablo. *Gallos y toros en Cuba.* Havana: Fundación Fernando Ortiz, 2002.

Ribó, José Joaquín. *Historia de los voluntarios cubanos.* 2 vols. Madrid: Imprenta de T. Fortanet, 1876.

Rivera, Raquel Rosario. *La Real Cédula de Gracias de 1815 y sus primeros efectos en Puerto Rico*. San Juan: First Book Publications, 1995.

Roach, Joseph. *Cities of the Dead: Circum-Atlantic Performance*. New York: Columbia University Press, 1996.

Robert, Karen. "Slavery and Freedom in the Ten Years' War, Cuba, 1868–1878." *Slavery and Abolition* 13:3 (1992): 181–200.

Robertson, William Spence. "The Recognition of the Spanish Colonies by the Motherland." *Hispanic American Historical Review* 1:1 (1918): 70–91.

Rodríguez, Mario. *The Cádiz Experiment in Central America, 1808–1826*. Berkeley: University of California Press, 1978.

Rodríguez, Rolando. *Cuba: La forja de una nación*. 2 vols. Madrid: Caja Madrid, 1999.

———. *La revolución inconclusa: La protesta de los Mangos de Baraguá contra el Pacto del Zanjón*. Havana: Editorial de Ciencias Sociales, 1999.

Rodríguez Altunaga, Rafael. *Las Villas: Biografía de una provincia*. Havana: Imprenta "El Siglo XX," 1955.

Rodríguez O., Jaime E. *The Independence of Spanish America*. Cambridge: Cambridge University Press, 1998.

Roig de Leuchsenring, Emilio. *La Casa de Gobierno o Palacio Municipal de la Habana* Havana: n.p., 1961.

———. *La colonia superviva: Cuba a los veintidós años de república*. Havana: El Siglo XX, 1925.

———. *Weyler en Cuba: Un precursor de la barbarie fascista*. Havana: Páginas, 1947.

Rojas, Rafael. *Las repúblicas de aire: Utopía y desencanto en la revolución de Hispanoamérica*. Mexico City: Taurus Historia, 2009.

———. "The Moral Frontier: Cuba, 1898. Discourses at War." *Social Text* 59 (1999): 145–160.

———. *Motivos de Anteo: Patria y nación en la historia intelectual de Cuba*. Madrid: Editorial Colibrí, 2008.

Roldán de Montaud, Inés. *La restauración en Cuba: El fracaso de un proceso reformista*. Madrid: CSIC, 2001.

Román, Reinaldo L. *Governing Spirits: Religion, Miracles, and Spectacles in Cuba and Puerto Rico, 1898–1956*. Chapel Hill: University of North Carolina Press, 2007.

Roseberry, William. "Hegemony and the Language of Contention." In *Everyday Forms of State Formation: Revolution and the Negotiation of Rule in Modern Mexico*, 355–366. Ed. Gilbert Joseph and Daniel Nugent. Durham, N.C.: Duke University Press, 1994.

Rosell y Malpica, Eduardo. *Diario del Teniente Coronel Eduardo Rosell y Malpica (1895–1897)*. 2 vols. Havana: Imprenta "El Siglo XX," 1949.

Rossell, Agustín. *Opúsculo que trata de materias muy interesantes para la Isla de Cuba*. Madrid: Imprenta de M. Minuesa, 1860.

Rousseau, Pablo, and Pablo Díaz de Villegas. *Memoria descriptiva, histórica y biográfica de Cienfuegos*. Havana: Imprenta "El Siglo XX," 1920.

Rovira González, Violeta. *Cienfuegos desde el Pacto del Zanjón hasta 1902*. Cienfuegos: Consejo Científico de la Sección de Investigaciones Históricas del PCC Provincial Cienfuegos, n.d.

Rubiera Castillo, Daisy, and Inés María Martiatu Terry, eds. *Afrocubanas: Historia, pensamiento y prácticas culturales.* Havana: Editorial de Ciencias Sociales, 2011.

Ruiz Zorrilla, Manuel. *Sobre el cumplimiento de la Ley Preparatoria (de Julio de 1870) para la abolición de la esclavitud en las Antillas españolas.* Madrid: Secretaría de la Sociedad Abolicionista Española, 1872.

Russell-Wood, A.J.R. "'Acts of Grace': Portuguese Monarchs and Their Subjects of African Descent in Eighteenth-Century Brazil." *Journal of Latin American Studies* 32:2 (May 2000): 307–332.

Sábato, Hilda. *The Many and the Few: Political Participation in Republican Buenos Aires.* Stanford: Stanford University Press, 2001.

———. "On Political Citizenship in Nineteenth-Century Latin America." *American Historical Review* 106 (2001): 1290–1315.

Saco, José Antonio. *Carta de un patriota: O sea clamor de los Cubanos.* Cádiz: N.p., 1835.

———. *Examen analítico del informe de la comisión especial nombrada por las Cortes (sobre la exclusión de los actuales y futuros diputados de ultramar, y sobre la necesidad de regir aquellos países por leyes especiales).* Madrid: Oficina de D. Tomás Jordan, 1837.

———. *La situación política de Cuba y su remedio.* Paris: Impr. de E. Thunot, 1851.

Sáenz y Sáenz, Eusebio. *La Siboneya, o episodios de la Guerra de Cuba.* Cienfuegos: Imp. de Manuel Muñiz y García, 1881.

Sánchez, Joseph P. "African Freedmen and the Fuero Militar: A Historical Overview of Pardo and Moreno Militiamen in the Late Spanish Empire." *Colonial Latin American Historical Review* 3 (1994): 165–184.

Sánchez Baena, Juan José. *El terror de los tiranos: La imprenta en la centuria que cambió Cuba (1763–1868)* Castellón: Publicacions de la Universitat Jaume I, 2009.

Sanders, James E. *Contentious Republicans: Popular Politics, Race, and Class in Nineteenth-Century Colombia.* Durham, N.C.: Duke University Press, 2004.

———. "The Vanguard of the Atlantic World: Contesting Modernity in Nineteenth-Century Latin America." *Latin American Research Review* 46 (2011): 104–127.

Santamaría García, Antonio, and Luis Miguel García Mora. "Colonos, agricultores cañeros, ¿Clase media rural en Cuba? 1880–1898." *Revista de Indias* 58:212 (1998): 131–161.

Sartorius, David. "Limits of Loyalty: Race and the Public Sphere in Cienfuegos, Cuba, 1845–1898." Ph.D. dissertation, University of North Carolina, 2003.

———. "My Vassals: Free-Colored Militias in Cuba and the Ends of Spanish Empire." *Journal of Colonialism and Colonial History* 5, no. 2 (2004): 1–25.

———. "Race in Retrospect: Thinking with History in Nineteenth-Century Cuba." In *Race and Blood in the Iberian World,* 169–190. Ed. María Elena Martínez, David Nirenberg, and Max S. Hering-Torres. Berlin: LIT Verlag, 2012.

Savage, Kirk. *Standing Soldiers, Kneeling Slaves: Race, War, and Monument in Nineteenth-Century America.* Princeton, N.J.: Princeton University Press, 1997.

Schama, Simon. *Rough Crossings: Britain, the Slaves, and the American Revolution.* New York: Ecco / HarperCollins, 2006.

Schmidt-Nowara, Christopher. *The Conquest of History: Spanish Colonialism and National Histories in the Nineteenth Century*. Pittsburgh: University of Pittsburgh Press, 2006.

———. *Empire and Antislavery: Spain, Cuba, and Puerto Rico, 1833–1874*. Pittsburgh: University of Pittsburgh Press, 1999.

———. "'Spanish' Cuba: Race and Class in Spanish and Cuban Antislavery Ideology, 1861–1868." *Cuban Studies* 25 (1995): 101–122.

Schorske, Carl E. *Thinking with History: Explorations in the Passage to Modernism*. Princeton, N.J.: Princeton University Press, 1998.

Schulman, Ivan A. "Reflections on Cuba and Its Antislavery Literature." SECOLAS *Annals* 7 (1976): 59–67.

Schultz, Kirsten. *Tropical Versailles: Empire, Monarchy, and the Portuguese Royal Court in Rio de Janeiro, 1808–1821*. New York: Routledge, 2001.

Scott, David. *Conscripts of Modernity: The Tragedy of Colonial Enlightenment*. Durham, N.C.: Duke University Press, 2004.

Scott, James C. *Domination and the Arts of Resistance: Hidden Transcripts*. New Haven, Conn.: Yale University Press, 1990.

Scott, Julius. "The Common Wind: Currents of Afro-American Communication in the Era of the Haitian Revolution." Ph.D. dissertation, Duke University, 1986.

Scott, Rebecca J. *Degrees of Freedom: Louisiana and Cuba after Slavery*. Cambridge: Harvard University Press, 2006.

———. "The Provincial Archive as a Place of Memory: Confronting Oral and Written Sources on the Role of Former Slaves in the Cuban War of Independence (1895–98)." *New West Indian Guide/Nieuwe West-Indische Gids* 76 (2002): 191–209.

———. "Race, Labor, and Citizenship in Cuba: A View from the Sugar District of Cienfuegos, 1886–1909, *Hispanic American Historical Review* 78:4 (November 1998): 687–728.

———. "Small-Scale Dynamics of Large-Scale Processes." *American Historical Review* 105, no. 2 (April 2000): 475–477.

———. *Slave Emancipation in Cuba: The Transition to Free Labor, 1860–1899*. Princeton, N.J.: Princeton University Press, 1985.

———. "Slavery and the Law in Atlantic Perspective: Jurisdiction, Jurisprudence, and Justice." *Law and History Review* 29 (2011): 915–924.

Scott, Rebecca J., and Michael Zeuske. "Property in Writing, Property on the Ground: Pigs, Horses, Land, and Citizenship in the Aftermath of Slavery, Cuba, 1880–1909." *Comparative Studies in Society and History* 44 (2002): 669–699.

Scully, Pamela, and Diana Paton, eds. *Gender and Slave Emancipation in the Atlantic World*. Durham, N.C.: Duke University Press, 2005

Sección de Educación de la Sociedad Patriótica de la Habana. *Instrucciones morales y sociales para el uso de los niños*. Havana: Oficina del Gobierno y Capitanía General por S.M., 1824.

Seigel, Micol. "Beyond Compare: Comparative Method after the Transnational Turn." *Radical History* 91 (2005): 62–90.

———. *Uneven Encounters: Making Race and Nation in Brazil and the United States*. Durham, N.C.: Duke University Press, 2009.

Serra, Rafael. *Ensayos políticos*. New York: Imprenta Porvenir, 1892.

———. *Ensayos políticos.* New York: Imprenta de P.J. Díaz, 1896.

———. *Ensayos políticos.* New York: Imprenta de A. W. Howes, 1899.

———. *Para blancos y negros: Ensayos políticos, sociales y económicos.* Havana: Imprenta El Score, 1907.

Serrano, Carlos. *Final del imperio: España 1895–1898.* Madrid: Siglo XXI, 1984.

Sevilla Andrés, Diego. *África en la política española del siglo XIX.* Madrid: Consejo Superior de Investigaciones Científicas, 1960.

Sevilla Soler, Rosario. "'¿Opinión pública' frente a 'opinión publicada'? 1898: La cuestión cubana." *Revista de Indias* 63:212 (1998): 255–276.

Sheller, Mimi. *Democracy after Slavery: Black Publics and Peasant Radicalism in Haiti and Jamaica.* Gainesville: University Press of Florida, 2000.

———. "Sword-Bearing Citizens: Militarism and Manhood in Nineteenth-Century Haiti." *Plantation Society in the Americas* 4 (1997): 233–278.

Sierra Madero, Abel. *La nación sexuada: Relaciones de género y sexo en Cuba (1830–1855).* Havana: Editorial de Ciencias Sociales, 2002.

Silva, Eduardo da. *Prince of the People: The Life and Times of a Brazilian Free Man of Colour.* Trans. Moyra Ashford. London: Verso, 1993.

Sinha, Mrinalani. *Colonial Masculinity: The "Manly Englishman" and the "Effeminate Bengali" in the Late Nineteenth Century.* Manchester: Manchester University Press, 1995.

Solís, Ramón. *El Cádiz de las Cortes: La vida en la ciudad en los años 1810 a 1813.* Madrid: Alianza Editorial, 1969.

Souleré, Emilio A. *Historia de la insurrección en Cuba.* Barcelona: Est. Tip de Juan Pons, 1879.

Spain. Cortés. *Diario de sesiones de las Cortes Constituyentes.* 15 vols. Madrid: Imprenta de J. A. García, 1870.

Spain. Cortés. *Diario de sesiones: Senado.* Madrid: Imp. y Fundación de los Hijos de J. A. García, 1887.

Spence, Jonathan D. *Treason by the Book.* New York: Penguin, 2001.

Stanley, Amy Dru. "Instead of Waiting for the Thirteenth Amendment: The War Power, Slave Marriage, and Inviolate Human Rights." *American Historical Review* 115 (2010): 732–765.

———. "Wages, Sin, and Slavery: Some Thoughts on Free Will and Commodity Relations." *Journal of the Early Republic* 24 (2004): 279–288.

Stilz, Anna. *Liberal Loyalty: Freedom, Obligation, and the State.* Princeton, N.J.: Princeton University Press, 2009.

Stock, Brian. *Listening for the Text: On the Uses of the Past.* Baltimore: Johns Hopkins University Press, 1990.

Stoler, Ann Laura. *Along the Archival Grain: Epistemic Anxieties and Colonial Common Sense.* Princeton, N.J.: Princeton University Press, 2009.

———. *Carnal Knowledge and Imperial Power: Race and the Intimate in Colonial Rule.* Berkeley: University of California Press, 2002.

———. "Colonial Archives and the Arts of Governance: On the Content in the Form." *Archival Science* 2 (2002): 87–109.

———. "On Degrees of Imperial Sovereignty." *Public Culture* 18:1 (winter 2006): 125–146.

Stolke, Verena. *Racismo y sexualidad en la Cuba colonial.* Madrid: Alianza Editorial, 1992.

Storey, Margaret M. "Civil War Unionists and the Political Culture of Loyalty in Alabama, 1860–1861." *Journal of Southern History* 69:1 (February 2003): 71–106.

Stoyle, Mark. *Loyalty and Locality: Popular Allegiance in Devon during the English Civil War.* Exeter: University of Exeter Press, 1994.

Suárez y Romero, Anselmo. *Francisco.* New York: N. Ponce de León, 1880.

Subrahmanyam, Sanjay. "Imperial and Colonial Encounters: Some Comparative Reflections." In *Lessons of Empire: Imperial Histories and American Power,* 217–228. Ed. Craig Calhoun, Frederick Cooper, and Kevin W. Moore. New York: New Press, 2006.

Sueiro Rodríguez, Victoria María. "Apuntes sobre la vida teatral cienfueguera del siglo XIX." *Ariel: La Revista Cultural de Cienfuegos* 2:1 (1999).

Sundiata, Ibrahim. *From Slaving to Neoslavery: The Bight of Biafra and Fernando Po in the Era of Prohibition, 1827–1930.* Madison: University of Wisconsin Press, 1996.

Sweet, James H. *Recreating Africa: Culture, Kinship, and Religion in the Afro-Portuguese World, 1441–1770.* Chapel Hill: University of North Carolina Press, 2003.

Tanco y Bosmeniel, Félix. *Petrona y Rosalía.* Havana: Editorial Letras Cubanas, 1980 [1838].

Tannenbaum, Frank. *Slave and Citizen: The Negro in the Americas.* New York: Knopf, 1946.

Tarragó, Rafael E. "La lucha en las Cortes de España por el sufragio universal en Cuba." *Colonial Latin American Review* 18 (2009): 383–406.

Taussig, Michael. *Mimesis and Alterity: A Particular History of the Senses.* New York: Routledge, 1992.

Thomas, Hugh. *Cuba, or The Pursuit of Freedom.* 2nd ed. New York: DaCapo Press, 1998.

Thompson, Peter. *Rum Punch and Revolution: Taverngoing and Public Life in Eighteenth-Century Philadelphia.* Philadelphia: University of Pennsylvania Press, 1998.

Thornton, John K. "'I am the Subject of the King of Congo': African Political Ideology and the Haitian Revolution." *Journal of World History* 4 (1993): 282–214.

Thurner, Mark. *From Two Republics to One Divided: Contradictions of Postcolonial Nationmaking in Andean Peru.* Durham, N.C.: Duke University Press, 1997.

Tomich, Dale. "The Wealth of Empire: Francisco Arango y Parreño, Political Economy, and the Second Slavery in Cuba." *Comparative Studies in Society and History* 45 (2003): 4–28.

Tone, John Lawrence. *War and Genocide in Cuba, 1895–1898.* Chapel Hill: University of North Carolina Press, 2006.

Torrente, Mariano. *Política ultramarina que abraza todos los puntos referentes a las relaciones de España con los Estados Unidos, con Inglaterra y las Antillas, y señaladamente con la Isla de Santo Domingo.* Madrid: Compañía General de Impresos y Libros del Reino, 1854.

Torres-Cuevas, Eduardo. *Félix Varela: Los orígenes de la ciencia y con-ciencia cubanas.* Havana: Editorial de Ciencias Sociales, 1995.

———. *Historia de la masonería cubana: Seis ensayos.* Havana: Imagen Contemporánea, 2004.

———. *Historia del pensamiento cubano.* 2 vols. Havana: Editorial de Ciencias Sociales, 2006.

Trelles, Carlos. *Matanzas en la independencia de Cuba.* Havana: Imprenta Avisador Comercial, 1928.

Trouillot, Michel-Rolph. *Silencing the Past: Power and the Production of History.* Boston: Beacon Press, 1995.

Turits, Richard Lee. *Foundations of Despotism: Peasants, the Trujillo Regime, and Modernity in Dominican History.* Stanford: Stanford University Press, 2003.

Twinam, Ann. *Public Lives, Private Secrets: Honor, Gender, Sexuality, and Illegitimacy in Colonial Spanish America.* Stanford: Stanford University Press, 1999.

———. "Racial Passing: Informal and Official 'Whiteness' in Colonial Spanish America." In *New World Orders: Violence, Sanction, and Authority in the Colonial Americas,* 249–272. Ed. John Smolenski and Thomas J. Humphrey. Philadelphia: University of Pennsylvania Press, 2005.

Ukpabi, S. C. "West Indian Troops and the Defence of British West Africa in the Nineteenth Century." *African Studies Review* 17:1 (April 1974): 133–150.

Uralde Cancio, Marilú. *Voluntarios de Cuba española (1850–1868).* Havana: Editorial de Ciencias Sociales, 2011.

Urban, C. Stanley. "The Africanization of Cuba Scare, 1853–1855." *Hispanic American Historical Review* 37:1 (February 1957), 29–45.

Uribe-Uran, Victor M. "The Birth of a Public Sphere in Latin America during the Age of Revolution," *Comparative Studies in Society and History* (2000): 425–457.

Valle, Adrián del. *Tradiciones y leyendas de Cienfuegos.* Havana: Imprenta "El Siglo XX," 1919.

Van Young, Eric. *The Other Rebellion: Popular Violence, Ideology, and the Mexican Struggle for Independence, 1810–1821.* Stanford: Stanford University Press, 2001.

Venegas Fornias, Carlos. *Cuba y sus pueblos: Censos y mapas de los siglos XVIII y XIX.* Havana: Centro de Investigación y Desarrollo de la Cultura Cubana Juan Marinello, 2002.

Villaverde, Cirilo. *Cecilia Valdés o el Ángel Hill.* Trans. Helen Lane. New York: Oxford University Press, 2005 [1882].

Villena Espinosa, Rafael. "El asociacionismo cubano antes de la independencia." In *Sociabilidad fin de siglo: Espacios asociativos en torno a 1898,* 281–323. Ed. Isidro Sánchez Sánchez and Rafael Villena Espinosa. Cuenca: Ediciones de la Universidad de Castilla-La Mancha, 1999.

Vinson, Ben. *Bearing Arms for His Majesty: The Free Colored Militia in Colonial Mexico.* Stanford: Stanford University Press, 2001.

Viotti da Costa, Emilia. *The Brazilian Empire: Myths and Histories.* Chicago: University of Chicago Press, 1985.

———. *Crowns of Glory, Tears of Blood: The Demerara Slave Revolt of 1823.* New York: Oxford University Press, 1994.

Vivanco, Julián. *Crónicas históricas de San Antonio Abad de los Baños.* Havana: Editorial El Sol, 1955.

Voelz, Peter M. *Slave and Soldier: The Military Impact of Blacks in the Colonial Americas.* New York: Garland, 1993.

Walker, Charles F. *Smoldering Ashes: Cuzco and the Creation of Republican Peru, 1780–1840.* Durham, N.C.: Duke University Press, 1999.

Walker, James W. St. G. *The Black Loyalists: The Search for a Promised Land in Nova Scotia and Sierra Leone, 1783–1870.* New York: Africana / Dalhousie University Press, 1976.

Warner, Michael. *Publics and Counterpublics.* New York: Zone, 2002.

Watts, David. *The West Indies: Patterns of Development, Culture and Environmental Change since 1492.* Cambridge: Cambridge University Press, 1987.

Weinstein, Barbara. "The Decline of the Progressive Planter and the Rise of Subaltern Agency: Shifting Narratives of Slave Emancipation in Brazil." In *Reclaiming the Political in Latin American History: Essays from the North,* 81–101. Ed. Gilbert M. Joseph. Durham, N.C.: Duke University Press, 2001.

Weyler, Valeriano. *Memorias de un general: De caballero cadete a general en jefe.* Ed. María Teresa Weyler. Barcelona: Ediciones Destino, 2004.

———. *Mi mando en Cuba.* 5 vols. Madrid: Imprenta de Felipe González Rojas, 1910–1911.

Williams, Claudette M. *The Devil in the Details: Cuban Antislavery Narrative in the Postmodern Age.* Kingston: University of the West Indies Press, 2010.

Williams, Lorna Valerie. *The Representation of Slavery in Cuban Fiction.* Columbia: University of Missouri Press, 1994.

Wilson, Ellen Gibson. *The Loyal Blacks.* New York: Capricorn Books, 1976.

Wilson, James H. *Under the Old Flag,* 2 vols. New York: D. Appleton and Co., 1912.

Wolf, Donna. "The Caribbean People of Color and the Cuban Independence Movement." Ph.D. dissertation, University of Pittsburgh, 1973.

Yun, Lisa. *The Coolie Speaks: Chinese Indentured Laborers and African Slaves in Cuba.* Philadelphia: Temple University Press, 2009.

Zaragoza, Justo. *Las insurrecciones en Cuba.* 2 vols. Madrid: Imprenta de Miguel G. Hernández, 1872–1873.

Zeuske, Michael. "Hidden Markers, Open Secrets: On Naming, Race-Marking, and Race-Making in Cuba." *New West Indian Guide / Nieuwe West-Indische Gids* 76:3–4 (2002): 211–235.

———. "'Los negros hicimos la independencia': Aspectos de la movilización afrocubana en un hinterland cubano. Cienfuegos entre colonia y República." In *Espacios, silencios y los sentidos de la libertad: Cuba entre 1878 y 1912,* 193–234. Ed. Fernando Martínez Heredia, Rebecca J. Scott, and Orlando F. García Martínez. Havana: Ediciones Unión, 2001.

———. *Sklavereien, Emanzipationen und atlantische Weltgeschichte: Essays über Mikrogeschichten, Sklaven, Globalisierungen und Rassismus.* Leipzig: Leipziger Universitätsverlag, 2006.

Montejo, Esteban, 187–88

Montoro, Rafael, 162–63, 173, 223

Moreno Fraginals, Manuel, 70: and José Moreno Masó, 188

Moret Law (1870), 95, 107–9, 123, 125–26; Article 3, 107–126; Cortes debates over, 107–8; estimates of numbers of slaves freed by, 125; interrogations of slave-soldiers, 110–15, 118–20; press reaction to, 108–9, 254n86. *See also* emancipation, slavery, slaves, Ten Years' War

Morúa Delgado, Martín, 154–55, 197

Napoleonic invasion (1808), 15, 21, 54, 58

Nápoles Fajardo, Antonio José, 120

nation and nationalism, x, 1–2, 65, 71, 127, 130, 218; and loyalty, 8–11; 64, 145, 215, 219; national identity, 81, 95, 145, 162, 186; race and, x, 86, 127,133, 150, 211–12, 220–23; Spanish, 23–31, 51. *See also* citizenship, empire, liberalism

"national integrity," 94, 96, 99–100,102, 122, 126–27, 162, 187–88, 195, 202, 207, 209, 214–15. *See also* empire

naturaleza, 24–26, 30, 41; letters of, 24, 39, 41–42, 44. *See also* citizenship (Spanish), *vecindad*

oaths of loyalty, 39–41, 57

O'Donnell, Leopoldo, 74, 85, 90

O'Gavan, Juan Bernardo, 72

Oriente, 119

Ortiz, Fernando, vii–xi, 196, 265n29

Pact of Zanjón, 125, 128–131; reforms after, xii, 130, 133, 135–36, 156, 160, 167, 169, 182, 196

Palace of the Captain General, vii–ix, 46, 74, 200, 217, 219, 227n2

Paraguayan War, 109, 126

Partido Liberal Autonomista. 158, 161–67, 173–77, 183–85; and Autonomist government, 208; Rodolfo de Lagardere and, 195–96; members' gravitation to independence movement, 202; popular support, 173, 175, 185; race and racism in, 184, 195; support among Cubans of color,

154, 178–79, 194–95, 197. *See also* autonomy, elections, liberalism

Partido Revolucionario Cubano, 131

Partido Unión Constitucional, 131, 145, 161–62, 163, 169, 174–79, 182–83, 195

passports, 22

patronato, 129, 140, 149, 159–63, 166, 175, 195. *See also* emancipation

Pedroso, Federico, 171–72

peninsulares, 17, 40, 95, 161–63

Pérez, Louis A., Jr., 201, 215

Peru, 29–30

Philippines, 1, 101

Pí y Margall, Francisco, 212–14

Piqueras, José A., 151

Plácido (José de la Concepción Valdés), 81–82

post-Zanjón reforms. *See* Pact of Zanjón.

Prendergast, Luis, 138

press: 56, 59, 69, 71, 80–81, 154; black newspapers, 146–48, 194, 196–201; after Pact of Zanjón 134, 138, 146–150; significance to public sphere 150–53, 162, 178; Spanish, 108–9, 125, 192. *See also* associations, censorship, public sphere.

prestación (lending of slaves), 121–24, 126. *See also* slaves, Ten Years' War

protector de indios, 36–38. *See also* Indian pueblos

public sphere: xii, 12–13, 16, 79–80, 93, 96, 155–57; critical liberalism and, 129–130; political valences of, 52–53, 132, 137; and press, 146–150; race and, 73–76, 80–82, 134–35, 151–55; restrictions on, 69–73, 135–36. *See also* associations, censorship, Pact of Zanjón, press, theaters

pueblos de indios. See Indians.

Puello, Eusebio, 101–6, 250n16, 250n24

Puerto Príncipe, 32–33, 50, 73, 88–90, 97, 102–3, 107, 114, 118–19, 124

Puerto Rico, 1, 91, 196, 208

race: terminology, 17–19, 150, 206; and empire, 26–30, 34–38, 48, 50, 136, 138, 156, 178, 214; Rodolfo de Lagardère defining, 139, 196; Latin, 213–14; and liberalism, 27–30, 47, 184; and public sphere, 73–76, 80–82, 134–35, 151–55; racial ideology, 17–20, 37–38, 193, 219–20. *See also*